THE ⚜ TIMES
THE SUNDAY TIMES

Telephone 08701 608080 (The Times)
         08701 658585 (The Sunday Times)

CUSTOMER:	DELIVERY:
Mr E Towne	Mr E Towne
53 Roebuck Road	53 Roebuck Road
Rochester	Rochester
Kent	Kent
ME1 1UE	ME1 1UE

PICK LIST NO. 0559584

CUSTOMER NO.	ORDER NO.	DESPATCH DATE	DOCUMENT NO.	DELIVERY BY
0003882090	2331505	26/02/2002	83541	UK Single Item T&M Despatch

CATALOGUE CODE	DESCRIPTION	QUANTITY	VALUE
1HOE	History of Europe	1 EACH	13.59

Thank you for your cash payment of 15.54
Thank you for your order

D0543457

Payment for your order has been taken by Grenville Books Ltd.

TOTALS

GOODS & VAT	13.59
POSTAGE & PACKING	1.95
TOTAL	15.54

RETURNS POLICY: Please call our customer service team before returning any items.
We cannot accept liability for items returned without authorisation.

THE  TIMES
HISTORY
OF
EUROPE

THE TIMES

HISTORY

OF

EUROPE

TIMES BOOKS

First published in 2001 by
TIMES BOOKS
HarperCollins*Publishers*
77-85 Fulham Palace Road
London W6 8JB

First published in 1994 as
The Times Atlas of European History
Second edition published 1998

© Times Books 1994, 1998, 2001

The HarperCollins website address is
www.**fire**and**water**.com

Editorial Direction:
Thomas Cussans
Philip Parker
Barry Winkleman
Cicely Oliver
Jane Cheverton

Maps prepared by:
Bartholomew, Edinburgh

Cartographic Direction:
Gavin James
Alistair Calder
Janet Mykura
Jackie Galloway
Martin Brown

Place-name consultant, index:
Pat Geelan

Design:
Ivan Dodd
Lesley Branscombe

Printed in Hong Kong

All rights reserved
No part of this publication may be
produced in any form or by any means
without permission in writing from
the Publisher

British Library Cataloguing in
Publication Data
A catalogue record for this book is
available from the British Library

ISBN 0-0071-3161-5

Front Cover:
Europe in 1387 (map); sarcophagus
with battle between Romans and bar-
barbarians (Scala/Museo delle Terme,
Rome).
Back cover:
Population movements in Europe
after WWII (map).

CONTRIBUTORS

Mark Almond
*Fellow of Oriel College, University of Oxford, and of the Institute for
European Defence and Strategic Studies*

Jeremy Black
Professor of History, University of Exeter

Felipe Fernández-Armesto
Faculty of Modern History, University of Oxford

Rosamond McKitterick
Professor of Early Medieval European History, University of Cambridge

Geoffrey Parker
Andreas Dorpalen Professor of History, The Ohio State University

Chris Scarre
McDonald Institute, University of Cambridge

Richard Vinen
Department of History, King's College London

Maps conceived and compiled by
András Bereznay

CONTENTS

INTRODUCTION

HISTORY today has come increasingly to be written in terms of societies rather than states, communities rather than dynasties, cultures rather than countries, and economies or even ecologies rather than politics. This atlas puts the politics back in. Unashamedly, it is a work of political history, narrowly defined.

The atlas concentrates on mapping the frontiers of Europe's states at key dates over the last 3,000 years. At each date, frontiers are drawn on identical base maps of the whole continent, allowing the evolution of its nations, states and empires – their appearance and growth, their contraction and disappearance – to become immediately clear. After every principal map, two pages of subsidiary maps at larger scales highlight the major processes which led to the condition of Europe as it appears on the main maps and focus on details too small to be shown on them. The accompanying text provides background and draws attention to the principal changes to borders.

Some redress in favour of a neglected traditional discipline may well be salutary. But the reason for adopting this resolutely state-based approach goes to the heart of the European historical experience. The complex state-system, in which a large number of competing, sovereign, territorial states have been crammed together, pushing and tugging at each other's frontiers, wresting and re-educating each other's populations, is an almost unique feature of European history, one which sets the continent apart from most of the rest of the world. Only Southeast Asia has had a long experience of anything similar. For other continents, it represents a model of what to avoid, or a reservoir of lessons for the future. Like other European vices and virtues, the state system was exported as empire builders extended the reach of Europe to other parts of the world.

The withering of the traditional European state has been widely predicted in one form or another. Marx thought it would disappear in favour of proletarian internationalism. More recent visionaries have hoped it would blend into a united Europe or fragment into a "Europe of regions" or a "Europe of the peoples". At the moment, the existing framework continues to appear unconquerably robust. Even if one of these predictions came true, it would probably mean only that the state-system continued in a new guise. As a glance through this atlas shows, the state is always with us, however much borders – and names – may change. Without knowledge of it, no one can hope to understand Europe today.

Because European history has taken place within a framework of states, the reach of cultural, social, intellectual and economic change has been directed or deflected, influenced or ordained by powerful state institutions. But in concentrating on political borders, *The Times History of Europe* is not meant to belittle non-political history or those kinds of political history – movements and mentalities, party-strife and popular revolutions – which cannot be represented on maps of this kind. On the contrary, the purpose of this work is to provide a view of the network of frontiers inside which the rest of European history has been trapped. It is a starting-point, not a substitute, for the study of these and other themes.

TIMES BOOKS
June 2001

The First States

The story of European societies in the centuries before 900 BC is largely dependent on the evidence of archaeology. The first European written records are the Linear A tablets, bureaucratic documents produced by the Minoan palace administration on Crete during the first half of the 2nd millennium BC. These are in an unknown language which has not yet been translated, but judging from their general appearance they are inventories of palace storerooms, lists of rations, and the like. The same is true of the Linear B tablets which succeeded them in the 15th century BC. These are written in an early form of Greek for the Mycenaean rulers who took control of Crete at this time. Linear B in turn went out of use with the demise of the Mycenaean palaces on both Crete and the Greek mainland during the 12th century BC. The Greek world then entered a "Dark Age" which lasted until the 8th century BC, when the Greeks adopted and adapted the use of the alphabet from their eastern trade rivals, the Phoenicians. From the Greeks the alphabet was passed to the Etruscans and Romans early in the 7th century BC, and thence to the Celts and Scandinavians.

What we know of European societies around 900 BC therefore comes almost entirely from the evidence of archaeology. This reveals a varied pattern consisting largely of small-scale farming societies, known as Urnfield societies from their custom of burying the ashes of their dead in pottery vessels (or "urns") grouped in cemeteries. Warfare was a conspicuous component of these Urnfield societies. They built hilltop fortresses – perhaps more as refuges than settlements – and leading members of society armed themselves with bronze breastplates and helmets, and wielded long bronze swords. The Mycenaean rulers of 2nd millennium Greece were in a sense merely one of these Bronze Age warrior societies, with a more sophisticated material culture than most. The demise of the Mycenaean aristocracies was not echoed in other parts of Europe, however, where the Urnfield societies continued to develop until the 1st millennium BC.

But Europe on the threshold of the 1st millennium BC was beginning to change in a number of important respects. By 900 BC, communities on the Greek mainland had re-established their trading links with the Near East. In Greece, as in northern Italy, the foundations were being laid of the city-states which were to arise during the 8th century BC. Political developments in the Near East were also shortly to have important repercussions on the West Mediterranean, for the spectacular growth of Assyrian power in the 9th century encouraged the Phoenicians to seek new markets overseas. By the 8th century BC Greeks and Phoenicians were fierce commercial rivals, and Greek and Phoenician colonies were already established around the shores of the central and western Mediterranean. Thus around 900 BC Mediterranean societies in Italy and the Aegean were already embarking on that dynamic of development which was to lead to the rise of city-states and the establishment of a fully literate civilisation. Under the Romans this was ultimately to permeate the greater part of the continent.

At the beginning of the 1st millennium BC, however, northern Europe was set on its own separate trajectory of development, its warrior societies the direct ancestors of the later Celts, Germans and Thracians. Meanwhile, on the steppelands north of the Black Sea, were the Cimmerians, one the many horse-riding nomadic peoples who were to terrorise and control the settled farmers of Eastern Europe until the defeat of the Mongols in the 16th century.

Teutonic
peoples

F i n n o - U g r i a n s

Volga

BALTIC
SEA

B a l t i c   p e o p l e s

Oder

Elbe

Vistula

S l a v s

Don

Volga

Danube

Dnieper

Dniester

C i m m e r i a n s

C a u c a s i a n   p e o p l e s

I l l y r i a n s

T h r a c i a n s

Danube

BLACK SEA

uscans

I l l y r i a n s

I t a l i c   p e o p l e s

URARTU

Tigris

Gordium ○ PHRYGIA

Sicily

Nineveh
○
ASSYRIA
Ashur
○

GREEK

Phocaea
○

NEO-HITTITE
CITY-STATES

Euphrates

Thebes
Corinth ○   ○ Megara
Argos ○   Athens

Ephesus
○

○ Halicarnassus

Sparta ○   CITY

Aradus
○
PHOENICIA

Malta   S E A

Cyprus
○
Byblos
○
Berytus ○   ISRAEL

A r a m a e a n s

Crete ○   S T A T E S

Gortyn

9

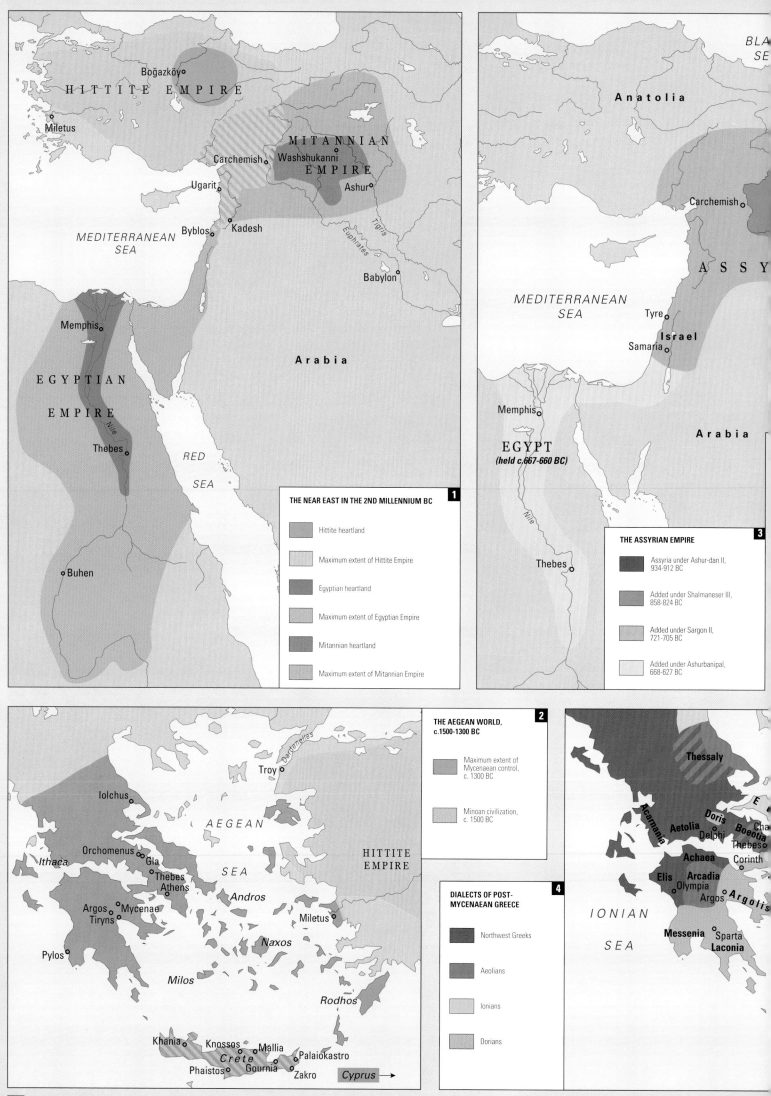

THE NEAR EAST IN THE 2ND MILLENNIUM BC `1`

Hittite heartland

Maximum extent of Hittite Empire

Egyptian heartland

Maximum extent of Egyptian Empire

Mitannian heartland

Maximum extent of Mitannian Empire

THE ASSYRIAN EMPIRE `3`

Assyria under Ashur-dan II, 934-912 BC

Added under Shalmaneser III, 858-824 BC

Added under Sargon II, 721-705 BC

Added under Ashurbanipal, 668-627 BC

THE AEGEAN WORLD, c.1500-1300 BC `2`

Maximum extent of Mycenaean control, c. 1300 BC

Minoan civilization, c. 1500 BC

DIALECTS OF POST-MYCENAEAN GREECE `4`

Northwest Greeks

Aeolians

Ionians

Dorians

The Near East in the 2nd Millennium BC

1 By the middle of the 2nd millennium BC, urban societies had existed in the Near East for some 2,000 years. The first cities had arisen in Sumer, in southern Mesopotamia, around 3500 BC. These were self-governing polities known as city-states, and were often at war with each other. Within a few centuries, cities had developed in the lands to the north and west, in northen Syria, Mesopotamia and the Levant. These, too, became involved in the power politics of the 3rd millennium, when the Akkadian rulers of southern Mesopotamia sought to extend their power as far as the Mediterranean.

By 3000 BC or a little later, a major new kingdom had formed in the Nile valley, that of ancient Egypt, and during the 2nd millennium the Egyptians cast their eyes northwards to the cities of the Levant and Syria. In the 15th century BC Egyptian armies of the New Kingdom period (1550-1070 BC) advanced as far as the River Euphrates. This brought them into conflict with the kingdom of Mitanni in Upper Mesopotamia and with the Hittites of central Anatolia. For a while, a careful three-hand game of war and diplomacy was played, until in the 14th century BC the Hittites destroyed Mitanni and took control of its territories west of the Euphrates. The division between Hittite and Egyptian zones was drawn by mutual agreement after the Battle of Kadesh (1286 BC). Within a century or so, both Hittites and Egyptians had been crippled by foreign attack and internal unrest. The Hittite kingdom collapsed, while the Egyptians retreated to the Nile valley.

The Aegean World, c.1500-1300 BC

2 The first European civilisation arose on the island of Crete early in the 2nd millennium BC. It takes its name, "Minoan", from the legendary King Minos, who annually fed Athenian youths and maidens to the savage Minotaur. Crete may have been divided into a number of separate states, governed from impressive palaces such as those at Phaistos, Mallia and Knossos. The rulers kept records of their administration in the form of clay tablets inscribed with a still-undeciphered script known as Linear A. The development of the Cretan states was brought to a sudden end during the 15th century BC, when the palaces were destroyed. Only one, at Knossos, was rebuilt after this destruction, and when the dust clears we find that Mycenaean Greeks rather than indigenous Minoan rulers are in control.

Mycenaean Greece was a land of small independent kingdoms centred on palaces or small fortresses. These tiny states arose during the 16th century BC by a process of internal development, as local war-leaders became increasingly powerful, agriculture improved and foreign trade fed new wealth into the economy. The most famous of the palace-fortresses is that of Mycenae in the north-western Peloponnese, from which site the whole civilisation of Mycenaean Greece takes its name.

In the 15th century the Mycenaeans took control of Crete, and by the 14th century they were the dominant power in the Aegean region, raiding the coasts of Asia Minor and perhaps (if legend is to be believed) attacking the strategic city of Troy at the mouth of the Dardanelles. Soon afterwards, the Mycenaean rulers were in crisis, and by the end of the 12th century their palaces had been abandoned.

The Assyrian Empire

3 Assyria – the land around the city of Ashur on the River Tigris – had been an important state throughout most of the 2nd millennium BC. In the 14th century the destruction of Mitanni gave the Assyrian kings their first great opportunity for territorial expansion, and during the 13th century BC they extended their frontiers as far west as the Ephrates. However, by the 10th century Assyrian control had declined and was once again limited to the core area around Ashur and Nineveh.

Assyrian kings began a new campaign of expansion in the 9th century BC. Two powerful rulers, Ashurnasirpal II and Shalmaneser III, campaigned as far west as the Mediterranean coastlands and struck deep into southern Mesopotamia. The Euphrates again became the Assyrian border, and the proceeds of conquest went to build elaborate palaces at Nimrud, the new capital city of Assyria. Then, after the accession of King Tigath-pileser III in 744 BC, the Assyrians seized control of more extensive territories than ever before, from Israel in the west to the Persian Gulf. It was the greatest empire the Near East had seen, but it survived for little more than a century. Ashurbanipal, the last great Assyrian ruler, invaded Egypt and conquered Elam, but his power was weakened by civil war. Within a mere two years of the Medes' invasion from Iran in 612 BC, the once mighty empire was destroyed.

Dialects of Post-Mycenaean Greece

4 With the abandonment of the Mycenaean centres between 1200 and 1100 BC Greece entered a "Dark Age". Tradition held that during this period of some 300 years, before the rise of the city-states in the 8th century, southern Greece was conquered and colonised by newcomers from the north known as the Dorians. For many years it was thought that the Dorians had introduced the Greek language. The deciperment of Mycenaean texts in Linear B has shown, however, that the Mycenaeans themselves spoke a form of Greek, and many people now argue that there were no Dorian invasions.

When literacy returned to Greece in the 8th century BC, a patchwork of dialects had emerged, with Doric dominant in the old heartlands of the Mycenaean kingdoms in the Peloponnese, Ionic in Attica, the Aegean islands and the colonies of western Asia Minor, while to the north and west Aeolic and other local dialects were spoken. There is no reason to believe that any of these dialects, or the people who spoke them, were recent arrivals from beyond Greece.

The Rise of Greece

By the 6th century BC, the Mediterranean and Black Sea European coasts were dominated by a series of city-states. They were founded by three separate peoples: the Greeks (successors of the Bronze Age Mycenaeans); Phoenicians (founders of Carthage, from modern Lebanon and Syria); and Etruscans (from northern Italy). Meanwhile, north of the Alps, a new order of Celtic leaders had established themselves in eastern France and southern Germany, linked by trade in luxury goods with the Mediterranean world.

In Greece, the 8th century witnessed a whole series of crucial innovations. One of the most important was the adoption of writing using the alphabet, which was borrowed and adapted from that of the Phoenicians. Already in the 8th century writing was being used to record the first great works of Greek literature, the Iliad and Odyssey, attributed in their final form to Homer, a poet who may have lived on the island of Chios at this time. Equally if not more important was the rise of the Greek city-states, which again can be placed in the 8th century. Their development was fuelled by a growth in overseas trade, by a rise in population, and by a new ethos which banded the people of a region together as a single political entity in which all adult males had citizen rights. Democracy was not yet born, however, and government lay usually in the hands of aristocratic families, or of powerful self-made individuals referred to as "tyrants".

One highly visible result of the so-called "Greek renaissance" was the development of new artistic and architectural styles. Brightly painted pottery manufactured at Corinth and later at Athens was widely traded. A tradition of human sculpture in marble began which was to lead directly to the masterpieces of the Classical style. And great stone temples were built in several Greek cities during the 7th and 6th centuries. With the establishment of Greek colonies around the Black Sea and the west Mediterranean, from the 8th century onwards, these new styles and traditions spread also, and Greek goods were traded northward to the Celts and the Scythians. From the 9th century, the Phoenicians, too, had established colonies on the fringes of the Mediterranean. The most important of these was Carthage, but they also founded settlements in western Sicily, southern Sardinia and southeastern Spain.

In northern Italy, the development of city-states in the 8th century BC was associated with a native people known as the Etruscans. These had their own language and literature (now largely lost) in an alphabetic script they borrowed from the Greeks. During the 7th and 6th centuries they expanded their power into the Po valley, and southwards to Latium – taking control of Rome – and the region of Naples (Neapolis) and Pompeii.

Both Greek and Etruscan goods turn up in richly furnished Celtic graves during the 6th century. A whole series of princely centres developed at this time in eastern France and southern Germany, based in each case in fortified hilltop settlements which were the residences of the leading families or dynasties. These leaders derived their power and prosperity from control over the agricultural resources of the surrounding territory and from their trading relations with neighbouring regions and with the Mediterranean world. It was to be several centuries, however, before the first states and cities were to arise in Europe north of the Alps.

Teutonic Peoples

F i n n o - U g r i a n s

Volga

BALTIC SEA

B a l t i c p e o p l e s

Oder
Vistula
Elbe

S l a v s

Don

Volga

Danube

S c y t h i a n s

Dnieper

I l l y r i a n s

Dniester

Tanais

T h r a c i a n s

Olbia

Tyras

Panticapaeum Phanagoria

Theodosia

Chersonesus

Dioscurias

Danube

ETRUSCAN CITY-STATES

Istrus
Tomi
Callatis
Odessus

B L A C K   S E A

Phasis

C a u c a s i a n s

Cortona
Perusia
...nia
...nii
...nii
...ome

I l l y r i a n s

Mesembria
Apollonia

Sinope

Amisus Trapezos

E M P I R E   O F   T H E   M E D E S

(Persian conquest in progress)

Heracleia

Tigris

I t a l i c p e o p l e s

Epidamnus

Neapolis
Pompeii

Apollonia

Methone

Abdera Maronea Perinthus Byzantium
Acanthus Aenus
Sestus Cardia Cyzicus
Lampsacus
Potidaea

L Y D I A

C I L I C I A

Euphrates

Nineveh

Taras

Sybaris

Croton Ambracia

...anormus Himera

Selinus **Sicily** Rhegium

Akragas Catana

Syracuse

Malta

GREEK CITY STATES

Phocaea

Thebes
Corinth
Argos Athens
Sparta

Pisidians

Ephesus
Miletus

Halicarnassus

Lycians

Salamis
Cyprus

NEW BABYLONIAN EMPIRE

S E A

Crete Gortyn

Semites

─────
13

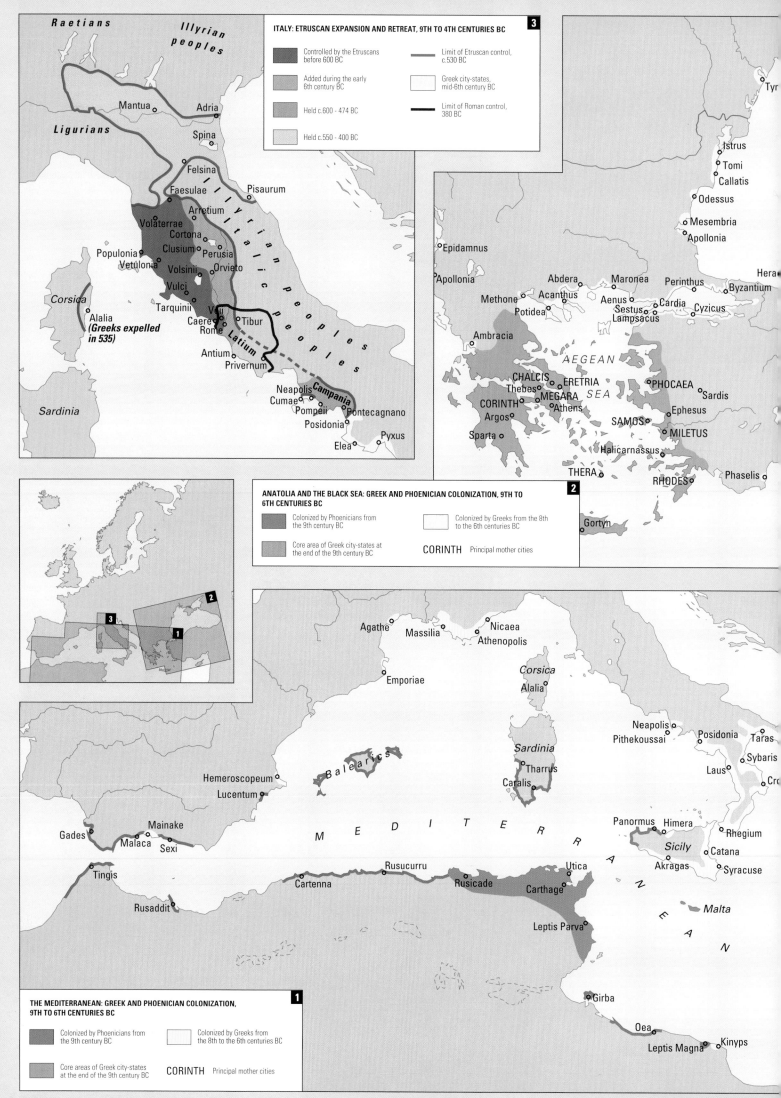

ITALY: ETRUSCAN EXPANSION AND RETREAT, 9TH TO 4TH CENTURIES BC

3

- Controlled by the Etruscans before 600 BC
- Added during the early 6th century BC
- Held c.600 - 474 BC
- Held c.550 - 400 BC
- Limit of Etruscan control, c.530 BC
- Greek city-states, mid-6th century BC
- Limit of Roman control, 380 BC

Raetians

Illyrian peoples

Ligurians

Mantua
Adria
Spina
Felsina
Faesulae
Pisaurum
Arretium
Volaterrae
Cortona
Clusium
Perusia
Populonia
Vetulonia
Volsinii
Orvieto
Vulci
Tarquinii
Veii
Corsica
Alalia
(Greeks expelled in 535)
Caere
Rome
Tibur
Antium
Privernum
Sardinia
Neapolis
Cumae
Pompeii
Posidonia
Pontecagnano
Pyxus
Elea

Illyrian peoples
Illyro-Italic peoples
Latium
Campania

ANATOLIA AND THE BLACK SEA: GREEK AND PHOENICIAN COLONIZATION, 9TH TO 6TH CENTURIES BC

2

- Colonized by Phoenicians from the 9th century BC
- Core area of Greek city-states at the end of the 9th century BC
- Colonized by Greeks from the 8th to the 6th centuries BC
- CORINTH Principal mother cities

Epidamnus
Apollonia
Methone
Potidea
Ambracia
Abdera
Maronea
Acanthus
Aenus
Sestus
Lampsacus
Cardia
Perinthus
Cyzicus
Byzantium
Hera
Tyr
Istrus
Tomi
Callatis
Odessus
Mesembria
Apollonia
AEGEAN SEA
CHALCIS
ERETRIA
Thebes
MEGARA
CORINTH
Athens
Argos
Sparta
PHOCAEA
Sardis
Ephesus
SAMOS
MILETUS
Halicarnassus
THERA
RHODES
Phaselis
Gortyn

THE MEDITERRANEAN: GREEK AND PHOENICIAN COLONIZATION, 9TH TO 6TH CENTURIES BC

1

- Colonized by Phoenicians from the 9th century BC
- Core areas of Greek city-states at the end of the 9th century BC
- Colonized by Greeks from the 8th to the 6th centuries BC
- CORINTH Principal mother cities

Agathe
Massilia
Nicaea
Athenopolis
Emporiae
Corsica
Alalia
Neapolis
Pithekoussai
Posidonia
Taras
Sybaris
Laus
Cr
Hemeroscopeum
Lucentum
Balearics
Sardinia
Tharrus
Caralis
Panormus
Himera
Rhegium
Sicily
Catana
Akragas
Syracuse
Gades
Mainake
Malaca
Sexi
Tingis
Rusaddit
Cartenna
Rusucurru
Rusicade
Utica
Carthage
Leptis Parva
MEDITERRANEAN
Malta
Girba
Oea
Leptis Magna
Kinyps

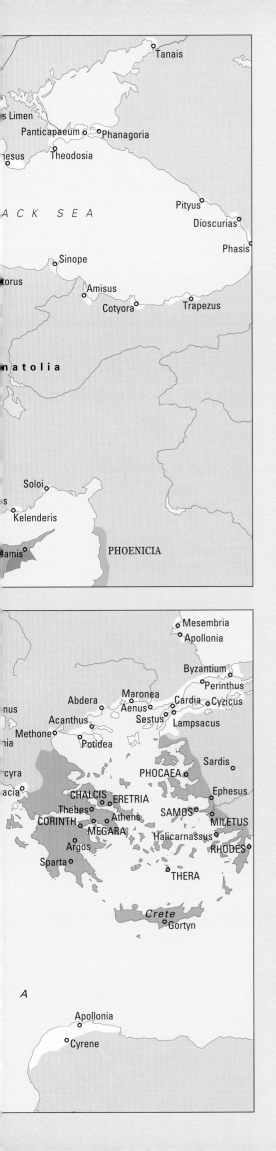

The Mediterranean: Greek and Phoenician Colonization from the 9th to the 6th Centuries BC

1 Greek and Phoenician settlers founded a number of colonies around the shores of the west Mediterranean from the 9th century BC. The Phoenicians concentrated their efforts on the North African coast and southern Spain. Their most important colony was the city of Carthage in modern Tunisia, traditionally founded in 814 BC, though the earliest archaeological evidence dates from the 8th century. The earliest Greek colony in the west was the settlement of Pithekoussai (c.750 BC), on the small island of Ischia off the coast of Italy, and Euboeans, Corinthians and Phocaeans went on to found a whole series of colonies in southern Italy, Sicily and southern France. Some of these, most notably Syracuse (733 BC) and Massilia (Marseilles, 600 BC), became major cities.

By the early 6th century, Greeks and Phoenicians had established separate spheres of interest in the west Mediterranean, but friction between them led to a number of wars, many of them focused on Sicily where the Greeks and Phoenicians occupied opposite ends of the island. In around 540 BC the balance of power was disturbed when Phocaean Greeks, who had been driven from their own city by the Persians, established a new home at Alalia on Corsica. The Carthaginians allied themselves with the Etruscans, and in a great sea battle forced the Phocaeans to abandon their settlement. Greek attempts to plant colonies in southern Spain (such as Mainake) were also suppressed by the Carthaginians as the latter strengthened their hold over the coasts and sea-lanes of the west Mediterranean basin. The Greek colony of Massilia continued to flourish, however, while southern Italy became so firmly hellenized that it was later known to the Romans as Magna Graecia, "Greater Greece".

Anatolia and the Black Sea: Greek and Phoenician Colonization from the 9th to the 6th Centuries BC

2 Greek merchants may have begun trading in the Black Sea as early as the 8th century BC, but the first permanent colonies were established only towards the end of the 7th century. The attraction of the region was the fertile cereal lands, especially those of what is now the Ukraine. The Greeks traded manufactured goods, some imported from Greece, to the native peoples in return for raw materials and foodstuffs. North of the Danube, political power over the interior was in the hands of the Scythians, a nomadic horse-riding people of the steppes, who acted as overlords to settled agriculturalists in the Crimea and in the valleys of the major rivers. Greek manufactures, including painted pottery and metalwork, were passed to Scythian leaders either as gifts or through trade, and they occur in the great Scythian burial mounds on the southern steppes. Greek craftsmen of the Black Sea colonies also produced metalwork to order, in a style designed specifically to appeal to their Scythian customers. Trade between the Black Sea and the Aegean made control of the sea-routes between them increasingly important, and a number of Greek colonies were founded on the coast there in the 7th and 6th centuries, including the key city of Byzantium (c. 660 BC). During the 5th century, Athens in particular came to rely heavily on Black Sea grain to support her large population, and it was loss of control over the straits to the Spartans that eventually brought her to defeat at the end of the Peloponnesian War (*see* page 20).

Italy: Etruscan Expansion and Retreat from the 9th to the 4th Centuries BC

3 The Etruscans became the leading power in northern and central Italy during the 6th century BC. United by a common language and culture, they were divided politically into a series of city-states. The most important of these were the members of the League of Twelve Cities, which met together for religious ceremonies and political discussions at the sanctuary of Voltumna, their principal goddess, near Volsinii.

The Etruscans soon began to extend their control into neighbouring regions of Italy. In the 7th century a line of Etruscan kings established themselves at Rome, turning the modest existing settlement of Latin farmers into a minor city. Further to the south, they won control of Greek colonies around the Bay of Naples, including Capua and Pompeii. This brought them into conflict with the Greeks, and in 535 BC the Etruscans fought a naval engagement in alliance with the Carthaginians, which resulted in the Greeks being expelled from Corsica. During the course of the 6th century, the Etruscans also cast their eyes northward, establishing colonies in the Po valley. The most important of these new cities were Spina and Adria, trading centres at the mouth of the Po which gave the Etruscans direct access to the Adriatic.

Etruscan power reached its peak in around 530 BC. The tide began to turn six years later, when they tried and failed to capture the Greek city of Cumae. In 510 BC, the Latins of Rome expelled their Etruscan king and established a republic. This cut the overland communications between Etruria and Campania, a problem which was compounded in 474 BC when the Greeks defeated the Etruscans in a sea battle off Cumae. Etruscan power was already sharply in decline when, in 396 BC, the Romans captured Veii, the first of the League of Twelve Cities to fall into foreign hands. By that time, the Etruscans had lost control of the Po Valley to the invading Gauls, while the cities of Campania had fallen to local Italic peoples. During the 4th and 3rd centuries, the remaining Etruscan cities were steadily absorbed by the expansionist Roman state.

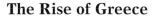

550 BC

The Battle of Salamis

The Persian Wars of the 5th century BC were a turning point in the early history of Europe. The victories over the Persians at Salamis in 480 BC and at Plataea the following year gave the Greeks new confidence and prosperity, leading to developments in art and literature which were the hallmark of the Classical age. Athens attained a particular prominence, taking her place alongside Sparta as one of the two leading city-states. This in itself was a marked change from the previous century, when Athens had been only a secondary power, with few warships to her name. Then in 483 BC a rich new seam was discovered in the Athenian silver mines at Laurium, and the Athenians used this new-found prosperity to build a fleet of 200 warships. These proved her salvation during the Persian invasion of 480 BC, and laid the foundations of the great Athenian maritime empire which survived until the capitulation of Athens at the end of the Peloponnesian War in 404 BC (*see* page 20).

The Greek cities of Ionia remained a significant force during the 5th century, though the conquest by Persia in 546-45 BC had damaged their power and prosperity. Still hankering after their lost freedom, they led an abortive revolt against Persian rule in 499 BC (beginning in the city of Miletus) which directed the wrath of the Persians against Greece itself. Two major Persian expeditions against the Greeks in 490 BC and 480 BC failed in the face of stiff resistance from Athens and Sparta, and the Persians gave up their attempts to subdue mainland Greece. Freed at last from Persian rule after the Salamis campaign (480 BC), the Ionian Greeks found all too soon that they had merely exchanged their old masters for new; and the Delian League, founded for their mutual defence, soon transformed itself into an Athenian empire (*see* map 1, page 23).

In the central Mediterranean, Greek interests were opposed by an alliance of Carthaginians and Etruscans. In 535 BC the two sides came to blows at the battle of Alalia, which forced the Greeks to abandon Corsica. But the Carthaginian attempt to expel the Greeks from Sicily in 480 BC ended in disaster when their invading force suffered crushing defeat at Himera. Nonetheless, the Carthaginians retained a significant presence in western Sicily. Their erstwhile allies, the Etruscans, seem to have played no part in this campaign, and indeed Etruscan power in central Italy was already past its peak. In 524 BC the Etruscans had attempted to extend their power deep into southern Italy by an assault on the Greek city of Cumae, but this was repulsed with heavy loss. A few years later, in 510 BC, the city of Rome broke free from Etruscan rule, expelling the Tarquins (an Etruscan dynasty) and establishing itself as an independent republic.

Europe north of the Mediterranean and Black Sea first entered the writings of Greek historians in the 5th century BC. They divided the continent between Celts (occupying Western and Central Europe) and Scythians (in the lands north of the Black Sea). Imports of Greek and Etruscan pottery and metalwork show that both Celts and Scythians were in contact with the Mediterranean world, though both peoples also had indigenous identities and traditions, as shown in the richly furnished burials of Celtic and Scythian leaders. It was the Scythians, together with their neighbours the Thracians and the Greek cities of the northern Aegean, who first encountered the expansionist ambitions of the Persian empire under Darius the Great.

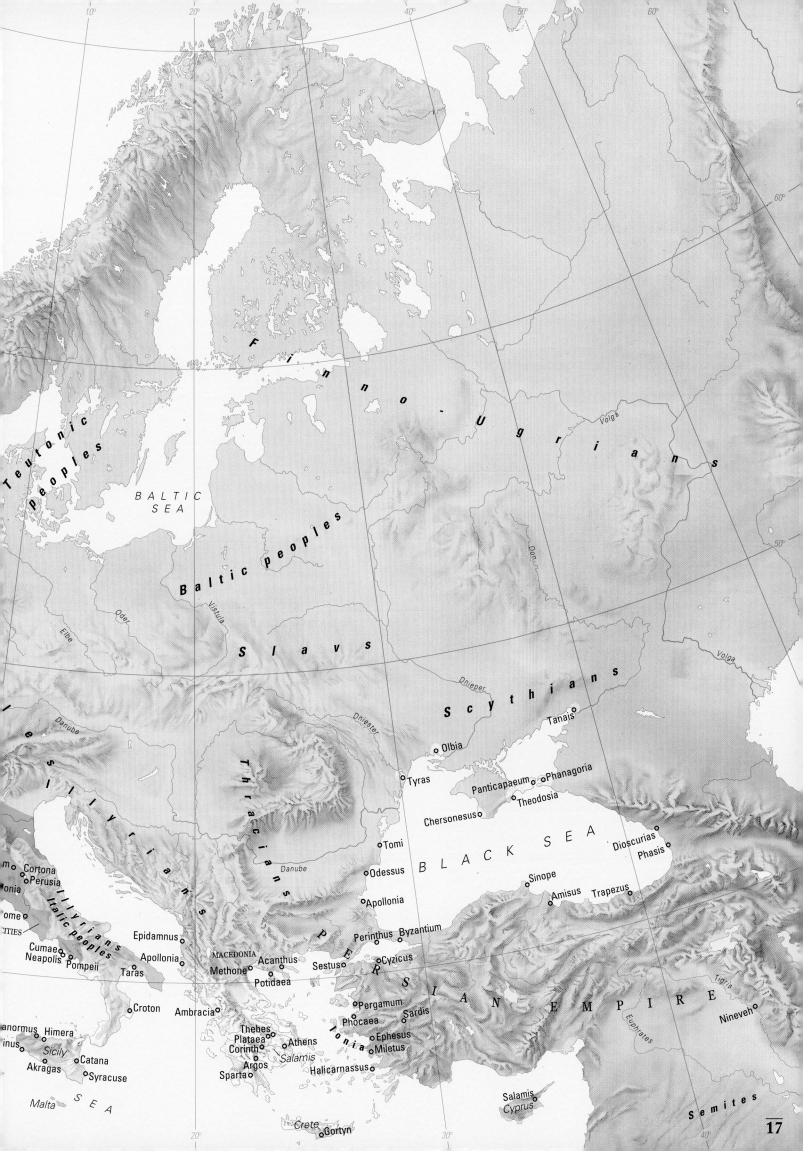

Teutonic
Peoples

BALTIC
SEA

Finno-Ugrians

Baltic peoples

Volga

Oder

Vistula

Elbe

Slavs

Don

50°

Danube

Dnieper

Scythians

Dniester

Tanais

Volga

Olbia

Thracians

Tyras

Panticapaeum
Phanagoria

Theodosia

Chersonesus

Dioscurias

Tomi

Phasis

Danube

Odessus

BLACK SEA

Apollonia

Sinope

Amisus
Trapezus

Illyrians

Cortona

Perusia

onia

Rome

Italic peoples

CITIES

Epidamnus

Perinthus Byzantium

Cyzicus

Cumae

Apollonia

Sestus

Neapolis

Pompeii

MACEDONIA

Taras

Methone
Acanthus

Potidaea

PERSIAN EMPIRE

Pergamum

Tigris

Croton

Ambracia

Phocaea
Sardis

Nineveh

Ionia

anormus Himera

Thebes

Ephesus

Euphrates

inus

Plataea

Corinth
Athens

Miletus

Sicily

Catana

Salamis

Halicarnassus

Akragas
Syracuse

Argos
Sparta

Malta

SEA

Salamis

Cyprus

Semites

Crete
Gortyn

17

MACEDONIA

PERSIAN

Thasos
Samothrace
Imbros
Sestus
Hellespont
Abydos
Lemnos

EMPIRE

AEGEAN

Epirus

Corcyra

Thessaly

SEA

Mytilene

Ambracia

Scyros

Artemisium
Oreus
Thermopylae
Euboea

Acarnania
Leucas

Aetolia

Delphi

Boeotia
Thebes
Plataea   Marathon

Eretria

Cyme

Erythrae

Cephallenia

Achaea
Sicyon
Corinth

Megara
Salamis

Attica
Athens

Andros

Ephesus

Zacynthus

Elis

Arcadia

Argolis
Argos

Tenos

Icaria

Miletus

Cyclades

Dodecanes

Tegea
Messenia   Sparta

Paros
Naxos
Naxos
Amorgos

Laconia

Asine

Melos

Cythera

SEA OF CRETE

Carpathos

Cydonia
Crete

Illyrians

Thracians

Istrus
Tomi
Callatis

Odessus

Mesembria
Apollonia

Thrace

PERSIAN

MACEDONIA
Abdera   Maronea
Potidaea

Perinthus
Lampsacus
Sestus

Byzantium
Cyzicus

EMPIRE

Thessaly
GREEK

Boeotia
Corinth   Marathon
Salamis   Athens
STATES
Sparta

Sardis
Ephesus
Miletus
Halicarnassus

Gortyn

THE AEGEAN AND THE BALKANS: PERSIAN EXPANSION, 513–480 BC

1

Secured by Persia by 540 BC

Added to Persia

in c. 518 BC

in 513 BC

by 480 BC

Persian vassal from 513 BC

Allied with Persia, 480 BC

Approximate Western frontier of Persian influence from 449 BC

GREECE AND THE PERSIAN WARS, 490–479 BC

The Persian Empire and vassal state, 490 BC

Conquered by Persia by 480 BC

Greek states allied with Persia by 480 BC

Greek states opposed to Persia

Neutral Greek states

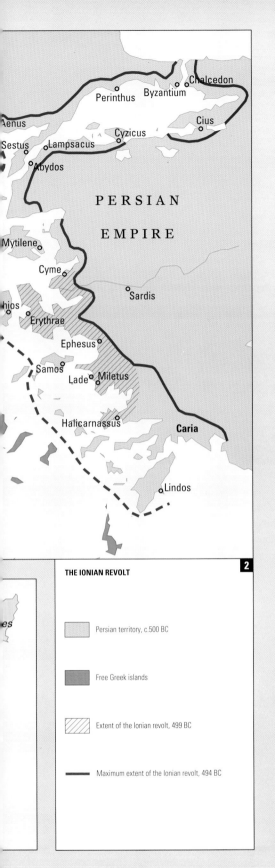

THE IONIAN REVOLT

Persian territory, c.500 BC

Free Greek islands

Extent of the Ionian revolt, 499 BC

Maximum extent of the Ionian revolt, 494 BC

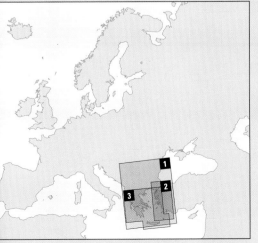

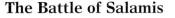

The Aegean and the Balkans: Persian Expansion 513-480 BC

1 The Persians made their first expedition into Europe during the reign of King Darius I (522-486 BC). In 513 BC Darius led a substantial Persian army across the Bosphorus to conquer Thrace and the lands south of the Danube. He then crossed the Danube and fought a wide-ranging but inconclusive campaign against the Scythians, who simply retreated before him, burning crops and blocking wells. It was only with difficulty that Darius managed to extricate his army. Despite this reverse, the Persians succeeded during the remainder of 513 BC in consolidating their hold on the northern shore of the Aegean and the Greek cities of the Hellespont. The Persians also reached the borders of the Kingdom of Macedonia in northern Greece, and accepted the submission of the Macedonian king Amyntas.

That remained the limit of Persian power until 480 BC, when Darius's son and successor Xerxes invaded Greece with an enormous army, receiving the submission of the Thessalians and Boeotians. By the end of August his forces had conquered Athens and Attica, but defeats at Salamis and Plataea forced them to withdraw, and within five years Persian possessions in Europe had been reduced to a handful of coastal cities. By 460 BC, even these had been lost, and Persian dreams of empire in Europe were over.

The Ionian Revolt

2 The Greek cities of western Asia Minor had been brought under Persian rule in 546-45 BC, during the reign of Cyrus the Great. They remained restless in their subjection, and in 499 BC broke out in open revolt against the Persians. The revolt was master-minded by Aristagoras, the ruler of Miletus, but soon spread to Caria in the southwest and northwards to the Greek cities of the Bosphorus. Aristagoras sought assistance from the free cities of mainland Greece, but Sparta refused assistance and only Athens and Eretria responded with men and ships. Mainland enthusiasm for the struggle petered out, however, after an abortive attempt to capture Sardis ended with heavy losses for the Greek side. The rebel fleet was eventually defeated by the Persians at the battle of Lade in 494 BC, and remaining resistance was soon stamped out. The Persians did not forget, however, that the Athenians had assisted the rebels, and it was to teach them a lesson that Darius in 490 BC sent an expeditionary force against Athens itself, only to encounter defeat at the battle of Marathon (*see below*).

Greece and the Persian Wars, 490-479 BC

3 In 490 BC the Persian king Darius I sent an expeditionary force by sea across the Aegean to punish Athens and Eretria for the help they had given to the rebels during the Ionian revolt. They captured Naxos and burned Eretria before moving south to Attica. They chose as their landfall the sandy bay of Marathon, on the opposite side of the peninsula to Athens. The Athenians mustered their forces and marched out against the enemy, and in a confused engagement won a resounding victory over a Persian army which was more than twice the size of their own force. The Persians lost several thousand men; the Athenians fewer than 200.

When next the Persians turned their attention to Greece their aim was to conquer the whole country. This was the famous expedition of Xerxes (486-464 BC), Darius's son and successor. The Greek historian Herodotus claims that the massive Persian invasion force numbered over five million men, and though the true figure was probably nearer 300,000, it was a truly formidable army, since even major Greek states such as Athens and Sparta could muster only 10,000 soldiers apiece .

In the spring of 480 BC Xerxes gathered his forces at the Hellespont and led them across to Europe over a bridge of boats. They marched along the northern shore of the Aegean as far as Macedonia, the Persian fleet shadowing them along the coast. Many states in northern Greece remained neutral, and Thessaly even entered an alliance with the invading Persians. North of the Peloponnese only Athens was a firm member of the anti-Persian alliance. Xerxes encountered the first serious resistance at Thermopylae, where a narrow pass barred the way to southern Greece. The Greeks had determined to defend the pass as long as possible, and for six days a force of 7,000 men, led by the Spartan king Leonidas, held the pass against the entire might of Xerxes' army. At last, on the seventh, they were surrounded and overcome by the weight of the Persians' superior numbers, Leonidas and his Spartans being killed in the fighting.

Xerxes next advanced to Attica, and captured Athens itself, though most of the Athenian citizens had already been evacuated to safety. Some of the Greeks were for staging a final stand at the Isthmus of Corinth, but the Athenians persuaded them to risk all on a sea battle in the narrow straits of Salamis. The result was a decisive Greek victory, which greatly discouraged Xerxes. The Persian king returned to Sardis in Asia Minor, leaving a reduced Persian force to continue the campaign under the command of his son-in-law Mardonius. When he too was defeated at Plataea in 479 BC and the Persian fleet was destroyed at Cape Mycale, the Persians finally gave up their hopes of conquering Greece. But they had stirred up a hornet's nest, and during the following decades the Greeks remained a thorn in their side, ejecting the Persians from Thrace and the Hellespont and chipping away at Persian territories in Asia Minor.

480 BC

Europe after Alexander

In the summer of 323 BC, on the eve of yet a further campaign, Alexander the Great died at Babylon. In a reign of only 13 years (336-323 BC) his Macedonian armies had defeated the Persian ruler Darius III and conquered the vast Persian realm. For a brief moment, the Greek and Persian worlds were united in a single mighty empire extending from the Adriatic to the River Indus.

The political power of the Greek city-states had passed its peak by the middle of 4th century BC. The defeat of the Persians in 480-479 BC had been followed by the establishment of the Delian League, under the leadership of Athens, in 478 BC. The league was soon transformed into an Athenian empire, and the growing power of Athens brought her into direct conflict with Sparta, Thebes and Corinth, which led to the outbreak of the Peloponnesian War in 431 BC. No match for Sparta on land, Athens was nonetheless secure as long as her fleet retained supremacy at sea. The turning point came with the ill-judged Athenian expedition against Syracuse in 415-413 BC. Crushingly defeated, the Athenians managed to struggle on for a further eight years, but finally lost their fleet and surrendered to the Spartans in 404 BC. The Athenian Empire was dissolved: she was forced to become an ally of Sparta; she had to give up her fleet; and her defensive walls were destroyed.

With the defeat of Athens, Sparta became the leading Greek state for over 30 years, until the Spartans in turn were defeated by the Thebans at Leuctra in 371 BC. But while the power of individual city-states rose and fell, Greece remained a divided land, and last-minute efforts to unite against Philip of Macedon were to no avail. Greece lost her political independence at the battle of Chaeronea in 338 BC and became a dependency within the empire of Philip and his son Alexander the Great. In 334 BC, Alexander crossed into Asia Minor. He defeated the armies of Darius in several engagements against overwhelming odds. By 330 BC he had conquered most of the Persian lands, and then pressed eastwards as far as the borders of India.

The story of the west Mediterranean during the 4th century BC can be summarised under two major themes: the continuing rivalry between Greeks and Carthaginians in Sicily; and the changing fortunes of Rome and the Etruscans in Italy. Rome grew as Etruscan power waned; the Etruscan city of Veii fell to the Romans in 396 BC. By 350 BC Rome controlled the whole of Latium and southern Etruria, and by 320 BC had extended her power far to the south, to the region of Capua and Naples.

The rise of Rome was not without its setbacks, however: in 390 BC the city was captured and sacked by the Senones, one of several peoples from north of the Alps known as Gauls to the Romans and Celts to the Greeks. Celtic expansion into Italy had begun in the 5th century, and though accompanied by raids on wealthy Italian cities, its main aim was to settle new territory. The Celtic heartland lay in eastern France and southern Germany, but Celtic incursions into northern Italy were so successful that the land beyond the Po became known to the Romans as Gallia Cisalpina, "Gaul this-side-of-the-Alps". It became part of Celtic Europe, a conglomeration of kingdoms and peoples known to us through their art, their princely burials, their fortified centres, and through the writings of Classical historians.

Carthaginian possessions

Greek city-states

Dependencies of Alexander's Empire

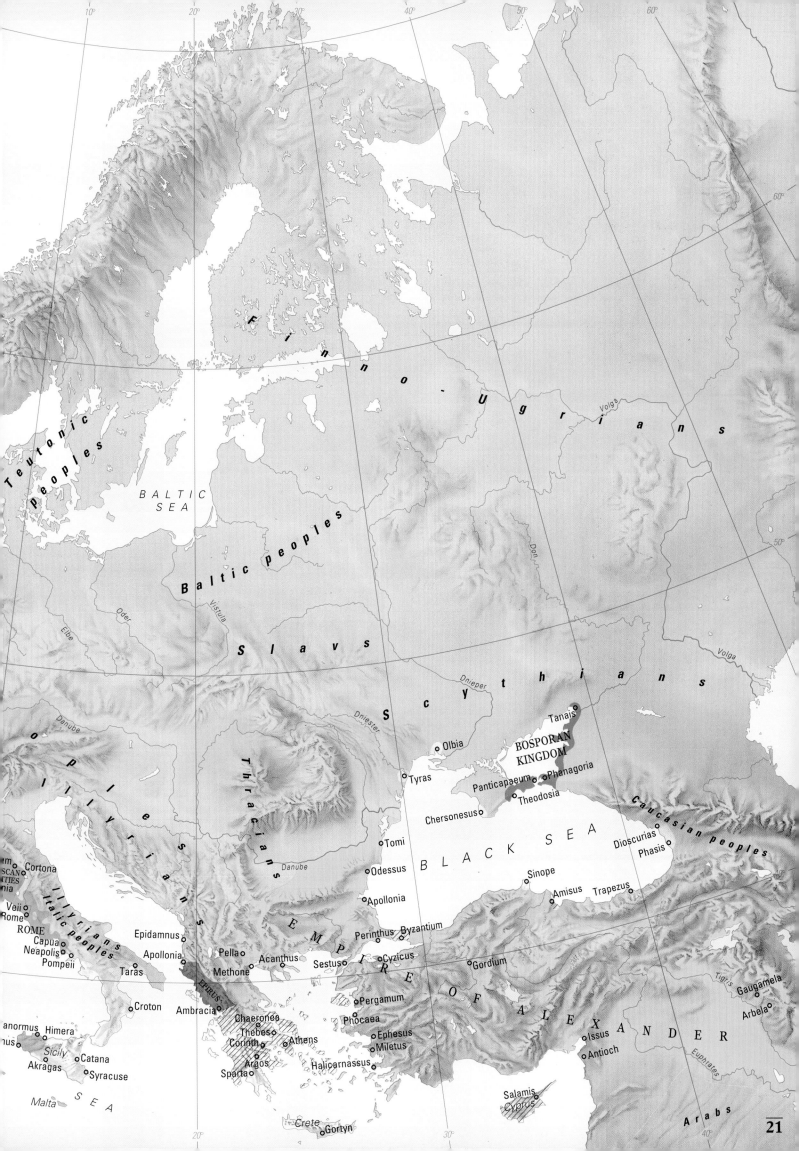

Teutonic
Peoples

BALTIC
SEA

Finno-
Ugrians

Volga

Baltic peoples

Oder

Elbe

Vistula

Slavs

Don

Dnieper

Danube

Dniester

Volga

Scythians

Tanais

Olbia

BOSPORAN
KINGDOM

Tyras

Panticapaeum

Phanagoria

Theodosia

Caucasian peoples

Thracians

Chersonesus

Dioscurias

Phasis

Tomi

Danube

Odessus

BLACK SEA

Sinope

Apollonia

Amisus   Trapezus

Illyrians

EMPIRE

Perinthus   Byzantium

Italic peoples

Cyzicus

Gordium

Tigris

um
SCAN
TIES
nia

Cortona

Veii
Rome

ROME

Capua

Epidamnus

Apollonia

Pella

Acanthus

Sestuso

Gaugamela

Neapolis

Methone

OF

Arbela

Pompeii

Taras

EPIRUS

Pergamum

ALEXANDER

Croton

Ambracia

Chaeronea

Phocaea

Issus

anormus   Himera

Thebes
Corinth

Athens

Ephesus

Antioch

us

Sicily   Catana

Argos

Halicarnassus

Miletus

Euphrates

Akragas   Syracuse

Sparta

Malta   SEA

Crete   Gortyn

Salamis
Cyprus

Arabs

21

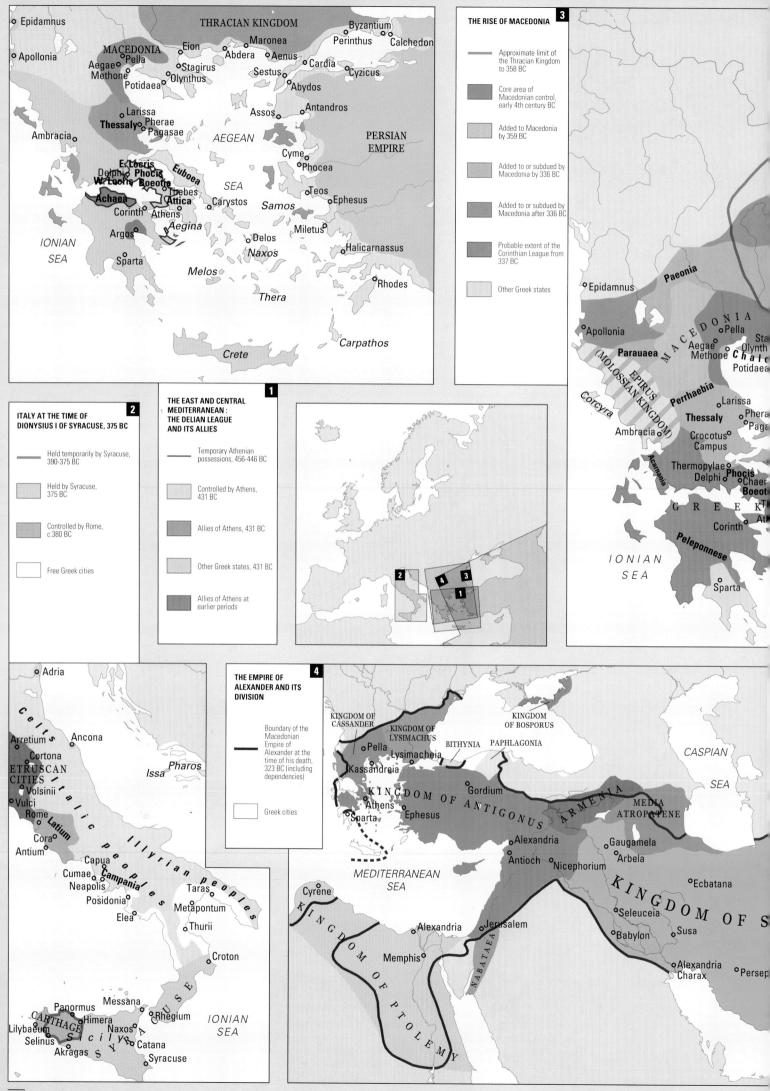

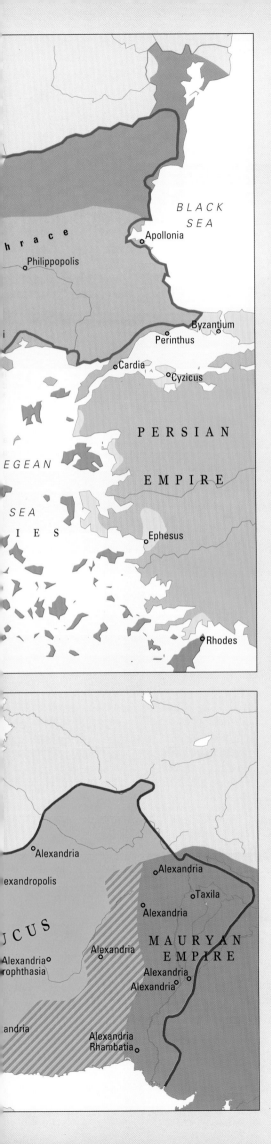

The East and Central Mediterranean: the Delian League and its Allies

1 The Persian invasion of Greece and its defeat had demonstrated the importance of uniting in the face of a powerful and aggressive neighbour. Individual Greek city-states could not hope to resist the might of the Persian Empire, which remained a serious threat even after the Greek victories at Salamis (480 BC) and Plataea (479 BC); *see* map 3, page 19. It was the continued need for mutual protection which led to the formation of the Delian League in 478 BC. The league had a treasury on the island of Delos, into which member-states paid an annual contribution. This revenue was used to support naval expeditions aimed at freeing the Greek cities of Thrace and Asia Minor from Persian control, and confronting Persian counter-attacks.

Leadership of the League fell to Athens, and such was the power of the Athenian fleet that by the middle of the 5th century what had begun as a voluntary defensive confederacy was transformed into an Athenian empire. In 454 BC, the treasury of the League was transferred from Delos to Athens, where some of it was used for the building of the Parthenon. A series of revolts were ruthlessly suppressed, but though many League members grew increasingly discontented, Athens steadily strengthened her position as the head of a maritime empire, covering most of the shores and islands of the Aegean. This led to direct confrontation with the cities of Peloponnesian League, led by Sparta, and the outbreak of the Peloponnesian War in 431 BC.

Italy at the Time of Dionysius I of Syracuse, 375 BC

2 The Greek victory at Himera in 480 BC had far from put an end to Carthaginian ambitions in Sicily, where Carthaginian cities continued to dominate the western end of the island. In 409 BC the Carthaginians staged a second major invasion of Greek Sicily, capturing the cities of Selinus and Akragas.

It was in this crisis that Dionysius, an able man of humble origin, seized power at Syracuse, the principal Greek city, and gradually extended his rule over the greater part of the island. In two hard-fought wars against the Carthaginians (398-397 BC, 392 BC), Dionysius drove them back again to the western end of Sicily. He then turned his attentions to the Italian mainland, and by 379 BC had conquered the southern peninsula, and made the Greek cities beyond this into dependencies of Syracuse. He even gained control of the distant Adriatic cities of Issa, Ancona and Adria.

Dionysius strengthened his hold over these territories by building up a powerful fleet, and protected himself at home by constructing a formidable ring of fortifications around Syracuse, which remained the capital of his empire. His reign ended in setback, however, for in 379 BC the Carthaginians once again won the upper hand in western Sicily, and Dionysius was still trying to recover his losses when he died 12 years later.

The Rise of Macedonia

3 The kingdom of Macedonia lay outside the core area of Classical Greece, and first rose to prominence only in the 4th century BC. The architect of Macedonia's greatness was Philip II, who came to power at a time when the kingdom was threatened by foreign enemies and internal unrest. He quickly established his authority, and by remodelling the Macedonian army created a fighting force which he then used to expand Macedonian power far beyond the frontiers he had inherited. By 352 BC he had conquered Thessaly and the Greek cities of the northern Aegean. By 341 BC he had added most of Thrace to his territories.

To counteract the growing power of Macedon the city-states of southern Greece formed an alliance led by Thebes and Athens, but their army was decisively defeated by the Macedonians at the battle of Chaeronea in 338 BC. The following year, Philip organised the Greek cities into the Corinthian League under Macedonian control. Each member of the League was to provide ships or men for a great expedition against the Persian Empire. It was on the eve of his departure for this campaign, in the summer of 336 BC, that Philip was assassinated, and his son Alexander came to power.

The Empire of Alexander and its Division

4 The conquest of the Persian Empire by Alexander the Great is one of the great hero-stories of ancient history. His army not only subjugated the vast Persian realm but also crossed the River Indus and fought against the rulers of the Punjab. Greek colonies were founded at strategic places, and Alexander endeavoured to bind his heterogeneous territories together by a policy of harmony and co-operation between Persians and Macedonians. His plans were cut short by his illness and death at Babylon in June 323 BC.

Though loyal generals attempted to hold Alexander's empire in trust for his infant son and heir, others were driven by personal ambitions and rivalry and division soon set in. By 300 BC the empire had broken into several independent kingdoms, the largest being those ruled by Seleucus, Ptolemy and Antigonus. Further fragmentation followed, as these generals devoted their energies to fighting each other in Greece and the Near East rather than to countering the secessionist tendencies of local rulers. The most significant losses were in the east, where Seleucus ceded the frontier provinces of his kingdom to the Indian ruler Chandragupta Maurya, founder of the Mauryan empire which dominated the subcontinent throughout the following century.

323 BC

The Rise of Rome

The struggle for supremacy between the generals of Alexander the Great continued during the first decades of the 3rd century BC. Egypt and many of the Aegean coasts and islands were ruled by the Ptolemies with their powerful fleet, though several smaller maritime states, such as the important island of Rhodes, managed to maintain their independence. The city-states of southern Greece, too, tried to regain their independence, playing off the larger powers against each other, and forming separate confederacies: the Achaean League in the north of the Peloponnese, and the Aetolian League on the opposite side of the Gulf of Corinth. But the Greeks were as often fighting each other as uniting against a common enemy, and periods of true independence were transitory and brief.

Greece was still overshadowed by the power of the kingdom of Macedon to the north which, after years of civil war and disputed succession following the death of Alexander, entered a new period of relatively stable rule under Antigonus Gonatas (276-239 BC). Eastwards again lay the enormous Seleucid Empire, comprising most of the Asiatic territories of Alexander's empire. Already by 270 BC, however, powerful centripetal forces were in motion, and independent kingdoms had formed in Asia Minor and Bactria. Particularly important in later years was the kingdom of Pergamum, in western Asia Minor, which declared its independence from the Seleucids in 263 BC.

In the central Mediterranean, the major powers of the early 3rd century BC were Rome and Carthage. For Rome, this was a period of conquest and consolidation, from which she emerged as ruler of virtually all peninsular Italy. Carthage, meanwhile, was still preoccupied with the threat posed by the Greek city-states of Sicily. In 310 BC, the Carthaginians had attempted to conquer the whole of the island, and came near to achieving their aim until Agathocles, ruler of Syracuse, turned the tables on them by invading the Carthaginian homeland in North Africa. Agathocles was eventually defeated in 307 BC, and the peace treaty which followed restored the previous balance of power between the Greeks and Carthaginians, with no significant gains for either side. The campaign launched against the Carthaginians by Pyrrhus in 278 BC likewise achieved no significant changes. The western Mediterranean remained largely a Carthaginian sphere until their defeat in the Punic Wars (*see* map 1, page 31), though the Greek colony of Massilia and its western outposts retained a hold on trade along the coasts of southern France and the Spanish Levant.

To the north of these lands lay the territories of the Celts, Scythians and Celtiberians. The Celts had already invaded the Mediterranean lands in the 4th century, and did so again during the 3rd. In 281 BC they defeated Ceraunus, king of Macedonia, and two years later mounted a major invasion of Greece, lured by the wealth of the cities and sanctuaries there. They were turned back at Delphi, and decisively defeated by the Macedonians at Lysimacheia in Thrace in 277 BC. But meanwhile another Celtic army had crossed the Hellespont into Asia Minor, where they established the kingdom of Galatia, and spread alarm and dismay among their neighbours by their raids and warfare. Eventually brought to heel by King Attalus of Pergamum in 240 BC, Galatia nonetheless survived as a separate kingdom until it was absorbed into the Roman Empire in 25 BC.

Teutonic
Peoples

BALTIC
SEA

Finno-Ugrians

Volga

Baltic peoples

Oder

Vistula

Elbe

Slavs

Scythians

Dnieper

Danube

Dniester

Volga

Thracians

Olbia

BOSPORAN
KINGDOM

Tanais

Don

Tyras

Panticapaeum

Phanagoria

Theodosia

Chersonesus

Caucasian peoples

Istrus
Tomi
Callatis
Odessus

Dioscurias

Phasis

BLACK SEA

Arretium

Perusia

Danube

Mesembria
Apollonia

Sinope

Amisus

Trapezus

ROMAN-LED

Rome

ITALIAN

Capua

Neapolis

Pompeii

ALLIANCE

Epidamnus

Apollonia

Tarentum

Croton

Ambracia

EPIRUS

MACEDON

AETOLIAN LEAGUE

ACHAEAN LEAGUE

Pella

Methone

Potidaea

Abdera

Acanthus

Maronea

Aenus

Delphi

Thebes

Corinth

Argos

Sparta

Chalcis

Athens

TYLISIAN
KINGDOM

Perinthus

Cardia

Sestus

Byzantium

Lampsacus

Cyzicus

PAPHLAGONIA

BITHYNIA

PONTUS

GALATIA

ARMENIA

CAPPADOCIA

MEDIA
ATROPATENE

PERGAMUM

Pergamum

Phocaea

Sardes

Ephesus

Miletus

SELEUCID EMPIRE

Euphrates

Tigris

Antioch

Halicarnassus

anormus

Himera

Sicily

Rhegium

Catana

Syracuse

Akragas

Malta

SEA

PTOLEMAIC EMPIRE

RHODES

Crete

Gortyn

Salamis

Cyprus

Arabs

Illyrians

Illyrians

25

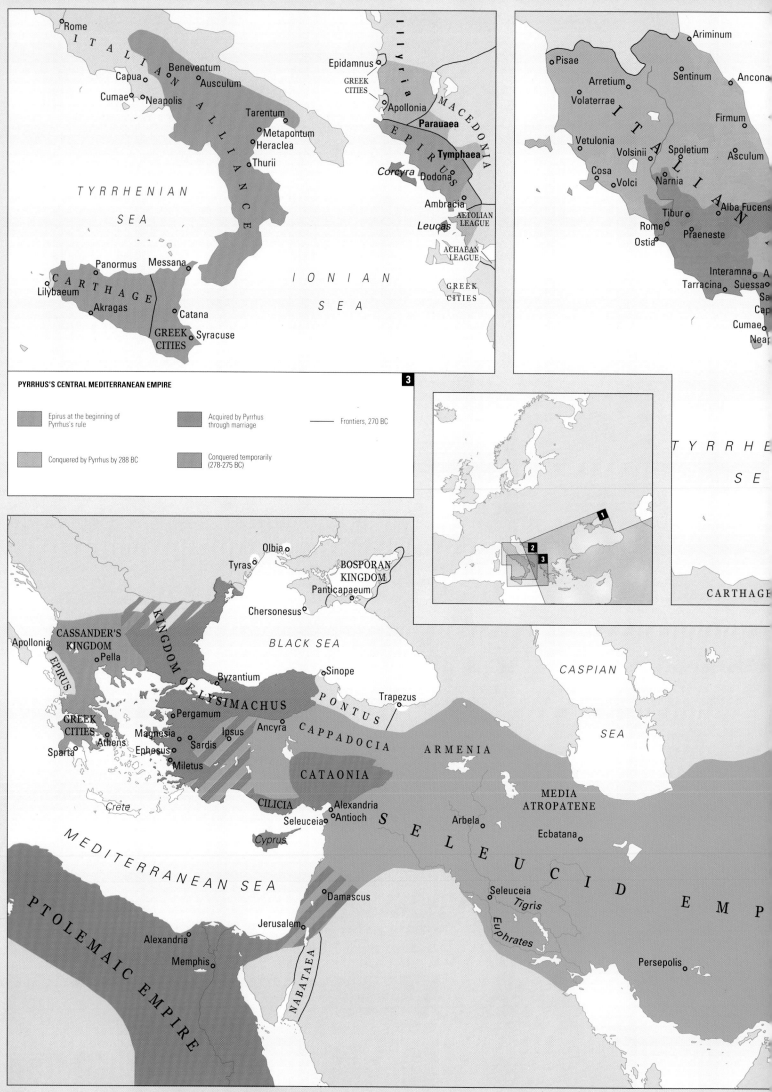

PYRRHUS'S CENTRAL MEDITERRANEAN EMPIRE

- Epirus at the beginning of Pyrrhus's rule
- Conquered by Pyrrhus by 288 BC
- Acquired by Pyrrhus through marriage
- Conquered temporarily (278–275 BC)
- Frontiers, 270 BC

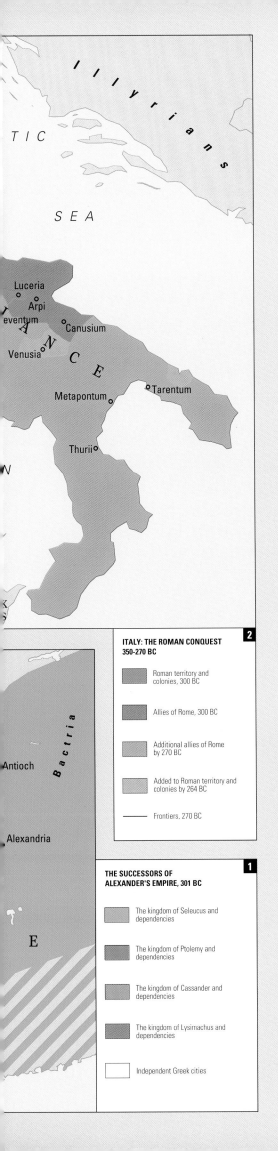

ITALY: THE ROMAN CONQUEST 350-270 BC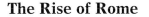

- Roman territory and colonies, 300 BC
- Allies of Rome, 300 BC
- Additional allies of Rome by 270 BC
- Added to Roman territory and colonies by 264 BC
- Frontiers, 270 BC

THE SUCCESSORS OF ALEXANDER'S EMPIRE, 301 BC

- The kingdom of Seleucus and dependencies
- The kingdom of Ptolemy and dependencies
- The kingdom of Cassander and dependencies
- The kingdom of Lysimachus and dependencies
- Independent Greek cities

The Successors of Alexander's Empire, 301 BC

1 The death of Alexander the Great at Babylon in June 323 BC was followed almost immediately by warfare between his generals over the division of the empire. The attempt to install Alexander's half-wit half-brother and infant son as joint kings of Macedon and overlords of the whole empire was soon overwhelmed by the forces of *realpolitik*. The political map shifted continuously as alliances were forged and broken and battles won and lost.

By 310 BC there were five main players left in the game: Ptolemy in Egypt and Palestine; Cassander in Macedon; Seleucus in Mesopotamia and most of the old Persian territories; Lysimachus in Thrace; and Antigonus in Asia Minor. The death of Antigonus at the battle of Ipsus in 301 BC reduced the main rivals to four; 20 years later Lysimachus was killed in battle at Magnesia.

The three major protagonists who survived – the Ptolemies, Seleucids and Macedonians – were to maintain an uneasy balance of power for the next 100 years. Native kingdoms reasserted their independence on the fringes of the vast Seleucid Empire, and smaller kingdoms broke away, most notably Pergamum, which came to dominate western Asia Minor in the mid-3rd century BC, and the remarkable kingdom of the Bactrian Greeks, which broke away from Seleucid control in the east. But the first real disturbance to this fragile political map came only when Roman armies began to interfere in the affairs of the region in the aftermath of the Second Punic War (218-201 BC).

Italy: the Roman Conquest, 350-270 BC

2 By the middle of the 4th century BC, the Romans had established their ascendancy over the Etruscan city-states and switched their attention to the peoples of southern Italy, notably the Samnites of the interior and the Greeks of the coast. The First Samnite War (343-341 BC), which the Romans fought in alliance with the Greek cities of Campania (around Neapolis), ended with no conclusive outcome, but paved the way for further Roman intervention in the region.

The Second War (328-304 BC) was an altogether more serious affair, and saw Roman armies operating for the first time on the Adriatic coast of Italy. By the end of the war Rome had extended its direct control from Latium south into Campania (the area round Capua), and had built the first and most famous of its all-weather roads, the Via Appia (312 BC), to speed the movement of its armies into southern Italy. Colonies of Latin citizens were established at strategic points (Luceria, Interamna, Tarracina, Saticula, Suessa Aurunca) to strengthen the Roman hold over the newly acquired territories.

The Samnites were not conquered, however, but merely forced to accept terms. Peace was soon broken by the Third Samnite War (298-290 BC). The

Romans fought a crucial battle against the Samnites and their Gaulish allies at Sentinum north of Rome, and after hard fighting they carried the day. The Samnites were reduced to the status of allies, and Rome was free to expand her power into the southernmost corners of peninsular Italy. Faced with resistance from some of the Greek cities, most notably Tarentum, the Romans still succeeded in defeating the forces of Pyrrhus, king of Epirus (*see* map 3, below), who came to their aid (280-275 BC).

With Pyrrhus's withdrawal from the scene, the Greek cities hastened to make alliance with the new regional superpower. To consolidate Roman gains, Latin colonies were established at Venusia (291 BC), Beneventum (268 BC) and Aesernia (263 BC) in the south, at Cosa (273 BC) in Etruria, and at Ariminum (268 BC) and Firmum (264 BC) on the Adriatic coast. The Roman conquest of peninsular Italy was, by the mid-3rd century, secure.

Pyrrhus's Central Mediterranean Empire

3 Pyrrhus, King of Epirus, is one of the more romantic figures of ancient history, a man in the mould of Alexander the Great, of huge ambitions and enormous energy, but without Alexander's military genius or good fortune. His greatest legacy, indeed, is the concept of the Pyrrhic victory, a technical win but at such enormous cost as to constitute a defeat.

Pyrrhus came to the throne of Epirus as a boy in 307 BC, but in the disturbed conditions of the time was twice exiled before securing his hold on that mountain kingdom in 297 BC. After attempts – only partially successful – to extend his power east into Macedonia, he switched his attention west to the Greek cities of Sicily and southern Italy. In May 280 BC Pyrrhus crossed into southern Italy with a substantial army, including elephants, to assist the Greek city of Tarentum against Roman encroachments in the Adriatic. With the help of his elephants he defeated the Romans at Heraclea in 280 BC, and again the following year at Ausculum to the north.

But the Romans refused to accept his terms, and in 278 BC he was lured to Sicily at the invitation of the Greek cities there to lead a campaign against the Carthaginians in the west of the island. Within 18 months he had reduced Carthaginian possessions in Sicily to the single fortress of Lilybaeum in the extreme west, but once again he could not bring himself to agree to terms, and after falling out with his Greek allies he returned to southern Italy in 276 BC. There he was decisively defeated by the Romans at the battle of Beneventum the following year and returned to Epirus. Tarentum fell to the Romans in 272 BC, and in the same year Pyrrhus was killed at Argos in Greece.

Roman Expansion in the Mediterranean

Between 270 BC and 121 BC the map of southern Europe was transformed by the steady expansion of Roman power. The first stage came in the conflict between Rome and her North African rival Carthage. Founded as a Phoenician colony on the north coast of Africa in the 9th or 8th century BC, by the early 3rd century BC Carthage had grown to become one of the greatest centres of the Mediterranean world, and under her leadership the Phoenicians had succeeded in retaining their hold on the west Mediterranean sea-lanes despite fierce competition from the Greek cities of Sicily and southern Italy. It was a dispute over control of the Sicilian city of Messana in 264 BC which first drew the Carthaginians and Romans into direct conflict.

The First Punic War, as it was called ("Punic" from the Latin word for Phoenician), was fought mainly in and around Sicily, by both land and sea, and rapidly developed into a large-scale war of attrition. It ended in 241 BC, when Carthage was finally obliged to come to terms. The peace that was reached lasted little over 20 years, however, and was broken by the outbreak of the Second Punic War in 218 BC. From southern Spain, the Carthaginian general, Hannibal, launched an invasion of Italy across the Alps, inflicting crushing defeats on Roman armies at the River Trebia in 218 BC, at Lake Trasimene in 217 BC, and finally at Cannae in 216 BC. He was unable to capture Rome itself, however, and was eventually forced to return to Africa, where he faced final defeat at the battle of Zama (202 BC). Carthage lost her Spanish possessions, and many of her North African territories were given to Rome's Numidian allies.

Further conquests in Spain occupied the Romans for another 70 years, but at the same time they became increasingly involved in Greece and the Balkans. The ambitions of the Macedonian king Philip V and the Seleucid ruler Antiochus III drew the Romans into wars with both in turn, but Roman victories over Philip at Cynoscephalae (197 BC) and over Antiochus at Magnesia (190 BC) were not immediately followed by any attempt to extend Roman territory in the Balkans. That development came later in the century, when repeated "provocations" led the Romans to make first Macedonia, and then Greece, into Roman provinces.

By 133 BC the Romans possessed an empire extending from the Atlantic to Asia Minor. This now included the former kingdom of Pergamum as well as North African territories annexed during the Third Punic War (149-146 BC) when Carthage itself was finally destroyed. But important developments were also taking place in northern Europe. By the 2nd century BC, powerful Celtic groups had emerged in some regions, and fortified Celtic towns were to be found across a broad band of territory from France in the west to Bohemia in the east. Rome had already subjugated the Celtic peoples of northern Italy; in the 120s the Celtic peoples of southern France were also drawn forcibly into the Roman sphere. The Mediterranean world was poised to extend its power yet further into northern Europe: Celts and Romans were destined to become still closer acquaintances in the century which followed.

Teutonic peoples

F
i
n
n
o
-
U
g
r
i
a
n
s

BALTIC
SEA

B
a
l
t
i
c

p
e
o
p
l
e
s

Volga

S
l
a
v
s

Don

I
r
a
n
i
a
n

p
e
o
p
l
e
s

Elbe
Oder
Vistula

Danube

Dnieper

Dniester

Volga

Dacians

Olbia

BOSPORAN
KINGDOM

Caucasian peoples

Tyras

Panticapaeum

I
l
l
y
r
i
a
n
s

Chersonesus

Aquileia
Verona

BLACK SEA

Ariminum

Tomi

Salonae

Danube

Narona

Odessus

GREEK
CITIES

Amisus Trapezus

ARMENIA

Rome

Mesembia

Thracians

Corfinium

Apollonia

Cannae

Dyrrachium

Stobi

Byzantium

PONTUS

Neapolis

Perinthus

BITHYNIA

Ancyra

Brundisium

Thessalonica

Prusa

PARTHIAN

Tarentum

Dorylaeum

Mazaca

Tigris

EMPIRE

Cynoscephalae

Demetrias

Alexandria

R E P U B L I C

Troas

Pergamum

Antiochia

CAPPADOCIA

Nicopolis

COMMAGENE

E   P   U   B   L   I   C

Panormus

Magnesia

Iconium

Euphrates

Messana

Patrae

Ephesus

PISIDIA

Tarsus

Antioch

Sicily

Corinth

Athens

Aphrodisias

Side

SELEUCID EMPIRE

Catana

Halicarnassus

CIBYRA

Syracuse

Sparta

LYCIA

Malta

Rhodus

S E A

RHODES

Cyprus Salamis

Arabs

Crete

PTOLEMAIC
EMPIRE

Gortyn

29

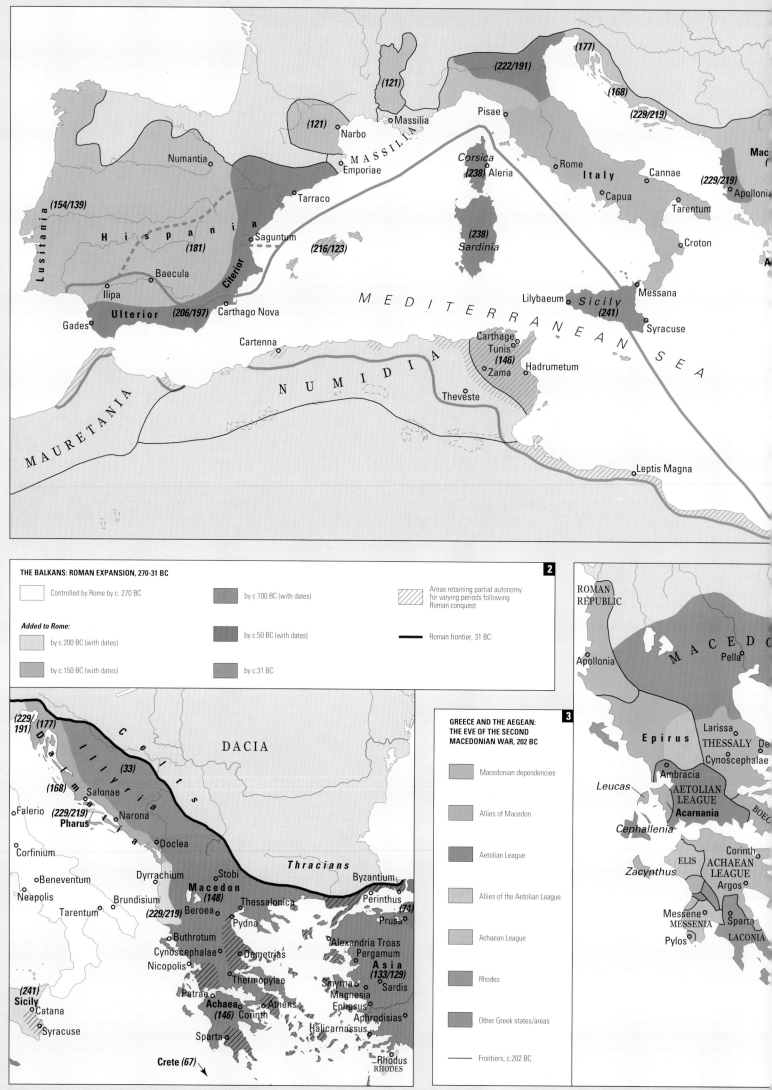

THE BALKANS: ROMAN EXPANSION, 270-31 BC `2`

Controlled by Rome by c. 270 BC

Added to Rome:

by c.200 BC (with dates)

by c.150 BC (with dates)

by c.100 BC (with dates)

by c.50 BC (with dates)

by c.31 BC

Areas retaining partial autonomy for varying periods following Roman conquest

Roman frontier, 31 BC

GREECE AND THE AEGEAN: THE EVE OF THE SECOND MACEDONIAN WAR, 202 BC `3`

Macedonian dependencies

Allies of Macedon

Aetolian League

Allies of the Aetolian League

Achaean League

Rhodes

Other Greek states/areas

Frontiers, c.202 BC

Map labels (main map, top):

Numantia · Narbo · Massilia · MASSILIA · Pisae · Corsica (238) Aleria · Rome · Italy · Cannae · Mac · (177) · (222/191) · (121) · (121) · (168) · (229/219) · (229/219) · Apollonia · Capua · Tarentum · Croton · Emporiae · Tarraco · Saguntum · Sardinia (238) · Hispania · Citerior · (181) · (216/123) · (154/139) · Lusitania · Baecula · Ilipa · Carthago Nova · Ulterior (206/197) · Gades · Cartenna · Lilybaeum · Sicily (241) · Messana · Syracuse · MEDITERRANEAN SEA · MAURETANIA · NUMIDIA · Carthage Tunis (146) · Zama · Hadrumetum · Theveste · Leptis Magna

Map labels (bottom-left, Balkans):

DACIA · Celts · Illyria · Dalmatia · (229/191) · (177) · (168) · (33) · Salonae · Narona · Doclea · (229/219) Pharus · Falerio · Corfinium · Beneventum · Neapolis · Tarentum · Brundisium · Dyrrachium · Stobi · Macedon (148) · (229/219) Beroea · Thessalonica · Pydna · Thracians · Byzantium · Perinthus · Prusa · (74) · Alexandria Troas · Pergamum · Buthrotum · Cynoscephalae · Demetrias · Nicopolis · Thermopylae · Smyrna · Sardis · Asia (133/129) · Magnesia · Ephesus · Aphrodisias · Patrae · Achaea (146) Corinth · Athens · Halicarnassus · Sparta · Rhodus RHODES · Crete (67) · (241) Sicily · Catana · Syracuse

Map labels (right, Greece):

ROMAN REPUBLIC · MACEDO · Pella · Apollonia · Larissa · THESSALY · De · Epirus · Cynoscephalae · Ambracia · Leucas · AETOLIAN LEAGUE · Acarnania · BOEO · Cephallenia · Corinth · ELIS · ACHAEAN LEAGUE · Argos · Zacynthus · Messene · MESSENIA · Sparta · Pylos · LACONIA

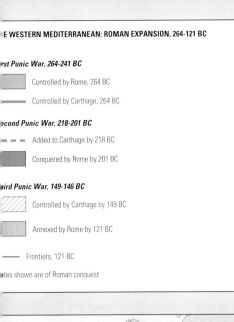

1

E WESTERN MEDITERRANEAN: ROMAN EXPANSION, 264-121 BC

rst Punic War, 264-241 BC

Controlled by Rome, 264 BC

Controlled by Carthage, 264 BC

econd Punic War, 218-201 BC

Added to Carthage by 218 BC

Conquered by Rome by 201 BC

ird Punic War, 149-146 BC

Controlled by Carthage by 149 BC

Annexed by Rome by 121 BC

Frontiers, 121 BC

tes shown are of Roman conquest

The Western Mediterranean: Roman Expansion, 264-121 BC

1 The 118 years between the outbreak of the First Punic War in 264 BC and the destruction of Carthage in 146 BC saw Rome grow from ruler of Italy to mistress of the Mediterranean. The peace terms which ended the First Punic War in 241 BC gave the Romans the island of Sicily. Three years later they were able to demand Corsica and Sardinia as well. The next expansionist move was the conquest of northern Italy, and the defeat of the Celtic peoples who had inhabited it since the 6th century. This was achieved in three major campaigns from 224 to 222 BC, and consolidated in 191 BC after a series of rebellions. Victory over the Carthaginians in Spain in 206 BC, during the Second Punic War, handed the coastal regions of the south and east to Roman rule, and in 197 BC the conquered territories were divided into two separate provinces (Hispania Ulterior and Hispania Citerior). That same year, however, the peoples of Spain mounted a general uprising against Roman rule, which was not finally suppressed until 181 BC.

This was far from being the end of the story, for in 154 BC the Lusitanians of western Spain invaded the conquered territories. Lusitania was annexed in 139 BC, but war dragged on until the fall of Numantia, the last independent stronghold, in 133 BC. Even then, Roman control did not extend to northernmost Spain. By that time, however, Rome had achieved final victory over Carthage in the Third Punic War, and the core Carthaginian territory had become the Roman province of Africa (146 BC). Rome completed her domination of the west Mediterranean by seizing the Balearic islands in 123 BC, and by campaigns against the Gauls in southern France in 125-121 BC, ostensibly in defence of her ally Massilia. These south French territories were ultimately to become the Roman province of Gallia Narbonensis.

The Balkans: Roman Expansion, 270-31 BC

2 Roman expansion east of the Adriatic began in 229 BC, when an army and a fleet were sent to suppress Illyrian pirates and a Roman protectorate was established over the Greek cities of the Adriatic coast. The piracy of Demetrius of Pharus in 219 BC was stamped out in a similar way. Soon afterwards, the Romans came into conflict with Philip V, King of Macedon. Their victory at Cynoscephalae in 197 BC forced him to pull back within his own frontiers, but they did not attempt to capitalize on this victory in territorial terms. Nor did they try to do so after their victories over Antiochus III at Thermopylae in Greece in 191 BC and at Magnesia in Asia Minor the following year.

Roman policy changed only after the Third Macedonian War (171-167 BC). Aemilius Paullus defeated Philip's son and successor Perseus at the battle of Pydna in 168 BC, and brought the kingdom of Macedon to an end. Macedonia was divided into four republics, and coastal Illyria into three, but 20 years more were to pass before further fighting at last forced Rome to reduce Macedonia to the status of a province. Greece itself was absorbed into the same province two years later. Roman control was finally extended to Asia Minor in 133 BC when the last king of Pergamum, Attalus III, bequeathed them his kingdom, which then became the Roman province of Asia.

Greece and the Aegean: the Eve of the Second Macedonian War, 202 BC

3 As the 3rd century BC drew to a close, two great monarchs dominated the Aegean region: Antiochus III, "the Great", ruler of the Seleucid Empire (223-187 BC), and Philip V, King of Macedon (221-179 BC). Both were men of boundless ambition. Antiochus dreamed of reconquering all the territories held by his predecessor Seleucus I a century before. His most spectacular undertaking was the reconquest of the eastern provinces in a seven-year campaign (212-205 BC) which took him as far as the borders of India. It was followed in 202 BC by a campaign in which Antiochus defeated the Ptolemaic army and seized control of the whole of the southern Levant up to the borders of Egypt.

Philip's eyes, meanwhile, were focused on Greece and the west. His attempts to subjugate Illyria and a foolish alliance with Hannibal and the Carthaginians led to the First Macedonian War with Rome (214-205 BC). The Romans allied themselves with Philip's enemies in Greece, the Aetolian League, but though the sporadic fighting continued for several years (marked by Aetolian atrocities), neither side made any significant gains and the peace which followed simply restored the status quo from before the war. Philip then turned his attention to the Aegean, attacking Rhodes and Pergamum (both friendly to Rome) and entering into a secret understanding with Antiochus.

The threat of an alliance between the two rulers was too much for the Romans. During the Second Macedonian War (200-196 BC), a Roman expeditionary force under the consul Flaminius defeated the Macedonian forces at the battle of Cynoscephalae (197 BC). Philip was forbidden to interfere any further in the affairs of Greece, and even Thessaly – which had long been his ally – was broken up into a series of independent leagues. Flaminius declared the Greek cities liberated from foreign control, and the Roman forces withdrew to Italy in 194 BC. Events were soon to show, however, that their involvement in Greece had only just begun.

Thracians

Maronea · Byzantium · Perinthus

asos · Aenus · Lysimachia

(to Ptolemaic Empire)

Thasos

Samothrace · Sestus · Cyzicus

Imbros · Abydos

Lemnos

PERGAMUM

EGEAN · Lesbos · Pergamum · Elaea

a SEA · Chios · SELEUCID EMPIRE

Chios · Ephesus

Andros

eos

nos *(to Ptolemaic Empire)*

Paros · Naxos

Cyclades · Rhodes

RHODES

Crete · Gortyn

31 BC

Roman Expansion Beyond the Mediterranean

The 90 years between 121 BC and 31 BC were marked by a dramatic further extension of Roman control, both around the shores of the Mediterranean and, for the first time, across large areas of Atlantic Europe. Rome grew steadily stronger and more prosperous as successive Roman commanders used military campaigns as a route to wealth and power at home. The political history of Rome during the 1st century BC is largely one of confrontation between leading generals, the factions who supported them, and the senate, which remained in principle the governing body of the state, but was often powerless in the face of military force.

The first of these over-mighty commanders, Gaius Marius, made his name in the war against the Numidian ruler Jugurtha in 111-104 BC. He gained still further renown in 102-101 BC when he defeated the Cimbri and Teutones, Germanic war-bands who had invaded southern France and crossed into northern Italy. After Marius, the position of leading general at Rome passed to Lucius Cornelius Sulla, an officer who had played a key role in suppressing the Italian rebellion of 90-88 BC and was then entrusted with the command of the war against Mithradates of Pontus. On his return to Rome in 82 BC he became absolute ruler until his abdication in 79 BC. With his demise the following year, Gnaeus Pompeius (Pompey) became the leading general, clearing the Mediterranean of pirates in 67 BC, finally crushing Mithradates in 66 BC, and later joining with Marcus Crassus and Julius Caesar in a power-sharing arrangement (known as the First Triumvirate) which completely overshadowed the traditional authority of the senate.

Crassus died fighting the Parthians at Carrhae in 53 BC and rivalry between Pompey and Caesar broke into open hostility in 49 BC. The civil war which followed lasted until March 45 BC, but the outcome was not in doubt after Caesar's victory at Pharsalus in 48 BC and Pompey's subsequent murder. Caesar became undisputed ruler of the Roman state, but his attempt to establish a lifelong dictatorship ended with his assassination on the Ides of March in 44 BC. There followed 13 more years of uncertainty and civil strife, during which Mark Antony and Caesar's adoptive son and heir Octavian first defeated Caesar's assassins at Philippi (42 BC), then became increasingly estranged from each other as Antony allied himself with the Egyptian queen, Cleopatra. The sea battle at Actium in 31 BC gave final victory to Octavian. Four years later, in a special arrangement with the senate, Octavian formally established the Roman Empire, taking the name Augustus and with it imperial powers over the government, the armies and the frontier provinces.

Beyond the Roman frontiers lay the Celtic peoples of Britain and the Alpine region, the Germans across the Rhine, and the Dacians and Thracians in the northern Balkans. A large part of Celtic Europe now lay within the empire, in northern Italy and the territories conquered by Julius Caesar in Gaul. Even before their conquest by the Romans, the Gauls were far from being disorganised barbarians, and had their own coins and kings, towns and trade, and sophisticated craftsmanship in bronze and gold. It was the less centralised Germanic peoples, however, which were to be the greatest threat to Rome's European provinces during the centuries which followed.

Finno-Ugrians

Teutonic peoples

BALTIC SEA

Baltic peoples

Elbe
Oder
Vistula

Slavs

Danube

Celtic peoples

Iranian peoples

Dniepr
Dniester

Don

Volga

Volga

num
Aquileia
Verona
Siscia
iminum
sae
tium
Rome
Corfinium
Neapolis
Tarentum
Panormus
Sicily
Catana
Syracuse
Malta

N

E

M

P

I

R

E

DACIA

Danube

Thracians

Doclea
Dyrrachium
Stobi
Philippi
Beroea
Thessalonica
Brundisium
Nicopolis
Demetrias
Actium
Pharsalus
Patrae
Corinth
Athens
Sparta

Tyras

Olbia

BOSPORAN KINGDOM

Panticapaeum

Heraclea

Tomi

GREEK CITIES

Byzantium
Perinthus
Prusa
Troas
Pergamum
Alexandria
Dorylaeum
Ephesus
Halicarnassus
Rhodus
LYCIA
RHODES
Side

Caucasian peoples

BLACK SEA

Amisus Trapezus

PONTUS

ARMENIA

Ancyra

GALATIA

Antiochia
Carrhae Iconium
Tarsus
Antioch

CAPPADOCIA

SOPHENE

COMMAGENE
OSRHOENE

CORDUENE

PARTHIAN EMPIRE

Tigris
Euphrates

Cyprus Salamis

Palmyra

Arabs

Crete
Gortyn

SEA

33

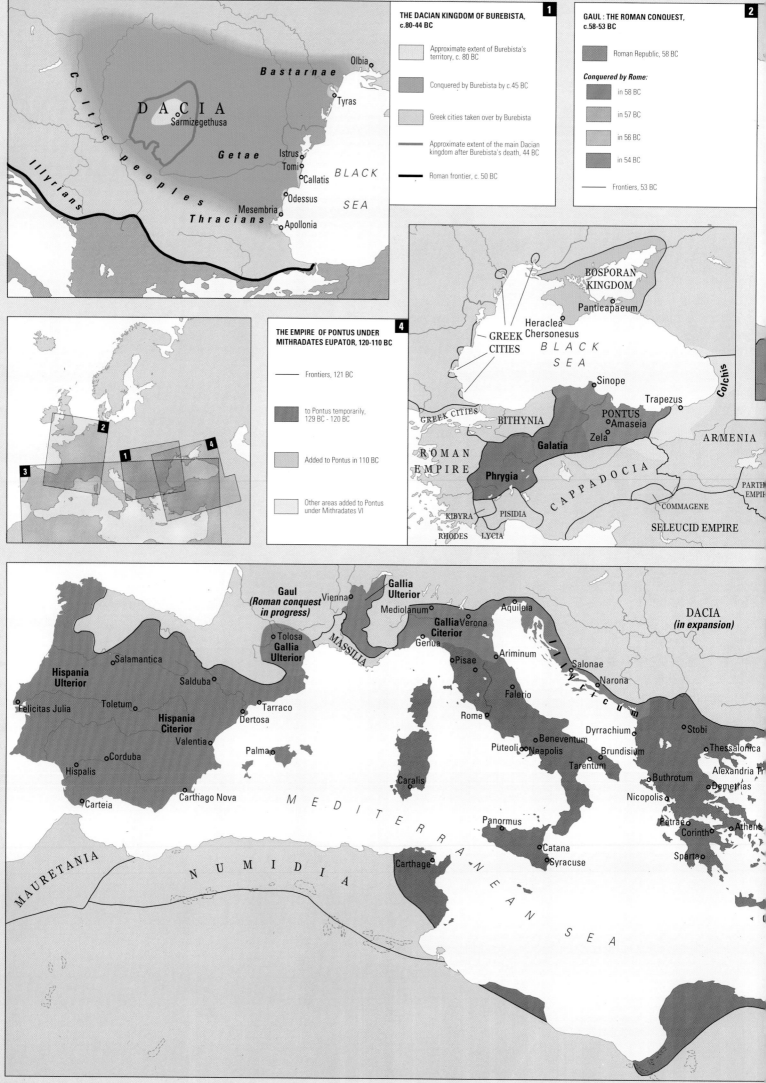

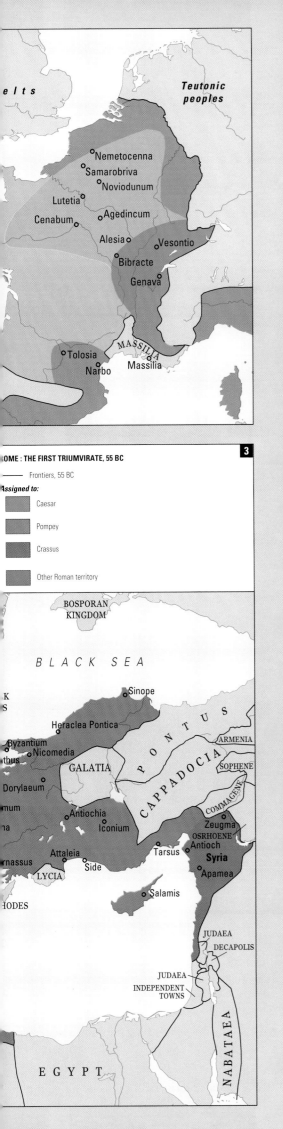

OME : THE FIRST TRIUMVIRATE, 55 BC   **3**

— Frontiers, 55 BC

Assigned to:

▢ Caesar

▢ Pompey

▢ Crassus

▢ Other Roman territory

The Dacian Kingdom of Burebista, c. 80-44 BC

1 The Dacian kingdom founded by the great war-leader Burebista lay north of the lower Danube in modern Romania. The peoples of this region had come under considerable pressure from the Celts during the 4th century BC, but by the beginning of the 1st century BC the Dacians, together with their eastern relatives the Getes, had re-established themselves as the major power in this region.

Unification came only with the rise to power of Burebista around 80 BC. He forged the Getes and Dacians into a single kingdom, with a new civil and religious capital at Sarmizegethusa in Transylvania, and embarked on a series of expansionist wars, beginning with the Celtic Scordisci. The defeated Scordisci then became allies of Burebista in his westward drive against other Celtic peoples. Dacian forces struck deep into central Europe, and in 60 BC they defeated the Boii, a Celtic people who gave their name to modern Bohemia.

Burebista also conquered the Greek cities of the Black Sea coast, but was careful to avoid confrontation with the Romans. Nonetheless, Julius Caesar viewed the Dacian kingdom as a danger, and made plans to attack it. It was saved by his assassination in 44 BC, and the death of Burebista in the same year. With the loss of its founder, the kingdom of Dacia disintegrated once again into warring tribes and factions.

Gaul: The Roman Conquest, c. 58-53 BC

2 Julius Caesar was a rising star of the Roman political world when he was appointed provincial governor of northern Italy and southern France in 59 BC. Not content to remain within the boundaries of his province, he immediately embarked on an ambitious campaign of conquest. At first, he posed as an ally of various Gallic peoples, aiding them in their struggles against their neighbours or against foreign aggressors, but he soon decided to conquer the whole country. He even made two celebrated forays across the Channel to Britain. The kingdoms of central Gaul were fairly easily defeated, but the warlike Belgae of the northeast put up a fierce struggle, and on more than one occasion came close to inflicting a serious defeat on the Roman legions. Six years of dogged campaigning yielded results, however, and by the winter of 53 BC Gaul was at last in Roman hands. Gallic resistance ended the following year with the siege of Alesia and the defeat of the war-leader Vercingetorix.

Rome: the First Triumvirate, 55 BC

3 The First Triumvirate was an accord reached between the three leading men at Rome, who effectively stripped the senate of its power and divided the most important Roman provinces between them. The cause was growing tension and confrontation between the senators and a series of powerful military commanders. Pompey had suppressed Mediterranean piracy, finished off the war against Mithradates of Pontus, and imposed a general political settlement on the Near East, but could not get the senate to grant land to his legionaries nor ratify his eastern settlement. Julius Caesar was standing for consul, only to find the senate changing the rules and refusing the provincial governorship which always followed. Crassus, the wealthiest man at Rome, desired a prestigious military command for himself.

By bribery and force, these three men overruled the senate to achieve their aims. In 60 BC Caesar was appointed governor of the two Gauls and Illyricum, while Pompey received the land-grant and treaty ratification he required. In 55 BC Crassus became governor of Syria, Pompey became governor of the two Spanish provinces, and Caesar's command was extended for a further five years. Crassus was captured and killed by the Parthians at Carrhae in 53 BC, but the accord between Pompey and Caesar lasted a further two years, and was only ended definitively when Caesar led his legions across the Rubicon and embarked on a civil war against Pompey and the senate in 49 BC.

The Empire of Pontus under Mithradates Eupator, 120-110 BC

4 Mithrades VI "Eupator", king of Pontus, was the last great independent monarch to oppose Roman ambitions in Asia Minor. His kingdom consisted of hill country and fertile plains on the southern shore of the Black Sea, with the former Greek colony of Sinope as its capital. Mithradates was only 12 years old when his father was murdered in 120 BC, and it was not until 112 BC that he was able to seize control in a palace coup. He soon expanded his power to the eastern end of the Black Sea, and in 110-107 BC he came to the rescue of the Greek cities of the Crimea, who were being threatened by Scythians and Sarmatians: so effectively, indeed, that he ended up controlling this region also. Mithradates' next move was to the east, conquering territory which included Colchis. He attempted to take the territory the Romans had granted to his father in 129 BC, but taken back to themselves on Mithradates' accession. He then installed his son as king of Cappadocia and married his daughter to the king of Armenia. During his campaigns he invaded much of Asia Minor and even Greece.

The Romans sought more than once to contain Mithradates' ambitions by threats and diplomacy, but it took three hard-fought wars (88-85 BC, 83-82 BC and 74-66 BC) to bring him finally to heel. Mithradates himself committed suicide in 66 BC, a sad ending to a spectacular career.

AD 180

The Triumph of Rome

The famous statue, which until recently stood on the summit of the Capitol in Rome, shows the Emperor Marcus Aurelius, who died in AD 180, victoriously horsed, baton in hand. No image of command has ever been so influential or so often copied for portraits of other rulers. It expresses the triumphant serenity of the Roman Empire at its height, spreading its peace through strength over an unprecedented swathe of the Western world. Yet the reign of Marcus Aurelius (AD 161-80) has also been traditionally regarded as the high point of Roman achievement, after which decline set in, punctuated only by lower peaks of recoveries.

Even after a long period of rarely interrupted success for Roman arms and Roman methods of control of subject-peoples, the empire bequeathed by Marcus Aurelius was not much bigger than that founded by the first emperor, Augustus, in 27 BC. True, Britain had been invaded by Claudius in AD 43 and by 160 was under Roman control as far as the Forth-Solway isthmus, and Dacia had been conquered by Trajan between 101 and 106. But many of the gains since Augustus's death had the nature of frontier adjustments: between the Rhine and the Danube; in North Africa (where Mauretania was annexed in AD 42) and on the eastern frontier. Augustus had established not only boundaries of surprising sustainability but also a remarkably enduring system of government. He founded an hereditary monarchy without offending the republican traditions of the Roman elite, using republican rhetoric to justify his personal power. Even so, the idea of an autocratic magistracy became compromised by associations with monarchical traditions. The power of the traditional republican institutions – the senate and the elective magistracies – was progressively weakened or by-passed. The imperial system had some advantages: unified command, strong leadership and popular appeal. But it carried with it a potentially fatal disadvantage: there was no enforceable method of ordaining the succession, and the army effectively usurped a constitutional role in making and unmaking emperors. No means was ever devised of forestalling the consequent dangers of fragmentation and civil war.

By the time of Marcus Aurelius two further dangers could be discerned. First, Christianity was making new converts and penetrating ever higher levels of society. From the perspective of most of the traditional elite, this was a development incompatible with the survival of the state, since – to the pious – Rome's greatness was at the disposal of the gods, while – to the practical – Roman political unity depended on adherence to the state religion and worship of the divine Emperor. Second, the subject peoples within the Empire and the barbarians on its borders were growing increasingly covetous of the status of Roman citizenship and the wealth of the Roman world. Already in AD 167, Marcus Aurelius had had to fight a three-year campaign to restore the Danubian frontier after a German horde invaded the Empire and besieged Aquileia.

Marcus Aurelius himself anticipated two ways in which the empire was to cope with these pressures. First, he embraced stoicism as his personal philosophy. He was a patron and practitioner of the culture, based on stoicism, in which Christians and pagans became reconciled and which made it possible in the long run for Christianity to replace the old religion at an official level. Second, he sensed the need to divide the unwieldy responsibilities of governing the vast empire, admitting his adoptive brother, Lucius Verus, to the rank of co-emperor in what was to be a recurrent formula for saving the state from crisis.

F i n n o

Teutonic peoples

BALTIC SEA

Baltic peoples

Oder

Elbe

Vistula

- U g r i a n s

Volga

Volga

Slavs

Dnieper

Dniester

Don

I r a n i a n p e o p l e s

Castra Regina
Augusta Vindelicum
Danube
Vindobona
Lauriacum
Carnuntum
Aquincum
Teurnia
Virunum
Savaria
Aquileia
Siscia
Sirmium
Patavium
Verona
Ariminum
Arretium
Salonae
Narona
Rome
Corfinium
Dyrrachium
Neapolis
Brundisium
Tarentum

Porolissum
Potaissa
Dacia
Sarmizegethusa

Oescus
Danube
Durostorum
Naissus
Serdica
Doclea
Stobi
Trimontium
Thessalonica
Beroea

Tomi

BOSPORAN KINGDOM
Panticapaeum

Chersonesus

Caucasian peoples

BLACK SEA

Sinope
Amisus
Trapezus
Heraclea Pontica
Amaseia
Perinthus
Byzantium
Nicopolis
Ancyra

ARMENIA

A
N
Panormus
Sicily
Catana
Syracuse
Malta
SEA

Nicopolis
Demetrias

Patrae
Corinth
Athens
Sparta
Halicarnassus
Rhodus

Crete
Gortyn

E
M
P
I
R
E

Prusa
Alexandria Troas
Pergamum
Sardis
Smyrna

Dorylaeum

Antiochia
Iconium

Caesarea
Melitene

Tarsus
Antioch
Side

Attaleia

Cyprus
Salamis

Apamea

Palmyra

Euphrates
Tigris

PARTHIAN EMPIRE

Arabs

10°   20°   30°   40°   50°   60°

60°

50°

40°

37

Borders of provinces, 180

The Roman Empire and dependencies, 180

Map 3 (top)

ATLANTIC OCEAN

Barbarians

Britannia

Germania Inferior

Barbarians

Belgica

Gallia Lugdunensis

Germania Superior

Raetia

Noricum

Pannonia Superior

Pannonia Inferior

Dacia

BOSPORAN KINGDOM

BLACK SEA

Aquitania

Alpes Graiae et Poeninae

Alpes Cottiae

Alpes Maritimae

Gallia Narbonensis

R O M A N I a

Dalmatia

Moesia Superior

Moesia Inferior

Thracia

Bithynia et Pontus

Cappadocia

ARMENIA

Lusitania

Tarraconensis

Corsica et Sardinia

Rome

M P I R E

Macedonia

Epirus

Asia

Galatia

Cilicia

PARTHIAN EMPIRE

Baetica

MEDITERRANEAN SEA

Achaea

Lycia et Pamphylia

Cyprus

Syria

Celtic

Mauretania Tingitana

Mauretania Caesariensis

Sicilia

Creta

Syria Palaestina

Africa Proconsularis

Barbarians

et

Arabia

Barbarians

Cyrenaica

Aegyptus

Map (bottom)

Barbarians

(c.AD 80-105)

(AD 142)

Eburacum

(AD 78)

(AD 78)

(AD 43)

Londinium

(12 BC)

Elbe

ATLANTIC OCEAN

Colonia Agrippina

(12 BC - AD 9)

Lutetia

Augusta Treverorum

Castra Regina

(AD 83)

Barbarians

Vindobona

(AD 57)

Burdigala

Lugdunum

Raetia (15 BC)

Noricum

Porolissum

(AD 57)

BOSPORAN KINGDOM (vassal state from 63 BC)

Cantabria (17 BC)

(AD 10)

Pannonia

(AD 107)

Verona

(15 BC)

BLACK SEA

R O M A N

Toletum

(29 BC)

Corduba

Rome

(AD 45)

Valentia

M

Neapolis

E M P I R E

Byzantium

Galatia (25 BC)

Carthago Nova

Actium

(AD 18)

(25 BC)

MEDITERRANEAN SEA

Pergamum

PAR

(25 BC)

Hippo Regius

Athens

(A

(AD 42)

Carthage

Syracuse

(AD 74)

Antioch

(AD 74)

(AD 115)

Barbarians

(AD 6)

Alexandria

(20 BC)

(30 BC)

Egypt

(AD 106)

Bar

The Expansion of the Roman Empire, 31 BC - AD 180

1 Too many battles have been called "decisive" but Octavian's victory at Actium (*see* page 32) certainly helped to re-shape the Roman Empire. The "imperial" provinces, which he governed directly, included eastern territories such as Egypt and Galatia (annexed in 25 BC); but his commitment to expansion on the northern frontier helped to make the empire more "western" than would have been the case had Antony triumphed, with his power-base and ambitions in the east.

Augustus – as Octavian was known after he became Emperor – added Cantabria (17 BC), Noricum and Raetia (15 BC), Illyricum and Pannonia (AD 10) to the Empire, planned the conquest of Britain and initiated those of Bohemia and Germany as far as the Elbe (9 BC). The need for military cuts and the demands of internal security forced the most ambitious of these plans to be aborted, and the conquests beyond the Elbe were abandoned. By the end of his reign, the empire had, on most fronts, attained its manageable limits. Apart from the conquest of Britain (*see* map 2, below), the acquisition of Mauretania in AD 42 and the annexation of Thrace in AD 45, the most important adjustment during the 1st century AD was made in the critical space between the upper Rhine and the sources of the Danube where the awkwardly shaped frontier could be shortened only by the laborious incorporation of heavily forested uplands. It was an arduous undertaking, not completed until the campaign of Domitian in AD 83.

The start of the new century, coinciding with an era of unprecedented prosperity and the accession of the aggressive and ambitious Emperor Trajan, initiated a brief period of further conquests. Victory over the Dacians in AD 107 stimulated Trajan's appetite and liberated resources for an assault on what was perceived as the greatest security problem of the time: the power of Parthia in the east. A new province of Arabia was created on the fringes of the Syrian desert, and in AD 114 Trajan's armies invaded Armenia and Meso-potamia, advancing as far south as the Persian Gulf. These gains could not be held, however, and Mesopotamia was already lost when Trajan died in 117.

Britain: The Roman Conquest, AD 43-185

2 The conquest of Britain, though hard to justify on grounds of military security or economic interest, became a dynastic obligation for Caesar's heirs. Repeatedly announced and deferred by Augustus, it was at last undertaken in AD 43 by Claudius (AD 41-54), who saw a chance of easy laurels. The rapid submission of the southeast was deceptive – procured by co-operation with local elites who already had close relations with Gaul, and who saw opportunities to profit as clients of Rome. Beyond the Humber native resistance proved much more stubborn. In the last quarter of the century, however, a new Roman governor, Agricola, inaugurated a decisive policy. He believed that to secure existing conquests, the whole island had to be subjugated regardless of cost, together with the offshore bastion of Anglesey and, if necessary, Ireland as well.

The effects of this policy were short-lived in the north of Britain. In AD 80, Agricola was recalled, the conquest of Scotland was halted and his remoter conquests were gradually abandoned, perhaps in the belief that the far north of Britain was too thinly populated to pose a serious threat to imperial security. If so, these expectations were misleading. Hadrian drew a frontier line from Tyne to Solway in 122 with the building of a wall, but by 142 the Romans had once again advanced to the Clyde and a second defence, the Antonine Wall, was built. This heavily fortified zone absorbed a garrison of at least 10,000 men. The history of the Roman frontier in Britain illustrates a problem of the Empire as a whole: there was no rational limit to expansion and frontier security was expensive.

The Roman Empire: Administrative Divisions, AD 180

3 The expansion of Roman rule under Augustus and his successors had made necessary administrative arrangements for the new provinces. In the far west, Hispania, the first conquest outside Italy, had been divided by Augustus into three provinces whose configurations reflected the heavy Roman colonisation of the southwestern regions of the peninsula in his day. The division of Gaul into six provinces was also the work of Augustus, but here he seems to have been guided more by geography and the boundaries of the pre-Roman native states.

Despite its remoteness and its active military frontier, Britain remained a single province from the start of the conquest, per-haps reflecting its relatively superficial Romanisation. Italy had been re-modelled as early as the time of Caesar, who extend-ed Roman citizenship to the inhabitants of the former "Cisalpine Gaul" between the Rubicon and the Alps. On its western edge, the mountainous terrain favoured the retention of small units, which became provinces in AD 64-5. Caesar wanted to incorporate Sicily into Italy, but it was left a separate province by his heirs. Sardinia and Corsica were constituted as a province under senatorial rule by Nero (AD 54-68), then retrieved for the direct rule of the emperor under Vespasian (AD 79-81).

Raetia, conquered in AD 39, always retained a marchland character, contrasting with neighbouring Noricum which was very accessible to Romanisation. Both these, together with Pannonia, Dalmatia and Moesia Superior, were carved out of the vast province of Illyricum after Augustus's death. Broadly speaking, the border of Noricum and Pannonia represented an eth-nic frontier between Celtic peoples to the west and a predominantly Illyrian popula-tion to the east. Beyond Illyricum again lay the anomalous Dacian province – a kingdom on the north bank of the Danube annexed by Trajan – and the provinces of "Greek Europe", where, except in Moesia, Greek and Thracian peoples predominated and where Roman rule and colonisation did not displace Greek language and culture.

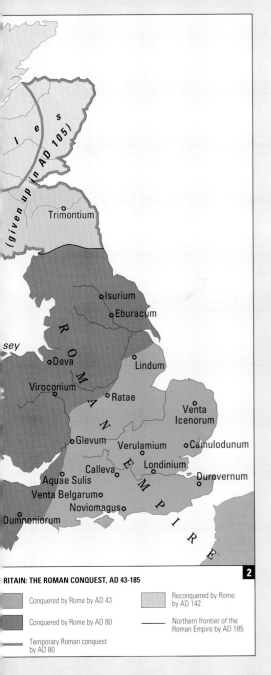

Trimontium
Isurium
Eburacum
Lindum
Deva
Viroconium
Ratae
Venta Icenorum
Glevum
Verulamium
Camulodunum
Calleva
Londinium
Aquae Sulis
Durovernum
Venta Belgarum
Noviomagus
Dumnoniorum

(given up in AD 105)
sey

ROMAN EMPIRE

RITAIN: THE ROMAN CONQUEST, AD 43-185

- Conquered by Rome by AD 43
- Conquered by Rome by AD 80
- Temporary Roman conquest by AD 80
- Reconquered by Rome by AD 142
- Northern frontier of the Roman Empire by AD 185

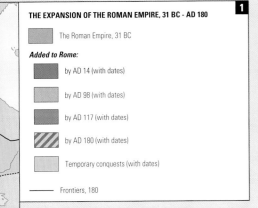

THE EXPANSION OF THE ROMAN EMPIRE, 31 BC - AD 180

- The Roman Empire, 31 BC

Added to Rome:
- by AD 14 (with dates)
- by AD 98 (with dates)
- by AD 117 (with dates)
- by AD 180 (with dates)
- Temporary conquests (with dates)
- Frontiers, 180

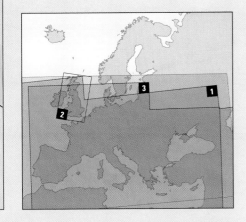

AD 180

The Decline of Rome

The empire bequeathed by Marcus Aurelius in AD 180 was recognisably the same state as that created by Augustus some two centuries before. After the lapse of two more centuries it had been transformed by "the triumph of barbarism and Christianity". The key changes had been the extension of Roman citizenship to all inhabitants of the Empire in 212 and the entry of Christians into the highest ranks of the ruling class – including, after the conversion of the Emperor Constantine, traditionally dated to 312, the Imperial throne itself. The rise of the Church from persecution to predominance was completed in 395, when the Emperor Theodosius proclaimed Christianity the official religion of the empire and reduced pagan traditions to the underprivileged status formerly imposed on Christians. The imperial elite was becoming more diversified: Christian bishops became servants of the state; the old ruling class was displaced by a new meritocracy; barbarian technicians were increasingly appointed to military commands; and the senatorial aristocracy began, especially in Italy, Gaul and Asia Minor, to withdraw from civic life and political responsibility and retire to the management of their estates.

On the borders of the empire – especially those with Germanic peoples – the pressure from barbarians for admittance to the empire, not just as mercenaries but as permanent settlers, grew ever more intense. The vast length of the frontiers could not be policed effectively and the trickle of immigrant communities could not be completely staunched. Raids *en masse* were almost as hard to cope with for the over-stretched imperial authorities. Those of the mid-3rd century, which devastated much of Gaul and penetrated Italy, coincided with internal political crisis (*see* map 1, page 43) and almost dissolved the empire.

Not until the late 4th century, however, did the struggle to exclude mass migrations of barbarians become hopeless. The Visigoths were the first people to be admitted *en bloc*. In about 275, when the Romans abandoned trans-Danubian Dacia, the Visigoths were settled in the vacated territory. After border trouble in the 320s they were granted federate (allied) status but by the late 360s relations had greatly deteriorated. Even so, long experience of life as the Romans' neighbours had profoundly influenced Visigothic culture: they had been converted to Christianity, although to Arianism, a heretical form. In 376 a Hun invasion obliged them to beg the Romans for refuge, and a reputed 200,000 were allowed over the Danube. But they were then left to starve, provoking a terrible revenge which culminated in the Visigoths' victory over the Romans at Adrianople in 378 and destroyed the Roman reputation for invincibility.

Henceforth, the empire could not guarantee to manage the barbarian war-bands whom it was forced to admit in increasing numbers. In Roman relations with other barbarian groups too, there were periods of tense collaboration; but from 395 to 418 the Visigoths undertook a destructive migration across the empire, terrorising the areas they traversed. Yet the Visigoths and other Germanic peoples did not come simply to destroy: they wished to share in the wealth and security of Rome. As the Roman armies came increasingly to depend on Germanic recruits and commanders, the difference between Roman and non-Roman diminished, especially in the west. After Theodosius' death in 395, when land was divided between his sons Honorius (west) and Arcadius (east), the Roman territories were never again ruled by a single emperor. In the decades which followed, the western provinces fell progressively under German control.

F i n n o - U g r i a n s

T e u t o n i c

BALTIC
SEA

Baltic peoples

S l a v s

Volga

Don

Dnieper

Dniester

Vistula

Elbe

Oder

Danube

a Regina
Augusta
Vindelicum
Lauriacum
Vindobona
Carnuntum
Aquincum
Teurnia
Virunum
Savaria
Aquileia
avium
Verona
Siscia
Sirmium

D a c i a

H u n s

Alans

Caucasian
peoples

Panticapaeum

Chersonesus

Tomi

Oescus
Durostorum
Danube

B L A C K   S E A

Sinope

Amisus
Trapezus

sae
tium

Ariminum
Salonae

Narona

Naissus

Serdica

Philippopolis

Adrianople

Perinthus
Constantinople

Heraclea Pontica

Amaseia

Nicopolis

M P I R E
Doclea

E A S T E R N   R O M A N   E M P I R E

Ancyra

Rome
Corfinium

Dyrrachium
Stobi
Beroea
Thessalonica
Neapolis
Brundisium
Tarentum

Prusa
Alexandria Troas
Dorylaeum
Caesarea
Melitene

PERSIA

(SASANIAN

EMPIRE)

Tigris

Euphrates

Demetrias
Pergamum
Nicopolis
Smyrna
Sardis
Antiochia
Iconium

Antioch

Panormus
Sicily

Patrae
Corinth
Athens
Tarsus
Apamea

Catana
Syracuse

Sparta
Halicarnassus

Attaleia
Side

Malta

S E A

Rhodus

Cyprus Salamis
Palmyra

GHASSANIDS

LAKHMIDS

Crete
Gortyn

41

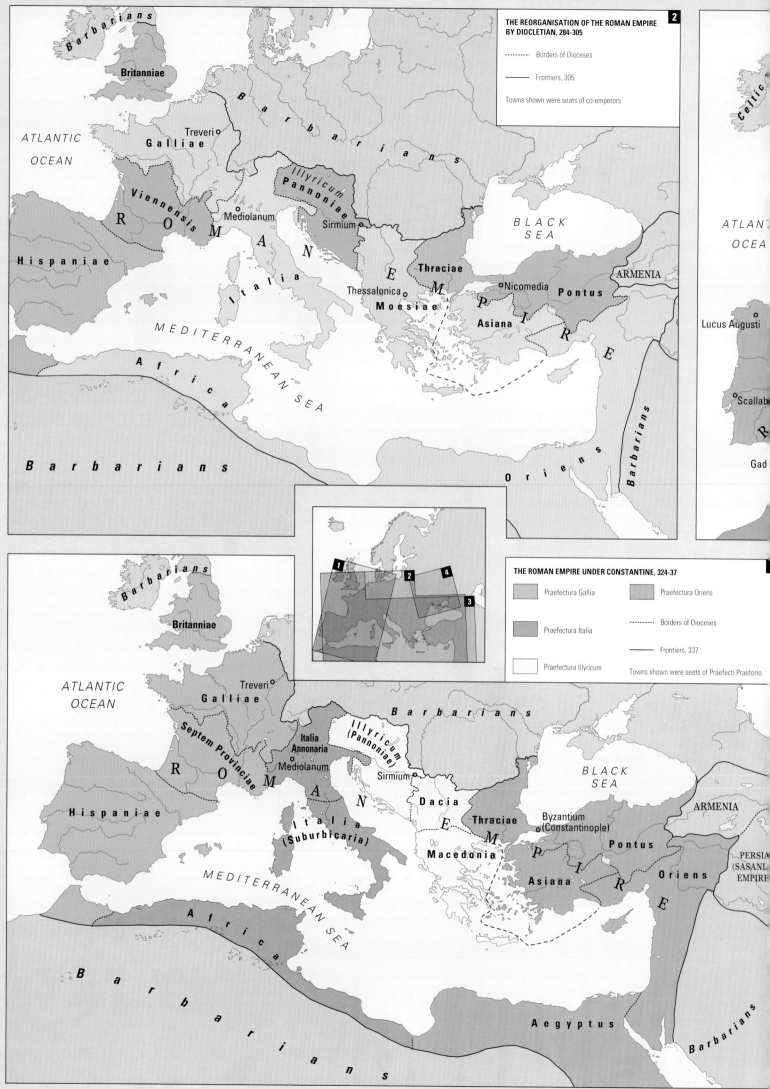

THE REORGANISATION OF THE ROMAN EMPIRE BY DIOCLETIAN, 284–305

- - - - - Borders of Dioceses

———— Frontiers, 305

Towns shown were seats of co-emperors

Map 2 (Diocletian)

Barbarians

Britanniae

ATLANTIC OCEAN

Treveri

Galliae

Barbarians

Viennensis

R O M A N

Mediolanum

Illyricum Pannoniae

Sirmium

BLACK SEA

Hispaniae

Italia

E M

Thraciae

ATLANTIC OCEAN

ARMENIA

Thessalonica

Moesiae

Nicomedia

Pontus

Lucus Augusti

MEDITERRANEAN SEA

Asiana

P I R E

Africa

Scallab

Barbarians

Oriens

Barbarians

Gad

Map inset (key)

1 2 4 3

THE ROMAN EMPIRE UNDER CONSTANTINE, 324–37

Praefectura Gallia	Praefectura Oriens
Praefectura Italia	- - - - - Borders of Dioceses
Praefectura Illyricum	———— Frontiers, 337

Towns shown were seats of Praefecti Praetorio

Map (Constantine)

Barbarians

Britanniae

ATLANTIC OCEAN

Treveri

Galliae

Barbarians

Septem Provinciae

R O M A N

Italia Annonaria

Mediolanum

Illyricum (Pannoniae)

Sirmium

BLACK SEA

Hispaniae

E M

Dacia

Byzantium (Constantinople)

ARMENIA

Italia (Suburbicaria)

Thraciae

Pontus

PERSIA (SASANL EMPIRE)

Macedonia

Asiana

P I R E

Oriens

MEDITERRANEAN SEA

Africa

Aegyptus

B a r b a r i a n s

Barbarians

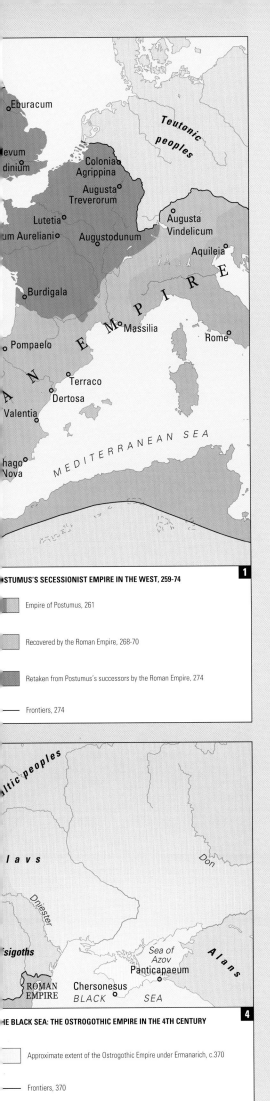

STUMUS'S SECESSIONIST EMPIRE IN THE WEST, 259-74

■ Empire of Postumus, 261

■ Recovered by the Roman Empire, 268-70

■ Retaken from Postumus's successors by the Roman Empire, 274

— Frontiers, 274

HE BLACK SEA: THE OSTROGOTHIC EMPIRE IN THE 4TH CENTURY

☐ Approximate extent of the Ostrogothic Empire under Ermanarich, c.370

— Frontiers, 370

Postumus's Secessionist Empire in the West, 259-74

1 In the mid-3rd century the Roman Empire endured its worst crisis yet. In 251 the Emperor Decius was slain by the Goths. In 260 Valerian was captured and humiliated by the Persians. His son, Gallienus, was confronted by a near-fatal combination: mutinous armies and invading barbarians. "Thirty tyrants" – in reality, 18 contenders for the purple – competed to usurp his throne. Empire-wide authority was effectively unenforceable and the state seemed about to dissolve into defensible regional networks of self-help.

The most promising of these was the "Gallic empire" which lasted for nearly 20 years after the election of the general Postumus on the Rhine frontier in 259 in a typical proclamation of the time, following a dispute over booty. He defeated Frankish and Alemannic raiders in Gaul and called himself "the saviour of the provinces". He was killed in a mutiny in 268, and his territories were reconquered from his successors by Aurelian in the 270s. Yet his experiment seemed to offer a glimpse of a workable future: the adherence of neighbouring provinces briefly pre-figured future administrative divisions; and his capital at Augusta Treverorum (Trier) became one of the centres of autonomous government under a the devolved system established by Diocletian (*see* below).

The Reorganisation of the Roman Empire by Diocletian, 284-305

2 The anarchy and invasions of the third quarter of the 3rd century were checked by the energy and generalship of Aurelian (270-5), but the next six emperors all ruled briefly and died violently. Diocletian, proclaimed emperor at Nicomedia in 284, was able to exploit reactions against instability. During the first 10 years of his reign he devised a new system for governing the Empire as a union of four effectively autonomous imperial territories.

In theory, the four Emperors formed a college under Diocletian's presidency but in practice each ruled his own area. In the west, Maximian's title of Augustus gave him direct rule over Italy and Spain; his subordinate "Caesar", Constantius, ruled Britain and Gaul. Diocletian was pre-eminent in the rest of the Empire, and his "Caesar", Galerius, shunted between marchland-areas of special responsibility in Illyricum and on the Persian front. Their capitals were close to theatres of frontier warfare but consciously rivalled Rome: Lactantius complained of Diocletian's "mania" for making his residence at Nicomedia the equal of Rome. By the force of Diocletian's personality and of their common interest in preventing rebellion, the four emperors remained loyal colleagues. In 305, Diocletian and Maximian were able to take the unprecedented step of "retiring" from imperial office, though the outcome was not entirely peaceful.

Diocletian continued and accelerated the tradition of "slicing" provinces into ever-smaller units: there were perhaps about 50 at the start of his reign and he seems roughly to have doubled their number. This made taxation, administration and jurisdiction more thorough but multiplied bureaucracy – especially when a layer of supervision was added to the provincial structure in the form of 13 "dioceses", groups of governorships overseen by imperial "vicars". Perhaps the most far-reaching aspect of his reforms was in personnel: the traditional senatorial elite was passed over in favour of a new "aristocracy of service", intended to be directly dependent on imperial patronage.

The Roman Empire under Constantine, 324-37

3 Constantine formalised the division of the Empire into eastern and western halves by founding a "second Rome" at Constantinople, where he resided, and devolving western government to his sons. In effect, by the 330s, his system resembled the system devised by Diocletian, with one "Caesar" ruling the "Prefecture" of Gaul, another Italy and two others commanding on the eastern fronts. He also continued the diocesan structure, splitting Moesia into two: Dacia (formerly the name of a province on the north bank of the Danube); and Macedonia. From his time onward, not only was the seat of the emperor transferred to the east, the centre of gravity of the empire as a whole shifted in the same direction. The last great imperial monument of Rome – the basilica of Maximian in the Forum – dates from just before his time; the Arch of Constantine, though impressive, is a second-rate construction, employing a lot of recycled reliefs. Constantine was the first Christian emperor and though Christianity was not definitively established as the official religion of the state until 395 AD, his patronage ensured its irreversible ascent.

The Black Sea: the Ostrogothic Empire in the 4th Century

3 The origin of the peoples collectively known in antiquity as the Goths has often been conjectured but never demonstrated. They were reputed to have crossed the Baltic from a Scandinavian homeland during the 1st century AD, in the time of Tacitus and Pliny. The Visigoths separated from the rest, perhaps because they baulked at crossing the Pripet marshes. The division known as the Ostrogoths pressed on to the Black Sea by the end of the 2nd century AD and founded an "empire" bounded by the Sea of Azov, the Black Sea and the lower Don. Though war bands split off and invaded the Roman world, the Ostrogothic state remained intact until it was destroyed by Hunnic invaders from the east on its vulnerable steppeland flank in 376, in the reign of King Ermanarich. After a series of bloody defeats, the Ostrogothic army was forced over the Dniester into the territory of the Visigoths who, unable to oppose the Huns, were forced to seek refuge in the Roman empire. The Ostrogoths remained in this area until their conquest of Italy in the 6th century (*see* map 2, page 51)

450

The Barbarian Settlements

Between 370 and 470, there was a steady build-up of Hunnic power on the fringes of Roman territory. Despite its brevity, this had profound consequences for the subsequent development of western Europe. Notwithstanding their ferocity in battle and their reputation for enduring cold, hunger and thirst "from the cradle", as the Roman historian Ammianus Marcellinus said, the Huns could not pose a serious threat to the Roman Empire nor construct a large state of their own while their primitive, pastoral economy rendered political integration impossible and united military action impracticable.

By the early 5th century, however, infusions of booty and fiscal exactions from subject-peoples were transforming the economic base of Hunnic society. The conquest of the Ostrogoths in 376 presupposed an unprecedented concentration of force. The Goths were permitted to cross the Danube and settle in Thrace. In 378 they inflicted a resounding defeat on the Emperor Valens, on the plains outside Adrianople. The Huns' advances forced other barbarian groups deeper into Roman territory, most notably in the winters of 395 and 405-6, when the Vandals, Sueves and Alans crossed the Rhine. These advances led indirectly to the creation of the barbarian kingdoms in Gaul, Italy, Spain and North Africa.

By about 420 a Hunnic confederacy was in being, which was further enriched in tribute, booty and land by supplying mercenaries to Rome and extorting "protection money". Under the rule of Attila, from the mid-430s, this system came under intolerable strain as the Huns' ambitions were fed by success and by the revenues of an empire which stretched from the Baltic to the Black Sea and the Caspian. In 445 Attila murdered his elder brother and co-ruler, Bleda. In 447, needing a continuous intake of plunder to sustain his warriors, he attacked the Eastern Roman Empire, at a time when an unusual combination of natural disasters – plague, famine and earthquakes – sapped resistance. In 451 he launched a similar attack on the Western Empire, on the unconvincing pretext that he intended to discipline the Visigoths on the Empire's behalf. Though severely beaten in Gaul on the Catalaunian Plains, by the united resistance of Romans and barbarians, he turned on Italy in 452. He seems to have fancied himself as the puppet-master of the whole Roman world, but the Empire was spared by his sudden death before the start of the campaign season of 453. Divided among his sons, the Hunnic state lasted only a dozen more years before being torn apart by internecine strife and swept aside by other Asiatic nomad-hordes.

Meanwhile, with the foundation of barbarian kingdoms within the territory of the Western Roman Empire, Europe was beginning to take on the configurations it was to display in medieval and modern times. The barbarians were often given the notional status of "federates" or allied peoples, but in practice came to rule over the areas in which they settled. Thus the Visigoths dominated southwestern France and the Sueves controlled the western half of the Iberian peninsula before being marginalized by the Visigoths in the early 6th century. North Africa, save for its westernmost reaches, was overrun by the Vandals early in the 5th century. In the late 5th century, the Ostrogoths settled in Italy. Gradually a series of effectively sovereign kingdoms took shape. The various elements of the cultural heritage of Europe were assembled when the Germanic traditions of these groups were fused with the Graeco-Roman and Judaeo-Christian legacies which formed the civilisation of 4th-century Rome.

F i n n o

U g r i a n s

Volga

n i c P e o p l e s

BALTIC
SEA

Oder

Elbe

rippina

Vistula

Don

Volga

Dnieper

Dniester

H u n n i c   p e o p l e s

a Regina

Augusta
Vindelicum

Danube

Vindobona

Lauriacum

Carnuntum

Aquincum

Teurnia

Virunum

Savaria

Aquileia

avium

Verona

Siscia

Sirmium

Panticapaeum

Chersonesus

n i c   p e o p l e s

sae

Ariminum

Salonae

Durostorum

Tomi

B L A C K   S E A

Lazi

tium

Oescus

Danube

AN EMPIRE

Narona

Doclea

Naissus

Serdica

Sinope

Amisus

Trapezus

Rome

Corfinium

Dyrrachium

Stobi

Philippopolis

Adrianople

Perinthus

Byzantium

Heraclea Pontica

Amaseia

Nicopolis

PERSIA

Neapolis

Brundisium

Beroea

Thessalonica

EASTERN   ROMAN   EMPIRE

Prusa

Alexandria Troas

Dorylaeum

Ancyra

Caesarea

Melitene

Tarentum

Demetrias

Pergamum

Smyrna

Sardis

Antiochia

Iconium

(SASANIAN

Nicopolis

Panormus

Patrae

Athens

Tarsus

Antioch

EMPIRE)

Sicily

Catana

Corinth

Attaleia

Side

Apamea

Syracuse

Halicarnassus

Palmyra

Sparta

GHASSANIDS

Malta

SEA

Rhodus

Cyprus

Salamis

LAKHMIDS

Crete

Gortyn

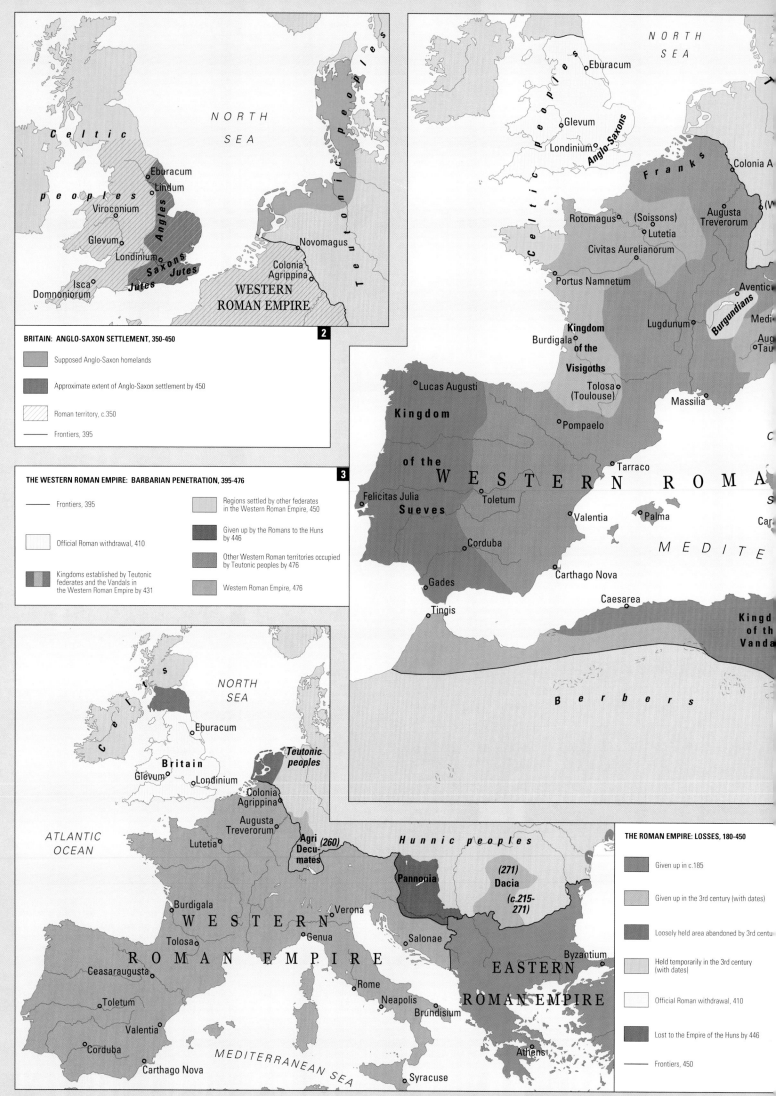

BRITAIN: ANGLO-SAXON SETTLEMENT, 350-450

	Supposed Anglo-Saxon homelands
	Approximate extent of Anglo-Saxon settlement by 450
	Roman territory, c.350
	Frontiers, 395

2

THE WESTERN ROMAN EMPIRE: BARBARIAN PENETRATION, 395-476

3

	Frontiers, 395			Regions settled by other federates in the Western Roman Empire, 450
	Official Roman withdrawal, 410			Given up by the Romans to the Huns by 446
	Kingdoms established by Teutonic federates and the Vandals in the Western Roman Empire by 431			Other Western Roman territories occupied by Teutonic peoples by 476
				Western Roman Empire, 476

THE ROMAN EMPIRE: LOSSES, 180-450

	Given up in c.185
	Given up in the 3rd century (with dates)
	Loosely held area abandoned by 3rd centu...
	Held temporarily in the 3rd century (with dates)
	Official Roman withdrawal, 410
	Lost to the Empire of the Huns by 446
	Frontiers, 450

Map labels

Britain: Anglo-Saxon Settlement
NORTH SEA · Celtic peoples · Eburacum · Lindum · Viroconium · Angles · Saxons · Jutes · Glevum · Londinium · Isca · Domnoniorum · Teutonic peoples · Novomagus · Colonia Agrippina · WESTERN ROMAN EMPIRE

The Western Roman Empire: Barbarian Penetration
NORTH SEA · Eburacum · Glevum · Londinium · Celtic peoples · Anglo-Saxons · Franks · Colonia A... · Rotomagus · (Soissons) · Lutetia · Augusta Treverorum · Civitas Aurelianorum · Portus Namnetum · Burgundians · Medi... · Lugdunum · Aug... · Tau... · Kingdom of the Visigoths · Burdigala · Tolosa (Toulouse) · Massilia · Lucas Augusti · Kingdom of the Sueves · Pompaelo · Tarraco · WESTERN ROMA... · Felicitas Julia · Toletum · Valentia · Palma · Car... · MEDITE... · Corduba · Carthago Nova · Gades · Tingis · Caesarea · Kingd... of the Vanda... · Berbers

The Roman Empire: Losses
Celts · NORTH SEA · Eburacum · Britain · Glevum · Londinium · Teutonic peoples · Colonia Agrippina · Augusta Treverorum · Lutetia · ATLANTIC OCEAN · Agri Decumates (260) · Hunnic peoples · Pannonia · (271) Dacia (c.215-271) · Burdigala · Verona · Genua · Salonae · Byzantium · WESTERN ROMAN EMPIRE · Ceasaraugusta · Tolosa · Rome · EASTERN ROMAN EMPIRE · Toletum · Neapolis · Brundisium · Valentia · Corduba · Carthago Nova · MEDITERRANEAN SEA · Athens · Syracuse

The Roman Empire: Losses, 180-450

1 The Western Roman Empire survived by adapting in the course of the 3rd, 4th and 5th centuries. The most striking examples are the extension of citizenship to former subject peoples in 212 and the domestication of Christianity– a potentially subversive religion which was converted to the service of the state. The leadership of the government itself was taken over by the barbarians, though much of Roman life and administration was only slowly transformed.

The defence of the vast frontier, employing limited resources in the face of ever-greater barbarian pressure, proved an impossible task. In 271 the exposed province of Dacia across the Danube was abandoned, and by the early 5th century Britain had, in effect, been left to defend itself. Barbarian pressure on the frontier increased in the late 4th century, when Gothic war-bands forced their way into the empire and proved difficult to control. Many Germanic groups, moreover, were established as "federates" with the function of military protection. A process of adaptation and assimilation got underway with a consequent gradual transformation of the Roman world. The Huns' own intrusion in imperial territory was short-lived, albeit proverbially destructive, although the loss to them of Pannonia in 446 proved permanent. Also, the effects of the many less spectacular invasions they helped to cause were long-enduring and included the fragmentation of the unity of the Roman Empire among numerous "sub-Roman" states and barbarian kingdoms within the frontiers.

Britain: Anglo-Saxon Settlement, 350-450

2 Writing *The History of the English Church and People* in the early 8th century, Bede divided the Germanic invaders of Britain into Angles, Saxons and Jutes. But though institutional peculiarities in medieval Kent have been ascribed to Jutish origins, the differences between these groups are conjectural and the validity of Bede's classifications are open to doubt. Evidence of localised Germanic communities scattered over a wide area by the mid-4th century suggests that the first settlements were of mercenaries imported with imperial connivance. Frankish mercenaries were employed in Gaul as early as 350, and the process of troops becoming settlers was probably similar in Britain.

In the early 5th century, the Emperor Honorius withdrew the last legions from Britain. The numbers of barbarian newcomers increased and their relations with the native authorities, who bore both Roman and Celtic names, is a matter for conjecture, though the outcome was the assertion 1of Anglo-Saxon dominance in eastern parts of Britain. The traditional date of the "Adventus Saxonum" ("arrival of the Saxons") is 449: this can perhaps be taken as the approximate starting-point for their establishment of kingdoms of their own in Britain, in which the fate of the British is unclear, though the assimilation process appears to have been thorough.

The Western Roman Empire: Barbarian Penetration, 395-476

3 With hindsight, the Roman empire in the west can be seen to have come to an end with the foundation of Germanic kingdoms inside the Roman frontier in the 5th century. At the time, this appeared by no means clear. Most of the Germanic kingdoms were founded by relatively small war bands, accommodated within the empire as uneasy allies, entrusted with tasks of imperial defence, quartered in rural garrisons at the expense of their host-communities and only gradually taking over the cities and usurping or accepting authority over the non-Germanic populations. The Empire had successfully absorbed non-Roman peoples at intervals in the past, and the Germanic settlers were all, in varying degrees, susceptible to Romanisation and their kings, in most cases, were prepared to show some measure of deference to imperial institutions.

Yet increasing territorial loss sapped Roman revenues, manpower resources and the will to resist. In 413 the Emperor Honorius had to reduce the taxation levels for southern Italy to one-fifth of their former level. As part of this movement, the Sueves (and Alans) invaded Spain and were only confined to the western part of the peninsula by the Roman employment of Visigothic troops. The Visigoths afterwards settled in Aquitaine and founded the Kingdom of Toulouse there in 418. Under Euric (466-84), the Visigoths greatly extended their kingdom to cover a large area of southern France. Their regime co-operated with the Gallo-Roman population, both in the administration of the region and in their participation in imperial politics by supporting candidates from southern France for the imperial throne.

The Vandals, who had followed the Sueves into Spain, crossed into Africa in 429, and in 439 captured Carthage. In 442 the imperial government recognised their possession of the richest provinces in Africa, leaving the Roman inhabitants under Vandal rule, which the Catholics among them, at least, deeply resented.

The Burgundians founded a kingdom around the city of Worms in about 410, but were settled in Savoy by the Roman Commander Aetius after Worms had been destroyed by the Huns in 437. On the whole they were allied to the Romans, but in the 460s they extended their territory by seizing Lugdunum (Lyons), which became their capital.

In northern Gaul, imperial authority was eroded by the gradual expansion of the Franks from their bases in the old Roman province of Belgica. Around 462 the general Aegidius withdrew recognition from the Emperor and he and his successors Paul and Syagrius governed an independent Roman enclave around Soissons. The Franks under Childeric seem to have co-operated with the Roman leaders there, although this stance was to be reversed under Childeric's son Clovis (*see* map 4, page 51), who eventually assumed control of the whole of northern Gaul.

The Barbarian West

Although the period from 450 to 526 saw the formal dissolution of the Western Roman Empire into various successor kingdoms under Germanic kings, in fact much of the fabric and structure of Roman life and provincial organisation remained and was even deliberately maintained and adapted by the Germanic rulers . From the mid-5th century there had been a succession of puppet emperors in the West, with real power in the hands of the *magister militum*, the leader of the Roman army, often, as in the case of Stilicho, Ricimer or Odoacer, a barbarian. After 476, when Odoacer overthrew the Emperor Romulus Augustulus, the Roman Senate sent a message to the Eastern Emperor Zeno informing him that there was no further need for a separate ruler in the West, though an eastern candidate, Julius Nepos, retreated to Dalmatia and held the title until 480.

The other provinces of the Western Roman Empire – Gaul, Spain and North Africa – had become gradually dissociated from the central government in Italy during the 5th century and military governors played an increasingly dominant role. Thus for much of the century the principal authority in Gaul had been the Roman military commander Aetius, and after 461 administrative links between Gaul and Italy no longer existed. The local populations reached their own *modus vivendi* with the barbarian groups who had originally been settled among them as military federates. In many cases, although the barbarian leaders emerged as the rulers, they were staunchly assisted by the Roman administrative classes, both civilian and ecclesiastical.

The Germanic kingdoms of Western Europe which emerged during the late 5th and the 6th centuries were the heirs of Rome in every sense. The evidence points to integration and adaptation in varying degrees, with much that was Roman – in government, law, administration, social organisation, religion and intellectual culture – maintained and even promoted under barbarian rule. Huneric (477-484), King of the Vandals, married the sister of the Roman Emperor Valentinian. Theodoric, the Ostrogothic king, had his daughter Amalsuintha taught both Greek and Latin. Carthage continued to expand under the Vandals, with King Thrasamund in particular initiating a number of new buildings on Roman models. Yet as the concerns of the barbarian successor kingdoms became increasingly regional and the Eastern Roman Empire became preoccupied with defending its eastern borders against the Sasanian rulers of Persia, trading and diplomatic links diminished.

The Christian church became a factor to be reckoned with in the political formation of Western Europe in the 5th century, not only in such missionary endeavours as St Patrick's in Ireland, but in collaboration between the church and the new Germanic rulers in Gaul and Spain. In Italy by the 540s, the bishops increasingly became powerful political leaders. The Papacy, too, began to emerge as a power, at least in Rome itself.

Of the development of much of the rest of Europe in the period, especially that of Scandinavia and the Slav regions, little is known. Britain was gradually being settled by groups of Angles, Saxons and possibly Jutes from northern Europe, though their penetration was limited and knowledge of their relations with the Romano-British population, as well as the nature of their social and political organisation, remains elusive. It is possible, too, that Frankish links with the southeast of England may have been quite strong.

F i n n o - U g r i a n s

Northmen

(Scandinavians)

BALTIC
SEA

B a l t i c   p e o p l e s

Volga

Don

ns
Thuringians

Oder
Elbe
Vistula

S l a v s

Dnieper

Dniester

Volga

T u r k i c   p e o p l e s

Danube

Lombards

KINGDOM
OF THE GEPIDS

Alans

num
Verona

Bononia
Iadera   Spalatum
ia   Dalmatia
Perusia

Rome

KINGDOM

OF THE

OSTROGOTHS

Naples   Barium
        Tarentum

normus
Messana
Sicily

Malta

Naissus

Serdica
Philippopolis

Danube

Odessus

Chersonesus

BLACK   SEA

LAZICA

Trapezus

E A S T E R N   R O M A N   E M P I R E

Adrianople   Constantinople

Salonica

Smyrna

Patras   Athens

SEA

Crete

Cyprus

PERSIA

(SASANIAN

EMPIRE)

Tigris

Euphrates

GHASSANIDS

LAKHMIDS

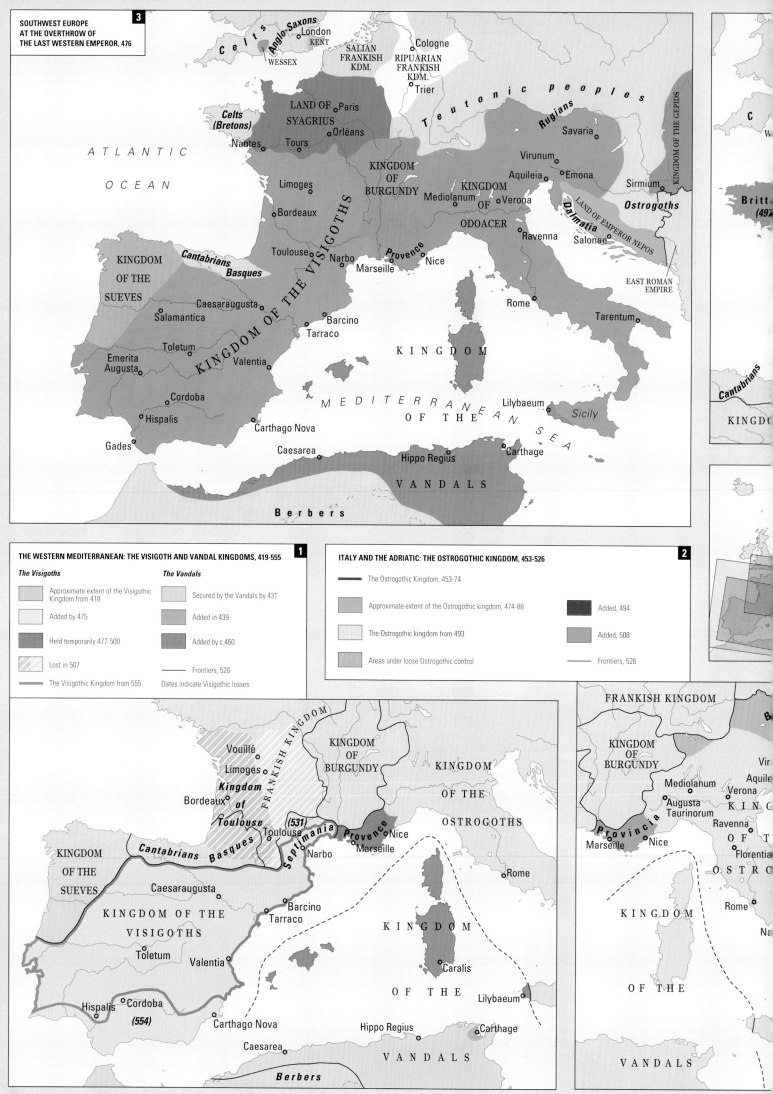

SOUTHWEST EUROPE
AT THE OVERTHROW OF
THE LAST WESTERN EMPEROR, 476

Map 3 – Southwest Europe at the overthrow of the last Western Emperor, 476

Celts
Anglo-Saxons
London
KENT
WESSEX
Cologne
SALIAN FRANKISH KDM.
RIPUARIAN FRANKISH KDM.
Trier
Celts (Bretons)
LAND OF SYAGRIUS
Paris
Orléans
Nantes
Tours
ATLANTIC OCEAN
Teutonic peoples
Rugians
Savaria
KINGDOM OF THE GEPIDS
Virunum
Emona
Aquileia
Sirmium
Limoges
KINGDOM OF BURGUNDY
KINGDOM OF ODOACER
Mediolanum
Verona
Ostrogoths
Britt... (497...)
Bordeaux
Dalmatia
Ravenna
Salonae
LAND OF EMPEROR NEPOS
KINGDOM OF THE VISIGOTHS
Toulouse
Narbo
Provence
Nice
Marseille
Cantabrians
Basques
EAST ROMAN EMPIRE
KINGDOM OF THE SUEVES
Caesaraugusta
Salamantica
Barcino
Tarraco
Rome
Tarentum
Toletum
Valentia
Emerita Augusta
Cordoba
KINGDOM
Hispalis
Gades
Carthago Nova
MEDITERRANEAN SEA
Lilybaeum
Sicily
OF THE
Caesarea
Hippo Regius
Carthage
VANDALS
Berbers

THE WESTERN MEDITERRANEAN: THE VISIGOTH AND VANDAL KINGDOMS, 419–555 — **1**

The Visigoths

Approximate extent of the Visigothic Kingdom from 418
Added by 475
Held temporarily 477–500
Lost in 507
The Visigothic Kingdom from 555

The Vandals

Secured by the Vandals by 431
Added in 439
Added by c.460
Frontiers, 526
Dates indicate Visigothic losses

ITALY AND THE ADRIATIC: THE OSTROGOTHIC KINGDOM, 453–526 — **2**

The Ostrogothic Kingdom, 453–74
Approximate extent of the Ostrogothic kingdom, 474–88
The Ostrogothic kingdom from 493
Areas under loose Ostrogothic control
Added, 494
Added, 508
Frontiers, 526

Map 1

FRANKISH KINGDOM
Vouillé
Limoges
Kingdom of Toulouse
Bordeaux
KINGDOM OF BURGUNDY
KINGDOM OF THE OSTROGOTHS
(531)
Toulouse
Septimania
Provence
Nice
Narbo
Marseille
Cantabrians
Basques
KINGDOM OF THE SUEVES
Caesaraugusta
Barcino
Tarraco
Rome
KINGDOM OF THE VISIGOTHS
Toletum
Valentia
KINGDOM
Caralis
OF THE
Lilybaeum
Hispalis
Cordoba
(554)
Carthago Nova
Caesarea
VANDALS
Berbers
Hippo Regius
Carthage

Map 2

FRANKISH KINGDOM
B...
KINGDOM OF BURGUNDY
Vir...
Aquile...
Mediolanum
Verona
Augusta Taurinorum
KIN...
Provincia
Ravenna
OF T...
Marseille
Nice
Florentia
OSTRO...
Rome
KINGDOM
Na...
OF THE
VANDALS

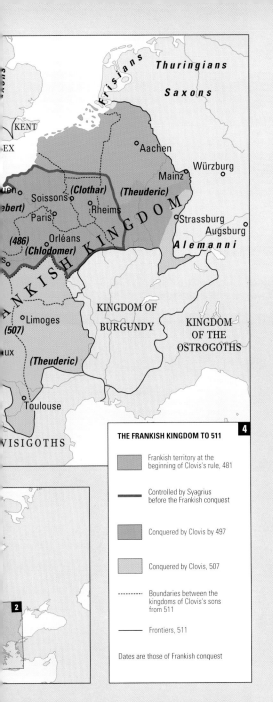

KENT

Thuringians

Saxons

Aachen

Würzburg

Mainz

(Clothar) (Theuderic)

Soissons

Rheims

Paris

Strassburg

Augsburg

(486)

Orléans

(Chlodomer)

Alemanni

FRANKISH KINGDOM

Limoges

(507)

KINGDOM OF BURGUNDY

KINGDOM OF THE OSTROGOTHS

(Theuderic)

Toulouse

VISIGOTHS

THE FRANKISH KINGDOM TO 511 4

- Frankish territory at the beginning of Clovis's rule, 481
- Controlled by Syagrius before the Frankish conquest
- Conquered by Clovis by 497
- Conquered by Clovis, 507
- Boundaries between the kingdoms of Clovis's sons from 511
- Frontiers, 511

Dates are those of Frankish conquest

uringians

Lombards

Slavs

Savaria

Gepids

Sirmium

Oescus

Novae

E A S T

R O M A N

Tarentum

E M P I R E

The Western Mediterranean: the Visigoth and Vandal Kingdoms 419-555

1 After their employment by the Romans to defeat the Sueves in Spain (*see* map 3, below), the barbarian Visigoths were settled in Aquitaine as a Roman allied army from 418. Gradually they came to rule over a defined area, the Kingdom of Toulouse. A pattern of Roman provincial administration was retained, with many senatorial aristocrats playing a major role in establishing the kingdom and working for the Visigothic rulers in running their government.

The Visigoths invaded Spain in 454, driving the Sueves, who had dominated the Iberian peninsula since 430, into the northwest. The Visigothic conquest of Spain was consolidated under Euric (466-84). In France, they expanded their control to the Mediterranean between 462-3, the Auvergne was ceded to them in 475 (by the Eastern Emperor) and Provence in 476 (by the barbarian ruler of Italy, Odoacer). In 507, however, the Visigoths suffered a crushing defeat by the Franks at Vouillé. The Franks then pushed the Visigoths out of most of Gaul except Septimania.

In 429 the Vandals crossed from Spain, to North Africa. They gained Mauretania and Numidia by treaty in 431, and took Carthage in 439. Although the Romans for a time retained a hold on the western regions, the Vandals by 442 occupied all the richest areas of North Africa and maintained their kingdom there until 534. The Vandal rulers, who, like the Visigoths, subscribed to Arianism, a heretical form of Christianity, conducted an allegedly vicious campaign of persecution against the Catholic church, but left Roman provincial life otherwise mostly undisturbed.

Italy and the Adriatic: the Ostrogothic Kingdom, 453-526

2 In 489, Theodoric the Ostrogoth and his people entered Italy. His initial arrival in 489 appears to have been a consequence of the Eastern Emperor again trying to intervene in western affairs by sending a ruler to replace Odoacer (*see* map 3). After four years of warfare, Odoacer was treacherously murdered at Ravenna. Theodoric then ruled Italy peacefully until 526. His precise constitutional position in Italy remained uncertain, however, though he styled himself "King of the Goths and Romans". In 497 the Emperor Anastasius conceded Theodoric's status as ruler of Italy. Like Odoacer before him, Theodoric appears to have worked from within the Roman system. He had high ideals of government, insisting on the rule of law, with Gothic law prevailing for Goths and Roman law for Romans. He was assisted in his administration by many aristocratic Romans, notably the scholar Boethius, and elevated many new men, such as Cassiodorus, to high office. Although himself an Arian Christian, Theodoric appears to have been tolerant of the Catholic church. Under Theodoric, many magnificent buildings were erected, especially in Ravenna. He established marriage ties with the Germanic rulers of Aquitaine, northern Gaul, Burgundy and North Africa. He was the effective ruler in Septimania and Provence from 508 to 521.

Southwest Europe at the Overthrow of the Last Western Emperor, 476

3 To view 476 as the "collapse" of the Empire in the west is a retrospective view. At the time, and in the context of the rapid succession of no fewer than 19 emperors in the west between 394 and 476, many of whom were the candidates of rival factions who held the throne for a very short time, the deposition of the teenage Emperor Romulus Augustulus by Odoacer would have seemed like yet another coup and temporary vacancy. Romulus was proclaimed emperor by his father Orestes in October 475 and thus "ruled" for only 10 months. The empire, moreover, had already suffered a series of reverses and territorial losses, so that by 476 the whole of the Iberian peninsula was ruled by the Sueves and Visigoths, and in Gaul the largest Roman-controlled area, that governed by Syagrius, did not acknowledge the authority of the Emperor.

Odoacer in fact maintained peace and stability in Italy between 476 and 493. He ruled from Ravenna, retained Roman administrative structures and personnel and rewarded many of the Roman senatorial families for their support. Although the 6th-century Greek historian Procopius says Odoacer "ceded his right" to Provence to Euric, ruler of the Visigoths, and a North African chronicler recorded the cession of Sicily to Gaiseric, king of the Vandals, Odoacer also made some attempts to expand his territory, conquering Dalmatia after the murder of the imperial claimant Julius Nepos in 480 and possibly conducting a campaign against the Rugians.

The Frankish Kingdom to 511

4 Clovis had ruled as king of the Franks from 481, gradually expanding the territories over which he ruled. In a contest for power in northern Gaul he had defeated the Roman Syagrius in 486. He ruthlessly eliminated his Frankish rivals, pushed the Visigoths out of southern Gaul in 507 and achieved a victory in battle against another barbarian group, the Alemans, between 486 and 508. Clovis's baptism as a Catholic has added a religious flavour to these campaigns for some historians. On the death of Clovis in 511, his hard-won kingdom was divided among his four surviving sons – Theuderic I, Chlodomer, Childebert I and Chlothar I. Each brother was given a portion providing equal revenues and in accord with current political circumstances. Each brother based himself in one of the old Roman centres within his territory: Childebert I at Paris, Chlodomer at Orléans, Chlothar I at Soissons and Theuderic I at Rheims. Control of the former Visigothic kingdom of Aquitaine, which was conquered after the battle of Vouillé in 507 (*see* map 1, above), was insecure and it is not clear how the area was divided among the brothers. The kingdom of Burgundy, meanwhile, retained its independence until 534.

526

The Frankish Kingdom

The first half of the 6th century saw the emergence of a strong Frankish kingdom in Gaul, ruled over by the Merovingian dynasty, and a Visigothic kingdom in Spain. In both of these much of the old Roman way of life survived. The roads, buildings, centres of population, and social institutions remained little altered at first, though in Gaul at least urban life appears to have been little favoured by the Franks. Latin remained the prevailing language throughout the former Western Empire, at least for religion, learning and the law. Its strength can be measured by the fact that with the exception of Britain, the tongues of the countries that were once within the Western Roman Empire are "Romance" languages descended from Latin. The incoming Franks, Visigoths, Ostrogoths, Sueves, and Burgundians adopted the language and mores, the institutions and culture of the peoples among whom they settled while the Roman Empire still flourished. They continued to use Latin as their principal language for communication, centuries after the Empire became simply a memory and an ideal. Latin was given new life after the introduction of Christianity to the Germanic and Slavic areas.

Although as a result of the reconquests of the Byzantine Emperor Justinian (*see* map 2, page 55), the Eastern Roman Empire's dominion was ostensibly restored across the whole of the Mediterranean, in practice each region was left to its own devices. The new political leaders, notably in Gaul and Spain, drew on what remained, or on what they wanted and seemed appropriate, from their Roman heritage and forged new political entities. In this they were undoubtedly assisted by many members of the Roman upper class families in these regions, who thereby maintained their social position, and no doubt their wealth. A notable feature of the period was the degree to which the Christian clergy, and especially the bishops, assumed positions of social and political responsibility.

These developments were not so marked in the eastern Mediterranean, where the Byzantine emperor was in any case pre-occupied with the attacks of the Persians. This was one reason, indeed, why Justinian failed to consolidate the western conquest with the resources and manpower needed for lasting success. Nevertheless, Persian success was limited to an area around the Black Sea. Internally, many reforms were instituted in the Eastern Empire. There were severe internal tensions which culminated in the Nika riots of 532 and which were exacerbated by the plague which wiped out a large portion of the population of Constantinople in 542. But Justinian was an administrative genius. His tax reforms and the wholesale reorganization of existing Roman law (Code and Digest of Justinian) as well as his own legislation (Novels) were a lasting legacy to Europe, though in the west the principal sources of Roman law until the 11th century remained the earlier Code of Theodosius and the Breviary of Alaric. The establishment of a silk monopoly in Constantinople boosted the economy.

Events in far off Mongolia and Asia among the Turks also impinged on Europe for they drove groups of steppe peoples, later to be known as the Avars, towards the west; they ferociously attacked the areas now known as the Ukraine and Bessarabia and established themselves on the lower Danube. In the far west, groups of Irishmen or Scoti established the kingdom of Dal Riada in what later became known as Scotland. The Scoti and the Picts clashed with the people of North Britain and the incoming Anglo-Saxons, as they pressed farther into Britain.

Finnic

Northmen

(Scandinavians)

BALTIC
SEA

peoples

Hungarians

Baltic peoples

Volga

Slavs

Don

Volga

Dnieper

Turkic peoples

Dniester

Oder

Vistula

Elbe

ns

ngians

st
nks

Bavarians

Danube

ns

KINGDOM
OF THE
LOMBARDS

KINGDOM
OF THE GEPIDS

Danube

Alans

Chersonesus

BLACK SEA

Verona

Bononia

Iadera

Spalatum

Perusia

ia

Rome

Naissus

Odessus

Trapezus

Serdica

Philippopolis

Adrianople

Constantinople

NTINE EMPIRE

PERSIA

Naples

Barium

Tarentum

Salonica

ERN ROMAN EMPIRE)

(SASANIAN

E

Smyrna

EMPIRE)

anormus

Sicily

Messana

Patras

Athens

Tigris

Euphrates

Malta

SEA

Cyprus

GHASSANIDS

LAKHMIDS

Crete

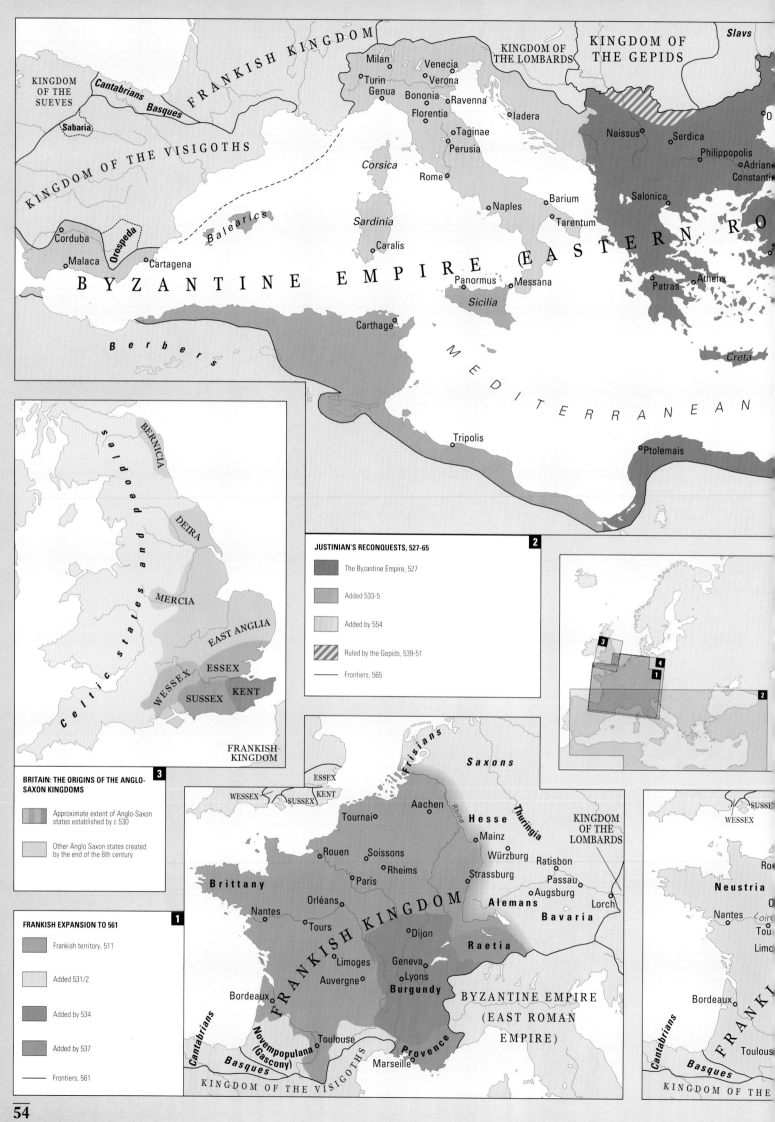

KINGDOM OF THE SUEVES

Cantabrians Basques FRANKISH KINGDOM

Sabaria

KINGDOM OF THE VISIGOTHS

Corduba
Orospeda
Malaca
Cartagena

Balearics

Corsica

Milan
Turin
Genua
Bononia
Florentia
Taginae
Perusia
Rome

Venecia
Verona
Ravenna
Iadera

KINGDOM OF THE LOMBARDS

KINGDOM OF THE GEPIDS

Slavs

Naissus
Serdica
Philippopolis
Adrian
Constanti

Salonica

BYZANTINE EMPIRE (EASTERN RO

Sardinia

Caralis

Panormus
Sicilia
Messana

Naples
Barium
Tarentum

Patras Athens

Creta

Berbers

Carthage

MEDITERRANEAN

Tripolis

Ptolemais

JUSTINIAN'S RECONQUESTS, 527-65 [2]

- The Byzantine Empire, 527
- Added 533-5
- Added by 554
- Ruled by the Gepids, 539-51
- Frontiers, 565

BRITAIN: THE ORIGINS OF THE ANGLO-SAXON KINGDOMS [3]

BERNICIA

Celtic states and peoples

DEIRA

MERCIA

EAST ANGLIA

WESSEX ESSEX
SUSSEX KENT

FRANKISH KINGDOM

- Approximate extent of Anglo-Saxon states established by c.530
- Other Anglo Saxon states created by the end of the 6th century

FRANKISH EXPANSION TO 561 [1]

- Frankish territory, 511
- Added 531/2
- Added by 534
- Added by 537
- Frontiers, 561

Frisians

Saxons

ESSEX
WESSEX SUSSEX KENT

Aachen
Tournai

Hesse Thuringia

Mainz
Würzburg
Ratisbon
Passau
Augsburg
Lorch

KINGDOM OF THE LOMBARDS

SUSSE
WESSEX

Rouen Soissons
Rheims
Paris

Strassburg

Alemans
Bavaria

Brittany

Nantes
Orléans
Tours

FRANKISH KINGDOM

Dijon

Raetia

Limoges
Auvergne

Geneva
Lyons

Burgundy

BYZANTINE EMPIRE (EAST ROMAN EMPIRE)

Neustria

Nantes
Tou

Bordeaux

Limo

Cantabrians
Novempopulana (Gascony)
Basques

Toulouse
Marseille

Provence

KINGDOM OF THE VISIGOTHS

Bordeaux

Cantabrians
Basques

FRANKI

Toulous

KINGDOM OF THE

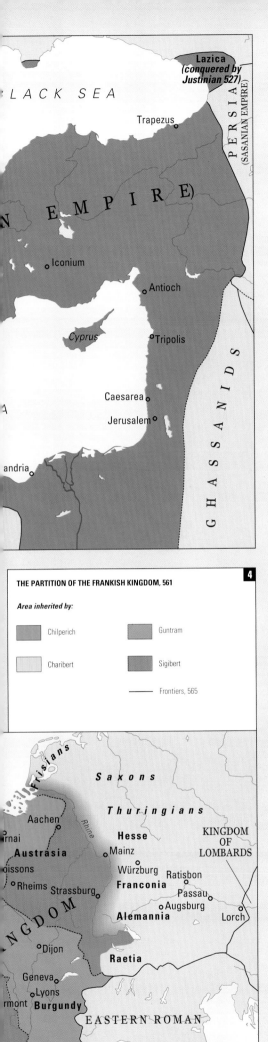

LACK SEA

Trapezus

Lazica
(conquered by
Justinian 527)

PERSIA
(SASANIAN EMPIRE)

E M P I R E)

Iconium

Antioch

Cyprus

Tripolis

Caesarea

G H A S S A N I D S

Jerusalem

andria

THE PARTITION OF THE FRANKISH KINGDOM, 561

4

Area inherited by:

Chilperich

Guntram

Charibert

Sigibert

Frontiers, 565

Frisians

S a x o n s

T h u r i n g i a n s

Aachen

Rhine

Hesse

KINGDOM
OF
LOMBARDS

rnai

Mainz

Austrasia

Würzburg

Ratisbon

oissons

Franconia

Rheims   Strassburg

Passau

Augsburg

Alemannia

Lorch

NGDOM

Dijon

Raetia

Geneva

Lyons

rmont   Burgundy

EASTERN ROMAN

(BYZANTINE)

Marseille

EMPIRE

Frankish Expansion to 561

1 With the death of Clovis in 511, his sons embarked on a ferocious expansion of Frankish territory. The Burgundian kingdom under Gundobad and Sigismund had been perhaps the strongest political presence in Gaul at the end of the 5th and in the early 6th century. In 523, however, Sigismund was murdered by the Frankish King Chlodomer (he later became the object of a saint's cult) and in 534 the Franks conquered the Burgundian kingdom. They gained Provence from the beleaguered Ostrogoths in 537, and consolidated their control of Gascony and the Auvergne.

The Franks, under the Merovingian dynasty, exercised influence over Brittany rather than direct rule. To the east they exercised at least nominal control over Alemannia (present day German- and French-speaking Switzerland) and to the north of Gaul as far as Utrecht, though in practice day-to-day administration may well have been left largely to the local inhabitants. For the time being, Bavaria retained its independence from the Merovingian rulers under the Agilolfing dukes, themselves, however, generally believed to be of Frankish origin.

In the Frankish areas, Roman administrative structures and institutions remain in evidence, most obviously in the organization of the church whose bishops were closely involved with secular government and whose dioceses were based on the old Roman *civitates*.

Justinian's Reconquests, 527-565

2 The Eastern Emperor Justinian embarked on a campaign of reconquest of the former Western Roman Empire in the second quarter of the 6th century, skillfully supported by propaganda from Constantinople which stressed the need to rescue the West from the barbarians and identified 476 as a crucial turning point.

Justinian seized on the excuse of internal political disputes in the west to intervene. In the short term the campaigns were a brilliant success. His military commander, Belisarius, conquered the Vandal kingdom of North Africa in 533. In Italy, Belisarius's initial campaign of 534 was followed up by a grim war of attrition under the general Narses until the last garrison of the Goths under their king Totila had fallen in 552. The Byzantines also occupied Cartagena and the southeast coast of Spain in 551.

Yet the irony of the reconquests was that much of the old Roman system in the areas "reconquered" appears to have been swept away in the course of the wars. It is from this period that archaeological evidence yields layers of destruction rather than from the earlier period of the so-called "barbarian invasions". Nor did the Byzantine reconquests last long. After fierce campaigns the Visigoths drove out the Byzantines in 624, while in Italy the arrival of the Lombards after 568 reduced Byzantine territory in Italy to the northeast portion around Ravenna and the southern tip of

Italy. Similarly, North Africa was lost to the Arabs by 700.

Britain: the Origins of the Anglo-Saxon Kingdoms

3 The tentative consolidation of various Anglian and Saxon tribal units to form territorial kingdoms was underway in the course of the 6th century, though political balances remained indeterminate and boundaries exceedingly ill-defined. Our information about the origins of Anglo-Saxon kingdoms largely stems from Bede, an early 8th-century source, who was writing at a time when there were indeed coherent kingdoms and when it may have been difficult to imagine a time when this was not the case. Still later, political writers and historians constructed genealogies of their kings in an effort to impose political structure onto a distant past.

Similarly, the later 7th-century kingdoms of the Northumbrians, the West Saxons, the men of Kent, the south Saxons, the east Saxons and the Mercians, the Hwicce, the Magonsaete, the east Angles, the middle Angles and others were reduced to seven (Wessex, Sussex, Essex, Kent, Mercia, East Anglia and Northumbria) in the 12th century and in the 16th century misleadingly entitled the "Heptarchy", thus distorting our understanding of the essential fluidity and diversity of the many early English kingdoms and implying a level of political coherence which did not exist at this early stage.

The institution of kingship itself, as well as the kingdoms, can only really be clearly discerned in the 7th century and, indeed, may not have been a form of social organization that the Angles and Saxons brought with them from north Germany and Denmark. Whatever the case, in the 7th century royal power began to be exercised over territories on which kings imposed fiscal and military obligations. In the 6th century, however, only the faintest glimmer of what were to become in due course the English kingdoms described by Bede can be made out.

The Partition of the Frankish Kingdom, 561

4 In 561 the grandsons of Clovis took over the kingdoms created in 511 (*see* map 4, page 51). Charibert I ruled from Paris, Guntram from Orléans, Chilperic from Soissons and Sigibert I from Rheims. Aquitaine and Burgundy were included in the partition, however, and in due course, especially after the further partitions of 567, the deaths of brothers without heirs meant the emergence of the three main political territories north and east of the Loire. These were to remain the principal focus of Frankish political activity for the next two centuries: Neustria in the west, Austrasia to the east, and Burgundy.

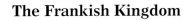

565

The Arab Advance

At the end of the 6th century, the Emperor Maurice of Byzantium assisted the Persian ruler Chosroes II to regain his throne, in return for which Byzantium was ceded Armenia and territory east of the Black Sea. But the days of Persian and Byzantine dominance of the eastern Mediterranean and Middle East were numbered. In 622 Mohammed fled from Mecca to Medina where he proclaimed the true religion devoted to one God, Allah, and Islam, submission to Allah's will. By Mohammed's death in 632 his teaching was widely accepted in Arabia and the Arabs then set out to spread the true religion. From 634 the Arabs embarked on a spectacularly successful and aggressive war of conquest, overrunning the Holy Land (Palestine) in 636, Mesopotamia in 637, Syria and Egypt in 640 and as far as the River Oxus in Central Asia by 651. The extent of the Byzantine Empire was thus drastically diminished while the Persian Empire was almost totally extinguished. However, though the Arabs went on to break the power of the Khazars, conquer Tashkent and push as far east as the province of Sind (modern Pakistan), they failed to conquer Constantinople itself or the Byzantine territories of Asia Minor.

Meanwhile, Byzantium's links with the western Mediterranean were significantly reduced, notably in Italy, with ties of respect and dependence increasingly weakened. The Imperial troops in Ravenna, Byzantium's foothold in northern Italy, rallied to the support of Pope Sergius (687-701) in his conflict with the Byzantine emperor, while Gregory III (731-41) was the last Pope to obtain the Byzantine mandate before his consecration as Pope.

The Arabs also moved westwards, capturing Carthage in 698 and converting the Berbers of the interior to Islam. Muslim troops had reached Tangier by 708 and, reinforced by Berbers, they crossed over to Spain in 711 under the leadership of Tariq ibn Ziyad, a Berber chief. The Visigoths fought bravely under their king Roderick, after a frantic march from the north of the kingdom to meet the invader, but Roderick was killed. Tariq took Cordova and Toledo. Mérida fell to Musa ibn Nusayr, Tariq's superior, in 713. By 716 virtually the whole peninsula, except for the Pyrenees and the northern region of the Asturias was under Muslim rule. Now known as El Andalus, the peninsula was ruled from Cordova by governors appointed by the governor of Qayrawan or his superior, the emir of Egypt. Raids into the Frankish Kingdom were conducted under the leadership of Abd al'Rahman but were definitively repelled by Charles Martel at the Battle of Poitiers in 732.

Since 567 the Franks had gone from strength to strength, consolidating their power under such rulers as Chlothar II, who reunited the realm in 613, and Dagobert I, while various Merovingian queens, such as Brunhild and Balthild, also played a conspicuously influential rule as adept politicians. They enjoyed a military strength which was admired and feared by their neighbours. But by the end of the 7th century control of the kingdom was slipping into the hands of the leading court officials, the "mayors of the palace" and other aristocrats in Neustria and Austrasia. Control of cross-Channel trade and the economy was also largely in the hands of the Frisians. The civil wars of the early 8th century, however, enabled the Carolingian mayor of the palace, Charles Martel, to seize power and start the steady process of winning back the areas that had once been under Merovingian control.

Northmen

(Scandinavians)

F i n n i c

p e o p l e s

Bulgarians

Hungarians

Volga

BALTIC
SEA

Baltic peoples

Oder

Vistula

S   l   a   v   s

Elbe

Don

KHAZAR KINGDOM

Sarkel

Volga

Dnieper

Ratisbon

Danube

Dniester

BAVARIA

Salzburg

AVAR KINGDOM

S
l
a
v
s

erona

Venice

Ravenna

Chersonesus

B L A C K   S E A

LAZICA

Tiflis

Bologna

Iadera

BULGARIA

Spalatum

Danube

Pliska

Varna

usia

Nish

Trapezus

Rome

STATE OF THE LOMBARDS

Serdika

Philippopolis

Vlachs

Adrianople

Constantinople

Naples

Barium

Tarentum

Salonica

B   Y   Z   A   N   T   I   N   E   E   M   P   I   R   E

Euphrates

Tigris

Mosul

ormus

Smyrna

Patrae

Athens

Sicily

Messana

S E A

U M A Y Y A D

C A L I P H A T E

Malta

Cyprus

Crete

Damascus

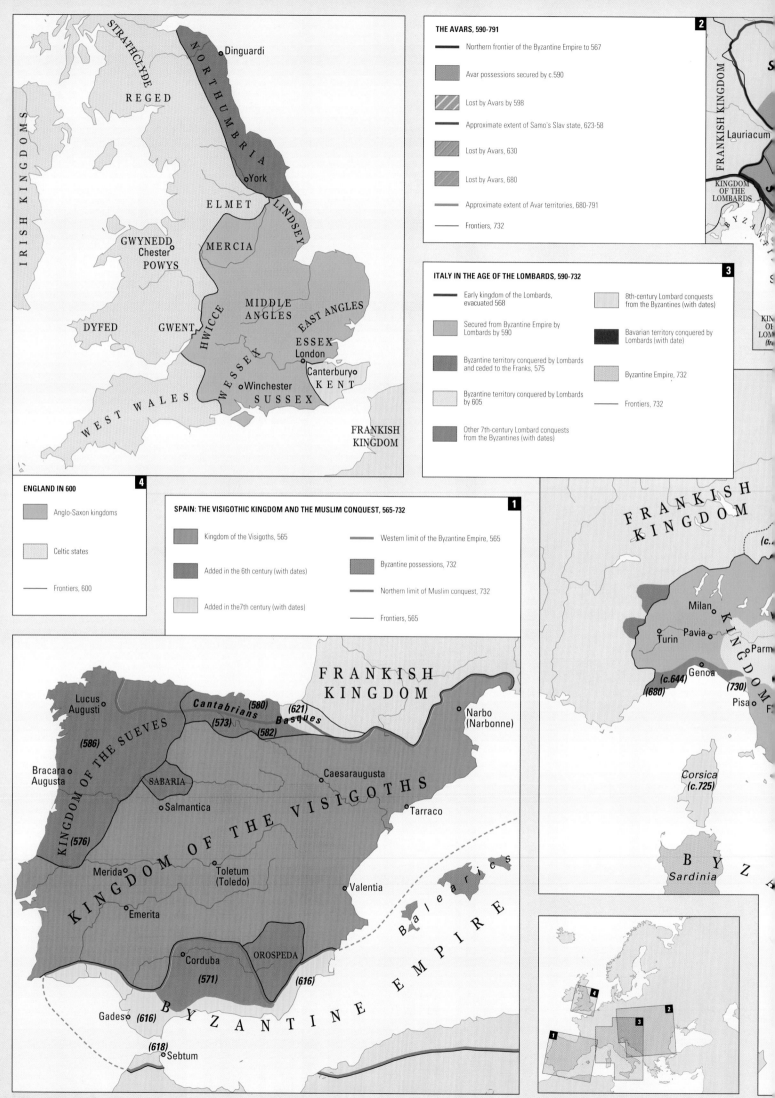

THE AVARS, 590-791

- Northern frontier of the Byzantine Empire to 567
- Avar possessions secured by c.590
- Lost by Avars by 598
- Approximate extent of Samo's Slav state, 623-58
- Lost by Avars, 630
- Lost by Avars, 680
- Approximate extent of Avar territories, 680-791
- Frontiers, 732

ITALY IN THE AGE OF THE LOMBARDS, 590-732

- Early kingdom of the Lombards, evacuated 568
- Secured from Byzantine Empire by Lombards by 590
- Byzantine territory conquered by Lombards and ceded to the Franks, 575
- Byzantine territory conquered by Lombards by 605
- Other 7th-century Lombard conquests from the Byzantines (with dates)
- 8th-century Lombard conquests from the Byzantines (with dates)
- Bavarian territory conquered by Lombards (with date)
- Byzantine Empire, 732
- Frontiers, 732

ENGLAND IN 600

- Anglo-Saxon kingdoms
- Celtic states
- Frontiers, 600

SPAIN: THE VISIGOTHIC KINGDOM AND THE MUSLIM CONQUEST, 565-732

- Kingdom of the Visigoths, 565
- Added in the 6th century (with dates)
- Added in the 7th century (with dates)
- Western limit of the Byzantine Empire, 565
- Byzantine possessions, 732
- Northern limit of Muslim conquest, 732
- Frontiers, 565

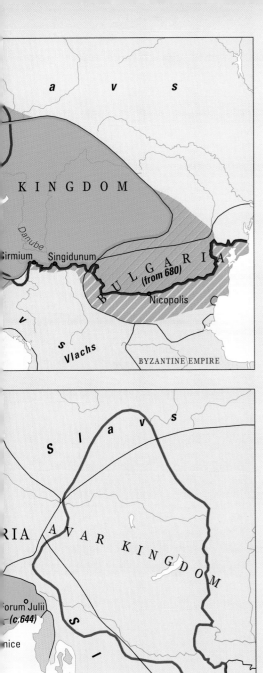

Spain: The Visigothic Kingdom and the Muslim Conquest, 565-732

1 In 589 the formal conversion of King Reccared and all the Visigoths from Arianism to Catholicism made the Catholic Hispano-Roman bishops their allies. Thereafter the Christian kings of Spain, whose authority was said to be bestowed by God, worked closely with the church to form a coherent and powerful ideology of kingship. This was reinforced by the firm basis which Reccared's predecessor Leovigild (569-86) had established for Visigothic royal power. In a series of campaigns, he subdued Cantabria, and in 586 conquered the Suevic kingdom and deposed the last king, Audeca. He also recaptured Corduba, which had been in revolt against the Visigothic kings since around 550. Leovigild, too, issued a law code, and introduced new regal styles and new coinage.

Under Sisebut (d. 621) campaigns were mounted against the Basques, and against the Byzantines, who had occupied a strip of southeastern Spain since the Emperor Justinian's expedition of 551 (*see* map 2, page 55), and who were finally expelled in 624. In the 7th century much anti-Jewish legislation was promulgated as well as the *Forum Iudicum*, a territorial law code which marked the thorough integration of Goths and Romans in the peninsula. Spain was nevertheless characterized by strong regional loyalties; internal dissension may well have contributed to the success of the Arab conquest in 711.

In that year Tariq ibn Ziyad crossed from Africa and routed and killed Roderick the Visigothic king. The Arab forces soon took Corduba, Toledo and Merida, and by 716 they had taken virtually the entire peninsula. They then destroyed the vestigial Visigothic kingdom which was based on Narbonne, and began raids into the territories of the Franks. A Visigothic remnant clung on in the northeast and began to forge the Christian kingdoms of Asturias, Leon, Pamplona and the County of Aragon, which in due course were to form the bases for the launching of the long centuries of the Reconquista, the Christian reconquest of Spain.

The Avars, 590-791

2 Almost nothing precise is known of the Avars in this period, save that they were a confederation of steppe peoples from inner Asia, whose base was situated near present-day Belgrade. There is, however, archaeological evidence of weapons in graves, suggesting that the Avars remained formidable well into the 8th century. Occasional references in written sources indicate a vast territory under their control, aggressive expansion and enormous wealth. Among their military triumphs were the eviction of the Gepids and Lombards from the Danube region in the 6th century and a major assault upon Constantinople in 626. Their rule came to an end in 791, when the Franks destroyed their massive military fortifications, the "Avar Ring".

Italy in the Age of the Lombards, 590-732

3 The Lombards settled in Pannonia (modern-day Hungary) in the early 6th century and first entered Italy as mercenaries in the pay of the Emperor Justinian's general Narses. In the aftermath of the Gothic wars (*see* map 2, page 55), Alboin and his armies re-entered the Po valley in 568-69, leaving dukes to govern from the major cities. Pavia was captured in 572 and by 571 the Lombards were forming duchies along the Italian peninsula in Spoleto and Benevento. Their kingship was essentially elective. King Rothari issued a law code in 643. Other kings, notably Liutprand (d. 742) directed their energies to expanding Lombard territory, presenting an aggressive front to the Byzantine exarchate of Ravenna and to Rome and the popes. The exarchate, although a local and to some degree isolated political entity comprising a local landed aristocracy of military officers, remained within the Byzantine orbit until its conquest by the Lombards in the mid-8th century. As well as consolidating their own secular power within the "Republic of St Peter" (*see* map 2, page 63), the popes had to contend with jurisdictional disputes with Byzantium over southern Italy and Illyricum as well as Lombard aggression. The Frankish kingdoms and the new missionary areas of England and Germany represented a further sphere in which they could begin to exert a spiritual influence.

England in 600

4 By 600 some of the English kingdoms, notably Kent, East Anglia, Mercia and Northumbria (made up of Deira and Bernicia), became a little better defined. In 597 Augustine, sent by Pope Gregory I from Rome, arrived in Kent and converted King Aethelbert (d. 616) and his people to Christianity. Aethelbert was married to a Christian Frankish princess who had been permitted to have her own chaplain. The marriage may be one indication of Merovingian Frankish hegemony in southeast England in this early period.

More is known of the other kingdoms from the early 7th century, especially about their reactions to Christianity. Raedwald (d. *c.*625) of the East Angles, who may be the king buried in the spectacular ship-burial at Sutton Hoo and was also almost certainly in contact with the Merovingian Franks, maintained both a Christian and a pagan altar. His son Sigibert (a Frankish name) fled into political exile in Francia and was there converted to Christianity. Aethelfrith of Bernicia (d.616 or 617) was a mighty warrior who defeated the Scots of Dal Riata at Degestan and the men of Powys at Chester, but it was his successor Edwin (d. 633 or 634) who was converted to Christianity.

The Death of Charlemagne

On his death in 814 the Frankish ruler Charlemagne left a vast territory, comprising most of Europe west of the Elbe and north of the Pyrenees. Many peoples had been brought under Frankish rule during his reign, and with law and religion as his principal tools and weapons, Charlemagne had forged a strong polity, with methods of government and principles of rulership, as well as many common elements of culture, which were to endure throughout the Middle Ages.

Charlemagne was fortunate in the pioneering work of his father, for it was Pippin III, king from 751 to 768, who had begun to forge a distinctive relationship with the Frankish church, and who had given the clergy a key place in the administration of the kingdom. He had also begun to develop effective instruments of government, including control of the coinage. The acquisition of the title of Emperor in 800 did little to affect Charlemagne's style of rulership or his actual power. For the most part he was an itinerant ruler, travelling the length and breadth of his empire to reinforce his authority with his presence, though towards the end of his reign he based himself principally at his new palace at Aachen. An immensely cultured man, Charlemagne promoted education and rewarded scholars throughout his realm, with the view of creating both a strong Church and an efficient network of administration based on the rule of law and written records. His surviving legislation is replete with his instructions on all matters, secular and ecclesiastical, within his kingdom. He was in touch with rulers as far afield as Cordova, Constantinople and Baghdad. Yet there were movements elsewhere in Europe which indicated new development ahead. Trade in the North Sea region was well established, with ports established on both sides of the English Channel at Hamwic, Ipswich, Quentovic and Dorestad, as well as in the Baltic at such places as Birka.

The late 8th century saw the beginnings of Viking raids in Europe. The Vikings were Scandinavian-based seafarers who had reached the Shetlands in about 790; subsequently, their first raid on England was the sack of the island monastery of Lindisfarne in 793. Charlemagne himself began to organise coastal defences against them.

In the Arab world, while the Umayyad emir Abd al'Rahman and his descendants ruled in Spain from 756, at the other end of the Mediterranean the Abbasids held sway in the Middle East well into the 9th century, though a diminution of their power was becoming evident, while the Arabs were active as a maritime power for the first time throughout the Mediterranean. The northern Christian kingdoms of Spain began their first efforts to push back the Arabs, with a gradual coalescence of the political divisions of the north into the kingdoms of the Asturias (León from the 10th century), Pamplona and the County of Barcelona, all of which fostered links with the Franks in different degrees. As a result of campaigns in the Septimanian region, the Franks secured the county formed by Vich, Cardona and Caseras and between 800 and 813 captured Barcelona, Tortosa and Pamplona. This marcher region was incorporated into the Frankish Kingdom.

Byzantium also began to acquire new territory, mounting successful campaigns in Thrace at the end of the 8th century, and subsequently in the early 9th century, in the Greek peninsular under Nicephorus I against the Slavs, who had overrun it since the 6th century, but meeting too formidable an enemy in the Bulgars led by Khan Krum (802-14).

Kaupango

Scandinavians

F i n n i c

p e o p l e s

Bulgar
VOLGA BULGARIA

DENMARK

BALTIC
SEA

Baltic peoples

Volga

Hungarians

eby

urg

Bremen

S l a v s

Oder

Vistula

Don

KHAZAR KINGDOM

t

Elbe

Dnieper

Volga

Sarkel

Danube

Dniester

Salzburg

IRE

Venice

Verona

Bologna

S
l
a
v
s

BULGARIA

Cherson

Danube

Pliska

LAZICA

Tiflis

Iadera

Spalatum

Nish

Varna

BLACK SEA

e

PAPAL STATE

Perugia

Sredets

Trapezus

ome

Philippopolis

Vlachs

Adrianople

Constantinople

PRINCIPALITY OF BENEVENTO

Naples

Barium

Salonica

Tarentum

Z
A
N
T
I
N
E

E M P I R E

Mosul

normus

Messana

Smyrna

Euphrates

Patrae

Athens

Tigris

Malta

SEA

Crete

Cyprus

Nicosia

ABBASIDS

Damascus

ITALY: THE DEVELOPMENT OF THE PAPAL STATE FROM 756

☐	Patrimonium Petri to 756	▨	Acquired in theory by 781
▨	Acquired in 756	▨	Acquired in theory by 787
▨	Acquired in theory by 757	▨	Acquired in theory by 789
▨	Acquired in theory by 774	—	Frontiers, 814

IRISH KDMS

WELSH STATES

MERCIA

WEST WALES

WESSEX

NORTHUMBRIA

NORTH SEA

DENMARK

BALTIC SEA

F r i s i a *(734)*

Saxony *(772/98)*

(lost 695, reconquered 722/804)

(789)

S l a v s

(805/6)

Aachen

Rouen

Soissons

Rheims

Paris

Metz

Mainz

Würzburg

Alemannia

Strassburg

Ratisbon

B a v a r i a *(lost late 7th century, reconquered 728; direct rule from 788)*

(direct rule from 744)

Salzburg

Danube

Steinamanger

Pannonia *(796)*

Mosapurc

BULGARIA

Brittany *(lost c.630 reconquered 786/99)*

Nantes

Tours

Orléans

Loire

Seine

F R A N K I S H   E M P I R E

Geneva

Dijon

Carinthia *(788)*

(799)

S l a v s

Dalmatia

BYZANTINE EMPIRE

BAY OF BISCAY

Limoges

Clermont

Lyons

(575)

(575)

Milan

Verona

Turin

Lombardy *(774)*

Genoa

Bologna

Rhône

Aquitaine *(lost c.670 reconquered 768)*

Toulouse

ASTURIAS

Roncesvalles

S p a n i s h   M a r c h *(795)*

(812)

Barcelona

Septimania *(759)*

Marseille

Nice

GULF OF LIONS

Florence

PAPAL STATE *(774)*

Perugia

Spoleto

Rome

DUCHY OF BENEVENTO *(787/9)*

Barium

Tarentum

Corsica

Sardinia

Balearics

EMIRATE OF CORDOVA

B Y Z A N T I N E   E M P I R E

THE GROWTH OF THE FRANKISH EMPIRE TO THE DEATH OF CHARLEMAGNE, 814

▨	Frankish territory, 565	▨	Added by Charlemagne (with dates)
▨	Added before the accession of Charlemagne in 768 (with dates)	▨	Brought into dependency by Charlemagne (with dates)
☐	Temporary Frankish possession (754-98)	—	Frontiers, 814

ENGLAND: THE SUPREMACY OF MERCIA, 625-796

▨	Mercia in c. 625	▨	Added by the end of Offa's rule, 796
▨	Mercian dependency from 777	—	Frontiers, 796

The Growth of the Frankish Empire to the Death of Charlemagne, 814

1 When Charles Martel died in 741, he divided the Merovingian kingdom between his sons Carloman and Pippin III. Although he still only occupied the position of "mayor of the palace", he had ruled without a king for the last four years of his life. Carloman and Pippin had to deal with revolts against Carolingian attempts to enforce their authority in Aquitaine, Alemannia, Alsace, Bavaria and Saxony.

Carloman's abdication in 745 to become a monk left the field free for Pippin, who deposed the last Merovingian king Childeric III in 751 and had himself crowned king, with the Frankish clergy adding a new element to the king-making ritual, namely, anointing. Pippin conquered Aquitaine between 759 and 768; he quelled the attempts of the Etichonid dukes of Alsace to assert their independence, and led campaigns against Brittany (in 753) and Burgundy (in 761) as well as a successful foray into the Lombard kingdom to protect the pope's interests.

Pippin III divided the kingdom in his turn between his sons Carloman and Charlemagne. A great military leader, the latter, left as sole ruler after 771, waged war energetically for the next 30 years, greatly expanding the borders of his realm. He confirmed the acquisition of Aquitaine and handed it on to his son Louis as a subkingdom in 781. He conquered the Lombard kingdom of Italy in 774. Charlemagne then led an expedition into Spain, which was defeated on the way home at Roncesvalles in 778, an episode immortalised in the *Song of Roland*. Bavaria was annexed in 788, and the power of the Avars destroyed between 791 and 793. Charlemagne waged war against the Lombard Duchy of Benevento in 787-9, and clashed with Byzantium for control of Venetia and Dalmatia. The Saxons, too, were hammered into submission after a long and very bloody series of campaigns between 772 and 798. Systematic evangelization, forced conversions and the establishment of new sees accompanied the military conquests of these new territories.

Italy: the Development of the Papal State from 756

2 In 754 the popes had taken the first crucial step towards realigning their sympathies away from Byzantium in favour of the Franks, for Pope Stephen II (or III) journeyed to France in order to re-anoint Pippin III, the Frankish ruler and his wife and sons as the legitimate line of rulers of the Franks and made Pippin the protector of the Roman church. The Frankish ruler's aid was thereafter invoked against the Lombards, whose attacks on the papal territories were particularly fierce under Aistulf (749-56) and Desiderius (757-774), culminating in the Frankish conquest of the Lombard kingdom in 774 by Charlemagne. Leo III strengthened the ties still further by crowning Charlemagne emperor and governor of the Romans on Christmas Day 800 in St Peter's, Rome. With Frankish protection and support, the popes consolidated their secular and independent rule of the Papal State, though Frankish protection was to become somewhat heavy-handed at times. The popes played an increasingly articulate role in the re-organization of the church in Western Europe, and in Rome itself the popes, especially Hadrian I (772-795) and Leo III (795-816) who erected and refurbished many magnificent churches and other buildings, extended the system of social welfare within the Papal State and streamlined the papal administration.

England: the Supremacy of Mercia, 625-796

3 The three strongest kingdoms in England at the end of the 7th century were Northumbria under Egfrith (670-85), Wessex under Caedwalla (695-8) and Mercia under Aethelbald (716-57). Egfrith waged successful campaigns against the Picts. Caedwalla tried to expand eastwards into Sussex and even Kent, but retired to Rome after only two years. Aethelbald appears to have attacked the Welsh, the Northumbrians and the East Saxons. Kentish charters suggest that he was in control of London and appears to have done much to establish the strength of Mercian rule in his 41-year reign from which his successors were to benefit.

Aethelbald was assassinated in 757 and buried at Repton; his successor Beornred held the kingdom for only a short time before Offa, with a tenuous family claim to the kingship, took power. Offa, firmly based in the Midlands, with a palace at Tamworth, set about expanding his territory in the Middle Saxon area and London, and by 770 London emerged as an important Mercian mint. The southern kingdoms were relatively stable in the earlier years of Offa's reign but later he was able to intervene successfully in Kentish affairs. In 764-5 Kent re-asserted its independence under King Egberht, only to lose it again on Egberht's death and with the subsequent decisive intervention of Offa in Kentish affairs. The local dynasties of Kent, Sussex, the Hwicce and East Anglia seem to have become subordinated to Mercia and Offa's daughters married the kings of Wessex and Northumbria.

Offa raided Wales and had the massive fortification known as Offa's Dyke erected on the Welsh border (possibly as a defence against further Welsh penetration), of which 80 miles of imposing earthwork are extant. Offa's power within England was no doubt considerable. He even went so far as to try and create a new ecclesiastical province based on Lichfield, independent of York and Canterbury. His relations with external rulers, however, seem to have been confined to a trade agreement with Charlemagne and arrangements for the protection of English pilgrims travelling through Francia. Offa died in 796 and was succeeded by his son Ecgfrith who survived his father by only five months. Mercia was unable to retain its dominant position and in due course it was Wessex that emerged as, and remained, the strongest kingdom of England.

814

910

The Viking Conquests

The start of the 10th century saw a marked increase in contacts between the Scandinavian and Slavic peoples to the north and east of Europe and the older established kingdoms of Western Europe, in both economic and political spheres. The Vikings were adventurers, originating in Scandinavia, who ranged far and wide across the North and Baltic seas, travelling vast distances in their sailing ships and using oars for short journeys, sea-fights and voyages through narrow waters. They moved down through Russia to Byzantium; across the Atlantic Ocean to establish farming communities in Iceland, Greenland and, for a short time, Vinland on the coast of Newfoundland; and colonized many territories in Britain, the Orkneys, Shetlands, Hebrides, Isle of Man, and on the western tips of Europe.

Despite their reputation as ferocious raiders, the Vikings in fact became closely involved in local politics and contributed constructively to the political development of every region they settled. The trading links they maintained in particular, and the enterprise of their explorations, opened up the North Sea and contributed substantially to the later mercantile and commercial development of northern Europe. The Danes in particular, who in the 9th century settled in England and in France, where they became known as Normans, ventured still further into southern Europe and the Mediterranean, and continued to make their mark on the map of medieval Europe well into the 12th century. Nonetheless, the Viking kingdoms of York and Dublin were reconquered in the 10th century by native rulers, though the Scandinavian presence remained strong in Scotland and the islands well into the 12th century.

The Frankish conquest of the Saxons at the end of the 8th century made them neighbours of the Danes. This led to clashes of interest with the Franks, particularly over the lands of Obodrites and other Slavs in northern Germany. The Franks therefore tried to influence Danish politics. One means was by intervening in the political succession within Denmark. Another was to send Christian missionaries: Ebbo had mixed success with the Danes; Anskar, in the mid-9th century, sent first to Denmark and later to Sweden, made some headway in establishing Christianity. This was later reinforced by missionaries from Germany and England in the 10th and 11th centuries.

West Frankish energies in the second half of the 9th century were directed both at maintaining the stability of the kingdom and defending its towns and monasteries from Viking raids. In the East Frankish Kingdom, in contrast, there was still room for expansion into the Slav regions, particularly under Louis the German (d.876) and his sons. The marches, or special stretches of territory in the frontier regions under military organization, constituted an important means of regulating relations with Slavic peoples on the Franks' northern borders, including the Obodrites, Linones, Sorbs and Daleminzi. In the south, the four peoples of importance were the Moravians, Bohemians, Bulgars and Slovenes. Relations involved tribute, supporting contenders for leadership in the regions and, again, infiltrating missionaries. The Moravians, particularly under Moimir I, Rastislav and Svatopluk (Zwentibald), proved formidable neighbours.

Western Europe, apart from Italy, had little contact with the Byzantine Empire at this time. Only Louis II in Italy asserted his rulership and imperial title, at a safe distance and in writing, against the claims of the Byzantine Emperor Basil I with any vigour, but for the most part he administered Italy efficiently as part of the Frankish realm.

NORWAY
Lade

Kaupang

SWEDEN

F i n n i c   p e o p l e s

Ugrians

Novgorod

Bulgar
VOLGA BULGARIA

Volga

DENMARK
Aarhus
Roskilde   Lund

BALTIC
SEA

Baltic peoples

K I E V A N   R U S

S l a v s

KHAZAR KINGDOM

by

urg

Oder

S l a v s

Vistula

Elbe

Don

Volga

50°

Kiev

Sarkel

NKISH
MY
Y)

Dnieper

Dniester

P e c h e n e g s

Danube

Salzburg

HUNGARY

Cherson

B L A C K   S E A

LAZICA

Tiflis

Venice
Verona

CROATIA

Iadera

Bologna

Spalatum

SERBIA

Nish

BULGARIA

Danube

Preslav

Varna

Trapezus

Perugia

PAPAL STATE

Rome

ITALY

PR. OF BENEVENTO

Sredets

Philippopolis

Scupi

Adrianople   Constantinople

Euphrates

Naples
Barium

Tarentum

Salonica

B Y Z A N T I N E   E M P I R E

Janina

Tigris

ormus

Messana

Sicily

Patrae   Athens

Smyrna

A B B A S I D S

Malta   SEA

Crete

Cyprus

Damascus

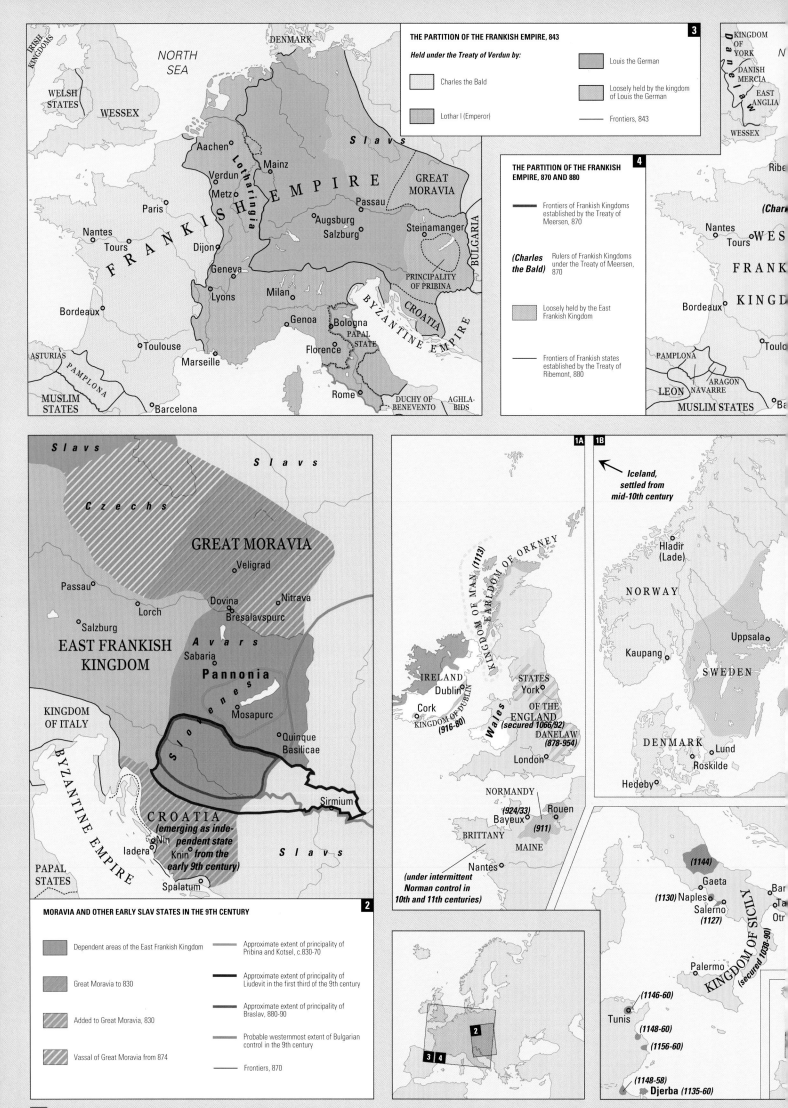

THE PARTITION OF THE FRANKISH EMPIRE, 843

Held under the Treaty of Verdun by:

Charles the Bald

Lothar I (Emperor)

Louis the German

Loosely held by the kingdom of Louis the German

Frontiers, 843

THE PARTITION OF THE FRANKISH EMPIRE, 870 AND 880

Frontiers of Frankish Kingdoms established by the Treaty of Meersen, 870

(Charles the Bald) Rulers of Frankish Kingdoms under the Treaty of Meersen, 870

Loosely held by the East Frankish Kingdom

Frontiers of Frankish states established by the Treaty of Ribemont, 880

NORTH SEA

DENMARK

IRISH KINGDOMS

WELSH STATES

WESSEX

Aachen

Verdun

Mainz

Metz

Paris

LOTHARINGIA

FRANKISH EMPIRE

GREAT MORAVIA

Passau

Slavs

Nantes

Tours

Dijon

Augsburg

Salzburg

Steinamanger

BULGARIA

Geneva

PRINCIPALITY OF PRIBINA

CROATIA

Lyons

Milan

Bordeaux

Genoa

Bologna

PAPAL STATE

BYZANTINE EMPIRE

Toulouse

Florence

ASTURIAS

PAMPLONA

Marseille

Rome

DUCHY OF BENEVENTO

AGHLA-BIDS

MUSLIM STATES

Barcelona

KINGDOM OF YORK

DANISH MERCIA

EAST ANGLIA

Danelaw

WESSEX

Ribe

(Charles

Nantes

Tours

WES

FRANK

KINGD

Bordeaux

PAMPLONA

LEON

NAVARRE

ARAGON

Toulo

MUSLIM STATES

Ba

Iceland, settled from mid-10th century

(1113)

EARLDOM OF ORKNEY

KINGDOM OF MAN

NORWAY

Hladir (Lade)

IRELAND

Dublin

Cork

KINGDOM OF DUBLIN *(916-80)*

Wales

STATES York

OF THE ENGLAND *(secured 1066/92)*

DANELAW *(878-954)*

London

NORMANDY *(924/33)*

Bayeux

Rouen *(911)*

BRITTANY

MAINE

Nantes

(under intermittent Norman control in 10th and 11th centuries)

Kaupang

SWEDEN

Uppsala

DENMARK

Lund

Roskilde

Hedeby

(1144)

Gaeta

(1130) Naples

Salerno

(1127)

Bar

Ta

Otr

KINGDOM OF SICILY

Palermo

(secured 1038-90)

(1146-60)

Tunis

(1148-60)

(1156-60)

(1148-58)

Djerba (1135-60)

Slavs

Slavs

Czechs

GREAT MORAVIA

Veligrad

Passau

Nitrava

Lorch

Dovina

Bresalavspurc

Salzburg

EAST FRANKISH KINGDOM

Avars

Sabaria

Pannonia

Mosapurc

KINGDOM OF ITALY

Slovenes

Quinque Basilicae

BYZANTINE EMPIRE

Sirmium

CROATIA (emerging as inde-pendent state from the early 9th century)

Nin

Iadera

Knin

Spalatum

Slavs

PAPAL STATES

MORAVIA AND OTHER EARLY SLAV STATES IN THE 9TH CENTURY

Dependent areas of the East Frankish Kingdom

Great Moravia to 830

Added to Great Moravia, 830

Vassal of Great Moravia from 874

Approximate extent of principality of Pribina and Kotsel, c.830-70

Approximate extent of principality of Liudevit in the first third of the 9th century

Approximate extent of principality of Braslav, 880-90

Probable westernmost extent of Bulgarian control in the 9th century

Frontiers, 870

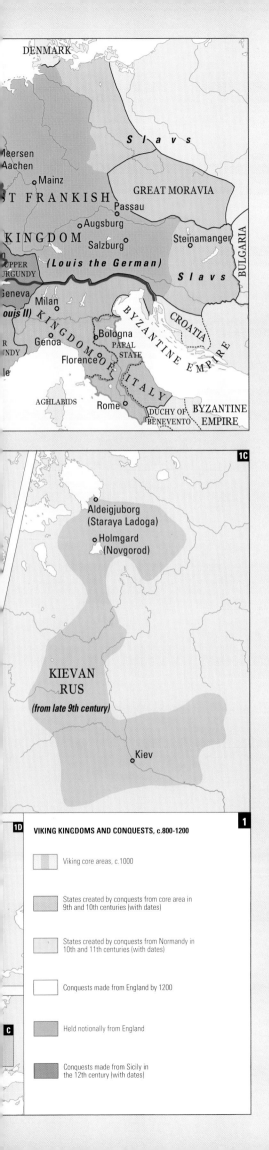

Viking Kingdoms and Conquests, c. 800-1200

1 Viking raids on France and the British Isles increased in intensity throughout the 9th century, with the Vikings establishing settlements there which later developed into polities. In 911 Charles the Simple, King of the West Franks, ceded Rouen and the lower Seine valley to a Viking group led by Rollo, who extended their authority to the west and took over the entire area now known as Normandy; they were later known as Normans. In 878, meanwhile, a frontier was agreed between the English king Alfred and the Danish leader Guthrum. This established much of the territory which became known as the Danelaw. The Vikings also settled extensively in East Anglia and set up a kingdom in Ireland based on Dublin.

By the 11th century, four independent kingdoms, in Denmark, Sweden, Norway and the Republic of Iceland had emerged. Danish power seems to have weakened in relation to Norway towards the end of the 9th century, and with it the limited influence over the Viking armies abroad which the sources suggest. Denmark recovered, however, under the Jelling dynasty of Kings Gorm and Harald in the 10th century; Harald established himself as overlord of Norway. The fortunes of Norway, Denmark and Sweden remained closely intertwined throughout the 10th and 11th centuries.

In the 12th century the Normans expanded farther from Normandy. Led by the brigand Robert Guiscard, they conquered Sicily from the Arabs and Apulia and Calabria from the Greeks, becoming a power of great importance under his successors Roger I (Count of Sicily 1072-1101) and Roger II (1105-54), the latter being accorded the title of king by the pope. The Normans also secured some short-term settlements on the North African coast.

Evidence of Scandinavian activity east of the Baltic in the 9th and 10th centuries is ambiguous. The large numbers of coins from north Russia found in Scandinavia may indicate trade, plunder, tribute or the payment of mercenaries. Islamic texts refer to the "Rus" as traders who were settled in Kiev as early as the middle of the 9th century. They also held bases at Novgorod and Staraya Ladoga. Links with Byzantium led to their conversion to Christianity.

Moravia and Other Early Slav States in the 9th century

2 The emergence of Moravia is connected with the collapse of Avar hegemony in the middle Danube region. In the 9th century, the Moravians expanded into the Nitrava region. Moravia's prince, Moimir, was, however, deposed by the Franks and Prince Ratislav imposed on the Moravians the Frankish king, Louis the German, in 846. But Ratislav's power grew so great as to cause the Franks unease. However, when he attempted to establish Christianity independent of the Franks, the pope refused to send a bishop. An appeal to the Byzantine Emperor then resulted in the short-lived but effective mission of Constantine and Methodius, who translated many church texts into Slavonic.

Frankish suzerainty in the area, over Pannonia and Croatia, dated from about 795, and over Dalmatia from about 803. Liudevit, a ruler of one of the Slav groups in the region, however, reneged on his oath of loyalty to the Franks and sought refuge with another Slavic group south of his territory, where he was murdered in 823. The western part of his territory remained within the Frankish sphere of influence, but the eastern area attracted the interest of the Bulgars, under whose "protection" it passed in 827.

Based at Pliska, the Bulgars under Omurtag allied with the Byzantine Emperor Michael II in 822-23. Later, Khan Boris (852-89 and 893) concluded a peace treaty with Byzantium. There were, however, serious tensions in Bulgar relations with Byzantium.

The Partition of the Frankish Empire, 843

3 Louis the Pious (814-840) inherited his father Charlemagne's entire empire in 814. With the *Ordinatio imperii* of 817, he tried to preserve both the idea of Empire and the Imperial title by dividing the lands between his three sons – Lothar, Louis (the German) and Pippin I (of Aquitaine) – and by making his eldest son Lothar co-emperor with him. By Louis's death in 840, however, the situation had been complicated by the death of Pippin I (though his son tried in vain to claim his father's portion) and by the birth of a further son, Charles (the Bald) to Louis the Pious and his second wife Judith in 823. Thus the fate of the Empire was bitterly contested between Lothar, Louis the German and Charles the Bald, and resolved after a fashion at the Treaty of Verdun in 843. The west and east portions created by this partition developed into France and Germany respectively. The Middle Kingdom, whose northern part became known as Lotharingia, remained a bone of contention between France and Germany, not finally resolved until the 20th century.

The Partition of the Frankish Empire, 870 and 880

4 The Emperor Lothar's portion, created in 843 (*see* above, map 3) had been divided between his sons Lothar II and Louis II on his death in 855. On Lothar II's death with no legitimate heirs, his uncles hastened to claim his kingdom. At the Colloquy of Meersen in 870, Charles the Bald divided Lotharingia with his brother Louis the German according to the number of counties, bishoprics and abbeys rather than natural boundaries or language. In this way Aachen, Charlemagne's great centre, became part of the East Frankish kingdom.

A further, short-lived partition was agreed in 880 in the West Frankish kingdom by the Frankish nobles between two of Charles the Bald's grandsons, Louis III and Carloman. An aristocrat called Boso, who had married a Carolingian, claimed a kingdom, while the east was ruled by Louis the German's youngest son, Charles the Fat, who took the title of Emperor. As kingdoms and territories were parcelled out, the position of Emperor outside Italy was becoming little more than an honorific title.

910

The First Russian State

After 888, many "petty kings" – Berengar in Italy, Rudolf in upper Burgundy, Guy and Louis in Gaul and Provence, Odo, son of Robert the Strong in Neustria and Ramnulf in Aquitaine – acted "as if they were kings". For a time it looked as if the fragmentation of Charlemagne's empire was complete and all semblance of unity lost. Yet many ties bonded the whole together, and the legend of Charlemagne himself, as well as surviving members of his family, proved resilient.

In the West Frankish kingdom, Carolingian rulers regained the throne and reigned throughout the 10th century, though the character of the monarchy was gradually changing in the face of developments towards greater autonomy of the territorial principalities which forged new bonds of loyalty to their royal overlord. The last Carolingian king, Louis V, died in 987 and in his place Hugh Capet was elected. Hugh inaugurated a new ruling dynasty in France, which was to last more than 800 years. Whatever the power of the nobles, the monarchy continued to exist as a political institution of significance. It rested firmly on its Carolingian foundations.

In the East Frankish kingdom, the last Carolingian ruler, Louis the Child, died in 911. In his place Count Conrad of Franconia was elected king. In 919, he was succeeded in turn by the Liudolfing Henry I, "the Fowler", the first of the Saxon or Ottonian dynasty, whose son Otto I, and grandson and great-grandson forged an empire in emulation of Charlemagne, which stretched from the Baltic to the Mediterranean. Otto I, who came to the throne in 936, made himself king of Italy in 951 and was crowned Emperor by Pope John XVI in 961. He established strong institutions of government and made clever use of ecclesiastical personnel and resources, both bishoprics and monasteries, within his system of administration. The royal women – mothers, wives, aunts and sisters of the reigning king – played a particularly conspicuous role in politics in this period, especially during the minority of Otto III when Queen Adelaide and Queen Theophanu acted as regents.

Otto I's son, Otto II, was greatly concerned with military consolidation in Italy, notably against the Byzantines, and died on campaign in 983. Otto II had, however, married a Byzantine princess, Theophanu, and asserted his title of Emperor in apparent competition to that of the Byzantine Emperor. Similarly their son Otto III developed imperial ideology still further before his premature death in 1002. It was left to his cousin Henry II to consolidate the practical government of the kingdom, especially in Germany itself and to forge a strong polity for his successors. Good relations were maintained with the West Frankish kingdom as well as the Kingdom of Burgundy and elsewhere which had broken away under their own rulers. It is striking how marriage alliances throughout the 10th century created links of varying strength between such kingdoms as England, France, Burgundy, Germany, Bohemia, Russia, Bulgaria and Byzantium, and how international many of the royal courts of Western Europe were at this time, welcoming scholars and ambassadors from many countries.

The 10th century was marked, too, by the emergence of political organizations in northern and eastern Europe. The marauders of the previous century (the Vikings in the north, the Magyars in the east) formed settled kingdoms; in England the successors of Alfred the Great conquered the Danelaw; in Poland the Piasts extended their rule to Cracow in the south, and east and west. Significant expansion by the Kievan Rus and their conversion to Christianity in 987 meant that their interests were increasingly pursued in the west and south towards the end of the 10th century.

NORWAY

(under Danish rule)

F i n n i c   p e o p l e s

Ladoga

Uppsala
Birka
Novgorod

SWEDEN

Pskov

Aarhus

BALTIC
SEA

Baltic peoples

Polotsk

Roskilde   Lund

DENMARK

Vitebsk   Smolensk

Hamburg

Slavs

Minsk

Bremen

K I E V A N   R U S

GDOM

Gniezno

Volga

Bulgar   VOLGA
BULGARIA

Suzdal

Vladimir

Oder

Vistula

Elbe

Meissen   POLAND
Wrocław

OF

K   I   E   V   A   N

Kiev

Prague   Cracow

ttgart

Dnieper

T u r k i c   p e o p l e s

Volga

Sarkel
(to Kiev)

MANY

Danube

Pozsony

Munich   Vienna
Salzburg   Esztergom

Fehérvár

Dniester

(to Kiev)

Tmutarakan

HUNGARY

Kalocsa

A l a n s

Kaffa

Venice   VENETIAN
REPUBLIC

Pécs

Ajtony

Cherson

Verona

CROATIA

Belgrade

B L A C K   S E A

GEORGIAN
STATES

SMALL
STATES

Bologna

Zara

sa

Florence

Spalato

Nissa

Danube

Varna

Perugia

BULGARIA

Preslav

Trebizond

ARMENIA

Serdica

Philippopolis

ome

PRINCIPALITY
OF BENEVENTO

Scupi

Adrianople

APAL
TATE

COUNTY
OF CAPUA

Barium

Salonica

Constantinople

Naples

Janina

PRINCIPALITY
OF SALERNO

Tigris

B Y Z A N T I N E   E M P I R E

BUWAYHIDS

normus

Messana

Smyrna

Catana

Athens

HAMDANIDS

Euphrates

KARMATIANS

SEA

Malta

FATIMIDS

Nicosia

Crete

Beirut   Damascus

69

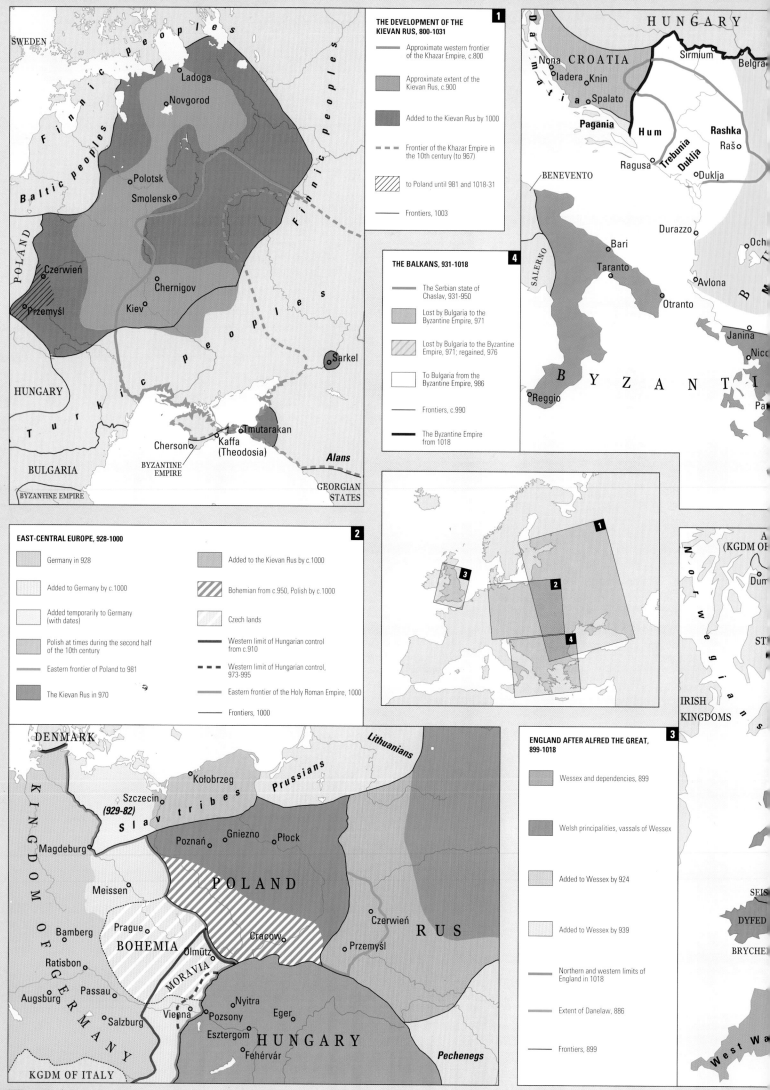

THE DEVELOPMENT OF THE KIEVAN RUS, 800-1031 `1`

- Approximate western frontier of the Khazar Empire, c.800
- Approximate extent of the Kievan Rus, c.900
- Added to the Kievan Rus by 1000
- Frontier of the Khazar Empire in the 10th century (to 967)
- to Poland until 981 and 1018-31
- Frontiers, 1003

THE BALKANS, 931-1018 `4`

- The Serbian state of Chaslav, 931-950
- Lost by Bulgaria to the Byzantine Empire, 971
- Lost by Bulgaria to the Byzantine Empire, 971; regained, 976
- To Bulgaria from the Byzantine Empire, 986
- Frontiers, c.990
- The Byzantine Empire from 1018

EAST-CENTRAL EUROPE, 928-1000 `2`

- Germany in 928
- Added to Germany by c.1000
- Added temporarily to Germany (with dates)
- Polish at times during the second half of the 10th century
- Eastern frontier of Poland to 981
- The Kievan Rus in 970
- Added to the Kievan Rus by c.1000
- Bohemian from c.950, Polish by c.1000
- Czech lands
- Western limit of Hungarian control from c.910
- Western limit of Hungarian control, 973-995
- Eastern frontier of the Holy Roman Empire, 1000
- Frontiers, 1000

ENGLAND AFTER ALFRED THE GREAT, 899-1018 `3`

- Wessex and dependencies, 899
- Welsh principalities, vassals of Wessex
- Added to Wessex by 924
- Added to Wessex by 939
- Northern and western limits of England in 1018
- Extent of Danelaw, 886
- Frontiers, 899

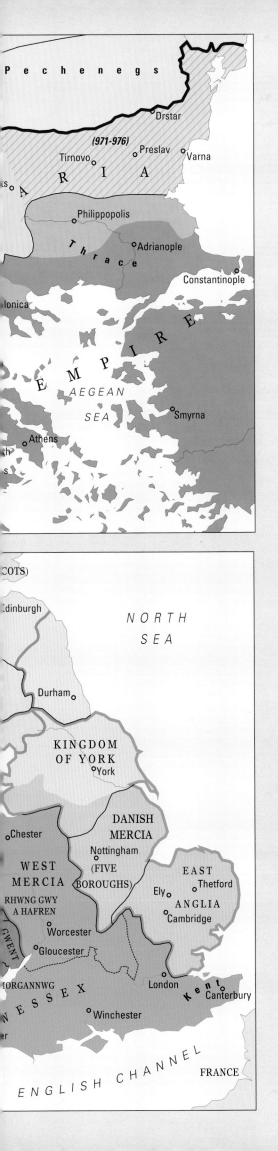

The Development of the Kievan Rus, 800-1031

1 Rapid expansion on the part of the Kievan Rus (*see* map 1, page 67) in the 10th century, notably under Igor in the 940s, enlarged the territories over which they had control at the expense of their Polish and Khazar neighbours. Later expeditions by Sviatoslav against the Khazars (965), Volga Bulgars (966) and the Bulgars on the lower Danube (967), however, resulted in mainly temporary gains.

Trade, too, played an important part in the growing importance of the Rus. From the coin evidence it is clear that the Samanid rulers of Transoxania had become very rich at the end of the 9th century as a result of the discovery of silver in Afghanistan. They minted vast quantities of coinage and their merchants began to trade with the Volga Bulgars, Rus, Ves, Lapps and Finns, though the Samanids themselves succumbed to the Turks in 998. Bulgar on the Volga developed rapidly as a trading centre. The Volga Bulgars were supplied in turn by the Rus. The Rus also traded actively with Constantinople and the Islamic regions.

Wealth had much to do with the political expansion of Kievan Rus, but the cultural links formed in the wake of mercantile connections were also crucial for political developments as Rus interests increasingly focused to the west and south towards the end of the 10th century. The formal conversion of Vladimir and the Rus to Greek Orthodox Christianity after 987, in the wake of the personal conversion of the regent Olga (d. 969, Igor's widow) and the marriage of Vladimir to the Byzantine princess Anna, provided an essential connection with Byzantium of great importance for Russia's future development.

East-Central Europe, 928-1000

2 The expansion eastwards of the German kings proceeded apace in the course of the 10th century. The establishment of the Christian church in newly created dioceses such as Magdeburg (968) and Bamberg (1007) was a fundamental component of political consolidation. Political relations with the princes of Poland, Bohemia, Moravia and Hungary were played out in the context of the conversion of the ruler and his people to Christianity. In the late 10th century, for example, a bishopric of Prague was created whose second bishop was Adalbert Vojtech, educated at Magdeburg and canonized in 990. In his position as national saint, he was soon joined by King Wenceslas.

By the second half of the 10th century, the Piast rulers of Poland, such as Mieszko (*c.* 963-992), had extended their rule to the east and south with Cracow occupying a vital strategic position.

England After Alfred the Great, 899-1018

3 By his death in 899, Alfred, who styled himself King of the English, had successfully consolidated the kingdom of Wessex; was in effect the overlord of the ruler of Mercia; reached a modus vivendi with the Danes in the Danelaw;

and in 886 occupied London. Alfred's methods of government, stressing the rule of law and encouraging learning, established a new style of kingship which became a model for future kings of England.

Alfred's sons and grandsons, Edward the Elder (899-924), Aethelstan (924-39), Edmund (939-46) and Eadred (946-55), extended the English kingdom. Edward established his rule over the entire area south of the Humber, and east of the Welsh and secured Mercia, thus effectively creating the kingdom of England consolidated by Aethelstan. He and his successors moved against the Vikings in the Danelaw and Northumbria; the last Viking ruler of the north, Eric Bloodaxe, fell in battle in 954 and the Viking kingdom of York was once more incorporated into the English kingdom. In 945, however, Cumbria was ceded to the Scots and Northumbria itself can never said to have been fully integrated with the south, as became clear in the years around the Norman conquest of the mid-11th century (*see* map 2, page 79).

The Balkans, 931-1018

4 In the 10th century, Bulgaria remained the principal rival to Byzantium in the Balkans. Symeon of Bulgaria (d. 927) brought particularly effective rule to Bulgaria. Moreover, by the treaty of 904, Byzantium recognized Bulgaria's possession of the greater part of Thrace and Macedonia. Between 913 and 927, Symeon asserted his status as an emperor equal in status and importance to the Byzantine ruler. He attacked Constantinople itself and was crowned as emperor in a ceremony whose significance has been much disputed.

The Serbs, too, had expanded their territory, especially under Vlastimir in the mid-9th century, but under Peter (d. 917) an alliance with Bulgaria was reached which lasted from 897 to 917. Thereafter Serbia attempted many times to break free of Bulgarian dominance, finally succeeding under Chaslav (d. *c.*960) after Symeon of Bulgaria's death. The Serbs, however, acknowledged Byzantine overlordship until about 976.

Symeon's successor Peter of Bulgaria (d. 969) confirmed peace with Byzantium by marrying Maria Lecapena and the borders were restored to those of 897 and 904. After his reign, however, Bulgaria was attacked by both Russia and Byzantium. Samuel (986-1014) fought back manfully and by 997 had secured a greatly enlarged territory. Not till 1000 or 1001 did the Byzantine counter-offensive of Emperor Basil II begin. Bulgaria was annexed to Byzantium in 1018.

Croatia, meanwhile, under Tomislav (d. 928), an ally of Byzantium, was a dangerous neighbour for the Bulgars and continued to pose a threat into the late 10th century under Stjepan Drzislav (d. 997) when it came under the overlordship of Venice with the doge ostensibly acting as the representative of the Byzantine emperor.

1003

Feudal Europe

Feudalism was the dominant system of political control and social organisation over much of 11th-century Western Europe. Its essential characteristic was a personal relationship between lord and vassal, cemented in an act of homage. The state in the modern sense – an agreed territory with sovereign powers and with a precise relationship with its citizens – did not exist. Instead, there was a series of individual rulers each effectively sovereign within his own lands, though each in turn nominally owing allegiance to a king or other ruler. As a consequence, the map of feudal Europe is complex. Given the disparate and many-sided relationships between lord and vassal, the political map of much of Europe was dominated by principalities, duchies and counties, so that countries such as France, while united in theory, were in practice far from being so. This fragmented authority nonetheless provided the political context for a marked rise in Europe's population, prosperity and culture. The Church, too, had an important impact on the map of Europe since many monasteries and bishops were landowners on a grand scale, often with correspondingly great political powers.

Even outside the lands of the former Carolingian Empire, where feudalism was at its strongest, "states" were dependent on successful military-political leadership. The death of a strong leader could easily lead to political collapse. This danger was amply demonstrated in the early decades of the 11th century by the fortunes of Kievan Rus and the Umayyad Caliphate of Cordova. The Kievan state dissolved after the death of Vladimir I of Rus (c.978-1015), who was succeeded by sons who ruled separate principalities based on Novgorod, Polotsk and Chernigov. Similarly, the death in 1002 of al-Mansur, who had effectively ruled Cordova since 981 and achieved many successes at the expense of the Christians, was followed by the fragmentation of Islamic Spain. A strong leader, by contrast, could rapidly restore the fortunes of a state. The Byzantine Emperor Basil II (976-1025), for example, destroyed the West Bulgarian Empire (1018), a bitter rival to Byzantium, and reduced the Serbs to vassalage. He gained his surname "Bulgar-slayer" from the battle of the Belasica mountains (1014) after which thousands of prisoners were blinded and sent home in groups of 100 each led by a one-eyed man. Shortly before his death in 1025 he even contemplated the re-conquest of Italy.

Because the existence of "states" often depended on the personal authority of a strong leader, large areas could be joined together in a single life-time. Thus in 1013, King Swein of Denmark conquered England, while the English king, Aethelred "the Unready" fled to Normandy. He returned when Swein died in 1014, but Swein's son Cnut continued the struggle, while divisions among the English handicapped the resistance. After Aethelred's death, England was divided between Cnut and Edmund, Aethelred's son, by the Peace of Alney (1016), with Cnut receiving Mercia and Northumbria. Edmund, however, died the same year and Cnut became King of all England (1016-35). On the death of his older brother, Harold, King of Denmark (1019), England became part of a Scandinavian empire, which further expanded with the conquest of Norway in the 1020s. In 1031 Cnut advanced to the Tay and received the submission of Malcolm II of Scotland.

The essentially personal and transient nature of authority was, however, demonstrated by Cnut's empire: he did not create any administrative structure to weld it together. Cnut was the king of a number of kingdoms, not a monarch seeking to enlarge one of them. After his death in 1035, his empire dissolved.

The Holy Roman Empire

Trondhjem

NORWAY
(To Denmark)

Finnic peoples

Uppsala

SWEDEN

Novgorod

Finnic peoples

Pskov

Aarhus
Roskilde

BALTIC
SEA

Polotsk

Vitebsk

Smolensk

Suzdal
Vladimir

Volga

Bulgar
VOLGA
BULGARIA

DENMARK

Slavs

Baltic peoples

Minsk

K I E V A N   R U S

Finnic peoples

Don

Poznań

Oder

Vistula

POLAND

Wrocław

Chernigov

Kiev

Prague
BOHEMIA

Cracow

Turkic peoples

Sarkel
(to Kiev)

Volga

GDOM

Elbe

MANY

Danube

Vienna

Salzburg

Pozsony

Esztergom

Fehérvár

Galich

Dniester

Dnieper

(to Kiev)

HUNGARY

Pécs

Zágráb

Tmutarakan

Alans

Verona
Venice
VENETIAN
REPUBLIC

CROATIA

Belgrade

Kaffa

Bologna

Zara

Spalato

Cherson

GEORGIAN
STATES

SMALL
STATES

Florence

Perugia

Naissus

Danube

Odessus

BLACK SEA

ARMENIA

Trapezus

PRINCIPALITY
OF BENEVENTO

Serdica

Rome

PAPAL
STATE

CIPALITY
OF CAPUA

COUNTY
OF APULIA

Philippopolis

Scupi

Adrianople

Constantinople

Ancyra

BUWAYHIDS

Naples

COUNTY
OF AVERSA

Barium

Ochrid

B Y Z A N T I N E   E M P I R E

Tigris

PRINCIPALITY
OF SALERNO

Tarentum

Salonica

Janina

Local

Euphrates

Mosul

Smyrna

dynasties

alermo

Messana

Athens

Catana

Sicily

SEA

Nicosia

Beirut
FATIMIDS
Damascus

Crete

KARMATIANS

73

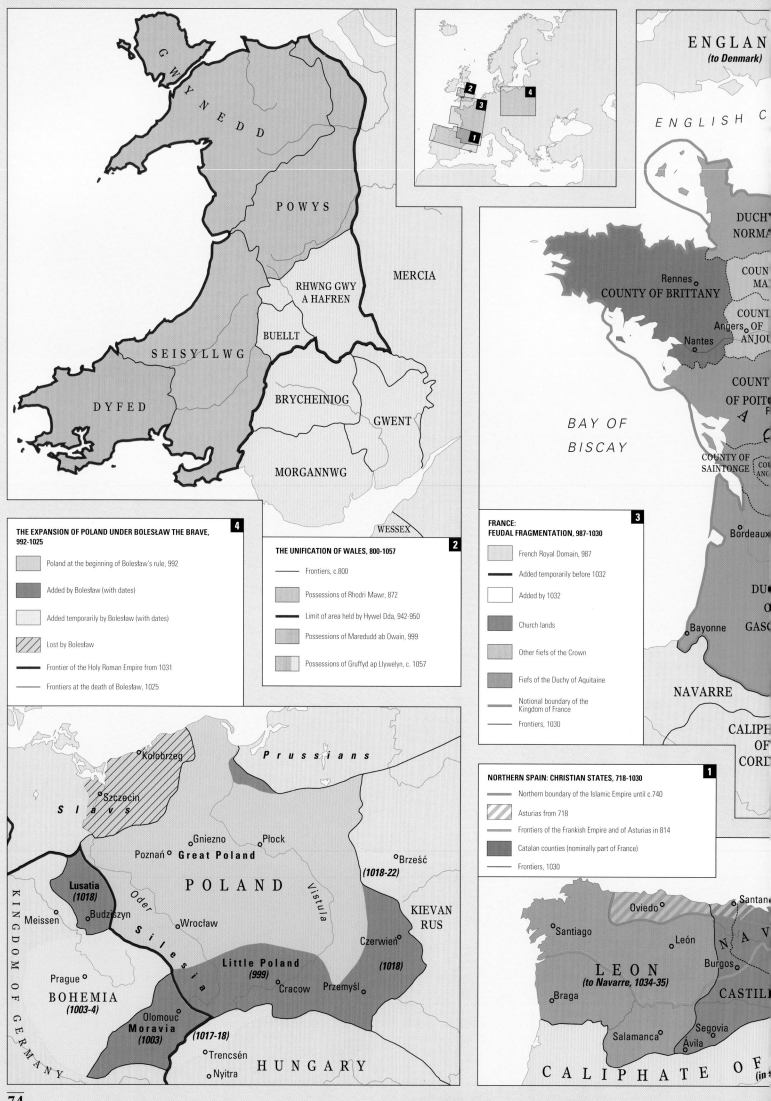

ENGLAND
(to Denmark)

ENGLISH C

DUCH
NORMA

Rennes
COUNTY OF BRITTANY

COUN
MA

COUNT
OF
ANJOU

Angers

Nantes

COUNT
OF POITO

BAY OF
BISCAY

Bordeaux

COUNTY OF
SAINTONGE

COU
ANG

DU
O
GASCO

Bayonne

NAVARRE

CALIPH
OF
CORD

MERCIA

RHWNG GWY
A HAFREN

BUELLT

SEISYLLWG

DYFED

BRYCHEINIOG

GWENT

MORGANNWG

WESSEX

G W Y N E D D

P O W Y S

**THE EXPANSION OF POLAND UNDER BOLESŁAW THE BRAVE,
992-1025**

4

Poland at the beginning of Bolesław's rule, 992

Added by Bolesław (with dates)

Added temporarily by Bolesław (with dates)

Lost by Bolesław

Frontier of the Holy Roman Empire from 1031

Frontiers at the death of Bolesław, 1025

THE UNIFICATION OF WALES, 800-1057

2

Frontiers, c.800

Possessions of Rhodri Mawr, 872

Limit of area held by Hywel Dda, 942-950

Possessions of Maredudd ab Owain, 999

Possessions of Gruffyd ap Llywelyn, c. 1057

**FRANCE:
FEUDAL FRAGMENTATION, 987-1030**

3

French Royal Domain, 987

Added temporarily before 1032

Added by 1032

Church lands

Other fiefs of the Crown

Fiefs of the Duchy of Aquitaine

Notional boundary of the
Kingdom of France

Frontiers, 1030

NORTHERN SPAIN: CHRISTIAN STATES, 718-1030

1

Northern boundary of the Islamic Empire until c.740

Asturias from 718

Frontiers of the Frankish Empire and of Asturias in 814

Catalan counties (nominally part of France)

Frontiers, 1030

Kołobrzeg

Prussians

Szczecin

Slavs

Gniezno
Poznań **Great Poland**
Płock

Brześć
(1018-22)

**Lusatia
(1018)**

Meissen
Budziszyn

P O L A N D

Oder

Wrocław

Silesia

Vistula

KIEVAN
RUS

Czerwień

(1018)

**Little Poland
(999)**

Prague
Cracow
Przemyśl
(1018)

**BOHEMIA
(1003-4)**

K I N G D O M   O F   G E R M A N Y

Olomouc
**Moravia
(1003)**

(1017-18)

Trencsén

Nyitra

H U N G A R Y

Oviedo
Santan

Santiago

León

L E O N
(to Navarre, 1034-35)

Braga

Burgos

NAV

CASTIL

Salamanca

Segovia

Ávila

C A L I P H A T E   O F
(in S

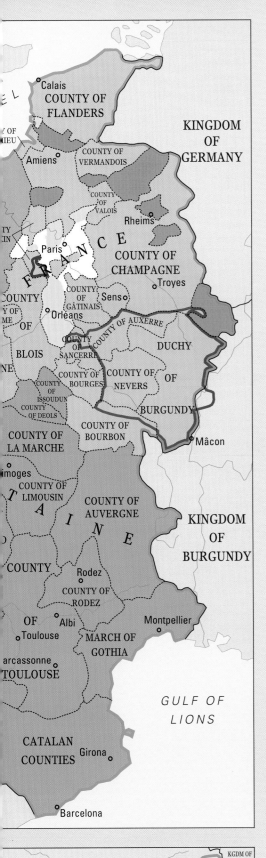

Northern Spain: Christian States, 718-1030

1 When Muslim Arab invaders swept through Spain in the decade after 711, the inhospitable lands of the north successfully resisted absorption into Islamic Spain. A nucleus of resistance formed in Asturias, following the victory of its first ruler, Pelayo, over the Muslims at Covadonga in about 722. Asturias expanded southwards in the 9th century and became, under Garcia I (911-14), the Kingdom of León. Alternative centres of Christian power developed further east in the Basque country, notably the Kingdom of Navarre, centred on Pamplona, under King Sancho I (905-26), and, from the mid-10th century, the County of Castile. Catalonia was a French fief, the "Spanish Marches", created by Charlemagne following his conquest of the territory from the Muslims around 801. Catalonia consisted of numerous small counties, the most important of which proved to be Barcelona, which steadily expanded at the expense of the others.

The southward expansion of the Christian states suffered a setback in the 10th century, as strong rulers of the Caliphate of Cordova resumed incursions into northern Spain. Under al-Mansur (976-1002) almost every Christian capital was sacked, but after his death the Caliphate of Cordova disintegrated into a series of independent lordships, ill-placed to resist the Christians' raids and forced to pay heavy tribute to them.

The Unification of Wales, 800-1057

2 Early-medieval Wales was divided into a number of small kingdoms. As in England, the tendency from the 6th century was for a decline in their number as the less successful kingdoms were absorbed by their more powerful neighbours, such as Dyfed and Gwynedd. They were based on fertile lowland, but also benefited from a degree of immunity from English attack. In contrast, Powys suffered from Mercian incursions.

Welsh inheritance customs – the division of property among sons – made it more difficult to translate territorial gains into more cohesive statehood. Rulers such as Rhodri Mawr of Gwynedd, who accumulated several kingships in the 9th century, allocated them to different sons. His grandson, Hywel Dda, however, came to rule most of Wales. He was the first Welsh king who definitely issued his own coinage. Hywel's death was followed by internecine conflict in which the English, with their growing pretension to overlordship in Britain, intervened ever more frequently.

The rise of Gwynedd under Llywelyn ap Seisyll (d. c. 1023) and his son Gruffyd ap Llywelyn (d. 1063) was the most critical development in Wales in the period preceding the Norman conquest of England. Both men had to fight to gain control of Gwynedd and both campaigned in south Wales, most of which was conquered between 1039 and 1055. The length of the process reflected the difficulty in obtaining a decisive "political" settlement short of slaying rivals, as Gruffyd twice did. The power of the rulers of Gwynedd rested on military success. Unlike their Anglo-Saxon counterparts in England – and like the Scottish kings – they did not build up any sophisticated administrative structures.

France: Feudal Fragmentation, 987-1030

3 Under the early members of the Capetian dynasty, which gained the French throne in 987, the effective power of the king was greatly limited by powerful feudal lords, and indeed by the end of the 10th century the king's writ was essentially confined to the Ile de France, the area around Paris. Elsewhere, the counties and their courts ceased to be public institutions and local official posts were absorbed into the patronage systems of the greater nobles. Counts wielded governmental powers: they minted coins, raised troops and built castles, the last a powerful expression of autonomy. The counts did not seek to replace the king: they scarcely needed to do so. Some, such as the Count of Toulouse and the Count of Champagne, were themselves as powerful as the king. Furthermore, Gascony and Toulouse, both south of the Loire, were sufficiently distant from Paris to be little concerned about its Capetian rulers. North of the Loire, however, rivalry between the powerful local feudatories and the crown was more important. As rulers of Blois and Champagne, the Counts of Champagne were powerful both to the east and west of the Ile de France. The Dukes of Normandy, meanwhile, competed with the Capetians for control of the Vexin to the northwest of Paris. The idea of a powerful monarchy was kept alive by the Church, but there was little basis to it in the 11th century.

The Expansion of Poland under Boleslaw the Brave, 992-1025

4 Boleslaw I Chrobry ("the Brave", 992-1025) of Poland built on the foundations laid by his father, Prince Mieszko I, who had converted to Christianity in 965. Boleslaw strengthened the centre by creating an administrative system based on counts, and used this as a base to expand Polish territory to the east, south and west, taking Cracow (formerly a Bohemian territory) in 999. Many of Boleslaw's conquests were temporary and involved long, debilitating wars on all frontiers. The conquest of Little Poland, which included Cracow, was permanent, however, and Casimir I (1038-58) transferred his residence there.

At first a dependent ally of the Holy Roman Emperor Otto III (who crowned Boleslaw king of Poland in 1000), Boleslaw broke with the Empire after Otto's death in 1002. He seized the imperial lands of Moravia (1003), Lusatia (1018) and Bohemia, though he controlled the latter for only two years (1003-4). Boleslaw further increased Polish influence in the east, when he placed his son-in-law, Svyatopolk, on the throne of Kiev in 1018. Boleslaw was again crowned king of Poland in 1024, this time by an Archbishop with the assent of the Pope, so symbolising his independence from imperial control.

1030

The Age of the Normans

In the late 11th century the conflict with the Muslim forces which had pressed at Europe's borders since the 7th century intensified once more. In Spain the Christians made gains, taking advantage of the dissolution of the Caliphate of Cordova into a variety of successor-states. Byzantium, however, proved unable to defend the frontiers won over the previous century by emperors such as Basil II. The Byzantine military machine found itself starved of funds, and a much-weakened Byzantine army was smashed by Seljuk Turks at Manzikert in 1071. The defeat was followed by the loss of almost all of Anatolia. The Byzantine Empire managed to retain its grip on most of the Balkans. Outside the Byzantine sphere of influence, however, there was instability as the Kingdom of Hungary gained Croatia in 1091.

At the other end of Europe, the Kingdom of England experienced particular turmoil during the 11th century. Cnut's empire (*see* page 72) fell apart in the 1030s: Norway rebelled successfully under Magnus the Good (1033-47), while Cnut's sons by different unions, Harthacnut and Harold Harefoot, competed to control England. Harthacnut succeeded to Denmark in 1035, and in 1040 gained the English throne when Harold died. On Harthacnut's death in 1042, he was succeeded by Aethelred's son, Edward "the Confessor" (1042-66).

In 1066 William Duke of Normandy conquered England with a small force, bringing to an end the Anglo-Saxon state and ushering in a new era in which England's fortunes would be tied to France and the south. Scandinavian involvement with England was not quite over, however: Harald Hardrada of Norway invaded England (unsuccessfully) in 1066, the Danes in 1069-70. But the Viking period of English history, which had begun when Norse ships were first recorded off the English coast in 789, was then over. For the Normans, by contrast, the conquest of England was just one of a series of successful military adventures, which brought them large territories in southern Italy and Sicily.

A divided succession characterized Kievan Rus as well as Cnut's empire. The Kievan principalities had been united under Iaroslav the Wise (1019-54) of Novgorod, who, after the death of his brother, the Prince of Chernigov, ruled them all save Polotsk. It was a period of particular Kievan political and cultural influence. However, on Iaroslav's death he left each of his sons an autonomous principality. The Great Principality of Kiev took precedence but it exercised little control over the others. Raids by Polovtsy nomads, who sacked Kiev in 1093, weakened the Great Principality, moving the centre of Rus activity farther north to the forest belt, away from the exposed steppes.

At the same time, in Italy and Germany a bitter power-struggle between the Holy Roman Empire and the Papacy raged: the Investiture Contest. At its height, Pope Gregory VII (1073-85), excommunicated and deposed Emperor Henry IV (1056-1106). Gregory condemned the practice of investiture by which newly appointed bishops and abbots were invested with symbols of spiritual office by the emperor, rather than by the Pope. At Canossa in 1077 Henry stood three days barefoot in the snow in the dress of a penitent to win the lifting of his excommunication, a powerful display of papal authority. Gregory helped to unite Henry's opponents and thus to weaken Imperial authority both in Germany and Italy. Meanwhile, Henry I (1031-60) and Philip I (1060-1108) sought to increase royal power in France, a goal challenged by the power of their vassals, especially the Dukes of Normandy, who were strengthened after 1066 by the Norman conquest of England.

NORWAY

Nidaros

gvin

Oslo

Uppsala

SWEDEN

BALTIC
SEA

Aarhus

Roskilde

DENMARK

urg
Bremen

Slavs

POMERANIA

Poznań

POLAND

Wrocław

NGDOM

urt

OF

Prague

Nuremberg

BOHEMIA

ttgart

MANY

Danube

Vienna

Salzburg

Innsbruck

Trieste

Venice

Verona

Y

Bologna

Pisa

Florence

Perugia

Rome
PAPAL
STATE

to Byzantine
Empire)

Naples

Bari

Taranto

Palermo

NORMAN PRINCIPALITIES

Messina

Catania

Malta

SEA

VENETIAN
REPUBLIC

CROATIA

Zara

Spalato

ZETA
(SERBIA)

Pozsony

Esztergom

HUNGARY

Pécs

Zágráb

Szeged

Temesvár

Gyulafehérvár

Belgrade

Nissa

Serdica

Scupi

BYZANTINE

EMPIRE

Salonica

Janina

Philippopolis

Adrianople

Constantinople

Smyrna

Athens

RÚM
(ICONIUM)

Finnic peoples

NOVGOROD

Novgorod

Pskov

Polotsk

Vitebsk

POLOTSK

Minsk

Brest

KIEV

Kiev

ROSTOV-
SUZDAL

Suzdal

Vladimir

SMOLENSK

Smolensk

CHERNIGOV

PEREYASLAVL

Dnieper

Dniester

Danube

Odessus

BLACK SEA

Cherson

Kaffa

(to Chernigov)

Finno-Ugrians

Volga

Bulgar

VOLGA
BULGARIA

Don

Sarkel (to Chernigov)

Volga

Turkic peoples

Alans

GEORGIA

Tiflis

Trapezus

Angora

SELJÜK EMPIRE

DANISHMENDS

Armenian
rulers

Manzikert

Mosul

Nicosia

Beirut

Damascus

Bedouins

Tigris

Euphrates

77

ATLANTIC OCEAN

EARLDOM OF ORKNEY

SCOTLAND
- Inverness
- Aberdeen
- Perth
- Dumbarton
- Edinburgh

KGDM. OF MAN (from 1075)

- Newcastle
- Durham
- Carlisle

Cumbria

ULSTER
- Armagh

CONNAUGHT
- Tuam

MEATH
- Tara
- Dublin

LEINSTER
- Kilkenny

MUNSTER
- Cork

GWYNEDD
POWYS
DEHEUBARTH
MORGANNWG
GWENT

- Chester
- York
- Ouse
- Derby
- Leicester
- Norwich
- Ely
- Shrewsbury
- Hereford
- Bristol
- Bath
- Salisbury
- Exeter

ENGLAND
- Oxford
- Thames
- London
- Canterbury
- Winchester
- Hastings

NORTH SEA

ST GEORGE'S CHANNEL

ENGLISH CHANNEL

- Rouen
- Bayeux
- Caen

N o r m a n d y

KINGDOM OF FRANCE

B r i t t a n y   *M a i n e*

LEON–CASTIL
- Coria
- Toledo

KINGDOM OF BADAJOZ
- Lisbon
- Badajoz
- Zallaca
- Mérida

KINGDOM OF SEVIL
- Cordova
- Seville

KIN Grana OF GR.
- Málag

EMPIRE OF THE

TUSCANY

PENTAPOLIS

PAPAL S
- Rome

NORMANDY AND THE BRITISH ISLES, 1062–92

Possessions of William the Conqueror, 1066	Added, 1092
Added by 1070	Limit of Norman-held areas in Wales, 1086

Possessions of Gruffyd ap LLywelyn, 1062

Norwegian possessions

Frontiers, 1062

RRE·ARAGON

COUNTY OF
BARCELONA
(with fiefs)

Saragossa
Lérida

Calatayud
Tarragona

KINGDOM OF
LÉRIDA

KINGDOM
OF SARAGOSSA

KINGDOM
OF TORTOSA

Tortosa

ALBARRAZIN

ALPUENTE

Palma

Valencia

KINGDOM
OF VALENCIA

KINGDOM OF THE BALEARES

Denia

KINGDOM
OF MURCIA

Murcia

IDS

IBERIA: SUCCESSOR STATES OF THE CALIPHATE OF CORDOVA, 1086

The Caliphate of Cordova, 1010

The Kingdom of Toledo, 1031-85

Muslim-held areas in 1030, lost to Christian states by 1085

Frontiers, late 1085

ADRIATIC
SEA

PR. OF
BENEVENTO

Capua

Benevento

COUNTY
OF APULIA

Bari

Naples

Salerno

Amalfi

PRINCIPALITY
OF SALERNO

Brindisi

Taranto

1127

TYRRHENIAN
SEA

Calabria

IONIAN
SEA

Messina

Reggio

Sicily
(empire of
Fatimids)

Taormina

Catania

Malta

NORMANS AND BYZANTINES IN SOUTHERN ITALY, 1030-1156

Frontiers, c.1030

Southern frontier of the Holy Roman Empire, 1030

Byzantine possessions, 1030

Temporary Byzantine expansion, 1036-43

Limit of Norman conquests by 1090

Counties secured by the Normans by 1042

Temporary Byzantine expansion, 1155-56

Further 12th-century Norman conquests (with dates)

The Normans and Byzantines in Southern Italy, 1030-1156

1 The Norman conquest of England (*see* below, map 2) was paralleled by other Norman conquests: of Sicily from the Arabs in 1090 and of Apulia and Calabria in southern Italy from the Byzantine Empire and from local principalities. These conquests all demonstrated the Norman genius for adaptability. Small groups of invaders, essentially adventurers, at first became important as professional soldiers, serving in the incessant conflicts in southern Italy. They then seized power. Richard of Aversa succeeded in becoming Prince of Capua, but the most dynamic was Robert Guiscard (*c.* 1015-85), the sixth of the 10 sons of Tancred d'Hauteville, a poor Norman noble, all of whom sought their fortune in southern Italy. In 1059 Pope Nicholas II recognised him as Duke of Apulia in return for the promise of Norman support against the Holy Roman Emperor. In 1060 Guiscard drove the Byzantines from Calabria; in 1071 he captured Bari and Brindisi, the main centres of Byzantine power in Italy. The Lombard principality of Salerno followed in 1077 and in 1081 Guiscard crossed the Adriatic, captured Corfu and defeated the Byzantine Emperor, Alexius Comnenus, at Durazzo. He died while preparing to attack Constantinople. The youngest of Robert's brothers, Roger, completed the conquest of Sicily: Messina had already fallen in 1061 and Catania in 1071, but the conquest was only completed in 1090. He also captured Malta. The basis of a powerful state had now been created. Roger II of Sicily (1105-54) gained control of the whole of southern Italy as well and in 1130 created a kingdom that united his dominions.

Where the Normans seized power they replaced the social elite, but there was no mass-displacement of the original population and much of the earlier administrative structure – whether Old English, Byzantine or Arab – continued. This was especially so in England, where a recognised political unit already existed, unlike southern Italy and Sicily, where one had to be created.

Normandy and the British Isles, 1062-92

2 In 1066, Duke William of Normandy ("the Conqueror") invaded England on the death of Edward the Confessor, claiming that Edward had bequeathed him the throne. He defeated the English forces at the Battle of Hastings in October, and 10 weeks later was acclaimed King of England in Westminster Abbey. The previous unification of the country by the House of Wessex ensured that it fell rapidly to William the Conqueror, in contrast to the more lengthy conquest of the Iron Age and Romano-British kingdoms by the Romans and Anglo-Saxons respectively. Even so, the conquest did not run entirely smoothly, and William did not crush the entire Anglo-Saxon elite: there was widespread rebellion, particularly in the north in 1068-70.

After 1066 England was part of a state that spanned the Channel, which found itself obliged to ward off the ambitions of other expanding territories. The Duchy of

Normandy had a long land frontier and, in the Kings of France and Counts of Anjou, aggressive neighbours. The continuous military effort that this entailed was to be a central theme, instrumental both in the development of government and in the domestic political history of the period. Though the Anglo-Norman realms were less a single state than a fortuitous conglomeration that had little in common in economic, administrative or legal terms, they were given common political direction by the interests of their ruler.

On the borders with their Celtic neighbours within Britain, the Normans faced a much less well-defined position. There were no clear geographical boundaries capable of preventing political expansion, and ethnicity could not serve as the basis for states. What eventually became Scotland was ethnically, geographically, economically and culturally diverse, and included Scots, Picts, the Britons of Strathclyde and the Angles of Lothian. Until the mid-12th century it was unclear whether much of what is now northern England, in particular Cumbria and Northumbria, would be part of England or of Scotland. The great ethnic and linguistic mixture of the population in both Cumbria and Lothian ensured that there was no obvious frontier in either respect. William II's conquest of Cumbria in 1092 played a major role in fixing the frontier.

In Wales, Gruffyd ap Llywelyn (*see* map 2, page 74) had been killed in 1063 as a result of the invasion of the country by Earl Harold of Wessex. It was not to be united again until the 13th century. William I did not seek to conquer Wales, but individual Norman adventurers seized land. These Normans were operating outside the kingdom of England and the "march" they created was a kind of no-man's-land between Wales and England. Initially the Normans advanced with great momentum, along the lowlands near the south and north coasts, and up the river valleys. The Welsh, however, benefited not only from their terrain, much of which offered little advantage to the feudal cavalry of the Normans, but also from the military skills honed by incessant conflict within their own ranks.

Iberia: Successor States of the Caliphate of Cordova, 1086

3 On the death of Abd ar'Rahman, Muslim Spain suffered two decades of civil war. The Caliphate of Cordova broke up into numerous independent kingdoms or *ta'ifas*. The most important of these was based on Seville, which gradually became pre-eminent in southern Spain. Elsewhere the *ta'ifas* were weakened by constant strife. They were forced to pay heavy tributes to the Christians, and this burden undermined them further. Their weakness led to the loss of Toledo to Castile in 1085. In order to resist the Christian advance, the Muslims called in the Almoravids, Saharan Berbers who had overrun Morocco in the 1060s. They defeated Alfonso VI of León at Sagrajas (1086) and put a temporary end to the Christian offensive.

Crusader Europe

In March 1095 an embassy from the Byzantine Emperor Alexius I asked Pope Urban II for help against the Seljuk Turks who had overrun most of the eastern provinces of the Byzantine empire following the Battle of Manzikert in 1071 (*see* page 76) and who were threatening Constantinople itself. Urban responded by summoning Western European knights to come to the aid of the Christians in the East. So began the First Crusade, spurred on by the aim of retaking the holy city of Jerusalem, which had been in Muslim hands for over 400 years. The Crusader ideal of fighting holy wars against the external or internal foes of Christendom remained a potent one into the 15th century and beyond.

The First Crusade led to the capture of Antioch and Edessa in 1098 and Jerusalem 1099, and to the establishment of four states, the Kingdom of Jerusalem, the County of Tripolis, the Principality of Antioch, and the County of Edessa. These gains were expanded with the capture of Tyre (1124) and Ascalon (1153), but in 1144 most of the County of Edessa was lost to the Muslims under Zangi, Atabeg of Mosul. This inspired the Second Crusade, but that led only to an unsuccessful attack on Damascus in 1148. In 1187 Jerusalem and most of the Crusading states were lost by the Christians after the Muslim leader Saladin's crushing victory at Hattin.

The Crusades also inspired a novel form of monastic organisation that had political overtones: the Military Orders. The Templars and Hospitallers had troops and castles and were entrusted with the defence of large tracts of territory in Palestine. The Crusades also contributed to an expansion of Byzantine control in western and southern Anatolia, but this faltered with the victory of the Seljuks of Rum at Myriocephalum (1176).

The Crusades demonstrated that Christendom could take the initiative: they were as important for relations with Eastern Europe, especially Byzantium, as for those with the Islamic world. Crusading activity played a crucial role at the margins of Europe. Crusading in Spain was the central theme of the Reconquista, while activity against pagan peoples in the Baltic was seen in the context of a Crusade: in 1147 the Wends, a Slavic people of northeast Germany, were attacked by the Danes, Saxons and Poles. Here, however, the campaigns were as much spurred on by demographic pressures as by religious idealism. In the period as a whole, German peasant settlement expanded eastward, especially in Saxony and Brandenburg, putting pressure on the Slavic peoples.

Elsewhere in Europe, monarchs struggled to expand their power. In southern Italy Roger II of Sicily created a powerful state. The death of a cousin led to his acquiring Apulia in 1127 and in 1130 he took the title of King. Louis VI (1108-37) and Louis VII (1137-80) struggled to expand the power of the Capetians in France, but a major setback occurred in 1152 when Louis VII allowed his divorced wife Eleanor of Aquitaine to marry Henry, Count of Anjou, soon to be Henry II of England, thereby losing effective control of a large portion of southern France. In northern Italy the Emperor, Frederick Barbarossa, was defeated by the Lombard League of Cities at Legnano (1176).

Further east, the centre of Rus activity continued to move towards the forest belt. A new principality, Suzdal, developed in this area, while in 1126 Novgorod became a republic: it soon extended its power to the White Sea. In 1169 Kiev was sacked by Suzdal and the title of Great Prince was transferred to the ruler of the latter, commonly known as Great Prince of Vladimir, after Suzdal's capital.

NORWAY

Nidaros

Oslo

SWEDEN

Uppsala

Åbo

Finns

NOVGOROD

FINNO-UGRIANS

Estonians

Pskov

Livs

BALTIC
SEA

Lithuanians

Polotsk

Vitebsk

POLOTSK

Minsk

VLADIMIR-SUZDAL

Vladimir Suzdal

Bulgar VOLGA
BULGARIA

Volga

SMOLENSK

Smolensk

Tula

MUROM-
RYAZAN

Aarhus

Roskilde Malmö

DENMARK

POMERELIA

Prussians

PRUSSIAN
SEA

CHERNIGOV

Don

Hamburg

Bremen

Hanover

POMERANIA

Vistula

Oder

GREAT
POLAND Poznań MAZOVIA

Brest

TUROV-
PINSK

NOVGOROD-
SEVERSK

GDOM

Elbe

SILESIA

Wrocław

LITTLE
POLAND

VOLHYNIA

KIEV

Kiev

PEREYASLAVL

Volga

OF

Nuremberg

Prague

KINGDOM OF
BOHEMIA Brno

Danube

Galich

GALICH

Dniester

Dnieper

C u m a n s

tgart

MANY

Munich Salzburg

Vienna

Pozsony

Esztergom

(to Kiev)

Innsbruck

Graz

HUNGARY

Szeged

(to Kiev)

Alans

Trieste

Venice

VENETIAN
REPUBLIC

Verona

Legnano

Pécs

Temesvár

Cherson

Bologna

Zágráb

Cumans

sa

Florence

Zara

BYZANTINE

Belgrade

Danube

BLACK SEA

GEORGIA

Perugia

Spalatum

Mostar

Naissus

Odessus

Trapezus

me

PAPAL
STATE

Serdica

Local
dynasties

Naples

Bari

Taranto

Philippopolis

Adrianople

Constantinople

RÙM
(ICONIUM)

Seljuk

Palermo

Scupi

Salonica

Janina

Myriocephalum

Iconium

Armenian
rulers

rulers

KINGDOM OF SICILY

Messina

Catania

Smyrna

PRINCIPALITY
OF ANTIOCH

Euphrates

Tigris

Athens

(Saladin)

COUNTY OF
TRIPOLIS
KINGDOM OF
JERUSALEM

Bedouins

Malta

SEA

Nicosia

Beirut Damascus

81

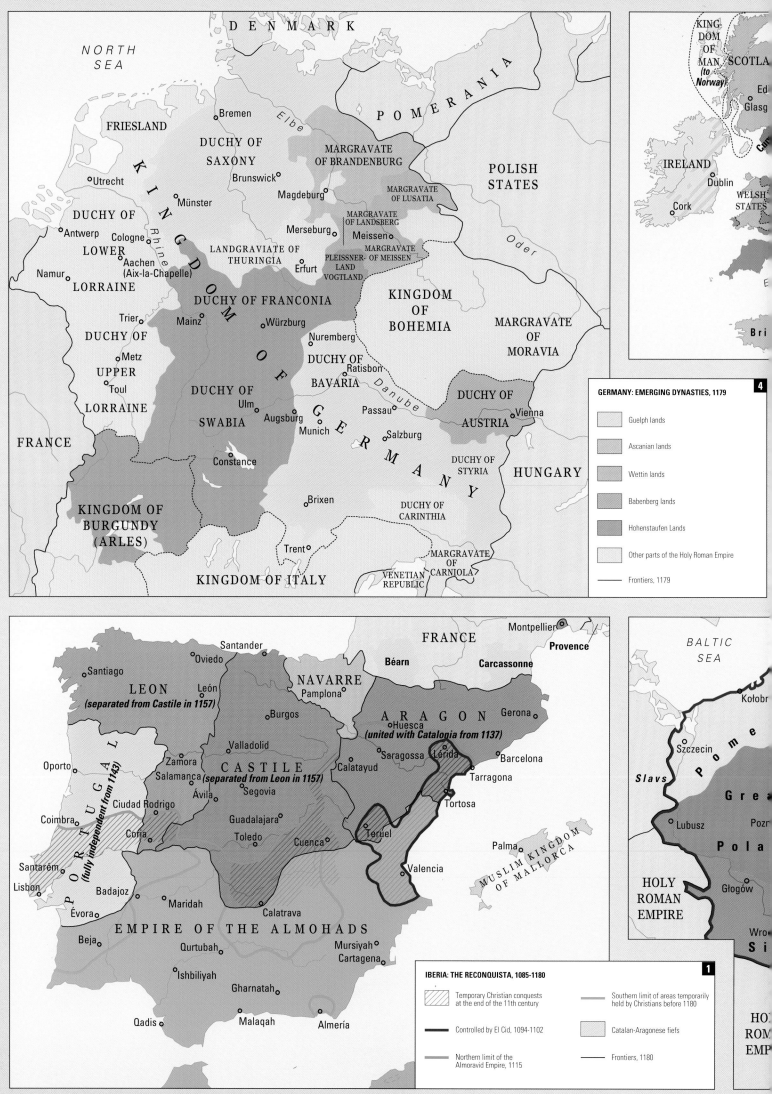

Map 4: Germany — Emerging Dynasties, 1179

NORTH SEA

DENMARK

POMERANIA

POLISH STATES

FRIESLAND

Bremen

DUCHY OF SAXONY

Brunswick

Elbe

MARGRAVATE OF BRANDENBURG

Magdeburg

MARGRAVATE OF LUSATIA

Utrecht

Münster

MARGRAVATE OF LANDSBERG

Merseburg

Meissen

Oder

Antwerp

Cologne

LOWER

Aachen (Aix-la-Chapelle)

LANDGRAVIATE OF THURINGIA

Erfurt

PLEISSNER-LAND VOGTLAND

MARGRAVATE OF MEISSEN

Namur

LORRAINE

KINGDOM OF GERMANY

DUCHY OF FRANCONIA

KINGDOM OF BOHEMIA

MARGRAVATE OF MORAVIA

Trier

Mainz

Würzburg

DUCHY OF

Nuremberg

DUCHY OF UPPER LORRAINE

Metz

Toul

DUCHY OF SWABIA

Ulm

Augsburg

BAVARIA

Ratisbon

Danube

Passau

DUCHY OF AUSTRIA

Vienna

FRANCE

Munich

Salzburg

Constance

DUCHY OF STYRIA

HUNGARY

Brixen

DUCHY OF CARINTHIA

KINGDOM OF BURGUNDY (ARLES)

Trent

MARGRAVATE OF CARNIOLA

VENETIAN REPUBLIC

KINGDOM OF ITALY

GERMANY: EMERGING DYNASTIES, 1179 [4]

- Guelph lands
- Ascanian lands
- Wettin lands
- Babenberg lands
- Hohenstaufen Lands
- Other parts of the Holy Roman Empire
- Frontiers, 1179

KING-DOM OF MAN (to Norway)

SCOTLA[ND]

Ed[inburgh]

Glasg[ow]

IRELAND

Dublin

WELSH STATES

Cork

Bri[tain]

Map 1: Iberia — The Reconquista, 1085–1180

Montpellier

FRANCE

Santander

Provence

Santiago

Oviedo

Béarn

Carcassonne

LEON *(separated from Castile in 1157)*

León

NAVARRE

Pamplona

ARAGON *(united with Catalonia from 1137)*

Gerona

Burgos

Huesca

Saragossa

Lérida

Barcelona

Oporto

Zamora

Valladolid

CASTILE *(separated from Leon in 1157)*

Calatayud

Tarragona

PORTUGAL *(fully independent from 1143)*

Salamança

Ávila

Segovia

Teruel

Tortosa

Coimbra

Ciudad Rodrigo

Guadalajara

Toledo

Cuenca

Santarém

Coria

Valencia

Palma

MUSLIM KINGDOM OF MALLORCA

Lisbon

Badajoz

Maridah

Calatrava

Évora

EMPIRE OF THE ALMOHADS

Beja

Qurtubah

Mursiyah

Cartagena

Ishbiliyah

Gharnatah

Qadis

Malaqah

Almería

IBERIA: THE RECONQUISTA, 1085–1180 [1]

- Temporary Christian conquests at the end of the 11th century
- Controlled by El Cid, 1094–1102
- Northern limit of the Almoravid Empire, 1115
- Southern limit of areas temporarily held by Christians before 1180
- Catalan-Aragonese fiefs
- Frontiers, 1180

BALTIC SEA

Kołobr[zeg]

Szczecin

Pome[rania]

Slavs

Gre[ater]

Lubusz

Pozn[ań]

Pola[nd]

HOLY ROMAN EMPIRE

Głogów

Wro[cław]

Si[lesia]

HO[LY] ROM[AN] EMP[IRE]

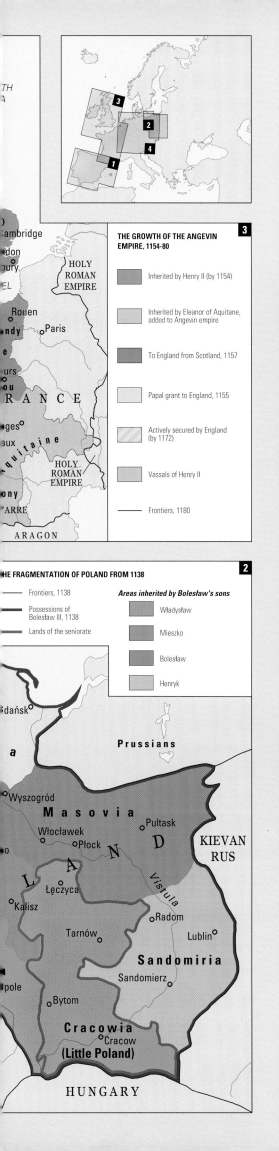

THE GROWTH OF THE ANGEVIN EMPIRE, 1154-80

▨	Inherited by Henry II (by 1154)
▨	Inherited by Eleanor of Aquitaine, added to Angevin empire
▨	To England from Scotland, 1157
▨	Papal grant to England, 1155
▨	Actively secured by England (by 1172)
▨	Vassals of Henry II
—	Frontiers, 1180

3

THE FRAGMENTATION OF POLAND FROM 1138

—	Frontiers, 1138
▨	Possessions of Bolesław III, 1138
▨	Lands of the seniorate

Areas inherited by Bolesław's sons

▨	Władysław
▨	Mieszko
▨	Bolesław
▨	Henryk

2

Iberia: the Reconquista, 1085-1180

1 The Christian advance into Spain which led to the capture of Toledo in 1085 had prompted the intervention of the Moroccan Almoravids in Spain (*see* map 3, page 79). The Almoravids took over most of the Muslim emirates in the early 1090s, Badajoz falling to them in 1095. The Almoravids, however, suffered a reverse when El Cid, a Christian soldier of fortune, captured Valencia in 1094.

Under Yusuf ibn-Tashfin and his son Ali (caliph 1106-43), the Almoravids overran the rest of Muslim Spain (1110-15) and recaptured Valencia from the Christians (1102), but, thereafter, the Christian states regained the initiative and expanded considerably. Under Alfonso VI and Alfonso VII León was particularly strong. In the 1140s Alfonso VII expanded his power to the Tagus and in 1147 he captured Almería on the Mediterranean coast. Aragon and Catalonia united in 1137 and then captured the lower Ebro (1148-9). Portugal expanded greatly with the capture of Lisbon (1147). This owed much to help of a fleet of Flemings, Rhinelanders, Normans and English which was taking part in the Second Crusade. They pressed on to take Faro (1147) and to help Aragon and the Genoese in the successful siege of Tortosa (1148).

From the 1150s the Almoravids were replaced by the Almohads, Shi'ite sectaries who had already conquered Morocco in the 1140s. They lent new energy to Muslim resistance and the Christians were further hindered by the division of León into three kingdoms: León, Castile and Portugal. Navarre had broken away from Aragon in 1134. Despite these divisions, Alfonso VIII of Castile took Cuenca in 1177.

The Fragmentation of Poland from 1138

2 The power of the Polish monarchy was gravely affected both by the rise in the power of the magnates and by the granting of provinces to members of the ruling Piast dynasty. In his will, Boleslaw III Krzywousty ("the Wrymouthed", 1102-38), divided Poland between his sons, a process that made it harder to resist the rise of the magnates. This began the so-called "Period of Fragmentation" which lasted until the coronation of Wladislaw I in 1320. During this time, politics revolved around the efforts of the regional princes to conquer the capital province of Cracowia and with it the title of *princeps* (senior prince). Fighting against each other, the princes were unable to mount effective resistance to German advances or to retain control over Pomerania.

The Growth of the Angevin Empire, 1154-80

3 Henry II (1154-89) of England created a powerful empire spanning the English Channel. His marriage to Eleanor of Aquitaine brought him control over most of southwest France. Combined with the Norman and Angevin (Anjou) inheri-tances, this made him the most powerful ruler in France, more so than his suzerain (feudal lord) for these French territories, Louis VII, king of France. In his first 12 years Henry used this power to resolve inheritance disputes in his favour, gaining control of Brittany and more of southern France. Angevin power was also dynamic in Britain. The Scottish frontier was settled in 1157, with Cumbria and Northumbria definitively part of England, and Henry campaigned actively in Wales.

Following initiatives by some of his nobles, particularly Richard de Clare, "Strongbow", who were creating powerful lordships for themselves, Henry intervened in Ireland in 1171. This was in order to establish his rights in accordance with a papal bull of 1155 from the English pope, Adrian IV. Like Wales, Ireland was far from unified, and this provided opportunities for aristocratic and royal ambitions. Henry successfully established the new lordship of Ireland, based on Dublin, created a large royal demesne for himself and bound the Anglo-Norman barons and most of the native Irish kings to him.

Germany: Emerging Dynasties, 1179

4 The unification of the kingdom of Germany with those of Italy (951) and Burgundy (1033) created a potentially powerful unit, although the Investiture Controversy with the papacy in the late 11th century (*see* page 76) exacerbated the natural difficulties of attempting to maintain authority over such a wide area. The Empire, however, regained its dynamism in the 12th century. The Salian dynasty had come to a close with the death of Henry V (1106-25) who settled the Investiture Controversy and was replaced by the Hohenstaufen dynasty, named after the Swabian castle of Staufen.

The first Hohenstaufen Emperor, Conrad III (1138-52), was succeeded by his nephew Frederick I Barbarossa (1152-90). He was a vigorous ruler, but his position was affected by the growing power of many of the leading aristocratic families, especially the Guelphs in Saxony. Henry the Proud, the head of the Guelphs, had resisted Conrad III, and his son, Henry the Lion, was a crucial figure in Barbarossa's reign. Duke of Saxony (1142-80) and Bavaria (1156-80), he helped to expand Germany eastwards and also founded Munich in 1158. Henry broke with Barbarossa in 1176, was deprived of his lands and exiled. The commitment of Frederick to maintaining and expanding Imperial power in Italy weakened his position in Germany, although the extent of the territorial power there of his family, the Hohenstaufen, remained considerable.

The Empire was altered by these dynastic rivalries on its eastern frontier too, where the Babenburg rulers of Austria were drawn in on the side of the Hohenstaufen. Even so, the Empire managed to expand: the Duchy of Pomerania was added in 1181.

1180

The Eve of the Mongol Invasions

The period after 1180 saw the Christians in Spain at first under severe pressure from the Almohads, but the victory of Alfonso VIII of Castille over the Muslim forces at Las Navas de Tolosa in 1212 opened the way for significant inroads into Almohad territory over the next 50 years. The Third Crusade (1190-1), in contrast, failed to regain more than a part of the conquests made by Saladin. The Fourth Crusade (1202-4), under Venetian influence, in fact attacked not the Muslims, but first Zara, which the Hungarians had captured in 1186, and then Constantinople: Alexius Angelus, the son of the deposed Byzantine Emperor Isaac II (1185-1195), offered 200,000 marks, help with the crusade and the union of the Orthodox Church with Rome if his uncle was removed. This was effected by the Crusaders in July 1203, but the new Emperor, Alexius IV, was unable to fulfil his promises and was deposed in an anti-Western rising. This led the Crusaders to storm the city, crown Count Baldwin of Flanders as first Latin Emperor of Constantinople and partition the Byzantine Empire between them.

Even before 1204, the Byzantine Empire had been severely weakened in the Balkans. Bulgaria, under Tsars Peter and Asen, had re-asserted its independence after 1185, and by 1204 had captured large areas of Thessaly, Macedonia and Thrace. Serbia, too, under Stepan Nemanja (d. 1196) and Stepan II (1196-1228), gained Byzantine recognition of its independence and steadily expanded its territory to the south and east. Both Serbia and Bulgaria for a time recognised the religious authority of the Pope, so diluting Byzantine and Orthodox influence even further.

The Byzantine Empire was dealt a shattering blow, if not a fatal one, by the Latin occupation of its capital. The Latins did not succeed in occupying the entire Empire, and centres of resistance grew up around the Trebizond (the Empire of Trebizond), Arta (the Despotate of Epirus), and Nicaea (the Empire of Nicaea). The Nicaean Empire under Theodore Lascaris prevented the Latins from gaining a permanent foothold in Anatolia, and ultimately proved the most successful focus for Byzantine opposition to the western invaders.

Further north the Swedes gained a foothold in Finland, while a crusading military order, the Sword Brothers, from a base on the river Dvina established in 1199, conquered Livonia. Meanwhile, in Italy, Emperor Henry VI (1190-7), the son of Frederick I Barbarossa (*see* map 4, page 83), married the heiress to the Kingdom of Sicily. Hohenstaufen authority was established in southern Italy in 1190-4 and in 1194 Henry's Genoese and Pisan fleet ensured control of Sicily: the Hohenstaufen became the wealthiest rulers in Europe.

To the east, the Mongols under Genghiz Khan (1206-27) were extending their sway and raiding on the Eurasian steppe. Fortunately for Christendom, Genghiz had concentrated on China and then the Muslim states of Central Asia, but the successful campaign against the Khwarizm Shah of Persia (1220-1) led Mongol forces to move west into the Caucasus, defeating the kingdom of Georgia, the Alans and Cumans to the north of the Caucasus, and the south Russian princes. This was achieved by a subsidiary Mongol force, and it indicated the vulnerability of Europe to the mobile peoples of Central Asia. The European states were ill-placed to resist the wave of invasion which was about to engulf them from the east, lacking the population, military resources and technology to face this new foe.

NORWAY

Nidaros

Oslo

SWEDEN

Uppsala

Åbo

Lapps

Finns

NOVGOROD

Novgorod

Reval **(to Denmark)**

Pskov

Estonians ORDER
OF THE
SWORD
Riga BROTHERS

(To Rostov)

VLADIMIR-
SUZDAL

ROSTOV

YURIEV

Suzdal

Vladimir

PEREYASLÁVL

Moscow

Volga

Bulgar

VOLGA
BULGARIA

Curonians

Aarhus

Roskilde Lund

BALTIC
SEA

Lithuanians

Polotsk

Vitebsk

SMOLENSK

Smolensk

Tula

Don

MUROM-RYAZAN

DENMARK

Prussians

POMERELIA

POLOTSK

Minsk

CHERNIGOV

Hamburg

Bremen *Elbe* Stettin

Hanover

CUJAVIA

GREAT
POLAND Poznań

MAZOVIA

TUROV-
PINSK

NOVGOROD-
SEVERSK

KGDOM

Meissen

Wrocław

SILESIA *Oder*

LITTLE
POLAND

Vistula

VOLHYNIA

KIEV Kiev

PEREYASLAVL

OF

Prague

KINGDOM OF
BOHEMIA

Brünn

Cracow

Dnieper

u

m

Volga

NUREMBERG

MANY

Munich

Salzburg

Danube

Pozsony

Vienna

Esztergom

Pest

Graz

HUNGARY

Galich

GALICH

Kolozsvár

Dniester

C

C

u

a

(to Kiev)

Alans

Pécs

Szeged

Temesvár

Brassó

**(to
Kiev)**

Zágráb

Belgrade

**(to
Venice)**

Bologna

Florence

VENETIAN REPUBLIC

Zara

Spalato

BOSNIA

Danube

BULGARIA Varna

BLACK SEA

GEORGIA

PAPAL

STATE

Rome

SERBIA

Nish

Serdica

Philippopolis

Trebizond

EMPIRE OF TREBIZOND

Scupi

Adrianople LATIN

KHWÁRIZM

Naples

Bari

Taranto

DESPOTATE OF EPIRUS

KINGDOM OF
SALONICA

Salonica

Janina

EMPIRE
(ROMANIA)

Constantinople

Nicaea

Angora

RUM
(ICONIUM)

Tigris

Euphrates

Mosul

KINGDOM OF SICILY

Palermo

Messina

Catania

DUCHY
OF
ATHENS

PRINCIPALITY
OF ACHAIA

Athens

EMPIRE OF NICAEA

Iconium

LESSER
ARMENIA

PRINCIPALITY
OF ANTIOCH

AYYUBIDS

SEA

VENETIAN
REPUBLIC

(to Venice)

(Gabalas)

KINGDOM
OF CYPRUS

Nicosia

COUNTY OF
TRIPOLIS

Beirut Damascus

Bedouins

85

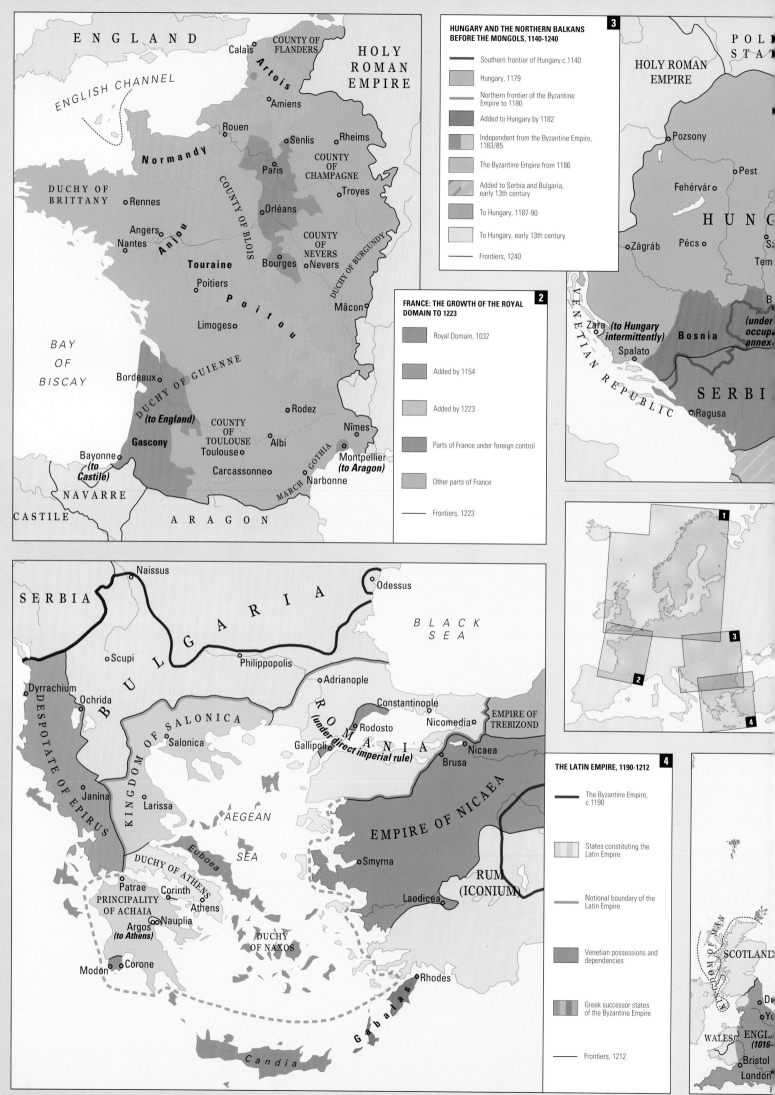

ENGLAND

COUNTY OF FLANDERS

Calais

HOLY ROMAN EMPIRE

Artois

ENGLISH CHANNEL

Amiens

Rouen

Senlis

Rheims

Normandy

Paris

COUNTY OF CHAMPAGNE

Rennes

Troyes

DUCHY OF BRITTANY

COUNTY OF BLOIS

Angers

Anjou

Orléans

Nantes

Touraine

COUNTY OF NEVERS

Bourges

Nevers

DUCHY OF BURGUNDY

Poitiers

Poitou

BAY OF BISCAY

Limoges

Mâcon

Bordeaux

DUCHY OF GUIENNE

Rodez

(to England)

Gascony

COUNTY OF TOULOUSE

Nîmes

Bayonne

Albi

Montpellier

(to Castile)

Toulouse

(to Aragon)

Carcassonne

MARCH OF GOTHIA

Narbonne

NAVARRE

CASTILE

ARAGON

HUNGARY AND THE NORTHERN BALKANS BEFORE THE MONGOLS, 1140-1240 **3**

- Southern frontier of Hungary c.1140
- Hungary, 1179
- Northern frontier of the Byzantine Empire to 1180
- Added to Hungary by 1182
- Independent from the Byzantine Empire, 1183/85
- The Byzantine Empire from 1186
- Added to Serbia and Bulgaria, early 13th century
- To Hungary, 1187-90
- To Hungary, early 13th century
- Frontiers, 1240

FRANCE: THE GROWTH OF THE ROYAL DOMAIN TO 1223 **2**

- Royal Domain, 1032
- Added by 1154
- Added by 1223
- Parts of France under foreign control
- Other parts of France
- Frontiers, 1223

HOLY ROMAN EMPIRE

POL STAT

Pozsony

HUNG

Pest

Fehérvár

Zágráb

Pécs

Tem

VENETIAN REPUBLIC

Zara (to Hungary intermittently)

Bosnia

(under occup annex

Spalato

SERBI

Ragusa

SERBIA

Naissus

Odessus

BLACK SEA

Scupi

BULGARIA

Philippopolis

Dyrrachium

Adrianople

Ochrida

Constantinople

EMPIRE OF TREBIZOND

DESPOTATE OF EPIRUS

KINGDOM OF SALONICA

Rodosto

Nicomedia

Salonica

Gallipoli

ROMANIA (under direct imperial rule)

Nicaea

Brusa

Janina

Larissa

AEGEAN SEA

EMPIRE OF NICAEA

Euboea

DUCHY OF ATHENS

Smyrna

Patrae

Corinth

PRINCIPALITY OF ACHAIA

Athens

Argos

Nauplia

RUM (ICONIUM)

(to Athens)

DUCHY OF NAXOS

Laodicea

Modon

Corone

Gabalas

Rhodes

Candia

THE LATIN EMPIRE, 1190-1212 **4**

- The Byzantine Empire, c.1190
- States constituting the Latin Empire
- Notional boundary of the Latin Empire
- Venetian possessions and dependencies
- Greek successor states of the Byzantine Empire
- Frontiers, 1212

1

3

2

4

KINGDOM OF MAN

SCOTLAND

WALES

ENGL (1016-

Bristol

London

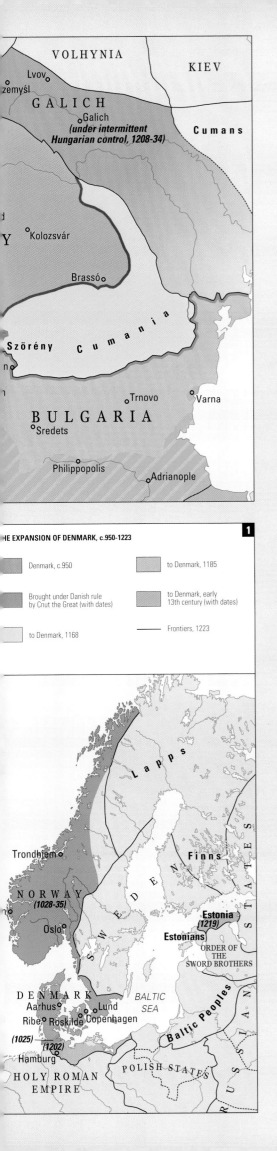

HE EXPANSION OF DENMARK, c.950-1223

Denmark, c.950

Brought under Danish rule
by Cnut the Great (with dates)

to Denmark, 1168

to Denmark, 1185

to Denmark, early
13th century (with dates)

Frontiers, 1223

The Expansion of Denmark, c. 950-1223

1 The Empire of Cnut (*see* page 72) and his successors had seen the king of Denmark also ruling England (1016-42) and Norway (1028-35). In the 1180s Denmark resumed an expansive role, this time in the Baltic. By 1185 the Danes, had occupied Pomerania, Mecklenburg and Holstein. King Valdemar Sejr (1202-41) captured the area around Lübeck and Hamburg, and during his reign the Danes played a major role in the crusading advance along the southern and eastern shores of the Baltic. In 1219-20 Denmark gained control of northern Estonia with their major base at Reval (Tallinn).

France: the Growth of the Royal Domain to 1223

2 The 12th century saw great expansion in the royal domain in France, that part of the kingdom under the direct control of the king rather than powerful feudal vassals. This growth was particularly at the expense of the Angevin monarchy. The determination and military success of Philip Augustus (1180-1223) led to King John of England's loss of most of his father's vast continental possessions, including Normandy and Anjou, in 1203-4. John's attempt to recover this continental inheritance ended in failure when his allies were defeated at Bouvines (1214). John's domestic opponents then offered the English throne to Philip's son Louis. His attempted invasion of England in 1217 was defeated by supporters of John's infant son, Henry III. French intervention in England was a logical consequence of the post-Conquest cross-Channel nature of the English monarchy. It was now plausible to attack England, or to support its rivals within the British Isles, in order to undermine the policy of England's monarchs, specifically their defence of their continental interests.

Whereas in Britain there were natural frontiers for most of the realm – the Anglo-Scottish and Anglo-Welsh land frontiers were far shorter than the marine frontiers – this was not the case to anywhere near the same extent on the continent. While the overlapping nature of feudal jurisdictions militated against the development of a national consciousness, within areas with a common sovereign, such as France, there were also important cultural, not least linguistic, divides.

In southern France the crusade against the Cathar (Albigensian) Christian heresy led eventually to an increase in royal power. Innocent III proclaimed a crusade in 1209, and Simon de Montfort overran much of Languedoc: Carcassonne fell after a short siege. In 1213 King Peter II of Aragon intervened. An orthodox Catholic, he was concerned about de Montfort's rising power, and backed Count Raymond VI of Toulouse with whom de Montfort was at war. Their united forces were defeated at Muret in September 1213. Peter was killed and the crusaders occupied Toulouse. Raymond regained the city in 1217 and his son was not forced to make peace until 1229. The war was important because expeditions in 1219 and 1226 by Louis, first as prince and then as Louis VIII, helped to strengthen royal influence in the region while the defeat of Aragon decisively weakened a long-lasting link between southern France and Catalonia.

Hungary and the Northern Balkans before the Mongols, 1140-1240

3 The growth in the power of Hungary was the most important development to the north of the Byzantine Empire in the 12th century. After having successfully fended off the attempts of Emperor Manuel I to conquer her, Hungary counterattacked following his death in 1180. The Hungarians gained not only southern Croatia and Bosnia, but also seized a frontier zone in the vicinity of Belgrade. At the start of the 13th century, the Hungarian kings extended their rule over the area known as Cumania (later Wallachia). The Hungarian kings also made attempts to take control of the Russian principality of Galich, but the enterprise proved too costly to sustain. The southern gains were more long-lasting. These areas were not annexed directly to Hungary, but administered by "bans", officials answering to the King of Hungary.

To the south Serbia regained her independence under Stefan Nemanja (1168-96). A successful revolt against Byzantium led to the restoration of Bulgarian independence in the mid 1180s too: the "Empire of Vlachs and Bulgars", or the Second Bulgarian Empire, had its capital at Trnovo. With the collapse of the Byzantine empire in 1204, both Bulgaria and Serbia made gains.

The Latin Empire, 1190-1212

4 The Latin Empire, known as "Romania", was created in 1204 after the Fourth Crusaders took Constantinople (*see* page 84), and comprised a number of feudal territories: the Principality of Achaia, the Duchy of Athens and the Kingdom of Salonica or Thessaly. The Venetians gained many of the Aegean islands, Candia (Crete) and a number of strategic points on the mainland that helped to give them command of coastal waters: the large crews required to man the oars of galleys needed a chain of bases to supply them. Part of the structure of a successful naval system was the existence of such bases, and it was these that Venetian expansion secured.

The Greeks were left with more peripheral parts of the Byzantine empire: the Empires of Nicaea and Trebizond, and the Despotates of Epirus and Rhodes (under the Gabalas). Nicaea, first under Theodore Lascaris (1206-22), was best placed to act as the Greek successor state as it was most able to challenge the Latins. The Latin empire rapidly encountered problems. Nicaea, which absorbed Rhodes, overran its Asian territories, while in 1223 Epirus took Salonica and made it the capital of the Empire of Salonica. The land route from Constantinople to Athens was therefore lost and the Latin Empire became dependent on maritime links.

1223

1270

The High Middle Ages

Eastern Europe suffered great turmoil in the 13th century, undergoing significantly greater territorial changes than occurred in Western Europe in the period. The Mongol invasions devastated the area: the northern principalities of Rus were overrun in 1233-9; Kiev was stormed and razed in 1240; in 1240-4 the Mongols tore through Hungary, taking Pest, while smaller forces poured into Poland, took Cracow and defeated a German-Polish army at Wählstatt in 1241. Only the death of the Great Khan Ogedai in December 1241 granted a respite to Europe as the Mongol hordes were recalled. The Byzantine Empire, meanwhile, had been restored with the capture of Constantinople from the Latins in 1261.

Another area of major change was the eastern Baltic, where the crusading movement still retained its vitality. The Teutonic Knights overran Prussia, their sovereign rights protected by Imperial (1226) and papal recognition (1234), the latter making their territory a papal fief. Königsberg was established as a base in 1255, Memel in 1252. The Knights of the Sword, however, were less successful. After their defeat by the pagan Lithuanians in 1236, they were absorbed by the Teutonic Knights. The latter, however, faced revolts in Prussia: their advance on Pskov was stopped by Prince Alexander Nevsky of Novgorod, who then defeated them on the frozen surface of Lake Peipus (1242); and they were defeated by the Lithuanians at Durben in 1260.

In Western Europe, the Muslims continued to lose ground in Spain, while the English Plantagenet kings were similarly on the defensive in France. Henry III (1216-72) failed to defeat the French and regain the lands lost by his father, John. In 1224 war with France resumed and Louis VIII successfully invaded Poitou and Gascony, though Bordeaux remained faithful to Henry, in part because of its commercial links with England. By the Treaty of Paris (1259), Henry III renounced his rights to Normandy, Anjou and Poitou.

Norway, too, suffered a reverse in its interests across its maritime empire. It obtained the submission of the Icelanders (1248), but lost territory to Scotland. In 1098 Magnus Barelegs had secured by treaty Norwegian rule of the islands to the west of Scotland. By the Treaty of Perth (1266), however, the Western Isles were regained by Scotland, a consequence of the failure of Hakon IV of Norway to overcome Alexander III of Scotland at Largs (1263), and the general failure of the entire campaign.

The increasing assertiveness of the Scottish kings provides a good example of the role of able monarchs, improved administrative and military mechanisms and the support of the Church in the formation of states, rather than of ethnic homogeneity. Though the authority of the kings over much of their kingdom, especially Galloway, the Highlands and the Isles, was limited, the fertile central belt was under secure control. Although ethnically diverse, Scotland was more politically united than Wales or Ireland. This was related to the introduction of Norman administrative methods and feudal tenures by David I (1124-53), who had been educated at the court of his brother-in-law, Henry I of England. Normanization also affected the Church, leading to new monastic foundations, the appointment of Anglo-French bishops, and thus to stronger Continental links. The Norman military machine of knights and castles, improved administrative mechanisms (especially the use of sheriffs), the skill of the rulers, and economic expansion served as the bases for an extension of royal power in the 13th century.

NORWAY

Nidaros

Oslo

SWEDEN

Lapps

Åbo

NOVGOROD

VELIKI USTYUG

BELOOZERO

GALICH

(to Denmark)
Reval

Lake
Peipus

Novgorod

KOSTROMA
YAROSLAVL

UGLICH
PEREYASLAVL
ROSTOV
YURIEV
SUZDAL-
NIZHEGOROD

Volga

Pskov

Riga

ORDER

Dünaburg

Polotsk

(to Novgorod)

TVER
DMITROV

SUZDAL
Vladimir

STARODUB
VLADIMIR

Aarhus

Roskilde

BALTIC
SEA

Königsberg

Vilnius

Vitebsk

POLOTSK

MUSCOVY
Moscow

MUROM

DENMARK

Hamburg
Bremen
Elbe
Hanover

Stettin

POMERELIA

TEUTONIC

LITHUANIA

SMOLENSK

Smolensk

Tula

RYAZAN

Don

MALL

GREAT
POLAND

Poznań

CUJAVIAN
PRINCIPALITIES
MAZOVIA

BERESTIE

TUROV-PINSK

CHERNIGOV

Meissen
Wahlstatt

SILESIAN

Wrocław

PRINCIPALITIES

LITTLE
POLAND

VLADIMIR

Oder

NOVGOROD
SEVERSK

Prague

BOHEMIA

Nuremberg

Brünn

MORAVIA

Cracow

ISYA-
SLAVL

SVIZH-
DEN

KIEV

Kiev

PEREYASLAVL

Sarai

Volga

KREMENETS

Galich

GOLDEN   HORDE

Munich

AUSTRIA

Pozsony

Eger

Kassa

GALICH

Dnieper

Salzburg

Vienna

Buda

Debrecen

Dniester

Innsbruck

STYRIA
Graz

HUNGARY

Kolozsvár

Pécs

Szeged

Temesvár

Brassó

Caffa
(to Genoa)

GEORGIA

Zágráb

BLACK   SEA

Bologna
Florence

VENETIAN REPUBLIC

Zara
Spalato

BOSNIA

Belgrade

PAPAL
STATE

Rome

SERBIA

Nish

Danube

BULGARIA

Tirnovo

Varna

Trebizond

EMPIRE OF TREBIZOND

Bari

Naples

Taranto

Scupi

Serdica

Philippopolis

Adrianople

Salonica

BYZANTINE   EMPIRE

Constantinople

Angora

RUM
(ICONIUM)

ILKHAN

EMPIRE

Tigris

Mosul

KINGDOM OF SICILY

DESPOTATE OF EPIRUS

DUCHY
OF
ATHENS
Athens

Smyrna

LESSER
ARMENIA

Euphrates

Palermo

Messina

Catania

PR. OF ACHAIA

SEA

COUNTY OF
TRIPOLIS

MAMELUKES

Malta

(to Venice)

Crete

KINGDOM
OF CYPRUS

Nicosia

KINGDOM OF
JERUSALEM

Beirut

Damascus

Bedouins

89

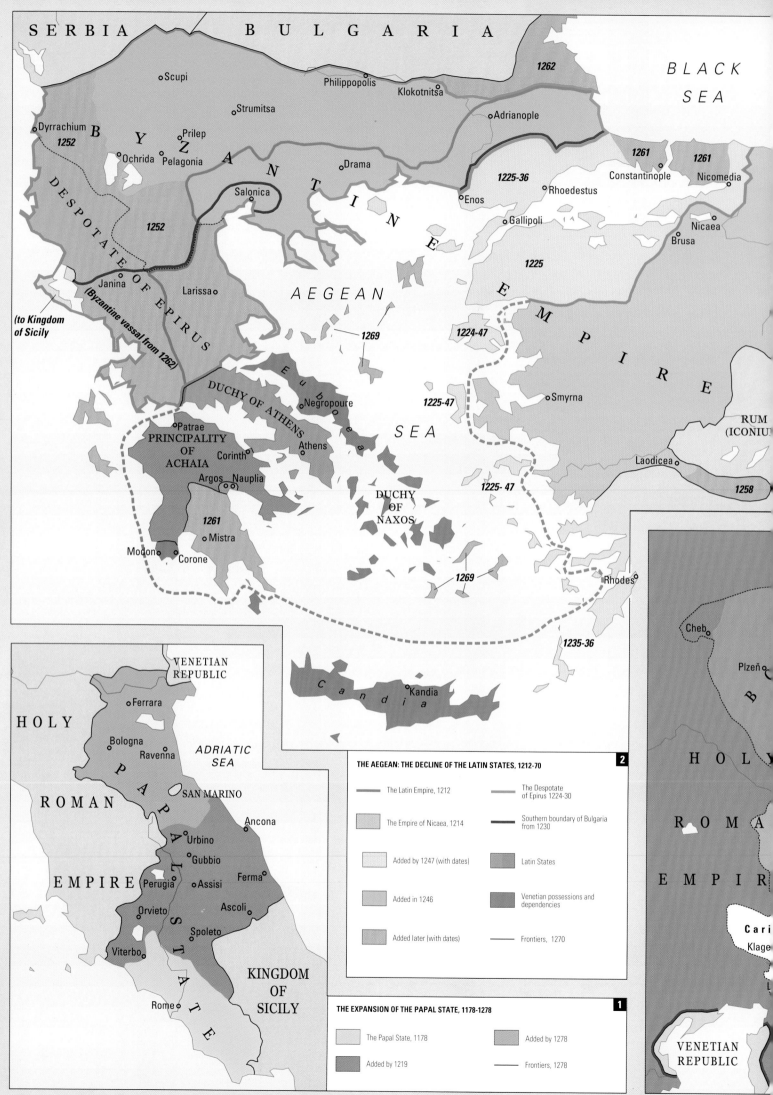

SERBIA   B U L G A R I A

BLACK
SEA

Scupi

Philippopolis
Klokotnitsa *1262*

Strumitsa

Dyrrachium B Prilep
1252 Y Ochrida Pelagonia
Z Adrianople
DESPOTATE OF EPIRUS A Drama *1261* *1261*
1252 N Constantinople Nicomedia
Salonica T *1225-36*
1252 I Rhoedestus
N Enos Nicaea
(Byzantine vassal from 1262) Janina E Gallipoli Brusa

(to Kingdom
of Sicily Larissa

A E G E A N *1225*

E

1269 M
1224-47 P
I
R
1225-47 E

DUCHY OF ATHENS E S E A Smyrna
u
b Negropoure
PRINCIPALITY Patrae o Athens RUM
OF e (ICONIU
ACHAIA Corinth a DUCHY *1225- 47* Laodicea
Argos Nauplia OF
NAXOS *1258*
1261 Mistra
Modon *1269* Rhodes
Corone

1235-36

Cheb

Plzeň

VENETIAN
REPUBLIC

Ferrara C
a
HOLY n
d
Bologna i
Ravenna a Kandia HOLY
ADRIATIC
SEA
ROMAN ROMA
SAN MARINO

Ancona THE AEGEAN: THE DECLINE OF THE LATIN STATES, 1212-70 **2** EMPIR
Urbino
EMPIRE Gubbio — The Latin Empire, 1212 — The Despotate
Perugia Ferma of Epirus 1224-30
Assisi
Orvieto The Empire of Nicaea, 1214 — Southern boundary of Bulgaria Cari
Ascoli from 1230 Klage
Spoleto KINGDOM
Viterbo OF Added by 1247 (with dates) Latin States
SICILY
Rome Added in 1246 Venetian possessions and
dependencies

Added later (with dates) — Frontiers, 1270

THE EXPANSION OF THE PAPAL STATE, 1178-1278 **1**

The Papal State, 1178 Added by 1278 VENETIAN
REPUBLIC
Added by 1219 — Frontiers, 1278

The Expansion of the Papal State, 1178-1278

1 The struggle between the Hohenstaufens and their opponents (*see* map 4, page 83) allowed the papacy to expand its territory in Italy. The Emperor Frederick II (1212-50) sought to consolidate Imperial power in Italy, but was excommunicated by the papacy and opposed by the Lombard cities. In Sicily, however, Frederick bloodily suppressed a Muslim rebellion that had begun in 1189, and which had left the mountainous interior of the island in practice an independent state that resisted the Christians and sought help from Muslim powers elsewhere. Between 1220 and 1246 Frederick launched a series of campaigns which destroyed the Muslim community of Sicily. His opponents elsewhere in Italy were more successful. Frederick's son Conrad IV (1250-4) continued the struggle with the papacy, but the position of his son Conradin was usurped by Frederick's second son Manfred, allowing the Pope to declare the throne forfeit and to offer it to Louis IX of France who passed it on to his brother, Charles of Anjou. As part of a crusade Charles defeated Manfred in 1266 and Conradin at Tagliacozzo (1268), ending the Hohenstaufen state in southern Italy and transferring the kingdom of Sicily to the Angevins. That transfer lasted only until 1282 when, in the Sicilian Vespers, Sicily revolted and turned to the house of Aragon. Thereafter Sicily and Naples were different states.

The papacy was able to benefit from the weaknesses of its Italian opponents to expand northwards, first into the Duchy of Spoleto and the March of Ancona, and then into the Romagna. The Frankish rulers had granted the papacy much of central Italy in the 8th century, but it had proved very difficult for the popes to wield effective control outside the area near Rome, and the lands to the east of the Apennines were in effect independent. Similar problems arose with the lands bequeathed to the papacy by the pious Countess Mathilda of Tuscany, who died in 1115. Under Innocent III (Pope, 1198-1216) there was a major attempt to give meaning to papal territorial claims and this was continued under his successors. This was achieved by obtaining Imperial renunciation of territory and by granting papal "bulls" of protection. The popes began to organize their territory more effectively, creating provinces governed by rectors.

The Aegean: the Decline of the Latin States, 1212-70

2 The Latin Empire created after the Fourth Crusade in 1204 faced Greek opposition divided between the Despotate of Epirus and the Empire of Nicaea. At first it seemed as if Epirus would be the most serious threat to the Latins. Epirus, however, was decisively defeated by the Bulgarians in 1230, leaving the way clear for the Empire of Nicaea to claim the Byzantine mantle.

Emperor John III Vatatzes (1222-54) played the crucial role in the firm establishment of the Empire of Nicaea. In 1225 he decisively defeated the Latins and occupied almost all their territory in Asia Minor. The Nicaean fleet then took the Aegean islands of Lesbos, Chios, Samos and Icaria. Vatatzes's army also captured much of eastern Thrace.

The Byzantines were soon able to recapture more land in the Balkans. The Mongol invasion in 1241 (*see* page 88) severely weakened the Bulgarians, and the Byzantine Emperor took advantage of this to extend his territory deep into Thrace and Macedonia: in December 1246 he entered Salonica; in 1252, as a result of an unsuccessful campaign against the Nicaean Emperor, the Despot of Epirus, Michael II, was forced to cede the eastern portion of his domains to Nicaea. It was the Nicaean Emperor Michael VIII (1258-82), who finally retook Constantinople in 1261, restoring it to Byzantine rule after the 45-year Latin occupation. As part of the surrender he acquired the area around Mistra in the Peloponnese.

Latin rule, however, still clung on in places. Venice retained many of its gains, particularly Crete which increased its power in the eastern Mediterranean, while the surviving Latin principalities, Athens and Achaia, were driven to seek the support of Charles of Anjou, the brother of Louis IX of France, who in 1266 had conquered southern Italy, killing its Hohenstaufen ruler at the battle of Benevento. With that base he wished to create a second Latin empire in the eastern Mediterranean. He gained Corfu and the Latin kingdom of Achaia (1267) and then conquered much of Epirus, being crowned King of Albania.

The loss of Constantinople marked a major defeat for Western Christendom, for the Latin Patriarch who had been installed in Constantinople was replaced by the Greek Patriarch, now returned from Nicaea. The Armenian Church remained faithful to the Papacy, but the Bulgars, who had agreed to transfer their allegiance to the Papacy in return for a patriarch of their own at Trnovo, reverted to Orthodoxy in 1235.

Bohemian Expansion under Ottakar II, 1250-69

3 The kingdom of Bohemia expanded greatly in the 13th century. Ottokar II (1253-78) did not become king until 1253, but in 1251 he had already been elected Duke of Austria and Styria. He suffered a setback when he lost Styria to Hungary in 1254. He regained it, however, in 1260, and, funded by the silver mines of Bohemia and Moravia, he continued his southward expansion, gaining Carinthia and Carniola. However, the new Holy Roman Emperor, Rudolf II (1273-91), drove him from all but the original provinces of the crown of Bohemia by 1276, and Ottokar's successors looked to the north and east instead. Wenceslaus II (1278-1305) was elected King of Poland (1306) and his son Wenceslaus III (1305-6) King of Hungary (1301).

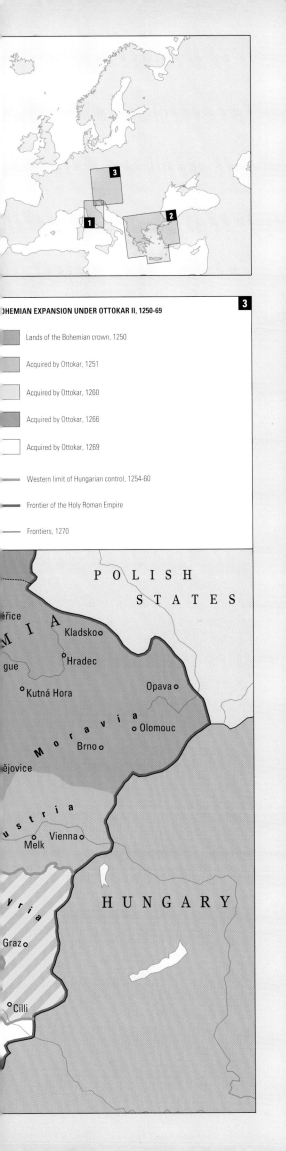

BOHEMIAN EXPANSION UNDER OTTOKAR II, 1250-69 **3**

- Lands of the Bohemian crown, 1250
- Acquired by Ottokar, 1251
- Acquired by Ottokar, 1260
- Acquired by Ottokar, 1266
- Acquired by Ottokar, 1269
- Western limit of Hungarian control, 1254-60
- Frontier of the Holy Roman Empire
- Frontiers, 1270

POLISH STATES

Kladsko

Hradec

gue

Kutná Hora

Opava

Moravia

Olomouc

Brno

ejovice

ustria

Vienna

Melk

yria

HUNGARY

Graz

Cilli

1270

The Consolidation of England

The fall of Acre in 1291 marked the end of the crusading presence in Palestine and Syria, but not the end of the crusading movement. The Knights of St John (Hospitallers) established a new base on Rhodes (1309), while Cyprus – which had been captured from its Byzantine ruler by Richard I of England and sold by him to his friend Guy of Lusignan, the former king of Jerusalem – remained under the Lusignan kings until acquired by Venice in 1489. Crusading also continued in the eastern Baltic. The Swedes proceeded with their conquest of southern Finland, where their position was recognised by Novgorod in 1323, while the Teutonic Knights moved their headquarters from Acre to Marienburg (1309) and waged war with the pagan Lithuanians. Meanwhile the French monarchy continued to expand, adding Flanders and several areas in the south to the royal domain by 1328.

The revived Byzantine Empire was unable to resist Ottoman advances in Anatolia, while there was also pressure on its northern frontier: under Tudor Svetoslav (1300-21), Bulgaria revived, after a period as a tributary of the Mongol Golden Horde, and expanded to include most of Macedonia and much of Serbia. These gains were, however, lost to the Serbs under Stefan Uros II (1282-1321) and Stefan Uros III (1321-31). The latter gained control over much of the strategic Vardar valley from Bulgaria and Byzantium.

Further north the power of the rulers of Hungary was greatly limited by the growth of aristocratic power. The native Arpad dynasty died out in 1301 and the first of the Angevin rulers was elected king in 1308. From his capital at Visegrád, Charles I (1308-42) reduced the power of the magnates, but it proved difficult to retain control of frontier areas: northern Serbia and Dalmatia were lost. In 1310, meanwhile, John of Luxemburg was elected king of Bohemia (1310-46). He held much of Poland too, particularly Mazovia (1329-51) and most of Silesia. John also expanded in other directions, gaining Upper Lusatia (1319) and, temporarily, the Tyrol (1335-42). Under Wladyslaw I (1305-33), Poland successfully resisted rule by kings of Bohemia, but lost territory to both Bohemia and Brandenburg. To the east, Lithuania under Gediminas (1316-41) was emerging as an important power, expanding into the Rus principalities, which were greatly weakened by the Golden Horde (the Mongols who settled the steppes of Russia after the invasion of 1240).

In Britain, the English rulers consolidated their position by the conquest of Wales. In 1277 Edward I (1272-1307) invaded with massive force and the support of other Welsh rulers: Llywelyn, who had been recognised by Henry III as Prince of Wales in 1267, was made to cede much of his territory. He rebelled and was killed in 1282. English power was then anchored by the building of a series of massive castles, while the independent Welsh principality was brought to an end. Edward I was less successful in Scotland. The death in 1286 of Alexander III of Scotland led to the succession of his young granddaughter, Margaret, the Maid of Norway. The Treaty of Salisbury (1289) secured Margaret's marriage to the heir of Edward I, the future Edward II. The rights and laws of Scotland were to be preserved, but 1289 prefigured the 1603 Union of the crowns. Margaret was succeeded in 1290 by John Balliol, chosen by Edward I as king and who swore fealty and did homage to him. For a while, the hegemony of the King of England over the British Isles seemed established. However, the eventual failure of his son, Edward II, to consolidate this position led to the recognition of Scottish independence (1328).

Habsburg possessions

Luxemburg possessions

Wittelsbach possessions

The Holy Roman Empire

Trondhjem

N O R W A Y

Oslo

S W E D E N

Åbo

Stockholm

(to Denmark)
Reval

Aarhus

Roskilde

BALTIC
SEA

Königsberg

Pskov

Riga

Danzig

Marienburg

Dünaburg

DENMARK

Hamburg

Stettin

Bremen

Hanover

BRANDENBURG

Leipzig

Dresden

Breslau

Poznań

Prague

Nuremberg

BOHEMIA

Brünn

Warsaw

Cracow

Vilnius

Vitebsk

Minsk

T E U T O N I C   O R D E R

MAZOVIA

L I T H U A N I A

POLAND

UPPER
LUSATIA

MORAVIA

BAVARIA

Munich

Salzburg

Innsbruck

AUSTRIA

Vienna

STYRIA

Graz

Pozsony

Buda

Visegrád

Debrecen

H U N G A R Y

Kolozsvár

Szeged

Pécs

Zágráb

Temesvár

VLADIMIR

ISYA-
SLAVL

SVIZH-
DEN

KREMENETS

G A L I C H

K I E V

Kiev

PEREYASLAVL

SMOLENSK

Smolensk

C H E R N I G O V

NOVGOROD-
SEVERSK

R Y A Z A N

NOVGOROD

N O V G O R O D

BELOOZERO

VELIKI USTYUG

GALICH

YAROSLAVL

KOSTROMA

UGLICH

ROSTOV

SUZDAL-NIZHEGOROD

STARO-
DUB

TVER

DMITROV

YURIEV

VLADIMIR

Moscow

MUSCOVY

MUROM

Kazan

Volga

G O L D E N   H O R D E

Sarai

Volga

Astrakhan

Don

Dnieper

Dniester

Venice

VENETIAN REPUBLIC

Zara

Spalato

BOSNIA

San Marino

PAPAL

STATE

Rome

NAPLES

Naples

Bari

Taranto

Belgrade

WALLACHIA

Danube

Tirnovo

Varna

Nish

B U L G A R I A

Burgas

SERBIA

Sofia

Skopje

Philippopolis

Adrianople

B Y Z A N T I N E   E M P I R E

Constantinople

(to Genoa)

Caffa

(to Genoa)

B L A C K   S E A

(to Genoa)

Trebizond

EMPIRE OF TREBIZOND

GEORGIA

ÇANDAR

Angora

I L K H A N   E M P I R E

Tigris

Mosul

Euphrates

OSMAN
(OTTOMAN)

KARASI

GERMIYAN

SARUHAN

SAHIPATA

LESSER
ARMENIA

Smyrna

AYDIN

LADIK

HAMID

KARAMAN

MENTEŞE

TEKE

DESPOTATE OF EPIRUS

DUCHY
OF
ATHENS

Athens

(to Genoa)

KNIGHTS OF ST JOHN

KINGDOM
OF CYPRUS

Nicosia

MAMELUKES

Beirut

Damascus

B e d o u i n s

Palermo

Messina

SICILY
(to Aragon)

Catania

Malta

S E A

Salonica

Crete

V E N E T I A N

R E P U B L I C

PRINCIPALITY OF ACHAIA

Lapps

10°

20°

40°

50°

60°

93

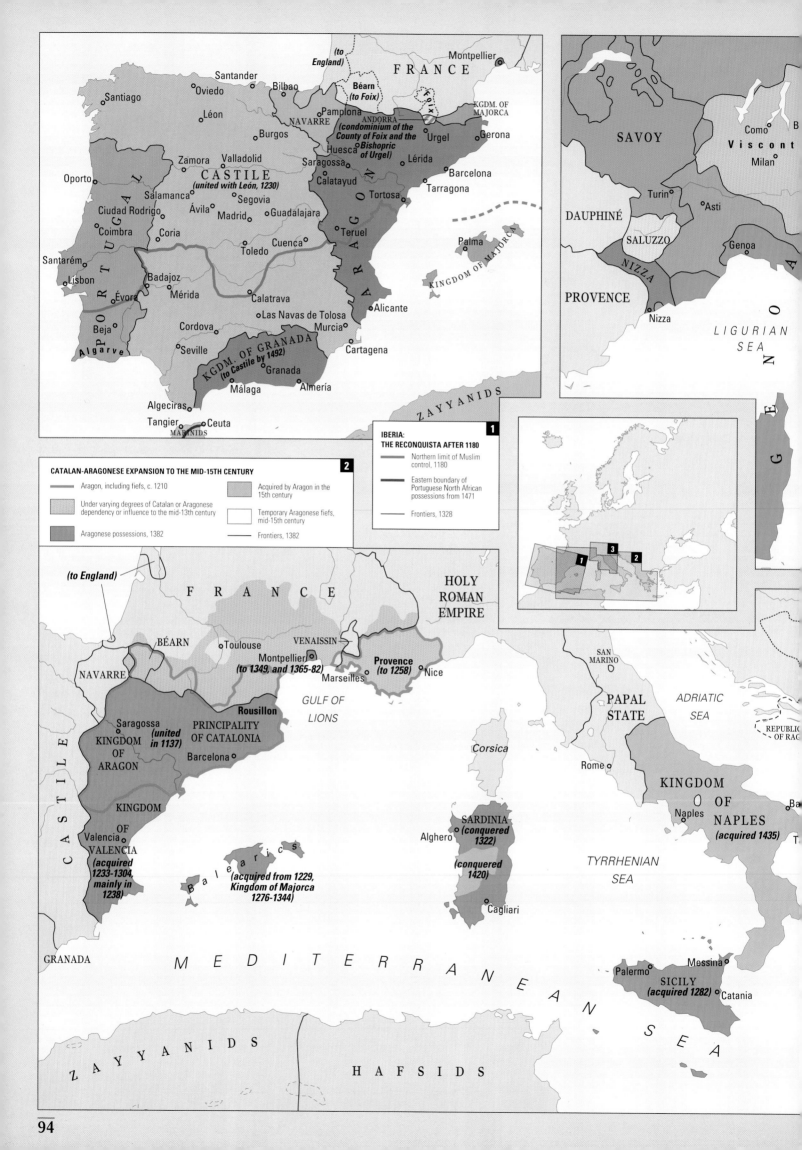

Montpellier

FRANCE

(to
England)

Santander

Oviedo

Béarn
(to Foix)

Santiago

Bilbao

Pamplona

KGDM. OF
MAJORCA

Léon

ANDORRA
(condominium of the
County of Foix and the
Bishopric
of Urgel)

NAVARRE

Urgel

Gerona

Burgos

Zamora

Valladolid

Huesca

Saragossa

Lérida

Barcelona

CASTILE
(united with León, 1230)

Calatayud

Tarragona

Salamanca

Segovia

Tortosa

ARAGON

Ciudad Rodrigo

Ávila

Madrid

Guadalajara

PORTUGAL

Coimbra

Coria

Teruel

Oporto

Cuenca

Toledo

Palma

Santarém

Badajoz

Calatrava

Lisbon

Mérida

KINGDOM OF MAJORCA

Évora

Alicante

Beja

Cordova

KGDM. OF GRANADA
(to Castile by 1492)

Murcia

Cartagena

Seville

Granada

Algarve

Málaga

Almería

Algeciras

Tangier

Ceuta

MARINIDS

ZAYYANIDS

SAVOY

Como

VISCONT

Milan

DAUPHINÉ

Turin

Asti

SALUZZO

NIZZA

Genoa

PROVENCE

Nizza

LIGURIAN
SEA

IBERIA:
THE RECONQUISTA AFTER 1180 ▮ **1**

— Northern limit of Muslim
control, 1180

— Eastern boundary of
Portuguese North African
possessions from 1471

— Frontiers, 1328

CATALAN-ARAGONESE EXPANSION TO THE MID-15TH CENTURY ▮ **2**

— Aragon, including fiefs, c. 1210

Acquired by Aragon in the
15th century

Under varying degrees of Catalan or Aragonese
dependency or influence to the mid-13th century

Temporary Aragonese fiefs,
mid-15th century

Aragonese possessions, 1382

— Frontiers, 1382

(to England)

FRANCE

HOLY
ROMAN
EMPIRE

BÉARN

Toulouse

VENAISSIN

NAVARRE

Montpellier
(to 1349, and 1365-82)

Provence
(to 1258)

Nice

Marseilles

SAN
MARINO

ADRIATIC
SEA

GULF OF
LIONS

Rousillon

PRINCIPALITY
OF CATALONIA

Saragossa

PAPAL
STATE

REPUBLIC
OF RAG

(united
in 1137)

KINGDOM
OF
ARAGON

Barcelona

Corsica

Rome

KINGDOM
O
OF
NAPLES

KINGDOM
OF

CASTILE

Valencia

VALENCIA
(acquired
1233-1304,
mainly in
1238)

Balearics

(acquired from 1229,
Kingdom of Majorca
1276-1344)

SARDINIA
(conquered
1322)

Naples

(acquired 1435)

Ba

Alghero

TYRRHENIAN
SEA

(conquered
1420)

Cagliari

GRANADA

M E D I T E R R A N E A N

S E A

Palermo

Messina

SICILY
(acquired 1282)

Catania

Z A Y Y A N I D S

H A F S I D S

NORTHERN ITALY, 1336 **3**

- States vassal to the Papacy
- Small states within the Holy Roman Empire
- Frontier of the Holy Roman Empire
- Frontiers, 1336

Iberia: the Reconquista after 1180

1 The Reconquista gathered pace again in the early 13th century, recovering the energy that had been shown in the late 11th century. The Almohads had displayed considerable vitality in the 12th century, heavily defeating Alfonso VIII of Castile at Alarcos (near Calatrava) in 1195. However, in 1212 Alfonso commanded the united armies of Castile, Aragon and Navarre and some crusaders in an advance south from Toledo which captured Calatrava and then crushed Caliph al-Nasir at Las Navas de Tolosa (16 July 1212), the crucial victory of the Reconquista. The exploitation of the victory was helped by the collapse of the Almohad Empire as a result of succession disputes. Most of southern Spain was overrun by 1275: Alfonso IX of León captured Badajoz in 1230; his son, Ferdinand III, King of Castile since 1217, inherited Léon in 1230. He captured Cordova in 1235 and Seville in 1248; his forces recaptured the valley of the Guadalquivir. Ferdinand's son, Alfonso X, conquered the emirates of Murcia and Niebla, leaving only the kingdom of Granada under the Muslims which, while in theory a vassal of Castile, was in practice independent. Meanwhile, James I of Aragon had captured the Balearic Islands (1229-35) and the Kingdom of Valencia, while the Portuguese advanced south to conquer the Algarve.

After this burst of activity, the Christian monarchs devoted most of their energies to attempting to resettle the lands they had conquered, from which many Muslims had fled or, as in the case of Andalusia and the cities of Valencia, been expelled; and to conflict with each other. This conflict was exacerbated by foreign intervention during the Hundred Years War between England and France (*see* map 3, page 103). English archers played a significant part in the battle of Aljubarrota (1385), where the Portuguese defeated a Castilian attempt at conquest. In 1386-87 Anglo-Portuguese forces jointly invaded Castile.

The Marinid Sultanate of Morocco, meanwhile, which had supplanted the Almohads in 1269, began attacking Christian Spain in 1275 and had some successes, but in 1340 Alfonso IV of Portugal and Alfonso XI of Castile decisively defeated the Marinids. The fall of Algeciras on the Straits of Gibraltar (1344) prevented further Moroccan intervention.

The advance against the Muslims resumed in the late 15th century. The Portuguese, who had expanded into Morocco, capturing Ceuta in 1415, added Arzila and Tangier in 1471. The marriage of Ferdinand of Aragon and Isabella of Castile in 1469 helped to unify Spain. Isabella inherited Castile in 1474, Ferdinand Aragon in 1479 and the two then ruled jointly. They turned against Granada from 1482 using artillery to capture the Muslim strongholds. Muslim disunity helped. One by one the remaining Muslim cities were taken. In 1492 the city of Granada itself fell. Spain no longer had a Muslim state. In 1497 a Spanish expedition captured Melilla on the Moroccan coast and the Reconquista was thus extended into Africa and the Mediterranean.

Catalan-Aragonese Expansion to the mid-15th Century

2 The opportunities for territorial expansion round the Mediterranean were demonstrated first by the expansion of Angevin power in the 13th century, and then by the house of Aragon. The Reconquista brought it Valencia and Majorca, the revolt known as the Sicilian Vespers (1282) led to the gain of Sicily, and in 1311 the Catalan Grand Company took the Duchy of Athens, which became a fief of Aragon in 1379. Meanwhile Aragon lost territory to the north of the Pyrenees. Provence was lost to Anjou, while James I renounced lands in France in 1258. The defeat of Peter I by Simon de Montfort at Muret in 1213, and the consolidation of French power in the Toulousain in the 1220s blocked any Aragonese hopes of expansion north of the Pyrenees. In 1435, on the death of the last Angevin ruler of Naples, Louis II, Naples passed to Alfonso of Aragon.

Northern Italy, 1336

3 Northern Italy owed nominal allegiance to the Holy Roman Empire. However, the cities of the region had for long had considerable rights of self-government and in some this had led to the development of republican communes. Other cities had fallen under the control of seignorial families. This was largely due to a need for stronger government, which led to a leading figure being given greater powers, or to an individual seizing these powers. Thus the Visconti came to dominate Milan, the Gonzaga Mantua, the Este Ferrara and Modena, and the della Scala Verona.

The della Scala family, which had ruled Verona since 1263, was at the height of its power in the mid-14th century. Cangrande I della Scala (d. 1329) extended their sway until, with the Visconti, they dominated Lombardy. Mastino II della Scala (1329-51) added control over Lucca, and later Parma, but fatally over-extended his resources, leading to the family's ultimate downfall. For the Visconti, Ottone Visconti, Archbishop of Milan (d. 1295), established the foundations of family power and from 1395 they were hereditary Dukes of Milan. Azzo D'Este (1205-64) established Este authority in Ferrara and the office of Signore of Ferrara was made hereditary in the family. Modena and Reggio were annexed by the Este. As yet, Venice had not begun to expand on the Italian mainland: her efforts were concentrated on the Dalmatian coast and in the Aegean. Only in 1339 did they change this policy with the annexation of Treviso.

This fragmented power structure of northern Italy contrasted with the more consolidated position in southern Italy. In the north the "state" was essentially a city or group of cities, while in the south the kingdoms of Naples and Sicily matched the governmental range, power and structure of developed states elsewhere in Europe.

1328

The Ottoman Advance

The Ottoman Empire was the most dynamic military power in Europe, western Asia and North Africa in the 14th, 15th and 16th centuries. Originating in Anatolia in the 13th century, this Muslim Turkish state expanded rapidly, helped by the ability of its ruling family, the house of Osman, and by the weaknesses of its opponents. The Byzantine Empire was unable to contest control of Anatolia and the Balkans effectively with them.

The Ottoman state originated as a frontier principality in the Byzantine-Seljuk frontier zone in north-western Anatolia. Under Osman I (c. 1281- c. 1324), the Ottomans expanded to the south of the Sea of Marmora. Under Orkhan (c. 1324-62) Bursa was conquered in 1326, becoming the Ottoman capital, and in 1354 Gallipoli, their first European foothold, was captured. From there, the Ottomans expanded in 1361 to capture Adrianople (Edirne), where they moved their capital in 1402. Under Murad (1362-89), expansion continued in Europe, particularly into Thrace, while in Anatolia the Ottomans expanded south towards the Mediterranean, completely absorbing the Emirates of Germiyan and Hamid by 1390 and 1392 respectively.

Further north, Moscow became the seat of a growing Russian principality, while Lithuania also expanded. To the west, the Danes sold Estonia to the Teutonic Knights (1346), and pawned their provinces in southern Sweden to the King of Sweden (they did, however, subsequently regain them), while King Valdemar Atterdag of Denmark conquered the Baltic island of Gotland from the Swedes (1360-1). The Danes were, however, defeated in 1370 by the cities of North Germany, who had joined together in the Hanseatic League . Meanwhile, France expanded its power in the Rhône valley, and in 1349 purchased the Dauphiné, a major gain to the east of the river. Further north, however, the Duchy of Burgundy, in theory a French fief, became more independent and powerful under Duke Philip the Bold (1363-1404), who gained the counties of Burgundy (1363) and Flanders (1384), both fiefs of the Empire. In the south of France, the Kingdom of Naples lost control of Provence in 1382.

Elsewhere, England and France were involved in the Hundred Years War from 1337 and the Scots became active as allies of the French. English power ebbed in Ireland. Though Edward Bruce's invasion of 1315 was crushed at the battle of Faughart (1318), and the scheme for a Scottish conquest of Ireland was thus wrecked, English lordship there did not recover. Despite major expeditions from England in the 1360s, 1370s and 1390, the situation continued to deteriorate. By the following century, direct English control was limited to the Pale, the area around Dublin, while the semi-autonomous Anglo-Irish lords and the independent Gaelic chieftains controlled most of the island.

Quite apart from the growing Ottoman threat, the 14th century was a period of crisis. The Black Death, an outbreak of bubonic plague which devastated Europe from 1346 to 1353, killed at least 20 million out of a European population of about 80 million. Further outbreaks later in the century prevented new population growth. This helped to exacerbate social and economic tensions: the socio-economic system of the "High Middle Ages" broke down, helping to cause a wave of rural and urban disorder. There was a sense of crisis in the Church, too: the transfer of the papacy to Avignon (1305-77) and the Great Schism (1378-1417) in western Christendom between areas owing allegiance to rival popes in Rome and Avignon challenged patterns of authority and obedience, contributing to a sense of fragmentation.

Trondhjem

N O R W A Y
(in personal union with Denmark)

Oslo

S W E D E N

Åbo

Stockholm

Reval

Estonia

Novgorod

N O V G O R O D

VELIKI USTYUG

MUSCOVY

Kazan

Gotland

Riga

Pskov

PSKOV

MUSCOVY

YAROSLAV

ROSTOV

SUZDAL-NIZHEGOROD

Volga

Aarhus
Copenhagen
Roskilde

Malmö

BALTIC
SEA

O R D E R

Dünaburg

TVER

Moscow

MUSCOVY

Nizhniy
Novgorod

Kazan

DENMARK

Königsberg

Vilnius

Vitebsk

(to Novgorod)

MUROM

Hamburg
Bremen

Stettin

Danzig

TEUTONIC

Smolensk

SMALL
PRINCIP-
ALITIES

RYAZAN

Don

BRANDENBURG

Berlin

Poznań

Vistula

Minsk

Hanover

Oder

SMALL
ATES

Leipzig

Dresden

Breslau

S I L E S I A

POLAND

Warsaw

Kiev

L I T H U A N I A

Sarai

kfurt

Prague

BOHEMIA

MORAVIA

Cracow

GALICH

Lvov

Dnieper

Volga

Nuremberg

Brünn

VLADIMIR

G O L D E N   H O R D E

tgart

Elbe

BAVARIA

AUSTRIA

Kassa

Dniester

Astrakhan

Munich

Salzburg

Pozsony

Vienna

STYRIA

Danube

HUNGARY

Buda

Graz

Debrecen

Kolozsvár

Suceava

nnsbruck

YROL

Venice

Pécs

Szeged

Temesvár

MOLDAVIA

(to Genoa)

VENETIAN
REPUBLIC

Zágráb

Belgrade

Brassó

Târgovişte

(to Genoa)

Caffa

San Marino

Zara

BOSNIA

WALLACHIA

PAPAL

Spalato

SERBIAN

Danube

B L A C K   S E A

GEORGIA

STATE

REPUBLIC
OF RAGUSA

Nish

B U L G A R I A N   S T A T E S

Varna

EMPIRE OF
TREBIZOND

Rome

NAPLES

Local rulers

Sofia

(to Genoa)

ÇANDAR

Trebizond

STATES

Skopje

Philippopolis

Adrianople

BYZANTINE
EMPIRE

ERETNA

Naples

Bari

Taranto

O T T O M A N

Salonica

Gallipoli

E M P I R E

Constantinople

Bursa

Angora

DULKADIR

Mosul

Palermo

Messina

MEGALO-
VLACHIA

BYZANTINE
EMPIRE

SARUHAN

GERMIYAN

Smyrna

KARAMAN

RAMAZAN

JALAYRIDS

SICILY
(to Aragon)

Catania

(Tocchi)

DUCHY
OF
ATHENS

(to
Genoa)

AYDIN

HAMID

Euphrates

TEKE

Tigris

Malta

PRINCIPALITY
OF ACHAIA

BYZANTINE
EMPIRE

Athens

VENETIAN
REPUBLIC

MENTEŞE

KNIGHTS OF
ST JOHN

KINGDOM
OF CYPRUS

Nicosia

MAMELUKES

Damascus

Bedouins

SEA

Crete

Lapps

97

NORTHERN ITALY AT THE PEAK OF VISCONTI POWER, 1390 `3`

— Held temporarily by the Viscontis (with dates)

Small states vassal to the Papacy

Other church states

Small Italian states and other states within the Holy Roman Empire

— Frontier of the Holy Roman Empire

— Frontiers, 1390

THE BALKANS ON THE EVE OF THE OTTOMAN CONQUEST, 1360

— The Byzantine Empire, 1340

— The Serb Empire, 1355

— Frontiers, 1360

States surrounded by the colour of Hungary were Hungarian fiefs

CENTRAL EUROPE: THE GROWTH OF ANJOU POWER TO 1382

Hungarian vassals, 1382 (with dates of final acknowledgement of Hungarian suzerainty)

Hungarian provinces governed intermittently by Bosnian and Wallachian vassal rulers

In personal union with Hungary, 1348-51

In personal union with Hungary from 1370

— Frontiers, 1382

Map 1 (Northern Italy): SAVOY · Como · Bergamo · BISHOPRIC OF TRENT · Trent · PATRIARCHATE OF AQUILEIA · Aquileia · Trieste · Milano · V i s c o n t i · Mantua · Padua · Verona · VENETIAN REPUBLIC · Venice · Chioggia · FRANCE · Turin · Asti · SALUZZO · *1347-82* · Gonzaga · Parma · Modena · Este · Ferrara · *1350-55* · HUNGARY · PROVENCE · Nizza · Genoa · GENOA · *1353-56* · Lucca · Bologna · SAN MARINO · Ancona · Pisa · Florence · PISA · FLORENCE · Siena · Visconti · PAPAL STATE · Perugia · Rome · KINGDOM OF NAPLES · SARDINIA *(to Aragon)* · Naples

Map 2 (Balkans): HOLY ROMAN EMPIRE · Zágráb · Pécs · Temesvár · Slavonia · HUNGARY · Belgrade · Croatia · Ozora · Só · Macsó · Dalmatia · BOSNIA · Lazar Hreblianovich · Vidin · Zara · Altoman · Nisho · Stra · Hum · Brankovich · Péc · SERBIA · Voislav Voinovich · Balshich · Vukasin & Ugliesha Marnavich · Dejanic · Skopje · Empres Helena · REPUBLIC OF RAGUSA · Ragusa · Durazzo · Charles Topia · Ochrida · Hlapen · Oliv Gerch · Saloni · Tom Prebliubovich · Simeon Urosh · Trikkala · Peter Liosa · KGDM OF NAPLES · Butrinto · Arta · Ian Spatas · DUC · Tocchi · Andravida · PRINCIPALITY OF ACHAIA · VENETIAN POS · Modon · Mistra

Map 3 (Central Europe): TEUTONIC ORDER · Poznán · Warsaw · HOLY ROMAN EMPIRE · POLAND · Cracow · GALICH-LODOMERIA *(to Hungary 1370)* · Galich · LITHUANIA · GOLDEN HORDE · Suceava · Baia · *(to Genoa)* · Buda · Fehérvár · Várad · Kolozsvar · MOLDAVIA *1372* · Zágráb · Pécs · HUNGARY · Temesvár · Brassó · Croatia · Belgrade · Dalmatia *(to Hungary 1358)* · Târgoviste · VENETIAN REPUBLIC · Ozora · Só · Macsó *(1339-42 to Serbia)* · Szörény · WALLACHIA *1365* · Zara · SAN MARINO · BOSNIA *1365* · Vidin · *1358 Lazar* · *1365 Stratsimir* · BULGARIAN STATES · Dobrotich · PAPAL STATE · REP. OF RAGUSA · Ragusa · *1358 Brankovich* · *1358* SERBIAN STATES · BYZANTINE EMPIRE · ADRIATIC SEA · *1358* · Cattaro · Local rulers · OTTOMAN EMPIRE · Manfredonia · Naples · Bari · KINGDOM OF NAPLES · Taranto · BYZANTINE EMPIRE · Megalovlachia · *(to Venice)* · *(to Genoa)* · SARUHAN · SICILY *(to Aragon)* · Tocchi · DUCHY OF ATHENS · PRINCIPALITY OF ACHAIA · *(to Knights of St John)* · BYZ. EMP. · AYDIN

98

The Balkans on the Eve of the Ottoman Conquest, 1360

1 On the eve of the Ottoman advance the most dynamic Balkan power was Serbia. Under the Nemanja dynasty, the role of the aristocracy was subordinated to royal power and territorial aggrandisement. Under Stefan Dušan (1331-55), Serbia expanded south and west to gain the rest of Macedonia, Albania, Epirus and Thessaly. Dušan also gained control of part of Herzegovina. He proclaimed himself Emperor of the Serbs, Greeks, Bulgarians and Albanians (1346), established a self-governing Serbian Orthodox Church with its own patriarch at Peć and moved his capital south to Skopje. Dušan had ambitions to supplant Byzantium in the Balkans and the expansion of his state clearly gained from its weaknesses. However, as so often in an age of hereditary monarchy, the fortunes of Serbia were compromised by weak successors, whose power was only nominal and under whom Serbia quickly disintegrated into local principalities, some of which became vassals of Hungary. At the same time Bulgaria fell into decline, and broke into three independent states.

The Balkans were now covered by more than 20 mini-states – including the Byzantine Empire in its terminal state of decline – all quarrelling with each other and ill-prepared to face the growing challenge of the Ottomans. Byzantium's remaining strength, in particular, was sapped by a bitter civil war which broke out on the death of Emperor Andronicus III in 1341. The loss of Epirus and Thessaly to the Serbs and Chios to the Genoese in 1346 left the Empire shrunken and unable to resist the Turkish advance. In 1354 the Ottomans seized Gallipoli, their first significant European foothold.

Central Europe: the Growth of Anjou Power to 1382

2 Charles I, the first of the Angevin rulers of Hungary (1308-42), had greatly increased royal authority and had also strengthened the economy. His successor, Louis the Great (1342-82), considerably extended Hungarian territorial power, greatly helped by the weakness of Serbia after the death of Stefan Dušan in 1355. To the east, Moldavia emerged under the suzerainty of Hungary (1372), which then gradually expanded its power towards the Dniester and the Black Sea. To the south suzerainty was again acknowledged by Wallachia and also, temporarily, by parts of Serbia and Bulgaria, and, reluctantly, by Bosnia. On the Adriatic the Republic of Ragusa accepted Hungarian sovereignty in 1358, while a bitter Hungarian war with Venice left Louis in control of Dalmatia.

Louis led two campaigns to Naples to revenge the murder of his brother, who had been King of Naples. He then took the crown for himself, and Naples was united with Hungary in a personal union (1348-51). To the north, Galich was gained by Hungary in 1370 and that year Louis succeeded the childless Casimir the Great as King of Poland. This amalgamation was not long to survive the death of Louis in 1382, an indication of the essentially transient nature of state-building, especially in Eastern Europe. Louis' authority had reached from the Adriatic to the Black Sea, from the Serbian valley of the Vardar to the frontier of Prussia, but there was no political, strategic, economic, geographical or ethnic logic to such a conglomeration and no real constituency of interest or opinion behind it. Louis left no son to maintain the union, but, instead, two daughters. The elder, Mária, married Sigismund, the son of the Holy Roman Emperor, Charles IV, heir to the Luxemburg lands in Germany, and brought the Hungarian Crown lands as her inheritance; but Poland remained apart from this under Louis' other daughter, Hedvig. Her marriage to the Lithuanian Jagiello united Poland and Lithuania and proved a crucial influence on Polish history until the 16th century.

Northern Italy at the Peak of Visconti Power, 1390

3 Venice with its far-flung foreign empire was the most successful of the Italian powers, which by 1390 ruled Crete, Euboea, Zara, Dubrovnik and most of Istria. As yet, however, Venice ruled little on the mainland bar Treviso, acquired in 1339. In 1378-81 Venice and Genoa fought a war over Chioggia, a city just to the south of the Venetian lagoon. Venice regained the city and thus drove Genoa from the northern Adriatic. The basis for Venetian expansion on the mainland had been laid.

However, the most powerful Italian state at this time was Milan under its Visconti dukes. The most dynamic was Gian Galeazzo Visconti (1351-1402). In 1378 he succeeded his father, Galeazzo II, as joint ruler with his uncle Bernabò, but in 1385 he had Bernabò seized and became sole ruler: Bernabò was killed the following year. Gian Galeazzo then rapidly expanded his inheritance, in particular by seizing Verona and Padua, which made him the most powerful ruler in northeast Italy. Visconti power was then extended into Tuscany. Bologna was temporarily captured, taking advantage of the weakness of Papal power to the east of the Apennines. The title Duke of Milan, purchased from the Emperor in 1395, confirmed Visconti power, but it was really based on the large army he built up. Gian Galeazzo compared himself to Julius Caesar, but his opponents saw him as a tyrant like Nero.

Neighbouring city-states, particularly Florence and Venice, feared Visconti expansion and when Gian Galeazzo died unexpectedly in 1402 they used the opportunity to increase their territories at the expense of Milan. Smaller city-states, such as Pisa, Lucca and Siena, which had survived as independent republics into the 14th century, increasingly became unable to preserve their status without powerful protectors. Pisa, for example, fell to Florence in 1406, in the aftermath of Gian Galeazzo's death.

1382

1430

The Hundred Years' War

In 1430 the Hundred Years' War between England and France was at its height and with it the struggle for primacy in Western Europe. Edward III's mother, Isabella, was the daughter of Philip IV of France. As already tense Anglo-French relations deteriorated over Gascony, Edward broadened his challenge to Philip IV's nephew, Philip VI, by claiming the French throne (1337). The fortunes of the ensuing war were mixed, but the use of longbowmen helped to bring victory at Crécy (1346) and Poitiers (1356), leading to the Peace of Brétigny (1360), in which Edward promised to renounce his claim to the French throne, to Normandy and to Anjou, but was recognized as duke of the whole of Aquitaine, as well as ruler of Calais. Edward's acquisitions proved difficult to maintain and, by the Truce of Bruges (1375), he was left with little more than Calais, Bordeaux and Bayonne.

The initiative was not regained by the English until Henry V invaded France in 1415: at Agincourt his longbowmen blunted the successive advances of the French, with very heavy losses. On his second expedition, in 1417, Henry conquered much of Normandy, and in 1419 its capital Rouen. He was helped by serious divisions in the French camp, and in 1419 he won the alliance of the powerful Duke of Burgundy. Throughout the conflict, the successes of the kings of England owed much to the existence of French allies. The Hundred Years' War was, indeed, in part an international dimension to a series of French civil wars. The Kings of England had supporters in Normandy, Brittany, Navarre and, in the early 15th century, Burgundy, without whose support they would have fared much less well. Henry's victories led in 1420 to betrothal to Catherine, the daughter of Charles VI of France (1380-1422), and, by the Treaty of Troyes, he was recognized as Charles's heir and as regent during his life. The French Dauphin, from 1422 Charles VII, continued to resist, and Henry V died in 1422, possibly of dysentry, while on campaign near Paris.

Meanwhile in the east, the Ottomans continued to push forward into the Balkans. The Christians seemed powerless in the face of the relentless tide of their advance. Bulgaria succumbed rapidly: in 1385 Sofia fell to the Turks; the next year they took Nish; in 1388 what remained of Bulgaria was forced to accept Ottoman overlordship. In 1389, the Serbian army of King Lazar was defeated by the Ottomans at Kosovo, breaking the back of Serbia's resistance. The Byzantine Empire was reduced to a rump area around Constantinople and the Peloponnese. The most bitter blow was the fall of Salonica to the Turks in 1387. In 1396 a Hungarian-French crusade sent to relieve the Byzantines was destroyed at Nicopolis: the Empire was only saved by the intervention of the Mongol leader Timur, who destroyed the Ottoman army near Ankara (Angora) and imprisoned Sultan Bayezid. The Ottoman hold on Thrace was weakened and the Byzantines even recovered some territory, most notably Salonica, which they held until 1423, when, with Imperial troops unable to secure its defence, it was handed over to the Venetians.

In Scandinavia, the late 14th century saw the emergence of the Union of Kalmar (1397). Eric of Pomerania had been recognized as king of Norway in 1389 and of Sweden and Denmark in 1396, and in 1397 the notables of the three countries gathered at Kalmar to agree the framework for a permanent Union. Although they did draft an agreement setting out measures to secure the unification, in practice the Union remained a personal one.

NORWAY

Nidaros

Oslo

(Union of Kalmar)

Aarhus
Copenhagen
Roskilde   Malmö

DENMARK

SWEDEN

Stockholm   Åbo

Lapps

NOVGOROD

MUSCOVY

Novgorod

Reval   Pskov

Riga

PSKOV

Dünaburg

Königsberg

Danzig

Stettin

Berlin

Bremen

Hanover

Poznań

Elbe

Oder   Vistula

SMALL   Leipzig
STATES   Dresden

Breslau

POLAND

LANDS OF
THE BOHEMIAN
CROWN

Prague

Nuremberg

Warsaw

Vilnius

Vitebsk   Smolensk

Minsk

LITHUANIA

ROSTOV

TVER   Moscow   SUZDAL

Nizhniy
Novgorod

Volga

Kazan

Tula   Ryazan

SMALL
PRINCIP-
ALITIES

RYAZAN

Don

GOLDEN HORDE

Sarai

Volga

Astrakhan

Brünn

Cracow

Lwów

Kiev

Dnieper

Munich   AUSTRIA
Salzburg   Vienna

Pozsony

TYROL   Graz

STYRIA

VENICE

Venice

SAN
MARINO

PAPAL

Zara

Spalato

STATE

Rome

NAPLES

Naples   Bari

Taranto

Palermo   Messina

SICILY
(to Aragon)   Catania

Malta

HUNGARY

Buda

Pécs

Zágráb

Bosnian
rulers

Debrecen

Kassa

Szeged

Belgrade

SERBIA

Nish

Kolozsvár

Temesvár

Danube

Sofia

Suceava

Jassy

MOLDAVIA

Brassó

Targoviste

WALLACHIA

Nicopolis

Tirnovo

Philippopolis

Dniester

Dniester

(to Genoa)

Tana

(to Genoa)

Caffa

Varna

BYZANTINE
EMPIRE

BLACK SEA

(to Genoa)

GEORGIA

EMPIRE OF
TREBIZOND

Trebizond

Local
rulers

REPUBLIC
OF RAGUSA

OTTOMAN   Kosovo

Úskúb

Adrianople

Constantinople

Angora

AK KOYUNLU

Local
rulers

Salonica

EMPIRE

Local
rulers

Janina

(Tocchi)

BYZANTINE
EMPIRE

DUCHY
OF
ATHENS   Athens

(to
Genoa)

Smyrna

KARAMAN

RAMAZAN

DULKADIR

KARA
KOYUNLU

Mosul

BYZANTINE
EMPIRE

REPUBLIC

KNIGHTS OF ST JOHN

KINGDOM
OF CYPRUS   Nicosia

MAMELUKES

Beirut
Damascus   Bedouins

Crete

TEUTONIC   ORDER

BALTIC
SEA

Euphrates

Tigris

Euphrates

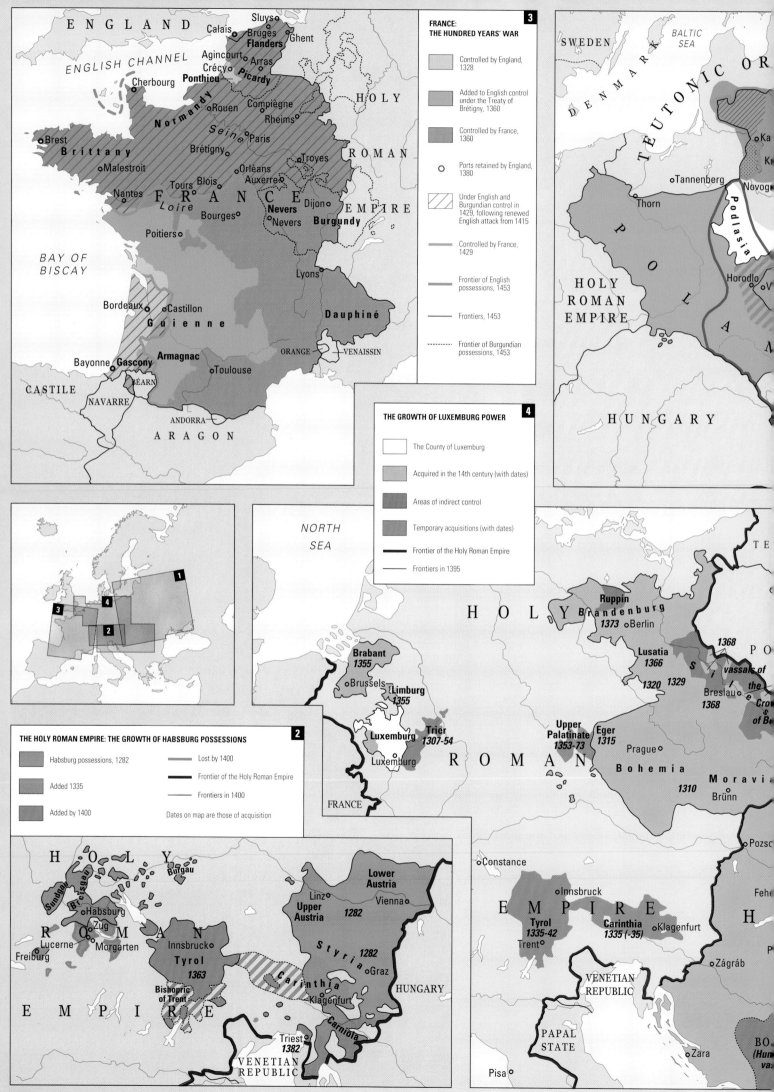

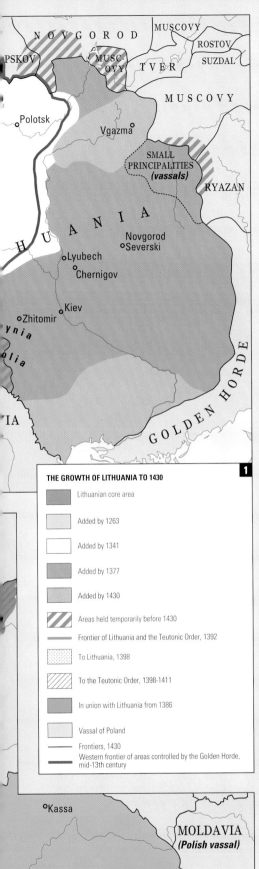

THE GROWTH OF LITHUANIA TO 1430

	Lithuanian core area
	Added by 1263
	Added by 1341
	Added by 1377
	Added by 1430
	Areas held temporarily before 1430
	Frontier of Lithuania and the Teutonic Order, 1392
	To Lithuania, 1398
	To the Teutonic Order, 1398-1411
	In union with Lithuania from 1386
	Vassal of Poland
	Frontiers, 1430
	Western frontier of areas controlled by the Golden Horde, mid-13th century

The Growth of Lithuania to 1430

1 The damage done to the Rus principalities by the Mongols and the continued pressure of their successors, the Golden Horde, created an opportunity for Lithuania to thrive. Founded in the 13th century by Mindaugas (d. 1263), this pagan state could not expand towards the Baltic because of the activity of the Teutonic Knights. Instead it expanded east, particularly in the earlier 14th century which saw the seizure of Polotsk as well as Podlasia. During the joint reign of Algirdas (1345-77) and Kestutis (1345-82), the southern lands of Kievan Rus were overrun: Novgorod-Severski fell in 1363 and Kiev in 1362-3. The Lithuanians thus expanded up to the lands of the Golden Horde. The Horde were then pushed back, so that by 1392 the Lithuanians had reached the Black Sea to the west of the Dnieper.

In 1385 a succession crisis in Poland led to a treaty at Krevo with Lithuania by which the Lithuanian Grand Duke, Jogaila, became King of Poland as Wladyslaw II Jagiello (1386-1434). In return the Lithuanians converted to Catholicism, although the two states continued to function as separate units. They united to fight the Teutonic Knights, who had been at war with Lithuania for much of the previous century. In 1410 the Polish-Lithuanian forces advanced into Prussia. At Tannenberg they crushed the Knights, killing the Grand Master, Ulrich von Jungingen, all but one of the commanders and 400 of the knight brothers. The Knights were greatly weakened, their period of expansion brought to a definitive close.

The Holy Roman Empire: the Growth of Habsburg Possessions

2 The Habsburgs were originally one of the second rank German princely families whose power expanded as the authority of the Holy Roman Emperor diminished. Their name is derived from the Habichtsburg (Hawk's Castle), built in about 1020 by the Bishop of Strassburg: the title Count of Habsburg first occurred in 1090. Initially, Habsburg power centred in Swabia, Alsace and northern Switzerland. In 1276, however, Rudolf I acquired Austria and Styria and this established the Habsburgs in the southeast of the Holy Roman Empire which, thereafter, was to be their centre of power. This advance was made at the expense of King Přemysl Ottakar II of Bohemia, who had been elected Duke of Upper and Lower Austria and had gained Styria, Carinthia and Carniola (see map 3, page 91). These were, however, only recent gains and thus the Habsburgs were able to advance into an area where there was no long-established state or dynasty to challenge their position. Rudolf's victory in battle in 1276 led, therefore, to a rapid transfer of control. From Austria and Styria the Habsburgs expanded to acquire Carinthia, Carniola and the Tyrol (in 1363). The Habsburgs also rose sufficiently in prominence for Rudolf I (1273-91) and Albert I (1298-1308) to become Holy Roman Emperors. In 1438 Albert II became Emperor and thereafter the Habsburgs held the title with only one short break until the end of the Empire in 1806.

In their Swiss heartland, however, the Habsburgs lost control to the demands of the Swiss cantons for autonomy. The Habsburgs had continued to expand their Swiss base in the 13th century, buying the lordship of Freiburg (1277), the town of Lucerne (1264) and Zug. In 1315, however, rising tension between the Habsburgs and the forest cantons led to warfare. Frederick of Habsburg's brother Leopold was routed at Morgarten. The Swiss cantons then rejected Habsburg seignorial rights. In 1385 Lucerne declared its independence. The Habsburg Leopold III was killed in battle against the Swiss near Zug in 1386, and a truce agreed in 1389 marked a permanent weakening of the Habsburg position in Switzerland as well as the creation of a strong Swiss confederation.

France: the Hundred Years' War

3 After the death of Henry V (see page 101), the tide of the Hundred Years' War turned against the English. Henry V's only son, Henry VI, became king when only nine months old and on the death of Charles VI was proclaimed King of France. The English strove to maintain Henry V's impetus and had some success until 1429. Charles VII, uncle of Henry VI, was, however, energized in 1429 by the charismatic Joan of Arc. That year, the English siege of Orléans was lifted by an army under Joan and Charles was crowned at Rheims. The balance of military advantage had shifted crucially and in 1435 the Burgundians abandoned Henry. Paris was lost in 1436 and the English were outmanoeuvred by the French, politically and militarily. In 1449-51, Normandy and Gascony fell swiftly to Charles VII's superior army, not least his artillery, and in 1453 an English riposte in Gascony was crushed at Castillon. The English were left holding only Calais.

The Growth of Luxemburg Power

4 The end of the Přemyslide dynasty in Bohemia (1306) was followed by an interregnum, and then by the election of John of Luxemburg (1310). Under John and his son Charles IV (1346-78) the power of the Luxemburg dynasty grew greatly. Charles was also Holy Roman Emperor and, by the Golden Bull outlining the imperial constitution (1356), the King of Bohemia was given precedence among the electors of the Empire. Charles also made Moravia, Silesia and Lusatia indissoluble parts of the Bohemian crownlands and acquired the Upper Palatinate (1353-73), Brabant and Limburg (1355), and Brandenburg (1373). His successor, Wenceslaus IV (1378-1419), lost Brandenburg (1411), however, and was opposed in Bohemia by the Hussites: a radical religious movement which gained support from Czech hostility to the Germans. Sigismund (1387-1437) became King of Hungary in 1387, Emperor in 1410 and King of Bohemia in 1419. He also conquered Bosnia. Sigismund took Luxemburg power to its greatest heights, but as with other dynastic accumulations, this was not to serve as the basis of a long-lasting state.

1430

1466

The Age of the New Monarchies

The later 15th century was in some senses the age of the "new monarchies" – consolidated states such as England, France and Scotland – where a number of changes helped to make political authority more clearly defined. One such was the general European trend towards more definite frontiers. This was partly responsible for much of the warfare of the 14th and 15th centuries, since lands whose status had been ill-defined for centuries were claimed and contended for by rival states. The implementation of firm frontiers was bound up with the existence of more assertive states and growing state bureaucracies, which sought to know where exactly they could impose their demands for resources and where they needed to create their first line of defence.

By 1466, the kings of England had lost virtually all their possessions in France, save Calais. The final stages of the Hundred Years' War saw the loss of Paris (1436), the surrender of Maine to the French (1448) and the French capture of Normandy by 1450. England became a typical "New Monarchy", based on a more-or-less precise territory, with an increasingly assertive central authority. This did not, however, mean that multiple kingdoms were redundant, more that the French empire of the English kings had been unsuccessful. There were a whole series of composite states or multiple kingdoms in Eastern Europe, for example Bohemia under Charles IV (1333-78), Poland-Lithuania from 1386, and Hungary under Matthias Corvinus (1458-90). At a lesser level, the marriage of James II of Scotland and Margaret of Denmark in 1469 led to the incorporation of Orkney and Shetland within the Scottish realm.

Central and Eastern Europe, however, experienced a time of particular turmoil, with the ever-present threat of the Ottoman forces diverting much-needed resources to the defence of Christendom. Bohemia, moreover, was rent by religious dissent. The followers of the Czech religious reformer, Jan Hus, who had been burnt at the Council of Constance in 1415, seized power in Bohemia in 1419. It was not until 1436 that Sigismund, the Hungarian king, was able to re-assert his authority there. In 1457, the Bohemians elected the Hussite George of Poděbrady as King of Bohemia. Pope Paul II preached a crusade against him, which led to an unsuccessful Hungarian invasion in 1468.

The danger posed by Turkish encroachments had grown so great that in 1443 a crusade set out, under the leadership of Wladislaw I, king of both Poland and Hungary. Initially the crusaders had great success, storming Nish and Sofia. The Ottoman Sultan was forced to agree a truce with the Christians in July 1444, but within a month Wladislaw had again advanced beyond the Danube as far as Varna. There Wladislaw perished and his army was routed. After this the Turkish advance recommenced. Setbacks such as the Ottoman failure to overcome Albania, defended resolutely by George Castriota (Skanderbeg) from 1443 to 1468, meant it was more difficult for them to tolerate the independence of Byzantine territory to their rear. In 1453, Mehmet II finally captured Constantinople, causing great consternation in the west. His army laid siege to Belgrade in 1456, but the siege was raised by the brilliant Hungarian leader, Janos Hunyadi. By 1460, the remaining Byzantine strongholds in the Morea had fallen and with the capture of Trebizond on the Black Sea in 1461, the last remnant of Byzantium was finally extinguished.

NORWAY

Nidaros

Oslo

SWEDEN

Åbo

Stockholm

BALTIC SEA

Reval

Novgorod

NOVGOROD

MUSCOVY

KHANATE OF SIBIR

Nizhniy Novgorod

Kazan

KHANATE OF KAZAN

(Union of Kalmar)

Aarhus
Copenhagen
Malmö

DENMARK

Riga

Dünaburg

Königsberg
Gdansk

Stettin

Hamburg

Elbe

Berlin

Hanover

SMALL

Dresden

SAXONY

LANDS OF THE BOHEMIAN CROWN

Prague

Brünn

Poznań

Vistula

Oder

POLAND

Warsaw

Wilno

Minsk

Vitebsk

Smolensk

Pskov

PSKOV

TVER

ROSTOV

Moscow

Tula

Ryazan

RYAZAN

SMALL PRINCIP-ALITIES

Don

GREAT KHANATE (GOLDEN HORDE)

Sarai

Volga

KHANATE OF ASTRAKHAN

Astrakhan

LITHUANIA

Kiev

Dnieper

Cracow

Lwów

Kassa

Munich
Salzburg

AUSTRIA
Vienna

Danube

Pozsony

Buda

Debrecen

Suceava

Dniester

KHANATE OF CRIMEA

Graz

STYRIA

HUNGARY

Szeged

Pécs

Kolozsvár

Jassy

MOLDAVIA

(to Genoa)

(to Genoa)

TYROL

Trieste

VENICE

Venice

FERRARA

SAN MARINO

Zara

Zágráb

Temesvár

Belgrade

Brassó

Târgoviste

WALLACHIA

Bucharest

Ruschuk

(to Genoa)

Caffa

SIENA

PAPAL

STATE

Rome

Mostar

Bosna Seray

HERZEGOVINA

Spalato

REPUBLIC OF RAGUSA

Nish

Sofia

Danube

Varna

BLACK SEA

GEORGIA

Trebizond

NAPLES

Naples

Bari

Taranto

OTTOMAN

Üsküb

Philippopolis

Adrianople

Constantinople

Angora

Tigris

KARA

Salonica

Janina

EMPIRE

Smyrna

KOYUNLU

DULKADIR

RAMAZAN

Mosul

Euphrates

Palermo

Messina

SICILY (to Aragon)

Catania

(Tocchi rulers)

REPUBLIC

Athens

(to Genoa)

Morea

KNIGHTS OF ST JOHN

MAMELUKES

KINGDOM OF CYPRUS

Nicosia

Bedouins

Beirut

Crete

Damascus

105

Map 4 — The Low Countries and Burgundy

NORTH SEA

ENGLAND

Friesland
Groningen
Amsterdam
Utrecht
Holland
Zutphen
Bishopric of Utrecht

HOLY
ROMAN
EMPIRE

Zeeland
Guelders
Bruges
Antwerp
Brabant
Calais
Ghent
Flanders
Boulogne
Artois
Brussels
Bishopric of Liège
Aix-la-Chapelle
Liège
Arras
Hainaut
Namur
Limburg
Picardy
Amiens
Pouthieu
Luxemburg
Luxemburg
Rethel
Verdun
Metz
Paris
Bar
Nancy
Strassburg
FRANCE
Troyes
Lorraine
Alsace

Duchy of Burgundy
Dijon
County of Besançon Burgundy
Nevers
Mâcon
Lyons

4

THE GROWTH OF BURGUNDY TO 1477

- Extent of Burgundian control, 1404
- Added by 1467
- Added by 1477
- Controlled by Burgundy, 1477
- Frontier of the Holy Roman Empire

THE GROWTH OF MUSCOVY TO 1466

SWEDEN

NOVGOROD
1478

TEUTONIC ORDER

Novgorod

Pskov
PSKOV
1510

GREAT
PRINCIPALITY

Yaroslavl
Rostov
PRINCIPALITY OF ROSTOV *1474*
Tver
Vladimir
Nizhniy Novgorod
OF
MOSCOW
GREAT PRINCIPALITY OF TVER *1485*
Moscow
Pereyaslavl Ryazansky
Ryazan
KHANATE OF KAZAN

LITHUANIA

GREAT PRINCIPALITY OF RYAZAN *1521*

GREAT KHANATE (GOLDEN HORDE)

- Muscovy, 1300
- Added by 1340
- Added by 1389
- Added by 1466
- Independent Russian states, with dates of later annexation by Muscovy
- Frontiers in 1466

Temporary acquisition is shown by crosshatching

ITALY: THE TREATY OF LODI, 1454

- Venetian Republic, c.1360
- Added by 1420
- Added by 1454
- Frontier of the Holy Roman Empire
- Frontiers in 1454

3

SWISS CONFEDERATION
HABSBURG POSSESSIONS
HABSBURG POSSESSIONS

SAVOY
FRANCE
VENAISSIN
Turin (Orléans)
Milan
MILAN
Lodi
MONTFERRAT
SALUZZO
TENDA
PROVENCE
MONACO
Genoa
REPUBLIC OF GENOA
MANTUA (Malaspina)
MODENA
Belluno
Verona
Vicenza
Venice
Padua
GÖRZ
VENETIAN
Ferrara
Ravenna
Bologna
LUCCA
Pisa
Florence
FLORENCE
Arezzo
SAN MARINO
Ancona
HUNGARY
PIOMBINO (protectorate of Florence)
Siena
SIENA
PAPAL STATE
Rome
NAPLES (to Aragon)
Naples
SARDINIA (to Aragon)
ADRIATIC SEA
REPUBLIC
Zara
HUM
REPUBLIC OF RAGUSA

(Balkans map)

Belgrade
Bosnia
Bosna Saray (Vrhbosna)
OTTOMAN
Herzegovina
REPUBLIC OF RAGUSA
Ragusa
Cattaro
MONTENEGRO
Serbia
Vidi
Nish
Kosovo Polje
Üsküb
Albania
Durazzo
Ochrida
Salonica
Otranto
VENETIAN REPUBLIC
Yanya (Janina)
Epirus
Thessaly
Patras
Morea
Modon
Mistra
NAPLES

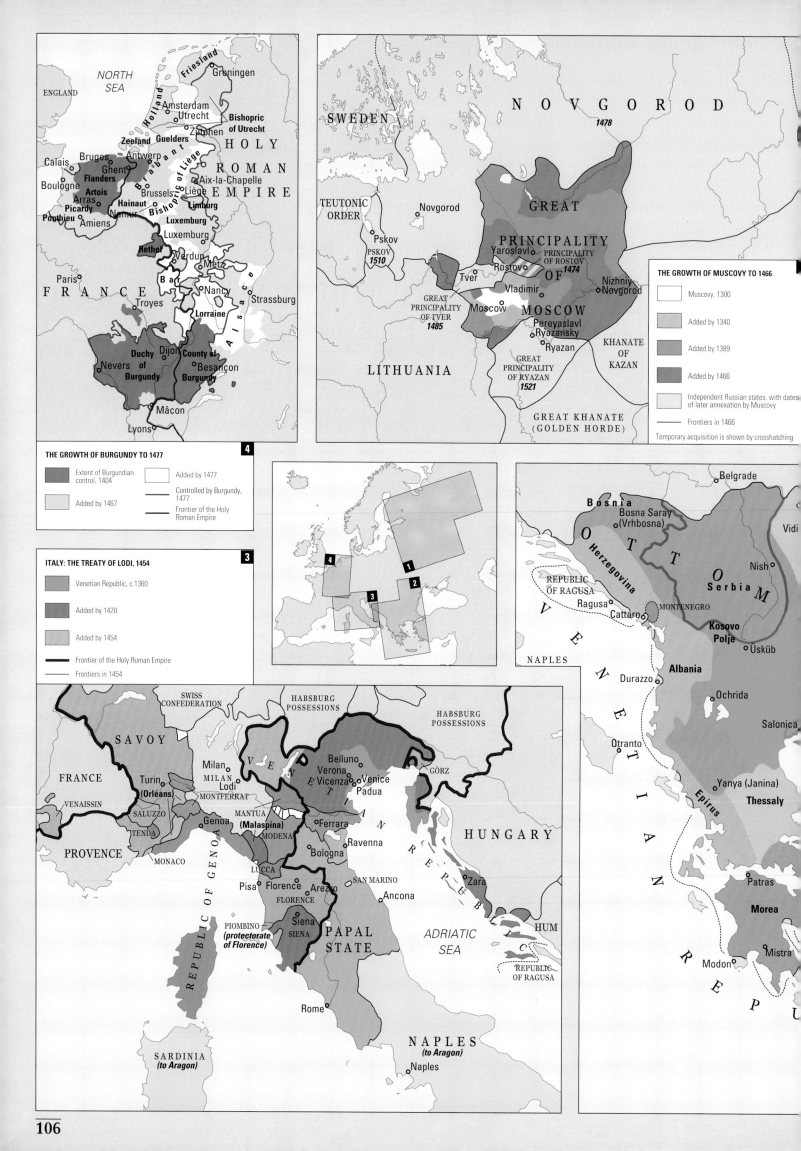

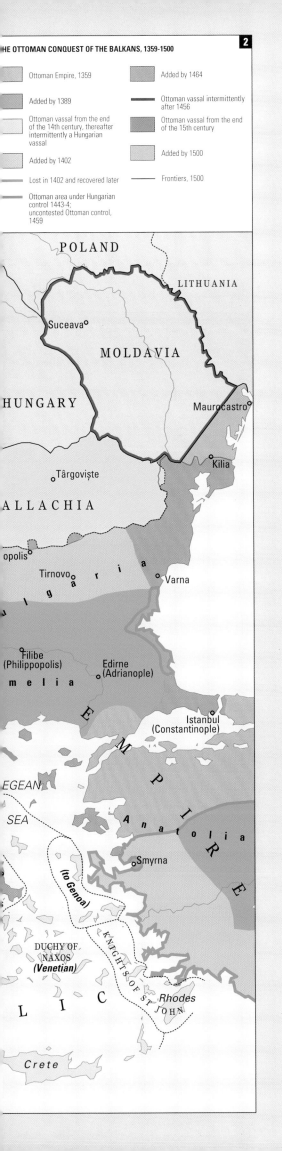

The Growth of Muscovy to 1466

1 The expansion of Muscovy was a slow process that owed much to the determination of its ruling house. Though the rulers of Rus were for long under the shadow of the Mongols and their descendants, the Muscovites were able to use this to their advantage: Ivan Kalita I (1328-41) gained the right to act as the tax collector of the Tatars and thus benefited from their power. This was not, however, a relationship free from tension and in 1445 the Tatars took Vasili II prisoner. Muscovy also faced challenges from other Rus rulers, such as the princes of Tver, who were not subdued until 1485. Other Rus states were unable to resist its expansion. Novgorod fell in 1478, Pskov in 1510. Ivan III, "the Great" (1462-1505), who conquered both Tver and Novgorod, refused to pay tribute to the Golden Horde and defied its attempt to intimidate him into doing so (1480). In 1493 he took the title "Sovereign of all Russia".

The Ottoman Conquest of the Balkans, 1359-1500

2 The crushing Turkish victory over the Serbs at Kosovo (1389) was the crucial triumph which anchored the Turks in the Balkans. The victor, Murad I (1360-89), added Rumelia (Thrace, Macedonia and southern Bulgaria) to the Ottoman Empire. After Kosovo, Serbia became a vassal state, the rest of Bulgaria was annexed (1389) and Wallachia, too, became a vassal state (1390). Constantinople was now completely surrounded, and from 1394 it was blockaded. Thessaly was then conquered. In 1396 a crusade to rescue Constantinople failed when a Hungarian-French army of 10,000 was routed at Nicopolis.

The move of the Ottoman capital to Adrianople (Edirne) in 1402 symbolised a shift in emphasis to Europe. Constantinople was reprieved for longer as a result of the advance of Timur (Tamberlaine) from Central Asia. Timur attacked and routed Bayezid in 1402 at Ankara. With Bayezid in captivity, the Turks made concessions to other opponents: Byzantium regained Salonica, and Wallachia, Serbia and Bosnia recovered their independence. Murad II (1421-44, 1446-51) restored the Turkish position. Wallachia, Serbia and Bosnia were subdued in the 1420s and 1430s, and Murad also expanded Turkish power into Epirus. In 1443 another crusade was launched. The Hungarians, under Janos Hunyadi, captured Nish and Sofia, Christians throughout the Balkans rebelled, particularly in Albania, and in 1444 an army of 20,000 under King Ladislas of Hungary advanced to Varna, only to be defeated by Murad II.

In 1453 Mehmet II (1451-81) laid siege to Constantinople, and finally took the city, putting an end to more than 1000 years of Byzantine history and inflicting a bitter psychological blow on Christendom. He then advanced on Belgrade in 1456, but his siege was broken by Hunyadi. Caffa in the Crimea was captured in 1475 and Albanian resistance was overcome in 1478. Mehmet also added the Morea (1458-60), the rest of Serbia (1459), southern Bosnia and Herzegovina (1463-82), and some of the islands in the Aegean. Wallachia became a permanent vassal state in 1476. In 1480 the Turks besieged Rhodes and landed at Otranto in southern Italy. Both initiatives were cut short by Mehmet's death, and under his successor, Bayezid II (1481-1512), the dynamism of Turkish expansion greatly slackened, although he conquered the important ports of Kilia and Akkerman (Maurocastro) on the Black Sea in 1484.

Italy: the Treaty of Lodi, 1454

3 Venice was the principal beneficiary of the collapse of Visconti power in northern Italy. After Gian Galeazzo Visconti died in 1402, Venice seized Belluno (1404), Vicenza (1404), Padua (1405) and Verona (1405). In another forward advance, Venice took Bergamo and Brescia in 1428. Ravenna was added in 1441. Milanese power was revived by Gian Galeazzo's son, Filippo Maria (1412-47), and the latter's son-in-law, Francesco Sforza, (1450-66), a *condottiere* (mercenary leader), who used his military strength to establish himself in Lombardy.

Further south, Florence expanded its power in Tuscany, acquiring Arezzo (1384) and the formerly powerful independent republic of Pisa (1406). The competing ambitions of these states led to much warfare, the costs of which encouraged peace negotiations, as did the Turkish challenge to Italy after the fall of Constantinople in 1453. This threat encouraged Pope Nicholas V to try to bring peace and form an anti-Turkish league. By the Peace of Lodi (1454) Italy's leading powers – Milan, Venice, Florence, Naples and the Pope – recognized each other's boundaries and laid the basis for over two decades of peace.

The Growth of Burgundy to 1477

4 The dynamism of its Dukes and the weakness of neighbouring states allowed Burgundy to expand greatly in the 15th century. The basis of its power was the marriage in 1369 of Margaret, the heiress of the County of Flanders, to Philip the Bold, Duke of Burgundy (1363-1404), the younger brother of Charles V of France, who had been established in Burgundy in 1363. Margaret brought Flanders, Artois and Nevers to Burgundy.

Philip the Bold's grandson, Philip the Good (1419-67), expanded Burgundian power in the Netherlands, acquiring Luxemburg (1451), Holland, Hainault, Friesland and Zeeland (all in 1433), Brabant-Limburg (1430) and the Somme towns with Ponthieu and Boulogne (1435). Most of this was by conquest or force, although Philip also bought Namur and obtained the reversion to Alsace from his aunt. His son, Charles the Bold (1467-77) gained Alsace, conquered Guelders and Zutphen (1472) and became involved in Lorraine. Burgundy was an expanding power, buoyed up by the commercial growth of the Low Countries which threatened France, but the Burgundian army was defeated by the Swiss at Nancy in 1477. Charles was killed, his army routed. The Burgundian inheritance was partitioned in the aftermath between the Habsburgs and Louis XI of France, who made important gains, including Burgundy and Picardy.

1466

The Later Middle Ages

The late 15th century saw a consolidation of many European states and a coalescence of Europe into the contours which were to shape it for almost 400 years, until the crisis of nationalism in the 19th century. In the southwest, the Spanish state emerged with the final conquest of Granada from the Muslims in 1492 and the Union of the crowns of Aragon and Castille. The French kings continued the process of expanding the royal domain, until by 1483 only the Duchy of Brittany remained more or less independent, and even this was to be absorbed early in the 16th century (*see* map 3, page 115). England, too, although she had lost her lands in France – except for Calais – by the Treaty of Arras in 1453 and was racked by a bitter civil war from 1453 to 1471, would begin to emerge under the Tudor dynasty from 1485 onwards as a maritime power, whose interests in terms of territorial expansion lay outside Europe.

Italy, after the Treaty of Lodi (1454, *see* map 3, page 107), experienced 20 years of relative calm, until the Venetians went to war with Ferrara from 1480. Although it faced a coalition of almost all the other Italian states, the settlement which ended the war in 1484 did leave Venice with some minor gains. More ominously, the Venetians had tried to induce the French king, Charles VIII, to invade Italy with the promise of their help to conquer Naples, an attempt which foreshadowed the French intervention in the catastrophic Italian wars of the next decade (*see* map 2, page 115).

In the east, Muscovy had emerged by the end of the 15th century as the predominant principality in Russia. The capture of Novgorod in 1478 and the adoption by Ivan III of the title "Sovereign of all Russia" marked the emerge of a new power in the east, and one which, with the disappearance of the Byzantine Empire in 1453, could claim to be the champion of Orthodox Christianity. The Ottoman advance which had swept away Byzantium slackened somewhat after the 1470s. A Turkish siege of Rhodes and the temporary occupation of Otranto in southern Italy in 1480-81 proved, however, that the threat was by no means over.

Throughout Europe in the Middle Ages, national boundaries were hardened and the concept of "statehood" was emergent, becoming politically more significant than the "nation", in its original meaning of a people of common descent. This development is most marked in the consolidation of England, France and Spain. The growth of national consciousness was not, however, dependent on the authority of a unitary state. The strong consciousness of Germanness and German nationhood evolved in a very different political context from that of England, France and Scotland. States which had developed by inheritance and conquest, such as Burgundy, while they were in theory subject to an individual ruler, in practice were too diverse to function as individual units. Their fragility was demonstrated by the partitioning of Burgundy after the defeat by the Swiss of Duke Charles the Bold at Nancy in 1477. The growth of the Swiss Confederation, too, demonstrates that national consciousness did not always develop hand-in-hand with a strong state, for the Swiss had no central authority, but still defended their lands tenaciously against threats from the Habsburgs and Burgundians, and extended the scope of the Confederation steadily in the last half of the 15th century.

NORWAY

Nidaros

Oslo

(Union
of
Kalmar)

Aarhus
Copenhagen
Malmö

DENMARK

SWEDEN

Åbo

Stockholm

BALTIC
SEA

Reval

Novgorod

MUSCOVY

Nizhniy
Novgorod

Kazan

Volga

KHANATE
OF
SIBIR

Pskov

PSKOV

Riga

TEUTONIC ORDER

Dünaburg

Moscow

KHANATE OF KAZAN

Königsberg
Gdańsk

Stettin

Wilno

Vitebsk

Smolensk

Tula

Ryazan

SMALL
PRINCIP-
ALITIES

RYAZAN

Don

GREAT KHANATE
(GOLDEN HORDE)

BRANDENBURG

Hanover
Berlin

Minsk

LITHUANIA

Poznań

Vistula

Warsaw

Dresden

Elbe

Oder

POLAND

Kiev

Sarai

Volga

KHANATE
OF ASTRAKHAN

Astrakhan

Prague

LANDS OF THE

Cracow

Lwów

Dnieper

BOHEMIAN CROWN

Brünn

Kassa

Dniester

Munich
Salzburg

Vienna

Pozsony

Buda

Debrecen

MOLDAVIA

Jassy

AUSTRIA

Graz

Trieste

Venice

HUNGARY

Pécs

Kolozsvár

Szeged

Temesvár

Brassó

KHANATE
OF CRIMEA

Kefe

Local rulers

Zágráb

Belgrade

WALLACHIA

FERRARA
SAN MARINO

Zara

Bosna
Serai

Bucharest

Danube

Ruschuk

LUCCA

PAPAL

Spalato

Mostar

Nish

Varna

BLACK SEA

GEORGIAN
STATES

STATE
Rome

REPUBLIC OF RAGUSA

MONTENEGRO

Üsküb

Sofia

Trebizond

Naples

Bari

Philippopolis

Adrianople

NAPLES
(to Aragon)

Taranto

Otranto

Janina

OTTOMAN

Constantinople

Angora

Tigris

EMPIRE

DULKADIR

AK KOYUNLU

Palermo

Messina

Smyrna

RAMAZAN

Mosul

SICILY
(to Aragon)

Catania

REPUBLIC

Athens
(to
Genoa)

Euphrates

Rhodes

MAMELUKES

SEA

KNIGHTS
OF
ST. JOHN

Nicosia

Beirut

Bedouins

Crete

Damascus

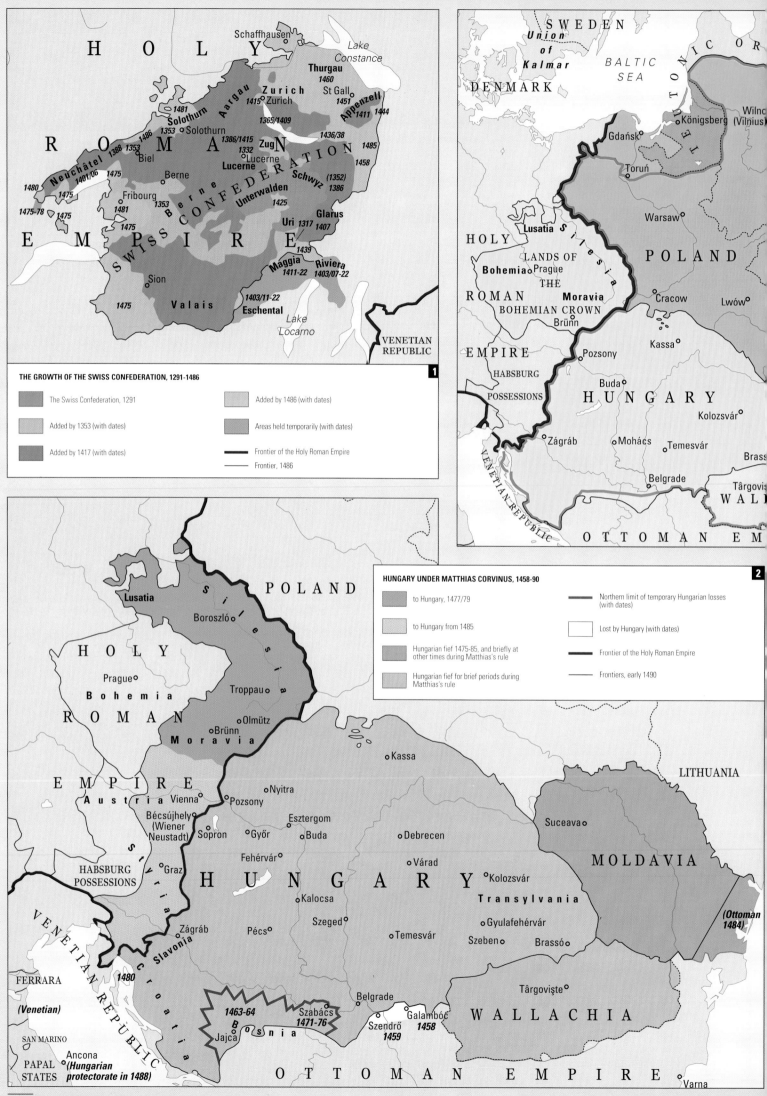

THE GROWTH OF THE SWISS CONFEDERATION, 1291-1486

H O L Y

Schaffhausen

Lake
Constance

Thurgau
1460

Zurich
1415 Zurich
St Gall
1451

Appenzell
1411 *1444*

1481
Solothurn
1353
Solothurn
1365/1409

1436/38

1485

R O M A N

1386 *1353*
Biel

1386/1415
1332
Lucerne

Zug

N

1458

1388 *1353*

Lucerne

1486

Neuchâtel
1401/06 *1475*

Berne

B
e
r
n
e

Unterwalden

Schwyz

(1352)
1386

1480

1475

1481

Fribourg

C
O
N
F
E
D
E
R
A
T
I
O
N

1425

E

1475-78 *1475*

1353

1407

Uri *1317*

Glarus
1407

E M P I R E

S
W
I
S
S

1475

Sion

1439

Maggia
1411-22

Riviera
1403/07-22

1475

Valais

1403/11-22
Eschental

Lake
Locarno

VENETIAN
REPUBLIC

1

▨ The Swiss Confederation, 1291	▨ Added by 1486 (with dates)
▨ Added by 1353 (with dates)	▨ Areas held temporarily (with dates)
▨ Added by 1417 (with dates)	▬ Frontier of the Holy Roman Empire
	── Frontier, 1486

SWEDEN
Union
of
Kalmar

BALTIC
SEA

T
E
U
T
O
N
I
C   O R

DENMARK

Wilno
(Vilnius)

Königsberg

Gdańsk

Toruń

Lusatia
S
i
l
e
s
i
a

Warsaw

H O L Y

LANDS OF
Bohemia Prague
THE
R O M A N
Moravia
BOHEMIAN CROWN
Brünn

P O L A N D

Cracow

Lwów

E M P I R E

Pozsony

Kassa

HABSBURG
POSSESSIONS

Buda

H U N G A R Y

V
E
N
E
T
I
A
N
-
R
E
P
U
B
L
I
C

Zágráb

Mohács

Kolozsvár

Temesvár

Brass

Belgrade

Târgovi
WAL

O T T O M A N   E M

HUNGARY UNDER MATTHIAS CORVINUS, 1458-90

2

▨ to Hungary, 1477/79	▬ Northern limit of temporary Hungarian losses (with dates)
▨ to Hungary from 1485	☐ Lost by Hungary (with dates)
▨ Hungarian fief 1475-85, and briefly at other times during Matthias's rule	▬ Frontier of the Holy Roman Empire
▨ Hungarian fief for brief periods during Matthias's rule	── Frontiers, early 1490

Lusatia

P O L A N D

Boroszló

S
i
l
e
s
i
a

H O L Y

Prague

Bohemia

Troppau

R O M A N

Olmütz

Moravia
Brünn

Kassa

E M P I R E

Nyitra

Austria Vienna

Pozsony

LITHUANIA

Bécsújhely
(Wiener
Neustadt)

Sopron

Győr

Esztergom

Buda

Debrecen

Suceava

S
t
y
r
i
a

HABSBURG
POSSESSIONS

Graz

Fehérvár

Várad

M O L D A V I A

Kolozsvár

Transylvania

H U N G A R Y

C
r
o
a
t
i
a

Zágráb

Kalocsa

Pécs

Szeged

Temesvár

Gyulafehérvár

Szeben

Brassó

V
E
N
E
T
I
A
N
R
E
P
U
B
L
I
C

1480

Slavonia

FERRARA

(Venetian)

SAN MARINO

PAPAL
STATES

Ancona
(Hungarian
protectorate in 1488)

B
o
s
n
i
a

1463-64

Jajca

Szabács
1471-76

Belgrade

Szendrő
1459

Galambóc
1458

(Ottoman
1484)

Târgovişte

W A L L A C H I A

O T T O M A N   E M P I R E

Varna

The Growth of the Swiss Confederation, 1291-1486

1 By the beginning of the 15th century the Swiss Confederation comprised eight *Orte* (territories): Berne, Glarus, Lucerne, Schwyz, Unterwalden, Uri, Zug and Zurich. Having freed itself from the abbey of St Gall, Appenzell joined in 1411. A truce with the Habsburgs negotiated in 1389 expired in 1415 and the Habsburgs were then driven from the Aargau. This did not become a canton, but instead a dependency. In the 15th century the Swiss Confederation expanded further, particularly to the southeast, northeast and west. Some of these gains were temporary: the expansion into Eschental, Maggia and Riviera, and thus to the shores of Lake Locarno, was reversed in 1422 as the Duchy of Milan recovered from the crisis caused by the death of Gian Galeazzo Visconti (*see* map 3, page 99), and the Swiss were not to advance in that area again until the 1510s. To the northeast Appenzell gained Rhinetal in 1444, St Gall became an allied district in 1451, Schaffhausen was acquired in 1454 and Thurgau occupied in 1460: Lake Constance had been reached; the Rhine crossed. In 1466 Berne made a defensive alliance with the Alsatian city of Mülhausen, a major extension in the territorial scope of Swiss commitments. The crucial Swiss role in the defeat of Charles the Bold of Burgundy in 1476-7 led to greater attention being paid to Swiss wishes and in the volatile situation created by the collapse of Burgundian power the Swiss Confederation made major gains. In 1481 Fribourg and Solothurn were accepted as additional members of the Confederation by the Agreement of Stans. In 1499 the Swiss were to force the Emperor Maximilian to acknowledge their effective independence. Their determination and fighting qualities had reaped their reward.

Hungary under Matthias Corvinus, 1458-90

2 Matthias Corvinus was the second son of Janos Hunyadi, the successful defender of Belgrade against the Turks (1456). From 1458 until 1490 he was King of Hungary. Corvinus was a renaissance ruler who promoted learning greatly, but also had to resist the Turkish advance. He maintained a largely defensive attitude, seeking to preserve his kingdom, without trying, as his father did, to push back the Ottomans to any great extent. He was, nonetheless, successful in retaking northern Bosnia from the Turks after they had conquered it in 1463.

Corvinus's main attention, however, was directed towards the west. With the standing (permanent) army he developed, he hoped to gain the crown of Bohemia and become Holy Roman Emperor. Bohemia was divided as a result of the Hussite troubles and in 1468 Corvinus obtained Papal support to conduct a crusade against its Hussite ruler, George of Poděbrady. This led to the partition of the Bohemian kingdom. Corvinus gained Moravia, Silesia and Lusatia as well as the title "King of Bohemia", though not Bohemia itself. Corvinus was opposed by the Emperor, the Habsburg Frederick III (1440-93), who had been elected ruler of Hungary in 1439 by a group of nobles. Corvinus was successful, gaining Lower Austria and Styria from Austria, and transferring his capital to Vienna. Under Corvinus the Hungarian state developed considerably, but he faced opposition from nobles concerned about their privileges.

East Central Europe: the Growth of Jagiello Power, 1440-1526

3 The Polish Jagiellonian dynasty had a long-standing connection with Hungary. Wladislaw I had been King of Hungary as well as Poland-Lithuania, ruling the countries in a personal union from 1440 until his untimely death in battle against the Turks at Varna in 1444. After the death of Matthias Corvinus in 1490, the Hungarians chose Wladislaw of the Polish Jagiellonian dynasty as their king, who had already been elected King Ladislav II of Bohemia in 1471. He rejoined to Bohemia those areas which had been conquered by Hungary under Matthias Corvinus (*see* map 3, below), namely Moravia, Silesia and Lusatia. The Habsburgs reversed Corvinus's conquests and regained Lower Austria and Styria. Hungary and Bohemia remained separate kingdoms, and it is unclear whether their joint rule by the Jagiellonians would have produced a closer union. After Wladislaw died he was succeeded in both by Louis II (1516-26; Ludvik I in Bohemia), but his reign was cut short, as was so much else in Eastern Europe, by the Turks. He was killed in 1526 when the more numerous and powerful invading forces of Suleiman the Magnificent destroyed Hungary's army and independence on the battlefield of Mohács. Although Suleiman set off for Hungary in April 1526, bad weather delayed him so that he did not cross the river Drava until late August. The Hungarians, however, divided, poorly led and short of infantry, failed both to contest the Drava crossing and to retire to Buda and allow the Turks to exhaust their resources in a difficult siege. Instead they deployed behind the Borza, a small tributary of the Danube. The Hungarian heavy cavalry pushed back the Turkish *sipahis* (Cavalry) of Rumelia, but stopped when Turkish troops advanced on their flank. Louis II then led the remainder of the cavalry in a second attack which pushed through the *sipahis* of Anatolia, but was stopped by the janissaries and cannon. Louis and most of his aristocracy died on the battlefield or in the nearby Danube marshes, though some of the army escaped north under the cover of darkness. Suleiman swept on to Buda. The days of independent Hungary were numbered. Louis had no children, and his inheritance was to be contested by his brother-in-law, Archduke Ferdinand, the brother of the Habsburg Charles V, and the Turks.

1493

EAST CENTRAL EUROPE: THE GROWTH OF JAGIELLO POWER, 1440-1526

Extent of Polish-Lithuanian-Hungarian personal union, 1440-44

Poland-Lithuania from 1466

Vassals of Poland-Lithuania by the end of the 15th century

Personal union under Jagiello kings, 1490-1526

Frontiers, end of 1490

Frontier of the Holy Roman Empire

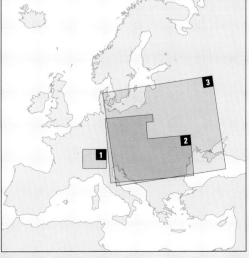

The Habsburg Ascendancy

In 1530, the triumph of the nation-state, whose beginnings are now conventionally traced to the start of the 16th century, would have seemed improbable. The most successful states appeared, instead, to be multinational ones, such as the Ottoman Empire in the east, or the "universal monarchy" built up by Charles V, which encompassed Spain, the Netherlands and the Austrian dominions of the Habsburgs. Small states prospered, too: the patchwork of hundreds of states which made up the Holy Roman Empire contained some of the most affluent parts of Europe. By contrast, the territorial kingdoms to the west, such as France and Spain, had seen their economic position badly affected by prolonged warfare and civil strife. The disparate inheritance of Charles of Habsburg seemed to represent the most acute threat to other monarchs in 1530 (*see* map 1, page 115). Charles had inherited, by quirks of marriage alliances and early deaths, the Burgundian Netherlands (1506), the united Spanish crowns (1516) and finally (in 1519), the lands of his grandfather Maximilian of Austria, after which he obtained the title of Holy Roman Emperor. The Imperial title, the secular counterpart of the Papacy, still carried immense prestige, giving its holder pre-eminence over other, lesser monarchs. Charles won it only in the face of a bitter challenge from Francis I of France, who saw the danger of Charles V, as Emperor, ruling a ring of territories around France (in Spain, Italy and Germany). The French king considered himself the legitimate successor of the first Emperor, Charlemagne, and tried unsuccessfully to play on this sentimental claim.

Having become Emperor, Charles V faced an immense task in keeping his domains united. The rise of Protestantism in the first half of the 16th century placed an additional strain on the Empire. Charles V failed to suppress it by force, despite temporary success in 1547-52, but held firm to Catholicism even though, in Germany at least, it might have been politically expedient to convert to Lutheranism. His power-base gradually shifted as a result, relying increasingly on Spain and her overseas empire to provide money and manpower for his wars against France and to counter the threat of the Turks in the Mediterranean and against Hungary. Overburdened, he could not support his brother-in-law, Christian II of Denmark, when in 1523 Gustavus Vasa led a successful rebellion in Sweden and founded an independent state.

The Ottoman Empire faced no such problems of religious dissent, and after 50 years in which the Sultans had consolidated their 15th-century Balkan conquests (*see* map 2, page 107), under Suleiman the Magnificent (1520-66) they renewed their drive against Christian territory. In 1521 Turkish forces captured Belgrade, and in 1526 Suleiman invaded Hungary, inflicting a crushing defeat on the Hungarian nobility at Mohács, and killing Louis II, the Hungarian king. In 1529, the Sultan's army besieged Vienna. This was a high-water mark of their advance. Though they failed to take Vienna, the Turks' gains confined the Habsburgs to Slovakia, Croatia and a thin strip of territory along the west bank of the Danube. This border area was to be the scene of battles between the Turks and Habsburgs for centuries to come, and the need to safeguard it meant that although the successors of Charles V enjoyed vast resources, they would have to fight on several fronts, against the infidel Muslim threat in the east and the heretical Protestant challenge in the west.

NORWAY
(Danish)

Lapps

SWEDEN

Nidaros

Oslo

Stockholm

Åbo

Reval

LIVONIAN
ORDER OF THE
BROTHERS OF
THE SWORD

Novgorod

M U S C O V Y

Nizhniy
Novgorod

Kazan

KHANATE
OF
SIBIR

Pskov

Riga

Dünaburg

Moscow

Volga

KHANATE OF KAZAN

Aarhus
Copenhagen

Malmö

BALTIC
SEA

Königsberg

Gdańsk

PRUSSIA

Wilno

Vitebsk

Smolensk

Tula

Kazakhs

Hamburg
Stettin

BRANDENBURG

Berlin

Poznań

Vistula

L I T H U A N I A

Minsk

Don

Wild fields

KHANATE
OF ASTRAKHAN

DENMARK

Warsaw

Oder

SILESIA

P O L A N D

Kiev

Volga

Hanover

Breslau

Dresden

Prague

BOHEMIA

MORAVIA

Brünn

Cracow

Lwów

Winnica

Dnieper

Astrakhan

Munich

AUSTRIA

Vienna

Salzburg

Pozsony

Kassa

Buda

Debrecen

MOLDAVIA

Dniester

KHANATE

OF

CRIMEA

Azov

Nuremberg

Danube

Graz

H U N G A R Y

(National King)

Kolozsvár

Jassy

Frankfurt

(Habs-
burg
King)

Mohács

Szeged

Brassó

Kefe

GEORGIAN
STATES

Tiflis

MANTUA

Trieste

VENETIA

Zágráb

Temesvár

Belgrade

WALLACHIA

Bucharest

B L A C K   S E A

Venice

FERRARA

SAN MARINO

Bologna

Lucca

DUCHY OF
URBINO

Zara

Bosna
Saray

O

T

Ruschuk

Danube

Varna

Trebizond

PERSIA

PAPAL
STATES

Rome

PONTECORVO

Spalato

Mostar

REPUBLIC OF
RAGUSA

MONTENEGRO

Nish

Sofia

T

Üsküb

Philippopolis

Adrianople

Constantinople

Angora

Tigris

Mosul

NO

BENEVENTO

Naples

Bari

NAPLES

Taranto

Janina

M

Salonica

A

Smyrna

N

(to
Genoa)

Athens

E M P I R E

Adana

Euphrates

Palermo

Messina

SICILY

Catania

R

E

P

U

B

L

I

C

Nicosia

P E R S I A

MALTA
(Knights of St. John)

SEA

Crete

Beirut

Damascus

Bedouins

113

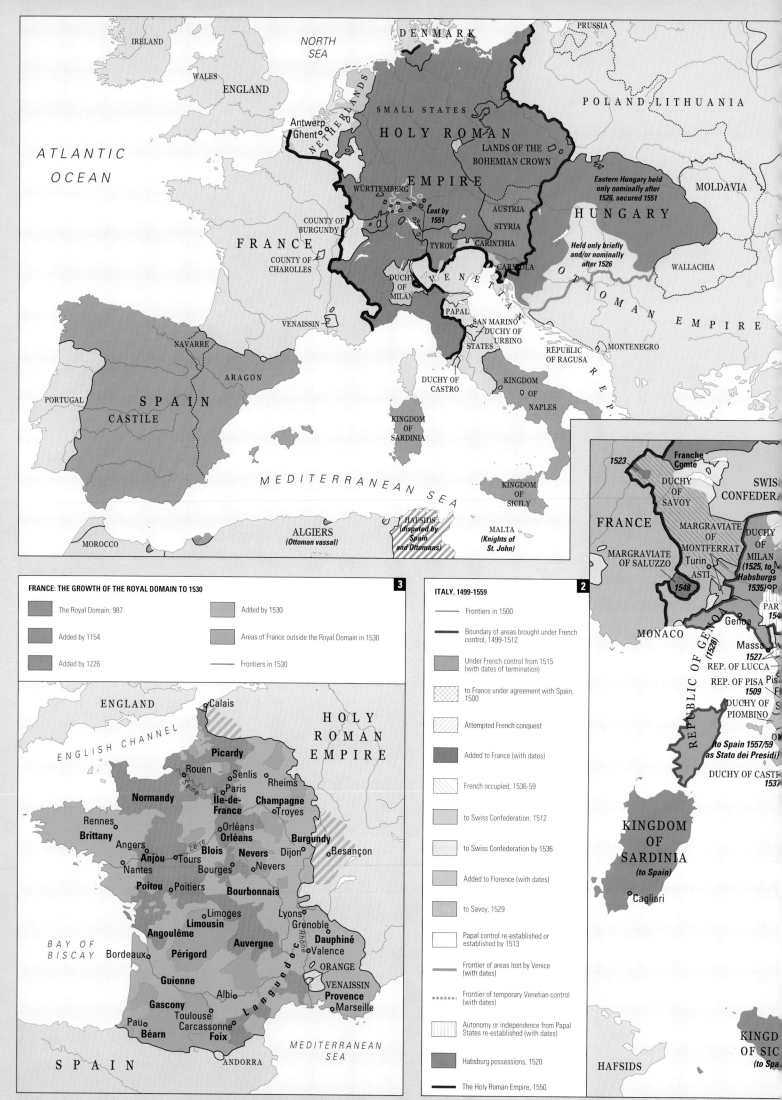

ATLANTIC OCEAN

NORTH SEA

IRELAND

WALES

ENGLAND

DENMARK

PRUSSIA

POLAND-LITHUANIA

NETHERLANDS

Antwerp

Ghent

SMALL STATES

HOLY ROMAN

EMPIRE

LANDS OF THE BOHEMIAN CROWN

WÜRTTEMBERG

AUSTRIA

STYRIA

CARINTHIA

TYROL

CARNIOLA

Lost by 1551

MOLDAVIA

Eastern Hungary held only nominally after 1526, secured 1551

HUNGARY

Held only briefly and/or nominally after 1526

WALLACHIA

OTTOMAN EMPIRE

FRANCE

COUNTY OF BURGUNDY

COUNTY OF CHAROLLES

VENETIA

DUCHY OF MILAN

PAPAL

SAN MARINO

DUCHY OF URBINO

STATES

MONTENEGRO

REPUBLIC OF RAGUSA

VENAISSIN

NAVARRE

ARAGON

PORTUGAL

SPAIN

CASTILE

DUCHY OF CASTRO

KINGDOM OF NAPLES

KINGDOM OF SARDINIA

MEDITERRANEAN SEA

KINGDOM OF SICILY

MOROCCO

ALGIERS (Ottoman vassal)

HAFSIDS (disputed by Spain and Ottomans)

MALTA (Knights of St. John)

FRANCE: THE GROWTH OF THE ROYAL DOMAIN TO 1530 3

The Royal Domain, 987

Added by 1154

Added by 1226

Added by 1530

Areas of France outside the Royal Domain in 1530

Frontiers in 1530

ENGLAND

ENGLISH CHANNEL

Calais

HOLY ROMAN EMPIRE

Picardy

Rouen

Senlis

Paris

Rheims

Normandy

Île-de-France

Champagne

Troyes

Rennes

Orléans

Brittany

Orléans

Angers

Anjou

Blois

Nevers

Dijon

Burgundy

Nantes

Tours

Bourges

Nevers

Besançon

Poitou

Poitiers

Bourbonnais

Lyons

BAY OF BISCAY

Limoges

Limousin

Angoulême

Grenoble

Dauphiné

Valence

Périgord

Auvergne

Bordeaux

Guienne

ORANGE

Albi

VENAISSIN

Gascony

Toulouse

Provence

Pau

Carcassonne

Marseille

Béarn

Foix

SPAIN

ANDORRA

MEDITERRANEAN SEA

ITALY, 1499–1559 2

Frontiers in 1500

Boundary of areas brought under French control, 1499–1512

Under French control from 1515 (with dates of termination)

to France under agreement with Spain, 1500

Attempted French conquest

Added to France (with dates)

French occupied, 1536–59

to Swiss Confederation, 1512

to Swiss Confederation by 1536

Added to Florence (with dates)

to Savoy, 1529

Papal control re-established or established by 1513

Frontier of areas lost by Venice (with dates)

Frontier of temporary Venetian control (with dates)

Autonomy or independence from Papal States re-established (with dates)

Habsburg possessions, 1520

The Holy Roman Empire, 1550

1523

Franche-Comté

DUCHY OF SAVOY

SWISS CONFEDERATION

FRANCE

MARGRAVIATE OF MONTFERRAT

DUCHY OF MILAN (1525, to Habsburgs 1535)

MARGRAVIATE OF SALUZZO

Turin

ASTI

1548

MONACO

REPUBLIC OF GENOA (1528)

Genoa

Massa

1527

REP. OF LUCCA

REP. OF PISA 1509

Pisa

DUCHY OF PIOMBINO

to Spain 1557/59 as Stato dei Presidi

DUCHY OF CASTRO 1537

KINGDOM OF SARDINIA (to Spain)

Cagliari

KINGDOM OF SICILY (to Spain)

HAFSIDS

114

MPIRE OF CHARLES V, 1551

Habsburg possessions acquired by 1477

The Burgundian inheritance, 1477 (secured by 1493)

The Spanish inheritance, 1516

The Jagiellonian inheritance, 1526

Other lands acquired by 1551

Areas of Holy Roman Empire held indirectly by Habsburgs

The Holy Roman Empire

Frontiers in 1551

The Empire of Charles V, 1551

1 What other dynasties achieved by conquest, the House of Habsburg gained through marriage. The emergence of an empire straddling the western half of Europe from the Netherlands to Gibraltar owed more to judicious marriages and opportunely timed deaths than to conquest. By the age of 20, the future Charles V had added the Holy Roman Empire and the various Spanish crowns to the 17 separate Netherlandish provinces of the Netherlands which he inherited on the death of his father Philip the Handsome in 1506. After his grandfather, Ferdinand of Aragon, died in 1516, Charles V inherited the Spanish kingdoms of Aragon and Castile.

Although he was elected Emperor in succession to Maximilian in 1519, the main source of Charles V's power increasingly lay not in Germany, but in Spain and his possessions in the Netherlands. The great commercial wealth of the Netherlanders made their taxes particularly valuable, even if their independent-mindedness meant Charles V had to treat them cautiously.

Charles V added Milan, Mexico, Peru and several Dutch provinces, notably Gelderland, to the territories he had inherited. However, his main aim was to preserve his disparate territories intact, although he subsequently divided his legacy between his son Philip (who received Spain), and his brother Ferdinand (who inherited the Imperial title), regarding the unity of his family as more important than that of his domain. He was able to retain and pass on such diverse territories to his successors in part because he had not encroached too far on their particular rights, a precaution Philip unwisely ignored, contributing to the Revolt of the Netherlands in the 1560s (*see* map 1, page 123).

Italy, 1499-1559

2 The late 14th and early 15th centuries saw a shift in the interests of the major Italian powers, which became less concerned with internal struggles, and sought instead to expand their territorial authority. Venice, for example, carved out an empire in Lombardy, seeking a secure food supply to offset Turkish advances against her Adriatic dominions. It was only a matter of time before the increased rivalry between states sucked in foreign powers.

In 1494, Ludovico il Moro, uncle of the legitimate Sforza duke of Milan, courted French assistance to seize control of the duchy. Charles VIII of France was all-too-pleased to intervene, as he himself had a family claim to both Milan and Naples. In October 1494, Charles invaded with a massive army of 30,000 men. Sweeping aside feeble resistance, he marched south and in 1495 occupied the Kingdom of Naples. The Spanish Habsburgs (in alliance with the Papacy, the Emperor and Venice) intervened, however, to halt the French advance. The struggle lasted nine years, and saw, in 1501, an attempt to partition the Kingdom of Naples, with France receiving the north (including Naples itself) and Spain the south. By 1504, however, the French had been dri-

ven out, and the whole of southern Italy lay under the Habsburg shadow.

Even Milan, which the French had occupied in 1499, could not be held for long. At the Battle of Pavia (1525), the Emperor Charles V drove out the French and restored the duchy to the native Sforza duke. But when he died in 1535, the Habsburgs took Milan, too. Even states such as Florence and the Papacy had to employ careful diplomacy to retain their independence. Charles V's troops sacked Rome in 1527, a devastating psychological blow to the Italians, and temporarily occupied Florence in 1529. The Florentines made a virtue out of necessity and in 1552-7, allied with Charles V, Duke Cosimo de Medici, they conquered the pro-French republic of Siena, traditional enemy of Florence. The Habsburgs, however, kept five Sienese seaports for themselves, organised as the "Stato dei Presidi."

Although Florence expanded her territory, the Papacy imposed its authority on areas of the Papal States which had become semi-autonomous, and Venice retained most of her land empire (save the Romagna, lost in 1530), the continued existence of these independent Italian states could not disguise the fact that after the Treaty of Cateau-Cambrésis (1559), it was a foreign dynasty, the Habsburgs, who were the real masters of the peninsula.

France: the Growth of the Royal Domain to 1530

3 One of the key sources of renewed French power after the Hundred Years' War was the growth of the royal domain – that part of the kingdom directly controlled by the king and not through feudal vassals – which made more money and men available to the King, resources which in turn helped him to assert his dominance. Victory in the Hundred Years' War against England gave the French king the opportunity to re-incorporate large areas, previously part of the royal domain built up in the early 13th century by Philip Augustus (*see* map 2, page 87). Two important territories, however, Brittany and the Bourbonnais, remained under their own dukes, owing only vague loyalty to the French kings.

Charles VIII set in motion the incorporation of Brittany by marrying its heiress, Anne in 1491. In order to keep Anne's duchy on Charles VIII's death in 1498, his successor, Louis XII, divorced his first wife and married her instead. Charles, Duke of Bourbon, controlled a compact bloc of land in central France, in which he was in effect in control of royal powers. However, he had inherited half the lands through his wife and on her death in 1521, Francis I used a dispute about her legacy to seize the lands of his over-mighty subject. By his death in 1547, only Calais (under English control), the county of Orange, the Papal enclave of Avignon (the Venaissin) and the south remained outside the French king's jurisdiction.

The Wars of Religion

On 24 August 1572, the French Regent Catherine de Medici, despairing of attempts to find a *modus vivendi* with her Protestant subjects, ordered a policy of savage repression instead. The resulting St Bartholomew's Day Massacre, in which many French Protestant grandees perished, plunged France into a generation of religious warfare. It was a potent symbol of a Europe where Catholic-Protestant divisions were hardening, fuelled by the determination of Catholic rulers inspired by the Counter-Reformation to establish religious conformity within their lands.

If the spread of Calvinism through key sections of the French nobility (and towns such as La Rochelle) had alarmed Catherine, Philip II of Spain faced a similarly grave Protestant challenge in the Netherlands. The rebels were inspired not only by religion, but also by hatred of Philip's attempts to impose an absolutist system of government on the Seventeen Provinces he had inherited. Philip II had been fatally distracted from this task by the need to fend off Turkish incursions in the Mediterranean. This was particularly so in 1565, when an outbreak of anti-Catholic Calvinist rioting and growing dissent even amongst Catholic nobles could not be contained because all available forces were deployed in the Mediterranean to protect southern Italy from the Turks and to lift the Turkish siege of Malta (1565). Only in 1567 could Spanish troops be sent northwards up the thin strip of Habsburg territory known as "the Spanish road" from Italy to Brussels.

Philip II's viceroy in the Netherlands, the Duke of Alva, enjoyed considerable success in pacifying the Dutch rebels, even defeating an invasion organised by one of their leaders, William of Orange, in 1568; but the taxes required to pay his troops soon caused more unrest. In 1572 Orange persuaded the French Calvinist leaders to join him in a new invasion: while he led an army from Germany in the east, his navy launched an assault on Holland in the north, and French forces captured Mons in the south. The St Bartholomew's Day Massacre cut off further aid from France, however, and allowed Alva to drive Orange back into Holland. There a long and expensive war of siege and counter-siege began, which failed to dislodge the rebels. Spain nevertheless refused to concede toleration to the Dutch and persisted in fighting a war it could not win.

Meanwhile, although the Turks failed to capture Malta from the Knights of St John in 1565, the Sultan's nominal subjects in North Africa continued to drain Spanish resources with their constant pirate raids on Spain and other Christian states. Even the Christian victory over the Sultan's fleet at Lepanto (1571) offered only temporary respite: in 1574 a new Turkish navy captured Tunis and enslaved all its Spanish defenders. Moreover, the Turks still posed a serious threat to the Habsburgs in the Balkans, although their efforts were in practice largely directed to the east.

Although Eastern Europe escaped the intense religious wars that plagued the west, stability eluded the rulers even there. The death of the last Jagiellonian king of Poland, Sigismund II, in 1572, left no obvious successor and set off a quarrelsome debate amongst the nobility as to who should become king. This left Poland, in particular Polish Lithuania, vulnerable to interference from Russia to the east. Even here, the spectre of religious difference as a tool of dynastic politics arose, as many of the inhabitants of Polish Lithuania were Orthodox, and Muscovy saw them as potential subjects.

N O R W A Y (Danish)

Trondhjem

Oslo

S W E D E N

Åbo
Helsingfors

Stockholm

R U S S I A

Novgorod

Reval
Estonia

Nizhniy
Novgorod

LANDS OF
PRINCE
MAGNUS

Livonia

Riga

Pskov

Volga

Moscow

KHANATE
OF
SIBIR

Aarhus

Copenhagen Malmö

BALTIC
SEA

COURLAND

Dyneburg

Tula

D E N M A R K

Hamburg Stettin

Königsberg

Wilno

Vitebsk

Smolensk

Kazakhs

Bremen

Gdansk

PRUSSIA

L I T H U A N I A

Minsk

Don

BRANDENBURG

Berlin

Poznań

Vistula

Warsaw

Leipzig
AL   Dresden

Elbe

Breslau

Oder

SILESIA

P O L A N D

Kiev

Volga

Astrakhan

Prague

Nuremberg BOHEMIA

MORAVIA

Cracow

Lwów

Dnieper

Frankfurt

Brünn

Danube

H U N G A R Y

Kassa

Winnica

Dniester

TES

Munich

Vienna Pozsony

AUSTRIA   Salzburg

Eger

Debrecen

MOLDAVIA

Azov

KHANATE OF
C R I M E A

Graz

Buda

Kolozsvár

Jassy

Circassians

Daghestan

Pécs

Szeged

TRANSYLVANIA

Verona Trieste

Venice

Zágráb

Temesvár

Brassó

FERRARA MODENA

Bologna

SAN MARINO
DUCHY OF
URBINO

Zara

Bosna
Seraj

Belgrade

WALLACHIA

Bucharest

B L A C K   S E A

PERSIA

Spalato

Danube

Ruschuk

Varna

Trebizond

ce

PAPAL

Perugia

STATES
Rome

Mostar

REPUBLIC OF
RAGUSA

MONTENEGRO

Nish

Sofia

Úsküb

Philippopolis

Adrianople

Constantinople

PONTECORVO

BENEVENTO

Naples Bari

NAPLES Taranto

Janina

Salonica

O T T O M A N

E M P I R E

Angora

Mosul

Tigris

Euphrates

Palermo

Messina

SICILY Catania

Smyrna

Adana

Athens

R E P U B L I C

SEA

MALTA
(Knights of St John)

Nicosia

Beirut
Damascus

Bedouins

117

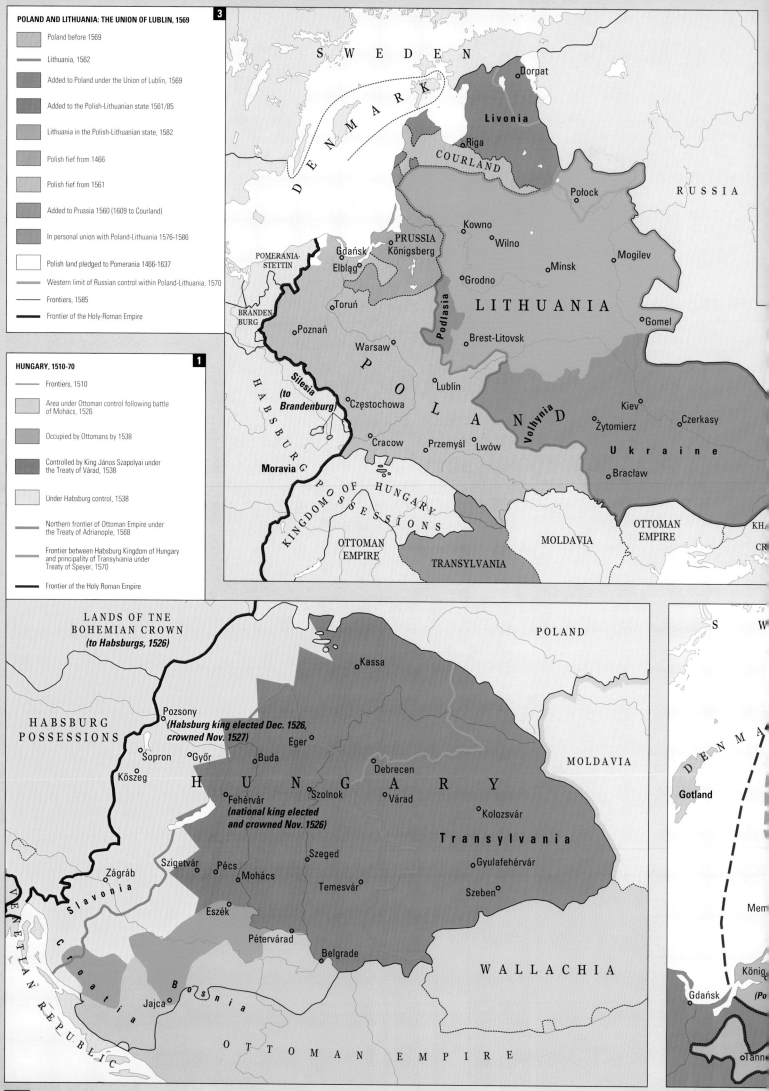

POLAND AND LITHUANIA: THE UNION OF LUBLIN, 1569 ③

- Poland before 1569
- Lithuania, 1562
- Added to Poland under the Union of Lublin, 1569
- Added to the Polish-Lithuanian state 1561/85
- Lithuania in the Polish-Lithuanian state, 1582
- Polish fief from 1466
- Polish fief from 1561
- Added to Prussia 1560 (1609 to Courland)
- In personal union with Poland-Lithuania 1576-1586
- Polish land pledged to Pomerania 1466-1637
- Western limit of Russian control within Poland-Lithuania, 1570
- Frontiers, 1585
- Frontier of the Holy-Roman Empire

HUNGARY, 1510-70 ①

- Frontiers, 1510
- Area under Ottoman control following battle of Mohács, 1526
- Occupied by Ottomans by 1538
- Controlled by King János Szapolyai under the Treaty of Várad, 1538
- Under Habsburg control, 1538
- Northern frontier of Ottoman Empire under the Treaty of Adrianople, 1568
- Frontier between Habsburg Kingdom of Hungary and principality of Transylvania under Treaty of Speyer, 1570
- Frontier of the Holy Roman Empire

SWEDEN

DENMARK

Dorpat
Livonia
Riga
COURLAND
Połock
RUSSIA
Kowno
Wilno
Mogilev
Minsk
Grodno
PRUSSIA
Gdańsk
Königsberg
Elbląg
POMERANIA-STETTIN
Toruń
Podlasia
Brest-Litovsk
LITHUANIA
Gomel
BRANDEN-BURG
Poznań
Warsaw
BRANDEN-BURG
Silesia
(to Brandenburg)
P O L A N D
Lublin
Kiev
Żytomierz
Czerkasy
HABSBURG
Częstochowa
Volhynia
Cracow
Przemyśl
Lwów
U k r a i n e
Moravia
Bracław
KINGDOM OF HUNGARY POSSESSIONS
OTTOMAN EMPIRE
MOLDAVIA
OTTOMAN EMPIRE
KHA
TRANSYLVANIA
CR

118

LANDS OF THE BOHEMIAN CROWN
(to Habsburgs, 1526)

POLAND

Kassa

HABSBURG POSSESSIONS

Pozsony
(Habsburg king elected Dec. 1526, crowned Nov. 1527)

Sopron
Győr
Eger
Buda
Debrecen
MOLDAVIA

Köszeg
H U N G A R Y
Szolnok
Várad

Fehérvár
(national king elected and crowned Nov. 1526)
Kolozsvár

Szigetvár
Pécs
Szeged
T r a n s y l v a n i a

Zágráb
Mohács
Gyulafehérvár
Slavonia
Temesvár
Szeben

Eszék

Croatia
Pétervárad
Bosnia
Belgrade
W A L L A C H I A
Jajca

VENETIAN REPUBLIC
O T T O M A N   E M P I R E

SWEDEN

DENMARK

Gotland

Memel

Königsberg
Gdańsk
(Po
Tann

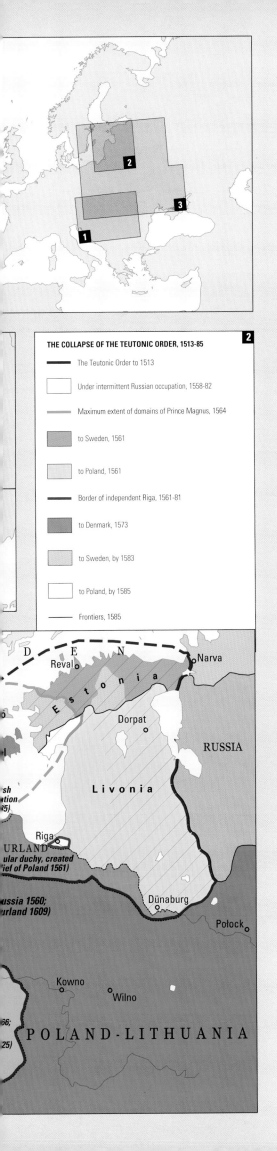

THE COLLAPSE OF THE TEUTONIC ORDER, 1513-85   2

— The Teutonic Order to 1513

☐ Under intermittent Russian occupation, 1558-82

— Maximum extent of domains of Prince Magnus, 1564

▨ to Sweden, 1561

☐ to Poland, 1561

— Border of independent Riga, 1561-81

▨ to Denmark, 1573

▨ to Sweden, by 1583

☐ to Poland, by 1585

— Frontiers, 1585

D E N ...
Reval ○   Narva ○

E s t o n i a

Dorpat ○

RUSSIA

L i v o n i a

Riga ○
URLAND
ular duchy, created
ief of Poland 1561)

ussia 1560;
urland 1609)

Dünaburg ○

Połock ○

Kowno ○
Wilno ○

66;
25)

P O L A N D · L I T H U A N I A

Hungary, 1510-70

1 Their crushing defeat by the Turks at Mohács in 1526 resulted in a split among the surviving Hungarian nobility about who should be elected in place of the dead king, Louis II. Although some opted for Ferdinand of Austria, others preferred a local candidate, János Szapolyai, who had led resistance to the prospect of a Habsburg succession as far back as 1505, when the Hungarian diet had ruled that a "foreigner" could not be elected. It was obviously convenient for the Ottoman sultan, Suleiman II, to recognise Szapolyai to prevent the Habsburgs from succeeding to the throne of Hungary. In the crisis after 1526, however, many of the Hungarian nobles felt they needed the foreigner Ferdinand – and the presumed assistance of the Empire against the Ottomans – more than he would gain by becoming their king.

For more than a decade, the forces of Hungary were caught in a civil war between the two kings, even after the Treaty of Várad (1538), when mutual acceptance was agreed on the basis of a dubious status quo. On Szapolyai's death, his supporters declared his infant son, John Sigismund, king. Ferdinand responded by laying siege to Buda, hoping to reclaim the east of Hungary, but this provoked Suleiman II into a counter-invasion. The Ottoman forces captured Buda, and a central strip of lowland leading to it from the south.

Hungary was now effectively divided into three parts. In the west, Ferdinand continued to rule less than one-third of the old kingdom (so-called "Royal Hungary"). In the east a new state of initially uncertain nature was emerging. This was at some times a Hungarian vassal kingdom of the Ottomans, at others it was united with Royal Hungary. With the Treaty of Speyer (1570), it crystallised into a new state of Hungarian character – Transylvania – loosely controlled by the Ottoman Empire. The third part of Hungary, the central plain, was ruled directly by the Sultan. He gradually extended the area he held directly until 1568, when new frontiers were agreed by the Treaty of Adrianople.

The Collapse of the Teutonic Order, 1513-85

2 The Teutonic Order had never entirely recovered from its defeat by Polish and Lithuanian forces at Tannenberg (Grünwald) in 1410. In 1513 the Grand Master of the Livonian Order of the Brothers of the Sword (which had been united with the Teutonic Order since 1237) purchased independence, leaving the latter with just East Prussia. In 1525 the Teutonic Grand Master, Albrecht von Hohenzollern, converted to Protestantism and secularised the remaining Teutonic lands as the Duchy of Prussia, the largest Protestant fief in the kingdom of Poland.

Meanwhile, the lands ruled by the Livonian Order remained independent and Catholic until, in 1556-7, a civil war came close to making the Order a

Polish client. This outcome was unacceptable to Tsar Ivan IV of Russia, who invaded in 1558 and captured most of Livonia and Estonia. However, this proved equally unacceptable to the other states of the area, which fought over the territory for the next two decades. The last Grand Master of the Order managed to secularise Courland, which became a Polish fief; Sweden gained most of Estonia; Poland wrested most of Russia's conquests from Ivan; and Denmark (which initially exercised her influence indirectly through Magnus Prince of Holstein, brother of the Danish king, and which began as a close ally of Russia) found her role reduced significantly by the end of the 16th century, losing all except the island of Ösel.

No hereditary German state survived in the Baltic lands, though noblemen of German origin played a central role in the region until 1918 and provided many of the civil servants of future rulers of the Baltic region.

Poland and Lithuania: the Union of Lublin, 1569

3 For nearly two centuries following the marriage between the Grand Duke of Lithuania, Jogaila, and the Polish Queen, Jadwiga, in 1386, the union between Poland and Lithuania was a personal one. However, by the 1560s it was clear that Sigismund II Augustus would be the last of the Jagiellonian line. For the Lithuanians, the prospect of the dissolution of the link with Poland was dire. Lithuania had been under threat from both the Ottomans, who had seized her territory on the lower Dnieper, and the Muscovites, who were pressing westwards under Ivan the Terrible (1533-1584). Only Polish support could guarantee Lithuania, while union with her offered the Polish nobility the prospect of fresh lands for settlement.

In 1569 at Lublin, a Lithuanian Parliament specially called into existence agreed with the traditional Polish Sejm to form an "indissoluble" union or "commonwealth" and to elect a common monarch after the childless Sigismund II Augustus's death. Initial resistance from the Lithuanian magnates, concerned that the proposed union would diminish their own power, was overcome. Poland and Lithuania remained distinct states, each with its own army, administration and laws.

In order to persuade the Poles to take on the burden of defending them in future, Lithuania agreed to turn Podlasia, Volhynia and the Ukraine over to Polish administration. Polish settlers, noble and common alike, moved into these territories, establishing new farms and great estates, and extending the influence of the Catholic Church. In turn, this helped to fuel conflicts with the other (Orthodox) groups living in these areas, especially the Cossacks of the Ukraine.

1572

1618

The Eve of the Thirty Years' War

The period following 1572 was characterised by continuing religious and dynastic wars, many of them exacerbated by foreign meddling such as that of Spain and England in the French Wars of Religion, and of England and France in the Revolt of the Netherlands. These also helped to reinforce nascent national identities, although the religious division of Europe following the Reformation had tended to cut across linguistic or ethnic lines. In places such as the Netherlands, where there was no clear-cut religious or ethnic divide and constitutional issues clouded the struggle, the conflict to determine who might believe what, and where, dragged on for years.

Indeed, because Philip II could bring to bear in the Netherlands so many of the resources of his vast trans-Atlantic and Mediterranean empire, Spain was able to fight for decades in the remote Netherlands rather than permit the revolt against Spanish rule, which began in 1566, to set the dangerous precedent of successful religious and political rebellion.

Ironically, it had been Philip II's efforts to impose a standard system of absolutist rule on the 17 provinces of the Netherlands in the face of their mutual rivalries which forced them together. It was to take his more diplomatically gifted generals, above all Parma, much effort and many years to split the French-speaking Catholic provinces from the Protestant Dutch-speaking areas. By identifying rebellion with religion, Parma and his successors were able to win back the bulk of the southern provinces, which had formed the Union of Arras in 1579. The decision of the Protestants in the northern Union of Utrecht to attack the south caused the southerners to appeal to Spain for troops to protect them and gave Philip II the excuse to carry through their re-Catholicisation.

The threat of a French invasion of the Spanish Netherlands in 1572 had distracted Philip II's soldiers from their campaign there and allowed the rebels to gain firm footholds in fortified towns. Philip's general, Parma, invaded France in 1589. But 10 years of war ended in 1598 without a clear victory for either side. Increasingly it was Elizabeth I's England which sent troops and money to support the Dutch. In 1604, however, Spain made peace with England, too. On each occasion no land changed hands. Only the war in the Netherlands dragged on. By 1609, the Spanish had recovered the great port of Antwerp as well as Flanders. Mutual exhaustion then persuaded Philip III to accept a 12-year truce with the rebels.

In Bohemia a movement of religious and political dissent against the Habsburgs similar to that in the Netherlands had developed during the early 17th century. By 1618, the largely Protestant Bohemian aristocracy was in open revolt. The decision to choose a non-Habsburg, Frederick V of the Palatinate, as King of Bohemia was seen as a challenge on the Dutch model to what the Habsburgs considered their divinely ordained right to rule. Control over wealthy and strategically central Bohemia, with its vote in choosing the emperor, was vital to the Austrian Habsburgs. With the Habsburgs' principal rivals – the Ottomans, France and England – unwilling or unable to restrain him, Ferdinand II, the new Emperor, was encouraged to undertake an ambitious war of reconquest to restore his authority to areas which had been lost to Protestantism since 1570. By 1620, Ferdinand had conquered Bohemia and installed himself as King there.

Trondhjem

N O R W A Y

(Danish)

Christiania

S W E D E N

R U S S I A

Archangel

Perm

Åbo   Helsingfors

Stockholm   Reval   Novgorod

Gothenburg

Nizhniy
Novgorod

Volga

Aarhus

Pskov   Moscow   Samara

Copenhagen   Malmö   Riga

BALTIC   COURLAND   Dyneburg   Tula   Kazakhs

ENMARK   SEA

Königsberg   Wilno   Vitebsk   Smolensk   Saratov   50°

Hamburg   Stettin   Gdańsk   PRUSSIA   L I T H U A N I A

Don

Minsk   Kursk   Astrakhan

ck   BRANDENBURG

Hanover   Berlin   Poznań   Volga

Oder   Warsaw

SAXONY   P O L A N D   Dnieper

frankfurt   Dresden   SILESIA   Breslau

erg   Prague   BOHEMIA   Cracow   Lwów   Kiev

ES   Brünn   MORAVIA   Winnica   Dniester   Azov

BAVARIA   Danube   Kassa   K H A N A T E   O F

Munich   Vienna   Pozsony   H U N G A R Y   Jassy   C R I M E A

AUSTRIA   Salzburg   Buda   Debrecen   M O L D A V I A   Circassians

Graz   Kolozsvár   Daghestan

V   Trieste   Pécs   Szeged   TRANSYLVANIA   Bakhchisaray

Venice   Zágráb   Brassó

MANTUA   Temesvár   W A L L A C H I A   Tiflis

MODENA   Zara   Belgrade   Bucharest   PERSIA

Bologna   San Marino   Bosna   B L A C K   S E A   Erivan

LUCCA   DUCHY OF   Serai   Danube   Ruschuk

NCE   URBINO   Spalato   Varna   Trebizond

PAPAL   Mostar   Nish

STATES   REPUBLIC OF   Sofia   Burgas

Rome   RAGUSA   Üsküb   Philippopolis   Adrianople

MONTENEGRO   Janina   Salonica   Constantinople

CHY   Naples   Bari   O T T O M A N   E M P I R E   Angora   Tigris

TRO   NAPLES   Taranto   Mosul

Palermo   Smyrna   Adana   Euphrates

SICILY   Messina   Athens

Catania

SEA   Nicosia

MALTA   REPUBLIC   Beirut   Bedouins

(Knights of   Crete   Damascus   121

St John)

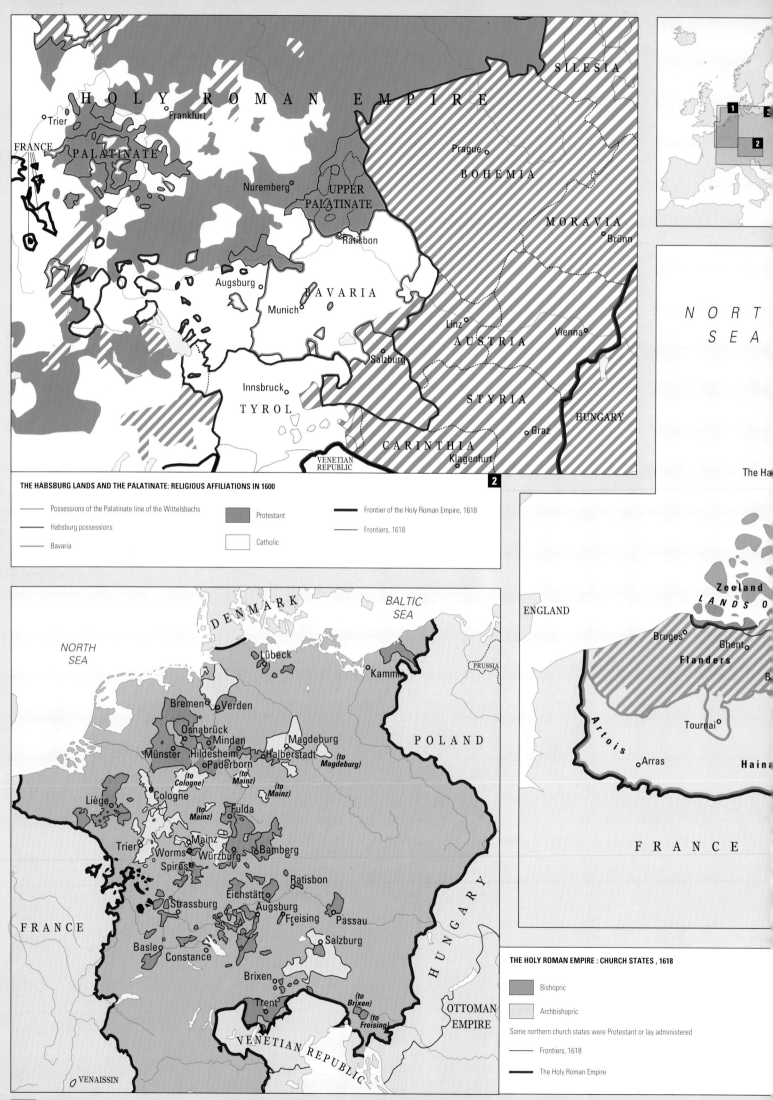

THE HABSBURG LANDS AND THE PALATINATE: RELIGIOUS AFFILIATIONS IN 1600

Possessions of the Palatinate line of the Wittelsbachs	
Habsburg possessions	
Bavaria	
Protestant	
Catholic	
Frontier of the Holy Roman Empire, 1618	
Frontiers, 1618	

THE HOLY ROMAN EMPIRE : CHURCH STATES , 1618

Bishopric	
Archbishopric	

Some northern church states were Protestant or lay administered

Frontiers, 1618

The Holy Roman Empire

THE NETHERLANDS, 1566-1648

▨ The Union of Utrecht, 1579	☐ Added to the United Netherlands, 1648
▨ The Union of Arras, 1579	▨ Spanish Netherlands, 1648
▨ Joined Union of Utrecht by 1581	▬ Frontier of the Holy Roman Empire
▨ Boundary of United Netherlands according to 1609 truce	▬ Frontiers, 1648

The Netherlands, 1566-1648

1 The revolt of the Netherlands against their Habsburg rulers after 1566 was a pivotal development in European history. Although William, Prince of Orange, played a major role in the revolt, its primary result was the creation of a republican regime drawing its strength from the mercantile wealth of Dutch cities such as Amsterdam. The rebellion was sparked by Philip II's attempts in the 1560s to centralise the government of the 17 provinces of the Netherlands. The rebels originally demanded a reversal of this and only turned to republicanism when it became clear that Philip II himself was personally behind the schemes to reduce the provinces' independence. Of course, Philip II's religious intolerance played a major part in promoting rebellion, because the Protestants in the north of the Netherlands could not compromise with him, whereas many Catholics were eventually bought off with concessions.

Renewed fighting began between the Dutch, led by Orange, and Spanish forces in 1572. In 1576 the royal army mutinied and Orange's supporters temporarily took over almost all the 17 provinces, but within three years unity among the rebels evaporated. In January 1579, the Union of Arras, committed to Catholicism and loyalty to the king, was formed in the south. In the same month the anti-Habsburg northern Union of Utrecht, which evolved into the United Provinces of the Netherlands, was formed.

Only in 1609 was Philip III prepared to accept a 12-year truce. The United Provinces of the Netherlands became *de facto* independent and France, England and other states hurried to recognise them as such. However, the Habsburgs still hoped to stifle the "rebels" and fought until 1648 to conquer them, only then finally recognising their independence.

If they failed with the seven northern provinces, by dint of military effort, religious zeal and playing on local identity, the Habsburgs managed to reconcile the 10 southern provinces to their rule. Dutch naval power and control of the islands at the mouth of the Scheldt meant, however, that the trade of Antwerp (recaptured by the Spanish in 1585) was strangled. In an attempt to stabilise the 10 loyal provinces, Philip II bequeathed them to his daughter Isabella, who was married to her cousin Albert of Austria, while the rest of his empire went to Philip III. At Albert's death in 1621, his possessions were returned to Spanish rule, but subsequent attacks, by both the Calvinist Dutch and the Catholic French, forged a new national identity in the South Netherlands, ancestor of modern Belgium.

The Habsburg Lands and the Palatinate: Religious Affiliations in 1600

2 The Austrian Habsburg lands had been devolved to various members of the family who had pursued the Catholic Counter-Reformation with varying degrees of intensity. It was the most vigorous persecutor of Protestants, Ferdinand of Styria, who became the family's champion as the more relaxed rule of Matthias waned. It was one thing to crack down on heresy in compliant Austria, but Bohemia had its own assertive local institutions which were strongly infiltrated by Protestantism.

By 1617, the Habsburg authorities were trying to push back the tide of Protestantism by ordering the closure and demolition of reformed churches in Bohemia, and the seizure of Protestant Church funds. This antagonised the Bohemian nobility, which prided itself on its independence. The fact that Bohemia had a Protestant neighbour in the Elector Palatine, whose eastern territories bordered Bohemia at Eger, meant that in the event of an election to the Bohemian throne there was a clear local Protestant counter-candidate to the Habsburgs.

Although the Bohemian estates had agreed to "accept" Ferdinand of Styria as their king in 1617 when Matthias died in 1619, the Bohemians chose Frederick V of the Palatinate to succeed him. Ferdinand of Styria ignored their choice and proclaimed himself king by hereditary right, using the Bohemian electoral vote to support his candidacy for the Empire and proceeded to invade and expel Frederick after only one winter as king. Ferdinand could rely on the equally staunch Catholic, Maximilian of Bavaria, to help him, not least because the Bavarian Duke coveted Frederick V's Upper Palatinate.

The Holy Roman Empire: Church States, 1618

3 Whereas even Catholic territorial monarchies such as France or Habsburg Spain had succeeded in abolishing separate ecclesiastical jurisdictions within their borders, many Church states survived as parts of the Holy Roman Empire. More controversially, one of the key consequences of the Reformation inside the Empire had been the secularisation of Church states by Protestant rulers. Both Catholic clerical rulers (such as the three clerical Electors of Cologne, Mainz and Trier) and Catholic lay rulers disliked such arbitrary secularisation (as they saw it) and wished to reverse it, while Protestant rulers who had benefited from it naturally resisted any reversion to the old order which could cost them land and income.

Neither the Catholics or Protestants accepted as definitive the Peace of Augsburg (1555), which brought a temporary halt to the first phase of the religious wars that followed the Reformation in Germany, and by 1618 they were manoeuvring for their own advantage. Conflict over the right of Protestants to build churches in Bohemia excited passions that spilled over into Germany and began the Thirty Years' War. The complexity of the Empire meant that there were always disputes over jurisdiction and historical rights, but the religious issue in particular and its European-wide implication meant that conflicts within the Empire soon spread and drew in other states.

1618

The Peace of Westphalia

The Thirty Years' War came to an end in 1648 after the most savage and destructive warfare yet seen in Europe. Peace was signed in the Westphalian towns of Osnabrück and Münster, where the Emperor negotiated separately with his Protestant and Catholic enemies. Yet whatever the convulsions of the long years of more or less general warfare, in the event strikingly few changes were made to the political map. The treaties, too, marked the final recognition that Catholic princes inspired by the Counter-Reformation would not be able to roll back entirely the gains that Protestantism had made in Europe since the early 16th century.

Although both France and Sweden gained lands inside the Empire, it was largely at the expense of minor princes and not the House of Habsburg. Of the Habsburgs' losses, the most important were those to the west of the Holy Roman Empire, where France gained Sundgau on the Rhine and Philippsburg, as well as a number of smaller territories. The result was that the Habsburg hold on the Spanish Road, the narrow strip of Habsburg controlled territory which linked Spain and the Spanish Netherlands, was cut.

Spain was forced to accept the independence and sovereignty of the seven United Provinces of the Netherlands some 80 years after the start of their revolt against Philip II. His grandson, Philip IV, retained the Southern Netherlands with their mixed Flemish and French-speaking populations and re-established Catholicism, which, despite linguistic differences within the newly reconquered territories, marked their identity for centuries afterwards and made even the southern Flemish-speakers reject the idea of unification with their Dutch-speaking cousins in the Protestant-dominated United Provinces.

From the mid-1630s Franco-Spanish conflict had been the central element of the Thirty Years' War. The war had begun as a battle for supremacy within the Empire between Catholic and Protestant in which outside powers had taken sides according to their dominant faith. Thus, first Lutheran Denmark, then Sweden supported the Protestant princes, while Catholic Spain backed the Emperor. But Catholic France's sympathies with the Protestant side changed the composition of the struggle. The pragmatic Cardinal Richelieu identified breaking Spain's ring of territories around France's land borders as the key to the rise of French power, overruling the arguments of a pro-Catholic *dévot* faction in France. Richelieu attempted to weaken the Habsburgs by subsidising their Protestant enemies, but after the catastrophic defeat of Sweden in 1634, France entered the war against Spain directly in 1635. Despite her previous disastrous set-back, Sweden emerged a victor from the war, largely as France's major ally. Her territorial gains in a girdle of lands to the south of Denmark put her traditional enemy at a disadvantage, but made further struggle between Denmark and Sweden for control of key trade routes through the Baltic much more likely. Sweden's position was additionally strengthened by her conquest of Livonia from Poland in 1629.

It soon became clear that Richelieu's successor, Mazarin, had overrated both the weakness of Spain and the capacity of the French population to support the expensive burden of the war. Mazarin's expectations of rapid victories against Spain were to be thwarted as the war dragged on for more than a decade.

NORWAY

Trondhjem

(Danish)

SWEDEN

Christiania

Åbo
Helsingfors

Stockholm

Reval

RUSSIA

Archangel

Nizhniy
Novgorod
Kazan

Volga

Gothenburg

Livonia
Pskov

Moscow

Samara

Aarhus

BALTIC
SEA

Riga

COURLAND
Dyneburg

Tula
Kazakhs

Copenhagen
Malmö

ENMARK

SWEDISH
POMERANIA

Gdansk

Königsberg

Wilno
Vitebsk
Smolensk

Saratov

Tsaritsyn

Hamburg
Stettin

PRUSSIA

LITHUANIA

Volga

Bremen

BRANDENBURG

Poznań

Minsk

Kursk

ick
Hanover
Berlin

Vistula

Warsaw

Kharkov

er

Elbe

SAXONY
Breslau

ALL
Leipzig
Dresden

SILESIA

Oder

POLAND

Kiev

Astrakhan

kfurt
White
Mountain

nberg
BOHEMIA

MORAVIA
Cracow

Lwów

Dnieper

ES
Brünn

Danube

Winnica

Azov

BAVARIA
Vienna
Pozsony

Kassa

Dniester

KHANATE OF
CRIMEA

Munich
AUSTRIA
Salzburg

HUNGARY

Buda
Debrecen

Jassy

Kolozsvár

MOLDAVIA

Graz

TRANSYLVANIA

Circassians

Daghestan

VENETIAN
Trieste

Pécs
Szeged

Brassó

Bakhchisaray

Venice
MANTUA
MODENA
Bologna

Zágráb

Temesvár

WALLACHIA

BLACK SEA

PERSIA

LUCCA
e
ANY

SAN MARINO
Spalato

Zara

Bosna
Seray

Belgrade

Bucharest

PAPAL
STATES

Mostar

Danube

Ruschuk

Varna

Trebizond

Rome

REPUBLIC OF
RAGUSA

MONTENEGRO

Üsküb

Nish

Sofia

Trebizond

UCHY
OF
STRO

Naples
Bari

NAPLES
Taranto

OTTOMAN

Philippopolis
Adrianople

Janina

Constantinople

Angora

EMPIRE

Tigris

Palermo
Messina

REPUBLIC

Smyrna

Adana

Mosul

SICILY
Catania

Salonica

Euphrates

SEA

Athens

MALTA
(Knights
of St John)

Crete

Nicosia

Beirut
Damascus

Bedouins

125

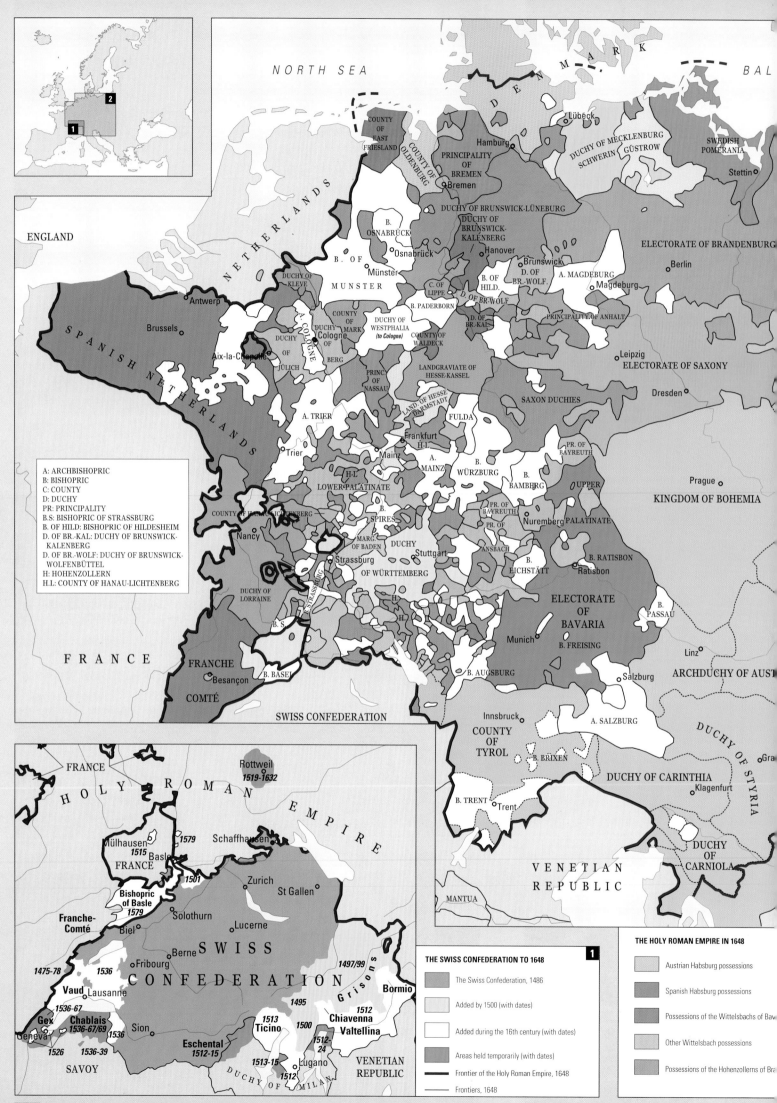

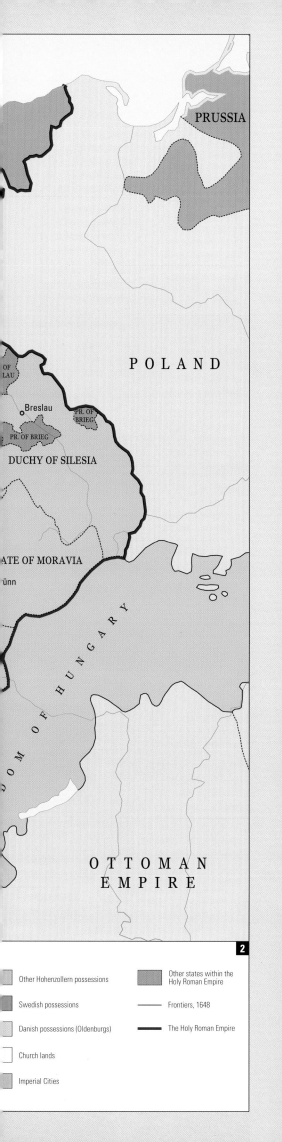

PRUSSIA

POLAND

OF LAU

Breslau

PR. OF BRIEG

PR. OF BRIEG

DUCHY OF SILESIA

ATE OF MORAVIA

ünn

KINGDOM OF HUNGARY

OTTOMAN EMPIRE

2

Other Hohenzollern possessions

Swedish possessions

Danish possessions (Oldenburgs)

Church lands

Imperial Cities

Other states within the Holy Roman Empire

———— Frontiers, 1648

━━━━ The Holy Roman Empire

The Swiss Confederation to 1648

1 Although the Emperor had in effect given up trying to bring the Swiss cantons back under his control as early as 1499, it was only in 1648 that the Holy Roman Empire renounced all claims over the 13 cantons and the city of Basle which together formed the "Community of the Oath" (*Eidegenossenschaft*).

At the same time that the Peace of Westphalia accorded independence to the Swiss cantons, by releasing their legal obligations to the empire, the generally poor Swiss cantons continued their involvement with Imperial politics by providing recruits to the great powers of Europe. Swiss mercenaries passed through the Gex corridor between Franche-Comté and Savoy into France, while others continued to serve the Pope and, from the Grisons in particular, the King of Spain.

The Holy Roman Empire, 1648

2 Historians have always found it difficult to define exactly what the Holy Roman Empire was. The very vagueness of the Empire's definition was part of its identity. It was clearly not a centralised absolutist state of the sort which France had become under the Bourbons. Unlike England, for instance, with its unified system of justice, the Empire contained more than 2,300 different jurisdictions. Given that the Empire was made up of somewhere between 294 and 348 different states after 1648 (historians disagree), it is clear that many of these jurisdictions were overlapping. This had been a source of conflict for centuries, and following the Reformation the issue of whether a prince could determine the faith of his subjects had been the cause of immense strife. Nonetheless, after 1648 most rulers were weary of using religion as the occasion of quarrel – a clear break with the past.

The most important and influential figures in the Empire were the seven Electors who chose the Emperor. Three of them were the Catholic Prince-Archbishops of the clerical states of Cologne, Mainz and Trier, while the other four were lay rulers. Until 1648, three of these were Protestants: the Electors of Brandenburg, the Palatinate and Saxony. Catholic Bavaria was granted the Electoral dignity in 1623. (In 1692, Protestant Hanover was added to the list of Electoral states, while in 1803, in the dying years of the Empire, Baden and Hesse acquired electoral status though neither had the chance to exercise their rights before the Empire's abolition in 1806.)

Despite the best efforts of Ferdinand III, the Habsburgs failed to preserve much real authority for the holder of the Imperial dignity. As a result, the idea that the different princes and states were subservient to the Emperor withered away. It was agreed that majorities in the Imperial Diet could not bind minorities, so no effective legislation was possible. Furthermore the Imperial "circles" (which authorised the raising of taxation) operated only by consent

and with no effective means of coercion, which should not, however, mask the occasions on which the members of given "circles" agreed on the need for common action. In addition, the multitude of weaker states looked to the Emperor as the guarantor of their status and rights. After all, their own standing depended on the same legal basis as that of the Emperor.

Voltaire's famous gibe that the Holy Roman Empire was neither holy, nor Roman, nor an empire applied especially well to the situation after 1648. Nonetheless, after the bloodletting within the Empire during the previous 30 years, it is perhaps more surprising that any Imperial institutions survived at all rather than that shadow instead of substance tended to predominate following the Thirty Years' War. For the Holy Roman Empire to survive more than 150 years after Westphalia suggests that its very vagueness served the purposes of its members (including the more powerful ones) rather better than a clear-cut definition of sovereignty on what was becoming the "modern" model for 17th-century Europe.

Out of the wreckage of the great Habsburg effort to assert Imperial predominance under Ferdinand II from 1618, his son, Ferdinand III, was able to preserve the continuity of the idea of the Empire and from his point of view, perhaps more importantly, to confirm the assumption that a Habsburg should be automatically elected to the throne. Partly because France was convulsed by the civil disorders known as the Frondes, Mazarin was unable to block Ferdinand III's nomination of his own successor, but a sudden death left the position of "King of the Romans" open at Ferdinand's death in 1656 and a bitterly contested election followed in 1657. The Habsburg Leopold I defeated his Bourbon rival, Louis XIV, but only at the cost of renouncing some of his father's rights.

In effect, a balance of power inside the Empire was established in 1648 by the Peace of Westphalia which was to last almost a century. The Habsburg lands did not give the Emperor a strong enough power base to seek to dominate the other rulers (as Ferdinand II had tried with Spanish help). The survival of the Habsburgs on the Imperial throne was offset by the expansion of Brandenburg – to include the Rhine duchies (1609), Prussia (1618) and much of Pomerania – and the acquisition of territories still formally inside the Empire by Sweden and France, as well as the acquisition of land by Bavaria in southern Germany.

The centre of gravity of Habsburg power shifted as a result of these changes towards their Austrian lands. Bohemia, which had been a centre of Protestant dissent, was almost wholly reclaimed for the Catholic Church, while in 1627 the Bohemian crown went from being elective to hereditary within the Habsburg family.

1648

The Siege of Vienna

The failure of the vast Ottoman army to capture Vienna in 1683 was a decisive event in European history. The victory of a mixed force of Imperial and Polish troops over the Sultan's army marked the point after which Christian Europe was never again threatened with conquest by an external enemy. Although the northwestern European powers played no part in the crisis and some German princes, like the Great Elector of Brandenburg-Prussia, studiously ignored the Emperor Leopold I's requests for help, it mattered a great deal to them who won. If the Sultan's forces had captured Vienna, the whole European balance of power would have been shattered. In the event, though 1683 saw the Ottoman Empire at the height of its European conquests, the Turks were already weakened by domestic divisions. Defeat served only to magnify them. Although Polish troops led by their king, Jan Sobieski, played a decisive part in raising the siege of Vienna in September 1683, it was not Poland but the Austrian Habsburgs who ultimately benefited most from the defeat of the Turks. The threat of rebellion in Habsburg-controlled Hungary was reduced, as the border with the Turks was pushed forwards to the south and east.

Yet however momentous the defeat of the Ottomans, the most significant change in the European balance of power after 1648 was the emergence of France as the mightiest country in western Europe. Following the Treaty of the Pyrenees (1659), Spain, formerly the pre-eminent European power, lost any vestiges of her previous position. By 1683, Louis XIV's France was nearing the peak of her power, and aggressively seeking to acquire land along her frontiers. France's power was based on her large population, which at 20 million far outstripped that of her neighbours. Numbers meant power: they provided large tax revenues and a rich source of recruits. Louis XIV's able ministers built on the legacy of Richelieu and Mazarin to create a large standing army, able to intervene swiftly against less well-prepared and well-funded enemies.

Although Louis XIV's France was seen as the arch-absolutist state, in fact it was smaller countries such as Brandenburg-Prussia and Sweden which exemplified the trend away from medieval constitutions to unified and centralised government. With only about two-million subjects, Sweden achieved much more, proportionately, than heavily populated France. In the later 17th century, an absolutist model of rule was imposed on Sweden by Charles XI (1660-97). Unlike his belligerent predecessor, Charles X, Charles XI concentrated on building up the financial power of the monarchy. Charles X's victories had marked the height of Swedish power, but his son's suppression of much of the influence of the nobility was vital in providing the secure base for Sweden's long struggle during the Great Northern War after 1700 (*see* page 136).

Large-scale wars in Eastern Europe, too, particularly involving Poland, had a major effect on the continental balance of power. In 1655, Charles X of Sweden invaded and temporarily took most of Poland, save Gdańsk and Lwów, in the Northern War. By the Truce of Andrusovo (1667), furthermore, Poland lost much of the Ukraine to Russia. By 1668, Poland had a population of only four million, down 45 per cent on that in 1618, while her economy had suffered devastating damage. Her increasing weakness opened up a tempting vacuum which drew in states such as Sweden and Moscow, as well as German princes, all eager for territorial acquisitions.

NORWAY

(Danish)

SWEDEN

Trondhjem

Christiania

Åbo

Helsingfors

Stockholm

Reval

Gothenburg

Riga

Pskov

BALTIC
SEA

COURLAND

Dyneburg

Aarhus

Copenhagen

Malmö

Königsberg

Wilno

Vitebsk

Smolensk

LITHUANIA

DENMARK

Hamburg

SWEDISH
POMERANIA

Stettin

Gdańsk

Minsk

BRANDENBURG

PRUSSIA

Bremen

Brunswick

Hanover

Berlin

Poznań

Vistula

Warsaw

SAXONY

Dresden

Breslau

POLAND

Leipzig

Oder

Elbe

SILESIA

Frankfurt

BOHEMIA

Prague

Cracow

Lwów

Hesse

Nuremberg

MORAVIA

Brünn

Winnica

Dniester

BAVARIA

Vienna

HUNGARY

Y Kassa

PRINC. OF THÖKÖLY
(in revolt against Habsburgs)

Munich

Salzburg

Pozsony

Buda

Debrecén

MOLDAVIA

AUSTRIA

Graz

Pécs

Szeged

Kolozsvár

TRANSYLVANIA

Jassy

MANTUA

Trieste

Zágráb

Danube

Temesvár

Brassó

Venice

VENETIA

Zara

Bosna
Saray

Belgrade

WALLACHIA

Bucharest

SAN MARINO

FLORENCE

PAPAL

Spalato

Mostar

Nish

Ruschuk

Danube

Perugia

REP. OF
RAGUSA

MONTENEGRO

Sofia

Philippopolis

Varna

STATES

Rome

Üsküb

Adrianople

Naples

Bari

Salonica

NAPLES

Taranto

Janina

OTTOMAN EMPIRE

Palermo

Messina

SICILY

Catania

REPUBLIC

Athens

SEA

MALTA
_(Knights of
St John)_

Crete

Archangel

Nizhniy
Novgorod

Kazan

Moscow

Volga

RUSSIA

Samara

Tula

Saratov

Kursk

Tsaritsyn

Kharkov

Volga

Kiev

HETMANATE

Don

Astrakhan

Zaporogian Cossacks

Dnieper

Azov

KHANATE
OF
CRIMEA

Circassians

Daghestan

Bakhchisaray

Tiflis

BLACK SEA

Erivan

PERSIA

Constantinople

Ankara

Trebizond

Smyrna

Adana

Mosul

Euphrates

Tigris

Nicosia

Beirut

Damascus

Bedouins

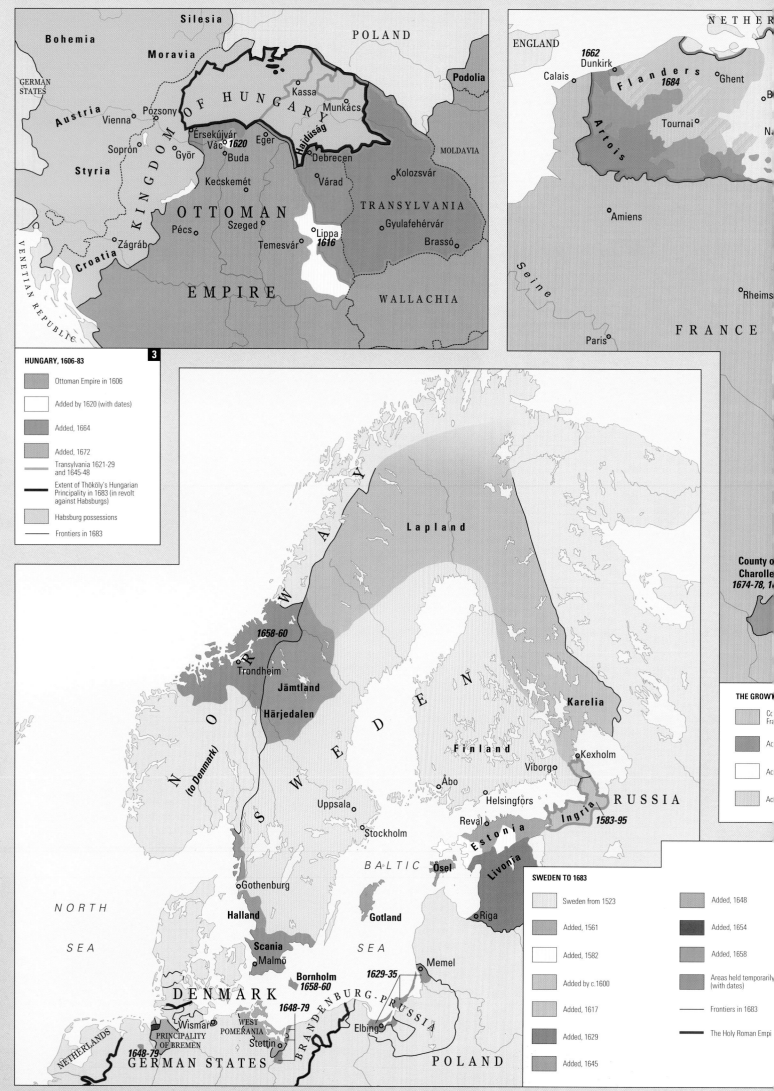

HUNGARY, 1606-83

- Ottoman Empire in 1606
- Added by 1620 (with dates)
- Added, 1664
- Added, 1672
- Transylvania 1621-29 and 1645-48
- Extent of Thököly's Hungarian Principality in 1683 (in revolt against Habsburgs)
- Habsburg possessions
- Frontiers in 1683

SWEDEN TO 1683

- Sweden from 1523
- Added, 1561
- Added, 1582
- Added by c.1600
- Added, 1617
- Added, 1629
- Added, 1645
- Added, 1648
- Added, 1654
- Added, 1658
- Areas held temporarily (with dates)
- Frontiers in 1683
- The Holy Roman Empi[re]

THE GROW[TH]

- Co[...] Fra[...]
- Ac[...]
- Ac[...]
- Ac[...]

County o[f] Charolle[...] 1674-78, 1[...]

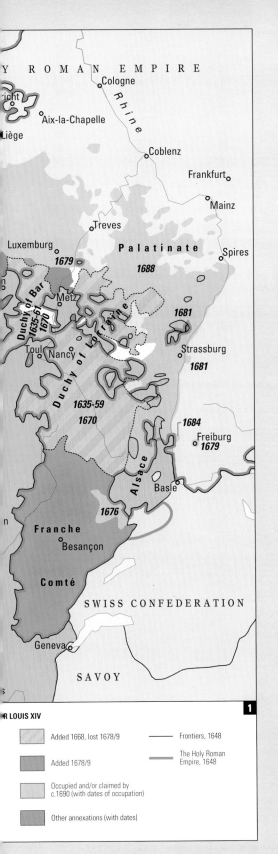

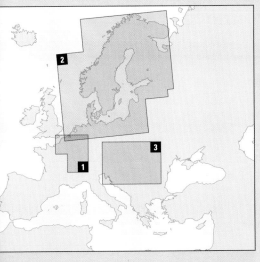

The Growth of France under Louis XIV

1 After the death of Mazarin in 1661, Louis XIV pursued a policy of diplomatic aggression. But it was only in 1667 that he first went to war. Claiming parts of the Spanish Netherlands by virtue of his Habsburg wife's rights as the elder sister of the new Spanish king, Carlos II, Louis XIV's troops quickly occupied the territory. Peace in 1668 gave France 12 fortresses along her borders with the Spanish Netherlands (to add to Dunkirk, bought from England in 1662).

Then, in 1672, Louis XIV turned on his former Dutch allies. They were saved from defeat only by opening the dykes as they had done a century earlier in their war against the Spanish. Although the Dutch survived until peace in 1678 and even recovered Maastricht by the Treaty of Nijmegen (1678-9), it was their weak Spanish allies who paid the price: France took more border fortresses plus the Franche-Comté and remained in occupation of the Duchy of Lorraine. France also kept Freiburg on the Rhine.

Louis XIV now adopted a complicated and essentially fraudulent legal procedure to claim sovereignty over many pockets of Imperial territory along his eastern border whose status after the Peace of Westphalia (*see page 124*) was ambiguous. Using his ever-growing army to back up the decisions of the so-called *chambres des réunions*, Luxemburg was repeatedly besieged and threatened as Louis nibbled at one part then another of the Duchy before seizing the fortress itself in 1684. Using the clerical jurisdiction of three bishoprics, Metz, Toul and Verdun, granted to France definitively at Westphalia, Louis XIV claimed political sovereignty over other places in their sees. Similarly, in Alsace French judges annulled the traditional rights of the German-speaking towns, seizing the great trading city of Strassburg in 1681.

Sweden to 1683

2 Sweden had expanded significantly from her core areas even before her gains from the Peace of Westphalia. By 1595, Sweden controlled the whole of Estonia. In 1617, under the Peace of Stolbovo, she added Karelia, cutting off Russia from all access to the Baltic. Sweden took Livonia from Poland in 1629, and occupied a string of Baltic ports on the Polish coastline between 1629 and 1635. In 1645 Denmark was forced to cede the Baltic islands of Ösel and Gotland to Sweden, as well as Jämtland and Härjedalen on the border with Norway. Although the peace settlement in 1648 gave her a string of territories around the southern borders of her old enemy Denmark, the Scania peninsula remained in Danish hands until 1658. Charles X waged a brilliant set of campaigns against a coalition of enemies, Denmark, Poland and Muscovy, and captured much of the remaining Danish territory on the northern side of the Baltic. In addition to Scania, Denmark had to cede parts of Norway around Trondheim and the island of Bornholm in the Baltic. Charles X how-

ever grew over-ambitious and tried to seize Copenhagen itself in a renewed war, hoping Sweden could control the traffic into the Baltic and therefore its tolls. But his sudden death and stiff Danish resistance led to a modified settlement in 1660, in which Denmark recovered Bornholm and parts of Norway. Sweden also had to renounce her demand that Denmark prevent foreign warships entering the Baltic.

During the minority of Charles XI (until 1672), Denmark started a war to recover Scania but the young king asserted himself and defeated the Danish invasion. Sweden fared less well against Brandenburg-Prussia, which had imitated some of her military and administrative measures, and put them to the test in a war in 1675. Only Louis XIV's pressure prevented Sweden losing more than small areas of Pomerania to Brandenburg. As the wars of the 1650s and 1670s showed, Sweden's Baltic empire was surrounded by envious neighbours and it was only a matter of time before the numerically weak Swedes lost the advantage of better organisation.

Hungary, 1606-83

3 By the early 17th century, the Turkish hold on central Hungary was weakening. Transylvania emerged during this period as an important and prosperous European power, ruled by Prince Bethlen Gábor (1613-29). He doubled the territory's revenues and acted as a staunch defender of Calvinism in Central Europe. His influence, and that of his successor Györgi I Rákóczi, meant that the Habsburgs could not enforce the Counter-Reformation as brutally in the parts of Hungary they controlled (Royal Hungary) as they did elsewhere.

Transylvania's brief flowering ended after 1657, when the army of Györgi II Rákóczi was destroyed by Tatars while attempting to seize the crown of Poland. Mehmet Köprülü, the Turkish Grand Vizier, took this chance to invade Transylvania, and seized important parts of the principality in the west, including Várad. The Habsburgs intervened and won a surprise victory against the Turks, but the peace settlement of Vasvár (1664) ratified most of the Ottoman gains.

The apparent increase in Turkish power encouraged anti-Habsburg plotting in Royal Hungary in the 1670s. A savage Habsburg reaction had the effect of driving the malcontents to more extreme measures. In 1678, Imre Thököly, a young Transylvanian, raised the standard of revolt and occupied a large part of central Hungary. The Turks took this opportunity to intervene and sent a huge army into Hungary in 1683. This laid siege to Vienna, putting the whole European balance of power in peril. By September, however, the siege had been lifted, in part through the intervention of King Jan Sobieski of Poland, and by 1699 Imperial forces had swept the Turks out of most of Hungary.

The Ascendancy of France

The defeat of the Ottoman army at Vienna in September 1683 by the Habsburgs was followed by the rapid advance of Emperor Leopold I's forces into Hungary, Transylvania and the Balkans. The Emperor formed the Holy League in 1684 with Poland and Venice to pursue the struggle against the Turks. Russia joined in 1686. However, war in the west gave the Turks a breathing space, as the Emperor, fearing a switch in the traditional pro-Habsburg majority in the Electoral College which chose Holy Roman Emperors, was forced to send soldiers westwards to the Rhine to resist a French threat to the Electorates there. Nonetheless, fighting dragged on until 1699 and the Turkish Sultan, who had recovered all of the Northern Balkans, was forced to cede Transylvania and most of Hungary to the Emperor by the Treaty of Carlowitz in 1699. His allies acquired territory, too. Poland regained Podolia and part of the Ukraine west of the Dnieper, while Venice took the Peloponnese and most of Dalmatia.

In Western Europe, Louis XIV's relentless nibbling away at the Spanish Netherlands and at the Imperial fringe territories turned his neighbours against him. In 1686, Catholic and Protestant German princes formed the League of Augsburg to resist further French penetration into the Holy Roman Empire. Louis XIV's revocation of the rights of French Protestants in 1685 also pushed traditionally pro-French, but firmly Protestant, Sweden into the League along with Catholic Austria, Bavaria and Spain.

France was already feeling the strain of enormous military expenditure even before the outbreak of war in 1688 (the Nine Years' War), when Louis XIV sent his troops into the Rhineland to secure his authority there. The war cost France dear. Famine and peasant discontent compounded the failure of the French armies to achieve victory. Instead, the improved forces of the German princes, backed by Anglo-Dutch troops and financial power, wore France down.

With the French in 1688 committed to their assault on the Rhineland, the Dutch were able to spare troops to assist in the overthrow of the Catholic James II of England. The Dutch Prince William of Orange gained the British crown, and the anti-French coalition was thereby greatly strengthened.

On the other hand, as the French threat declined, so rivalries between the allies grew. On the political horizon, the vital question of who would inherit the Spanish Habsburg throne when the childless Carlos II eventually died was becoming acute. William III (of England and the Netherlands), although in alliance with the Austrian Habsburgs from 1688, was anxious to avoid either a clear-cut French or Austrian succession. Peace in 1697 was meant to buy all the participants time to prepare for the next crisis.

In the east, another European succession crisis loomed when Charles XI of Sweden died in 1697, leaving his 15 year-old son, Charles XII, as king. Sweden's neighbours eyed her territory greedily, and none more so than Augustus the Strong of Saxony, who had additionally ruled Poland in personal union since 1697. By 1699, Augustus was preparing for a campaign to seize Sweden's territories to the south of the Baltic, despite bitter opposition from the Polish Diet (parliament).

Meanwhile, the young Tsar of Muscovy, Peter I, had captured Azov on the Black Sea from the Turks in 1696, giving his previously land-locked empire an outlet to the sea. Peter managed to retain Azov, despite the weakening of his strategic position when Austria and Venice, his Holy League allies, made peace with the Sultan by the Treaty of Carlowitz in 1699.

Spanish Habsburg possessions

Austrian Habsburg possessions

The Holy Roman Empire

NORWAY (Danish)

Trondhjem

Christiania

SWEDEN

Åbo Helsingfors

Stockholm

Reval

Pskov

Gothenburg

Riga

DENMARK
Aarhus
Copenhagen Malmö

BALTIC
SEA

COURLAND

Dyneburg

DUCHY OF SCHLESWIG
HOLSTEIN-GOTTORP
SWEDISH
POMERANIA

Wilno

Vitebsk

LITHUANIA

Hamburg Stettin

Königsberg

Minsk

Bremen

BRANDENBURG.

Gdańsk

PRUSSIA

Hanover

Berlin

Poznań

Warsaw

Brześć-Litewski

Frankfurt

SAXONY

Breslau

Łódź

Leipzig Dresden

SILESIA

BOHEMIA

POLAND

Prague

Cracow

(in Personal Union with Saxony)

MORAVIA

Brünn

Winnica

BAVARIA

Vienna

Munich

AUSTRIA

Salzburg

Pozsony

Buda Pest

Graz

HUNGARY

Debrecen

Venice Trieste

Zágráb

(Military administration)

Kolozsvár

Jassy

MOLDAVIA

Szeged

TRANSYLVANIA

Temesvár

Brassó

Modena

Bologna

SAN MARINO

Zara

Bosna Saray

Belgrade

WALLACHIA

Bucharest

TUSCANY

PAPAL

Spalato

Nish

Mostar

STATES

Rome

REP. OF
RAGUSA

MONTENEGRO

Sofia

Ruschuk

Danube

Varna

Philippopolis

Naples

Bari

Üsküb

Adrianople

NAPLES

Taranto

Salonica

Janina

Constantinople

Palermo

Messina

Angora

SICILY

Catania

Smyrna

Patras

Athens

Adana

SEA

MALTA
(Knights of
St John)

Crete

Nicosia

Beirut

Damascus

Bedouins

133

RUSSIAN EMPIRE

Archangel

Perm

Nizhniy
Novgorod

Volga

Moscow

Samara

Smolensk

Tula

Saratov

Kursk

Kharkov

Astrakhan

Don

Kiev

HETMANATE

Dnieper

Volga

Zaporogian Cossacks

Dniester

Azov

KHANATE OF CRIMEA

Great Kabardia

Daghestan

Bakhchisaray

Circassians

BLACK SEA

PERSIA

Trebizond

OTTOMAN EMPIRE

Mosul

Tigris

Euphrates

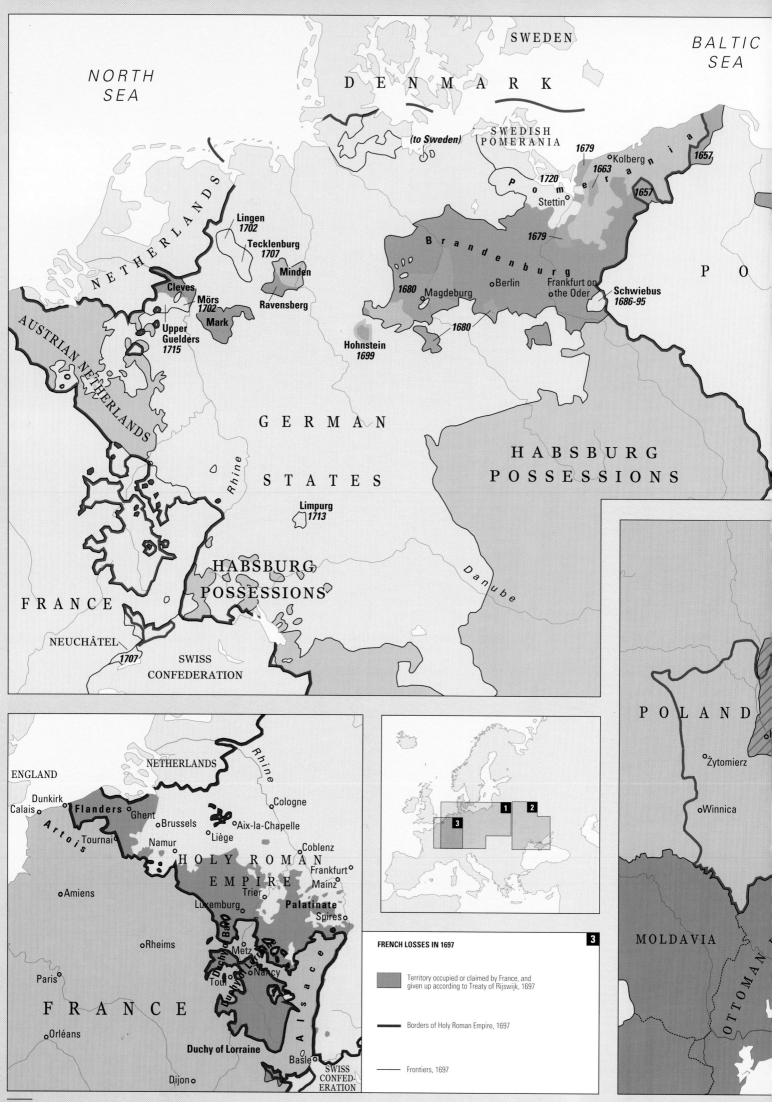

NORTH
SEA

SWEDEN

BALTIC
SEA

D E N M A R K

(to Sweden)

SWEDISH
POMERANIA

1679

°Kolberg

1657

P o m e r a n i a

1720

1663

1657

Stettin°

NETHERLANDS

Lingen
1702

Tecklenburg
1707

Minden

1679

B r a n d e n b u r g

P O

Cleves

Mörs
1702

Ravensberg

°Berlin

Frankfurt on
the Oder

Schwiebus
1686-95

AUSTRIAN NETHERLANDS

Upper
Guelders
1715

Mark

1680

°Magdeburg

Hohnstein
1699

1680

H A B S B U R G
P O S S E S S I O N S

G E R M A N

S T A T E S

Rhine

Limpurg
1713

HABSBURG
POSSESSIONS

D a n u b e

FRANCE

NEUCHÂTEL

1707

SWISS
CONFEDERATION

P O L A N D

°Żytomierz

°Winnica

ENGLAND

Rhine

NETHERLANDS

Dunkirk

°Cologne

Calais

Flanders

Ghent

°Brussels

°Aix-la-Chapelle

Artois

Tournai

Namur

°Liège

°Amiens

Coblenz°

H O L Y   R O M A N

°Frankfurt

E M P I R E

Mainz°

Trier°

Luxemburg

Palatinate

°Rheims

Metz

Spires°

°Paris

Nancy

Duchy of Bar

Alsace

Toul

FRANCE

Duchy of Lorraine

°Orléans

Basle°

Dijon°

SWISS
CONFED-
ERATION

MOLDAVIA

OTTOMAN

FRENCH LOSSES IN 1697

3

Territory occupied or claimed by France, and
given up according to Treaty of Rijswijk, 1697

Borders of Holy Roman Empire, 1697

Frontiers, 1697

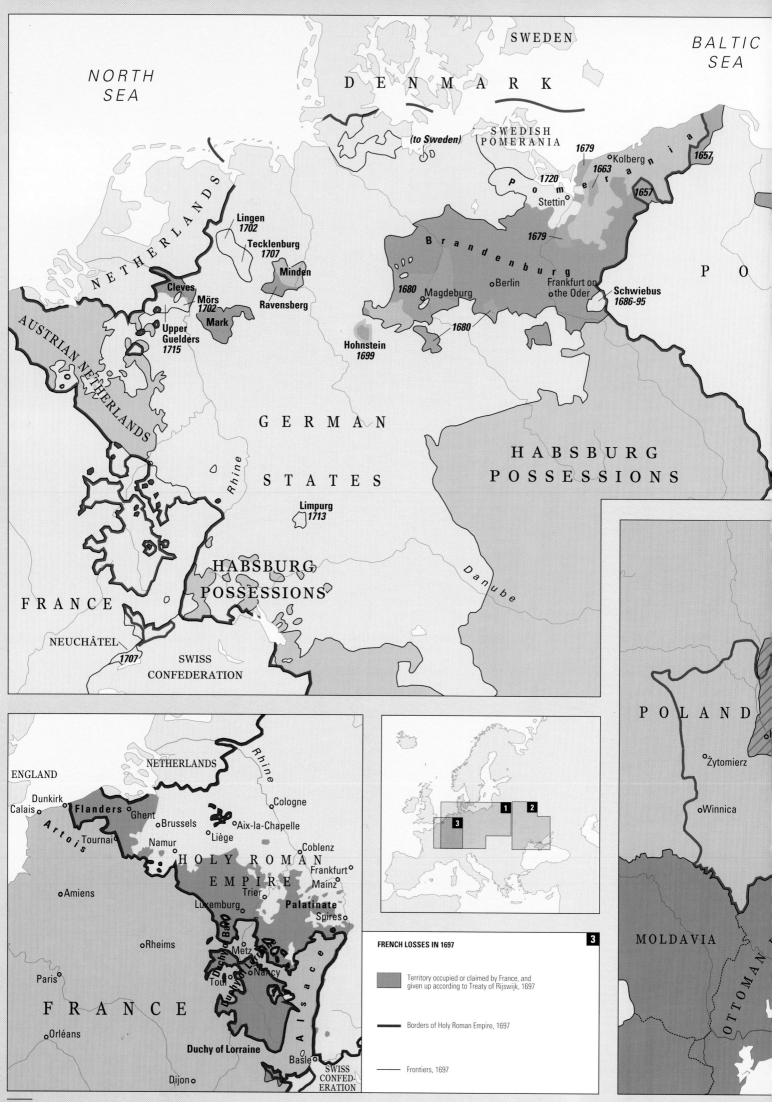

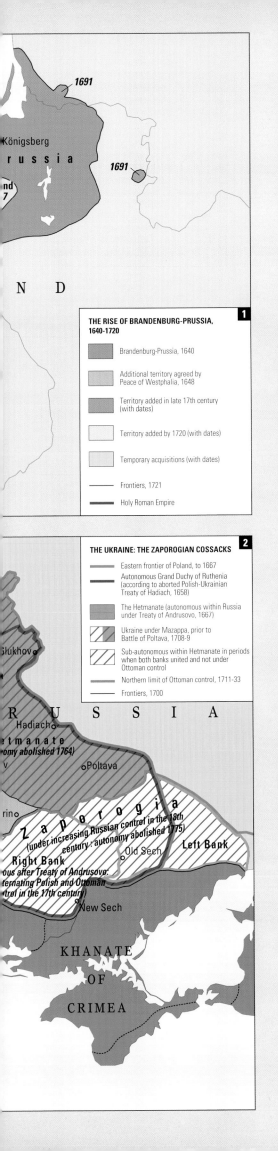

The map on the left includes the following labels and legend:

1691

Königsberg

Prussia

N D

THE RISE OF BRANDENBURG-PRUSSIA, 1640-1720

1

- Brandenburg-Prussia, 1640
- Additional territory agreed by Peace of Westphalia, 1648
- Territory added in late 17th century (with dates)
- Territory added by 1720 (with dates)
- Temporary acquisitions (with dates)
- Frontiers, 1721
- Holy Roman Empire

THE UKRAINE: THE ZAPOROGIAN COSSACKS

2

- Eastern frontier of Poland, to 1667
- Autonomous Grand Duchy of Ruthenia (according to aborted Polish-Ukrainian Treaty of Hadiach, 1658)
- The Hetmanate (autonomous within Russia under Treaty of Andrusovo, 1667)
- Ukraine under Mazappa, prior to Battle of Poltava, 1708-9
- Sub-autonomous within Hetmanate in periods when both banks united and not under Ottoman control
- Northern limit of Ottoman control, 1711-33
- Frontiers, 1700

Glukhov

R U S S I A

Hadiach

Hetmanate
(autonomy abolished 1764)

Poltava

rino

Zaporogia
(under increasing Russian control in the 18th century: autonomy abolished 1775)

Old Sech

Left Bank

Right Bank
(alternating Polish and Ottoman control in the 17th century)

New Sech

KHANATE

OF

CRIMEA

The Rise of Brandenburg-Prussia 1640-1720

1 When Frederick William inherited the Electorate of Brandenburg in 1640, it was one of the most devastated parts of the Holy Roman Empire. During the negotiations leading up to the Peace of Westphalia in 1648 he showed skillful obstinacy which eventually persuaded the other great powers, France and Sweden, to accept some of his ambitious demands in order to get a peace settlement agreed within the Empire. Although Sweden took the bulk of Pomerania, Brandenburg received Eastern Pomerania plus pockets of territory such as Minden and the reversion of Magdeburg on the death of its "administrator" (who died in 1680), which helped to link the core lands east of the Elbe with the possessions in the Rhineland, Cleve and Mark.

Frederick William recognised that without a standing army and therefore without the tax revenue to pay for it, he could never hope to assert himself in his inherited quarrels with dynastic rivals or to pursue his ambitions against what had become Swedish Pomerania after 1648. The Elector had first to make himself master over his own subjects. The two decades after 1648 were largely taken up with Frederick William's imposition of absolutist rule on each of his territories in turn. He persuaded or cajoled the local estates into granting him taxes to maintain a standing army, which in turn served to intimidate the local elites into obeying him.

In 1657, as a by-product of Poland's humiliation in the Northern War with Sweden, the Elector was able to make himself sovereign Duke of East Prussia instead of owing fealty to Poland. It was a significant step towards his son's assertion of the royal title of King in Prussia in 1701. At his death in 1688, the "Great" Elector's regular army numbered 30,000 – more than England's – and Brandenburg-Prussia was well on the way to being "an army with a state" rather than a state with an army. Prussia's position was further strengthened in 1720, with the acquisition of much of western Pomerania from Sweden by the Peace of Stockholm.

The Ukraine: the Zaporogian Cossacks

2 In the second third of the 17th century, Polish noblemen established great estates and even endowed Catholic (Uniate) churches well to the east of the Dnieper as far as Poltava. The Ukraine appeared set to become an integrated part of the Polish Commonwealth.

Local Cossacks were subordinated in theory to the Polish authorities but their obedience was often bought by encouraging them to raid their Tatar and Turkish enemies to the south. Most peasants found themselves enserfed. In 1648, thousands of peasants rose in revolt against their masters, encouraged by a simultaneous dispute between the Polish authorities and the leaders of the "free" Cossacks. Kiev fell to the rebels and was declared Orthodox again, while the Catholic clergy were driven out.

After winning dramatic victories, the Cossack leaders settled with the new King of Poland, Jan Casimir, much to the disgust of the peasantry. Fresh quarrels ensued. The Poles gradually whittled down the area of Cossack control as the Cossacks turned to Muscovy for support.

The Northern War (1655-60) left Poland much weakened and her control over the Ukraine, particularly in the south and east, was never secure after 1648. Wars with Russia (1654-6 and 1658-67) saw the Cossacks side with the Tsar against the Poles. The Treaty of Hadiach (1658) left Ukraine and Poland rejoined in a personal union, but renewed Russian-Polish fighting meant its terms were never effectively implemented. By the Treaty of Andrusovo (1667), Muscovy gained Smolensk and the Ukraine up to the Dnieper as well as ancient Kiev on the west bank. An autonomous region, the Hetmanate, was created on part of the territory added to Russia. The Cossacks of Zaporogia had autonomy within this area, which applied to their lands when they were not under Polish or Ottoman control.

The Cossacks proved almost as unruly as subjects of the Tsar as they had under the Poles. Under Peter the Great, Mazappa, the Hetman (commander) of the Tsar's Cossacks, tried to create an independent Cossack state in the Ukraine in alliance with the Swedes and the Zaporogian Cossack Host. Peter's victory in 1709 marked the conquest of the Cossacks. Many of the survivors were deported to distant parts of the Tsar's empire.

French Losses in 1697

3 Although the Nine Years' War (1688-97) soon reached stalemate, it took many years before Louis XIV was prepared to make sufficient concessions to buy peace from his enemies. In 1696, he gave up some areas in southern France around Nice to Savoy, in effect admitting that the duchy of Savoy could not be made into a French satellite.

By the Treaty of Rijswijk (1697), France returned Lorraine to her duke, but with the duchy surrounded by Louis XIV's territory, France retained effective military control. However, both Flanders and Luxemburg were returned to Spain (as was occupied Catalonia), probably because Louis was already manoeuvring for Madrid's favour over who would succeed to the Spanish throne when Carlos II died. Other parts of Imperial territory, including a section of the Palatinate, were also given up, though France kept Alsace and Strasbourg.

A key cause of the war after 1688 was Louis XIV's evident determination to dominate the key clerical electorates in the triangle between Trier, Cologne and Mainz. This would have made France dominant along the vital trade arteries of the Rhine and Main. By 1697, however, the greater problem of who would inherit the vast Spanish empire was looming on the horizon.

1699

The Rise of Russia

Though Spanish Habsburg power was in decline by the late 17th century, control of their vast empire in Europe and in the Americas remained a crucial prize. The death of the childless last Spanish Habsburg, Carlos II, in 1700 led to a struggle between his French and Austrian relatives for the succession. Europe's strategic balance was at stake, and the determination of the Austrian Habsburgs and their Anglo-Dutch allies to thwart Louis XIV's ambitions for French expansion led to the bitterly-contested War of the Spanish Succession (1701-14). Louis XIV's acceptance of Carlos II's will, which granted his entire empire to his grandson, the Bourbon Philip of Anjou, made war with Britain inevitable, as she could not tolerate the strategic Barrier Fortresses on the border with the Spanish Netherlands falling into French hands. Leopold I of Austria, meanwhile, sought to place his younger son, Charles, on the Spanish throne and fighting spread across western Europe from Italy, into Spain itself, and up the Rhine into the Low Countries.

After a decade of war, France engineered a compromise peace. Philip of Anjou retained the Spanish throne (as Philip V), but he and his heirs were denied the right to succeed Louis XIV in France. Leopold I's son, now Charles VI, had to accept the loss of Spain, particularly as his erstwhile British and Dutch allies saw little purpose in fighting to prevent a Bourbon hegemony only to restore a Habsburg version of it. The treaties of Utrecht (1713), Baden (1714) and Rastatt (1714) brought the conflict to an end. Charles VI did not, however, formally recognise the Bourbon Philip V as King of Spain until 1720.

The Austrian Habsburgs made up for this serious reverse in the west by continuing their advances into Ottoman territory in the east. By the Treaty of Passarowitz (1718), they gained Belgrade, the Banat of Temesvár, and parts of Serbia and Wallachia. The Turks were not entirely on the defensive, however, as in 1715 they forced the Venetians out of the Peloponnese.

In northern Europe, the young Charles XII faced a coalition of Sweden's neighbours intent on taking advantage of his minority. Unfortunately for Denmark, Saxony-Poland and Russia, the young king inherited a well-trained and officered army and possessed military genius, which came to the fore in the Great Northern War (1700-1721). He routed an ill-prepared Russian army at Narva in 1700 and then scattered his Danish and Polish/Saxon enemies, but his invasion of Russia led to disaster at Poltava (1709). Sweden lacked the resources to make up its heavy losses and afterwards was forced back into a defensive strategic position.

Britain and Russia emerged the winners from the two great wars at the start of the 18th century. Although in territorial terms, Britain gained little, only the fortress of Gibraltar and Minorca, her influence after Utrecht was still enormous because of her wealth from commercial gains outside Europe. France, though defeated, was too populous and wealthy to be reduced from her status as the greatest single power, but her long-term prospects of dominating the Continent were damaged by the financial exhaustion which Louis XIV bequeathed his infant successor in 1715.

Peter the Great of Russia (1682-1725) decisively altered the estimation of the previously vast but ill-organised Tsarist empire. By combining Western techniques with ruthless autocratic methods, he created a military system for Russia capable of wearing down his gifted Swedish rival. By 1721, Russia overshadowed the Baltic region: she gained greatly from the Treaty of Nystad (1721), taking Estonia, Livonia, Ingria, most of Karelia and part of Finland. A defeat by the Turks, however, led to the loss of Azov on the Black Sea in 1711.

Habsburg possessions

The Holy Roman Empire

NORWAY
(Danish)

SWEDEN

Karelia

RUSSIAN

EMPIRE

Trondhjem

Christiania

Trondhjem

Nystad
Åbo
Helsingfors
St. Petersburg
Narva **Ingria**
Revel
Estonia

Stockholm

Gothenburg

BALTIC
SEA

Aarhus
Copenhagen
Frederiksborg
Malmö
DENMARK

Livonia Pskov
Riga
COURLAND
Dyneburg

**SWEDISH
POMERANIA**
Stettin
HANOVER
Hamburg
Hanover
Frankfurt

Königsberg
Gdansk
PRUSSIA

Wilno
Vitebsk

LITHUANIA
Minsk

Moscow

Tula

Smolensk

Nizhniy
Novgorod
Volga

Samara

Saratov

PRUSSIA
Berlin
Poznań
Oder
Vistula
SAXONY
Dresden
SILESIA
Breslau
BOHEMIA
Prague
MORAVIA
Brünn

Warsaw
Łódź
Brześć-Litewski

POLAND
(in Personal Union with Saxony)

Cracow

Kiev

HETMANATE
Poltava

Winnica

Dnieper

Kursk

Kharkov

Don

Astrakhan

Volga

BAVARIA
Munich
Vienna
AUSTRIA
Salzburg
Graz

Pozsony
Buda Pest

HABSBURG POSESSIONS
HUNGARY
Debrecen
Szeged

Kolozsvár
TRANSYLVANIA
Temesvár Brassó

MOLDAVIA
Jassy

Dniester

Zaporogian Cossacks

Azov

KHANATE OF CRIMEA

Bakhchisaray

Great Kabardia

Circassians

Daghestan

Venice
Trieste
Zágráb
MODENA
Bologna
SAN MARINO
Zara
Bosna Saray
Spalato
Mostar
(Military administration)

WALLACHIA
Belgrade
Bucharest
Nish
Danube Ruschuk

PERSIA

VENETIAN REPUBLIC

TUSCANY
PAPAL
STATES
Rome

REPUBLIC
OF RAGUSA
MONTENEGRO
Üsküb

Sofia
Philippopolis
Adrianople

Varna
Burgas

BLACK SEA

Trebizond

Constantinople

**KINGDOM OF
NAPLES AND SICILY**
Naples
Bari
Taranto

Janina

Salonica

Smyrna

Angora

Tigris

Mosul

Palermo
Messina
Catania

Patras
Athens

Adana

Euphrates

OTTOMAN EMPIRE

MALTA
**(Knights of
St John)**

SEA

Crete

Nicosia

Beirut
Damascus

Bedouins

137

DENMARK
(to Sweden)

Friesland

Holland

NETHERLANDS

Zeeland

Brandenburg

POLAND

AUSTRIAN NETHERLANDS

○ Cologne
JÜLICH BERG

Hainaut

GERMAN STATES

Bohemia

FRANCE

Würzburg ○
Bamberg ○
Spires ○
PALATINATE
Nuremberg ○

Bayreuth ○

H A B S B U R G   P O S S E S S I O N S

Ratisbon ○
BAVARIA
Passau ○
Munich ○

Austria

HUNGARY

NEUCHÂTEL

SWISS CONFEDERATION

Tyrol

Salzburg ○

Carinthia

V E N E T I A N

KINGDOM OF SARDINIA

MILAN

MANTUA

R E P U B L I C

MILITARY FRONTIER

VENAISSIN

REP. OF GENOA

PARMA

MODENA

PAPAL STATES

SWISS CONFEDERATION

Tyrol

Savoy

MASSERANO
KINGDOM OF SARDINIA
Piedmont

BISHOPRIC OF

DUCHY OF Milan
MILAN

○ Veron

FRANCE

Genoa ○

SABIONETTA
PARMA
Parma

DUCHY OF MANTUA
GUASTALLA
NOVELLARA
Mantua ○

Modena ○

Nizza ○
MONACO ○

FOSDINOVO
MASSSA
LUCCA

○ Bol

○ Lucca
Florence ○

R E P U B L I C   O F   G E N O A

PIOMBINO

TUSCANY

STA

Rom

STATO DEI PRESIDI

○ Sassari
KINGDOM OF SARDINIA
(held by Habsburgs, 1714-20)

(to Pa

BAVARIA TO THE END OF THE 18TH CENTURY   **1**

▢ Bavaria, 955

▨ Wittelsbach possessions, c. 1350

— Frontiers,1721

▢ Bavaria, 1721

▢ 18th-century additions to Bavarian territory

▨ Bavarian territory lost in 1779

━ The Holy Roman Empire

PRUSSIA

Bohemia

Moravia

POLAND

GERMAN STATES

Austria

Kassa ○

Vienna ○
Pozsony ○

Styria

Sopron ○

Buda ○

P a r t i u m

MOLDAVIA

M E D I T E R R A N

Carinthia

Nagyvárad ○

Carniola

Zágráb ○
Croatia

H U N G A R Y

Pécs ○

Szeged ○

TRANSYLVANIA

Kolozsvár ○

Gyulafehérvár ○

Temesvár ○
Zenta ○
BANAT OF TEMES
(to Hungary 1779)

Nagyszeben ○

Brassó ○

V E N E T I A N

Eszék ○
Slavonia

Carlowitz ○

TUNIS
(Ottoman vassal)

PAPAL STATES

R E P U B L I C

Belgrade ○
Passarowitz ○

WALLACHIA

O T T O M A N   E M P I R E

3

THE HABSBURG REORGANISATION OF HUNGARY

━ Hungary, c.1500

— Ottoman frontier, 1683

┅ Ottoman frontier, 1699

▨ Status undecided until 1732, when united with Hungary

▨ Status undecided until 1732, when united with Transylvania

▨ Returned to Hungary from military administration in 1744 but then united with Croatia: status subsequently disputed

▢ Hungary by 1745

▨ Returned to Hungary from military administration, 1750

▢ Lands acknowledged by Habsburgs as part of the Hungarian Crown but administered separately

▨ Autonomous within Hungary

▢ Temporary Habsburg acquisition, 1718-39

▢ Other Habsburg territory

— Frontiers, 1752

ITALY, 1714-21   **2**

▢ Habsburg possessions

━ The Holy Roman Empire

— Frontiers, 1721

Bavaria to the End of the 18th Century

1 The origins of the Bavarian duchy lay in a 4th-century barbarian incursion into the Roman Empire. The Bavarians were ruled by the native Agilolfing dynasty until their last duke, Tassilo, was defeated by Charlemagne in 788 and his lands incorporated into the Frankish Empire. After the partitions of the Frankish empire in the 9th century, the Duchy of Bavaria became an East Frankish territory with a royal residence at Regensburg.

By the 11th century Bavaria came to be ruled by the Wittelsbach family, who held it until 1918. At first they ruled only the southeastern part of present-day Bavaria and political divisions in the 14th and 15th century led to a fragmentation of the duchy. Bavaria was only reunited by Duke Albert IV (1467-1508) with Munich as its capital.

During the Wars of Religion of the 16th century and in the Thirty Years' War, the Bavarian Dukes were staunch defenders of the Catholic cause. They were rewarded for their loyalty to the Imperial cause by the transfer of the Upper Palatinate to Bavaria in 1648, and with it the title of Elector. Bavarian influence was further enhanced by the acquisition of Julich-Berg, inherited by Charles Theodore of the Palatinate, Elector of Bavaria from 1777 to 1799. By the late 18th century, the duchy had become a serious rival to the Habsburgs in southern Germany.

The Austrian Habsburgs, indeed, sought repeatedly to draw Bavaria into their sphere of influence. In the War of the Spanish Succession, the Elector Max Emmanuel sided with Louis XIV, and was, for his pains, expelled by the Austrian Habsburgs, and only restored at French insistence. In 1777 the Elector Max Joseph II died and the Austrian Habsburg Emperor Joseph II put forward a distant claim of his own to the Bavarian crown. The Prussians reacted with large-scale troop movements to prevent this disturbance in the European balance of power. The Bavarian War of Succession which resulted between Austria and Prussia was not a long fought struggle, and from the Treaty of Teschen which ended it in 1779 no clear victor emerged, and only a small area of land to the north of Salzburg passed to the Austrians.

Italy, 1714-21

2 Despite the peace settlement which concluded the War of the Spanish Succession, the Habsburg Charles VI of Austria was still unwilling to accept the Bourbon Philip V as King of Spain, and the Mediterranean became the scene of tension and clashes after 1714 as the Emperor manoeuvred, apparently to pursue his claims to Spain, while Philip V and his Italian wife, Elizabeth Farnese, devoted much effort to interference in Italy and seeking to establish their children there as a way of reversing Vienna's hegemony.

An eventual compromise was reached, which granted Don Carlos, Elizabeth's son, the succession to Parma, while Sicily and Sardinia were swapped between the Austrian emperor and Victor Amadeus of Savoy in 1720. The Austrian Habsburgs now had a cohesive southern Italian kingdom of Naples and Sicily, while Savoy ruled over more distant Sardinia. Austria also possessed the key Tuscan ports (and the island of Elba) which had given their Spanish cousins dominance over much of Central Italy's trade for two centuries. Milan and Mantua, too, were Austrian Habsburg territory from 1714, although Savoy had received some border areas from Milan in 1713.

These uneasy compromises were the result of an unusual alliance between France and Britain which came into being in 1716 to force Spain into line. Philip V announced that Spain had no ambitions in Italy – even though his children by Elizabeth Farnese still had aspirations to rule in Parma.

The Habsburg Reorganisation of Hungary

3 The potential of Austrian Habsburg power was often diminished by the division of its attention between two fronts. In the west, the struggle against Louis XIV dragged on for decades, while in the east Leopold I and his successors pursued their ambitions against the Sultan. Only when Austria had support in the west from powerful allies like Britain and the Netherlands and when her own armies, under the generalship of Prince Eugene of Savoy, achieved levels of military efficiency comparable with the best in Europe, could she hope to overcome this division of her forces.

After the defeat of the Turks outside Vienna in 1683, Leopold I pursued the war against the Sultan and found new allies to join in his latter-day crusade. While the Venetians seized the Morea and Athens in 1690, Habsburg forces occupied Hungary and Transylvania. In 1687, the Hungarian Diet agreed that the Hungarian Crown should pass by hereditary right to the Habsburgs.

Although the Turks had recovered Belgrade in 1690, they suffered a crushing defeat by Prince Eugene at Zenta in 1697, and the Sultan made peace with the Emperor at Carlowitz in 1699. The land taken from the Ottomans was put initially under military administration. During the next half century it was gradually re-absorbed into Hungary, save for a strip by the Ottoman frontier which remained under military administration as the Military Frontier (*see* map 2, page 143). The War of the Spanish Succession distracted the Habsburgs from the Balkans, but between 1716 and 1718 Prince Eugene waged his most devastating war of conquest. By the Treaty of Passarowitz, the Sultan was forced to cede northern Serbia, Little Wallachia and the Banat to the Emperor. Charles VI lost much of this territory in 1739, but at the end of the second decade of the 18th century, the Habsburgs seemed set to make further inroads into the Balkans, gains which in the event eluded them.

The Eve of the French Revolution

An uneasy peace covered much of Europe at the start of 1789. Relations between most of the Great Powers were tranquil, although not cordial, following the deaths of Frederick II of Prussia (1786) and Maria Theresa of Austria (1780), the two principal protagonists of the Habsburg-Hohenzollern wars of 1740-8 and 1756-63.

The major development of the first half of the 18th century had been Brandenburg-Prussia's emergence from a subordinate position within the Holy Roman Empire to the status of principal rival to the Austrian Habsburgs. This led to bitter wars between them, particularly over the problem of the succession to Charles VI of Austria. Charles had only daughters, and needed acceptance by the other Great Powers of the Pragmatic Sanction (1713) by which he left his lands to his daughter Maria Theresa. He was especially vulnerable as Austria's war with Turkey had gone badly wrong and the Treaty of Belgrade in 1739, by which Austria ceded to the Turks much of the land gained at the Treaty of Passarowitz (1718), made clear the real weakness of the Habsburg armies.

Frederick II of Prussia refused to acknowledge the settlement and launched a surprise attack on Austria after the succession of Maria Theresa in 1740, seizing Silesia. Britain sided with Austria, hoping to prevent the Prussians' French allies gaining too much influence in central Europe. The Prussian success against Maria Theresa also encouraged the other Electors in 1742 to choose Charles Albert of Bavaria as the first non-Habsburg Emperor for 300 years.

In 1743, Charles Albert tried, with French assistance, to seize Maria Theresa's hereditary lands. Maria Theresa bought off Prussia with the concession of Silesia, and instead concentrated Austria's forces on recovering Bohemia and Austria from Franco-Bavarian occupation. By 1748, a classic war of coalitions had led to general exhaustion and a willingness to make peace. In 1756, the Austrians reversed a 250-year old policy of enmity towards France, and the old rivals performed a "diplomatic revolution" which was intended to allow Austria to recover Silesia while France concentrated on her colonial rivalry with Britain. The ensuing Seven Years' War (1756-63) almost shattered Prussia, but Frederick II earned his title "the Great" by defeating the combined forces of France, Austria and Russia.

France did gain Lorraine in 1766, which had been ruled since 1738 by Stanislaw Leszczyński, the candidate for the Polish crown whom the French had unsuccessfully supported during the War of the Polish Succession (1733-8), and who was also the father-in-law of Louis XV.

Russia, meanwhile, continued to expand around the Black Sea. The Treaty of Belgrade gave Russia Azov and the lands of the Zaporogian Cossacks. A further Russo-Turkish war in 1768-74 brought Russia Kerch and Yenikale in the Crimea and Kherson. The Treaty of Kutchuk-Kainardji which ended the war also gave the Tsar a vague duty to protect the Sultan's Christian subjects, the cause of much future Russo-Turkish friction.

Although Prussia and Austria did spar again over the issue of who should rule Bavaria in 1778 (*see* map 1, page 138), the Great Powers avoided another great land war after 1763 for more than 25 years. It seemed as if a balance between France, Austria, Prussia and Russia had been established, with Britain holding the ring offshore. Even small states seemed protected by the arrangement, although the First Partition of Poland in 1772 between Prussia, Russia and Austria was a taste of how cynically the Great Powers could treat their weaker neighbours.

N O R W A Y

Trondhjem

Danish

S W E D E N

Christiania

en

Åbo

Helsingfors

St. Petersburg

Stockholm

Revel

Archangel

Perm

Gothenburg

Pskov

Nizhniy
Novgorod

Volga

Aarhus

Riga

Moscow

Samara

NMARK

Copenhagen

Malmö

BALTIC
SEA

COURLAND

Dvinsk

Tula

R   U   S   S   I   A   N

Small
Horde

mburg

SWEDISH
POMERANIA

Königsberg

Vilna

Vitebsk

Smolensk

Gdańsk

LITHUANIA

Don

Saratov

P   R   U   S   S   I   A

Stettin

Minsk

Kursk

E   M   P   I   R   E

ANOVER

Hanover

Elbe

Berlin

Poznań

Brest-Litovsk

Volga

Łódź

Warsaw

SAXONY

Oder

Breslau

P   O   L   A   N   D

ALL

Dresden

Silesia

Kiev

Kharkov

Astrakhan

RMAN

BOHEMIA

Prague

GALICIA

Dnieper

Ekaterinoslav

TES

Nuremberg

MORAVIA

Cracow

rt

BAVARIA

Brünn

Dniester

Vinnitsa

Danube

Vienna

Pozsony

H   A   B   S   B   U   R   G   P   O   S   S   E   S   S   I   O   N   S

Munich

AUSTRIA

Debrecen

Salzburg

Buda

Jassy

HABSBURG

Graz

HUNGARY

Kolozsvár

MOLDAVIA

Crimea

Kerch

Great Kabardia

Daghestan

Trieste

Szeged

TRANSYLVANIA

Brassó

Circassians

Venice

Zágráb

Temesvár

GEORGIA

N

Military

Frontier

WALLACHIA

Sebastopol

B   L   A   C   K   S   E   A

MODENA

Belgrade

Bucharest

Bologna

SAN MARINO

Zara

Bosna Saray

Danube

Ruschuk

Trebizond

ce

PAPAL

Spalato

Mostar

Nish

Varna

ANY

STATES

REPUBLIC
OF RAGUSA

Sofia

Burgas

Rome

MONTENEGRO

Üsküb

Philippopolis

Adrianople

PERSIA

Naples

Bari

O   T   T   O   Constantinople

Tigris

Taranto

Janina

M   A   N   E   M   P   I   R   E

Mosul

KINGDOM OF NAPLES
AND SICILY

Salonica

Ankara

R

Palermo

E

Smyrna

Adana

Euphrates

Messina

P

Patras

Athens

Catania

U

B

L

I

C

MALTA
(Knights of
St John)

SEA

Crete

Nicosia

Beirut

Damascus

Bedouins

141

HABSBURG EUROPE, 1699-1789

	Habsburg territory, 1699-1789
	Church lands under Habsburg control
	Added by 1714 (with dates)
	Added by 1775 (with dates)
	Temporary acquisitions (with dates)
	Territory lost, 1742
	Frontier of Poland to 1770
	Frontier of Holy Roman Empire
	Frontiers, 1789

Map labels:

PRUSSIA

POLAND

NETHERLANDS • Utrecht

GERMAN STATES

SAXONY

Antwerp *1714*
Brussels
• Aachen
AUSTRIAN NETHERLANDS
• Luxemburg

FRANCE
Rastatt
Blenheim

• Breslau

Prague •
Bohemia
Olmütz •
Brünn •
Moravia

• Lemberg

1770

Galicia
1772

Kaschau (Kassa) •

Bukovina
1775

NEUCHÂTEL

BAVARIA

Austria
1779
Linz • Vienna •
Salzburg •

Pressburg (Pozsony) •

HUNGARY

MOLDAVIA

SWISS CONFEDERATION
Innsbruck •
Tyrol

Styria
Graz •

Ofen • Pest (Buda)

Grosswardein (Nagyvárad) •

• Klausenburg (Kolozsvár)

TRANSYLVANIA
Kronstadt (Brassó) •

KINGDOM OF SARDINIA
1714-38/48
1714
MILAN
1748
Milan •
1708

Carinthia
Klagenfurt •

Croatia

Fünfkirchen (Pécs) •

Temeschwar (Temesvár) •

Banat
1718

WALLACHIA

1714-38/48

PARMA
1735-48
MODENA

MANTUA
GUASTALLA

Agram (Zágráb) •

Esseg (Eszék) •

Little Wallachia
1718-39

Military Frontier

REPUBLIC OF GENOA

MASSA
LUCCA

Florence •

SAN MARINO

MONACO

TUSCANY
1737

PAPAL STATES

PIOMBINO

Belgrade • Passarowitz

Serbia

OTTOMAN EMPIRE

STATO DEI PRESIDI
1714-35

ADRIATIC SEA

REPUBLIC OF RAGUSA

MONTENEGRO

• Sassari

• Bari

KINGDOM OF SARDINIA
1714-20

Naples •
NAPLES
1714-35

• Taranto

• Cagliari

MEDITERRANEAN SEA

ALGIERS

Palermo •

SICILY
1720-35
• Catania

TUNIS (Ottoman vassal)

MALTA (Knights of St. John)

VENETIAN REPUBLIC

Inset 1 (right middle):

Moravia

Vienna •
• Pozsony

Zágráb •
Croatia

• Pécs

Esseg (Eszék)
Slavo

VENETIAN REPUBLIC

PAPAL STATES

ADRIATIC SEA

MONT

REPUBLIC OF RAGUSA

NAPLES

Inset 2 (bottom right):

NORTH SEA

SWEDEN

DENMARK

SWEDISH POMERANIA

• Kolbe

East Friesland
1744

(to Sweden)

Pomera

Stettin •

GREAT BRITAIN

NETHERLANDS

• Lingen

• Tecklenburg

Minden •

Brandenburg

Magdeburg •
• Berlin
Potsdam •
• Frankfurt on the Ode

Upper Guelders •

AUSTRIAN

• Cleves

Mark

Ravensberg

Mansfeld
1780
Rossbach •

SAXONY

• Dresden

NETHER LANDS

• Aachen

Sayn
1741-83

Pirna •

FRANCE

GERMAN STATES

Limpurg

BAVARIA

Prague •

Bohemia

• Kolin

Mo

NEUCHÂTEL

SWISS CONFEDERATION

Tyrol

Austria

HABSB

Habsburg Europe, 1699-1789

1 Following the Treaty of Carlowitz (1699), the Austrian Habsburg advance into the Balkans was slowed down by domestic difficulties. In 1703, Ferenc II Rákóczi, of the old ruling house of Transylvania, led a peasants revolt to drive out the Habsburgs. Hoped for assistance from the French failed to materialise, however, because of their defeat in 1704 at Blenheim by the Anglo-Austrian coalition in the War of the Spanish Succession. Any chance of a reconciliation with Vienna was destroyed by Rákóczi's election as Prince by the Transylvanian nobles in 1704. For a while Transylvania was effectively freed from Habsburg rule, until the revolt finally fizzled out in 1711.

Charles VI's reign (1711-40) saw the Austrian Habsburgs reach unparalleled heights of power, but by the end Austria's position was actually much weakened. Distant territories like the southern Netherlands and Naples (obtained in 1714) and Sicily (acquired in 1720) proved expensive to defend and administer. By the 1730s, it became clear that the triumphs of Prince Eugene had not led to any long-term increase in the strength of the Habsburg army. By the Treaty of Belgrade (1739) Charles VI had to give the city itself and those parts of Serbia gained by Eugene back to the Sultan, although he was able to preserve the territories in the Banat of Temesvár gained in 1718.

As for any dynastic state, the absence of a male heir to Charles VI opened the Habsburg lands to the threat of aggression from its neighbours. Charles's daughter, Maria Theresa, managed, however, to preserve the bulk of her father's legacy, despite a Prussian invasion at the start of her reign which led to the loss of Silesia.

After 1763, it was clear that Austria could not hope to recover Silesia from Prussia so Vienna turned instead to plans to acquire other territories to "compensate" for its loss. In 1772, Maria Theresa participated in the partition of Poland, gaining Galicia – although she "wept as she took", as Frederick of Prussia commented – and acquiring Bukovina from the Ottomans in 1775. However, for much of the 18th century, the Habsburgs and their advisers had regarded the acquisition of Bavaria as a natural strategic goal. The addition of Catholic and German-speaking Bavaria would round off the core Habsburg lands of Bohemia and Austria. In return for Bavaria, Vienna was prepared to offer the Southern Netherlands. However, when the crisis of Bavarian Succession arose in 1777, the spectre of revived Imperial authority in Germany proved sufficient to bring Prussian intervention on the side of the Bavarians. Out of a bloodless war, Austria had to be satisfied with the acquisition of a small area of land to the northwest of Salzburg.

In Italy, a re-division of territory saw the Habsburgs gain Tuscany in 1732 in exchange for Sicily, Naples and Parma, which went to the children of the Bourbon Philip V of Spain.

The Military Frontier from 1700

2 The land taken from the Ottomans by the Treaty of Carlowitz was initially put under military administration. Over the next half century much of it was reabsorbed back into Hungary, but a strip by the Ottoman frontier remained permanently under military administration. Its eastern section was, however, returned to Hungary when further lands were gained from the Ottomans by the Treaty of Passarowitz (1718). The Habsburgs freed another part of the frontier from military rule in 1751, but sought to prevent its incorporation into Hungary by organising the territory as a new crownland, which they named the Banat of Temesvár. In 1775, however, the Hungarian Diet persuaded the Habsburgs to return this land to Hungarian civil administration.

Transylvania retained a separate status, although strongly Hungarian in character. The old borderlands of Hungary proper were governed by Transylvania, and were the subject of a dispute with Hungary until 1732, when an agreement (the "Carolina Resolutio") allowed both countries to retain a share. The Transylvanian borderlands remained under military administration until 1851.

The Growth of Prussia under Frederick the Great

3 Unlike his father, Frederick William I (1713-40), Frederick II of Prussia (1740-1786) preferred to use his armies rather than just play at soldiers. Frederick William I had built up Prussia's military potential and left his son a standing army of 80,000 but had only fought in one major war (against Sweden from 1715 to 1721). Frederick II opened his reign by launching a surprise attack on neighbouring Silesia in 1740 and seizing it from the new Austrian ruler, Maria Theresa.

Frederick II's behaviour meant that Prussia's traditional alliance with the Habsburgs was completely reversed. Despite two great wars with Maria Theresa and her allies, Frederick II kept Silesia, although at enormous cost to Prussia. Frederick's state only survived by concentrating its resources on the army, and by emphasising the militarisation of life.

Out of the War of the Austrian Succession, Frederick gained not only Silesia but East Friesland in northwestern Germany. He was lucky to preserve his gains after the Seven Years' War (1756-63). He succeeded, however, in his ambition to link his East Prussian lands with his core territories around Brandenburg. Prussia's share of the first Partition of Poland in 1772 gave him West Prussia and the elbow of Ermeland, though not yet the strategic port of Danzig.

The Rise of Napoleon

Given the domestic political chaos in France after the outbreak of the Revolution in the summer of 1789, few observers would have predicted that French troops would dominate the western half of Europe only a few years later. In fact, although the monarchs of Russia, Austria and Prussia were alarmed by the collapse of Louis XVI's authority and outraged by his subsequent deposition and execution, they consistently underrated the power of revolutionary France well into the 1790s. Ironically, Louis XVI's lavish expenditure on the French army and navy, which had done so much to bankrupt the monarchy and precipitate the Revolution, provided his revolutionary successors with the military resources to wage a successful war of conquest, or "liberation" as they called it. However, as long as the French were content to maintain a defensive posture, the response of the Great Powers was half-hearted. In 1792, Prussia despatched a relatively small force to intimidate the French authorities and particularly the people of Paris into not harming the king or his wife Marie-Antoinette. In fact this bungled invasion – defeated at Valmy in September – spurred on the radicalisation of the revolutionaries and encouraged them to spread their creed of "liberty, equality and fraternity" by force into the dominions of what they saw as hostile monarchs.

The neighbouring lands of Louis XVI's Austrian in-laws, plus the clerical states of the Holy Roman Empire along the Rhine, made natural targets for "liberation", though even the republican Swiss were not immune to French attack. The youthful Napoleon Bonaparte made his name thwarting British assistance to the counter-revolutionaries based at Toulon, but it was his role as the youngest general in the French army in Italy in the mid-1790s which made his reputation as the most able and feared commander of his day.

Mutual rivalries continued to prevent a united monarchist front and many sovereigns hoped that others would bear the burden of restoring the divinely ordained order in France while they pursued their own interests elsewhere. Poland became a victim of this policy, gradually disappearing from the map as her lands were divided up between Austria, Prussia and Russia in three successive partitions (1772, 1792 and 1795); *see* map 1, page 147.

Meanwhile, Austria's army, which had hardly covered itself in glory in the war against Turkey after 1788 (fought in alliance with Russia), proved itself unable to withstand the French, either in the Netherlands or in Italy, where the Habsburgs lost the dominant position which they had spent so much of the 18th century securing.

For Russia, Austria's growing preoccupation with the French threat was quite convenient. It meant that she was in a position to dictate terms to Turkey after what had been a joint campaign with Austrian troops, who were then redeployed to the west. By the Treaty of Jassy (1792), Russia gained the Black Sea coast between the Bug and the Dniester and was able to establish the port of Odessa.

The Treaty of Campo Formio (1797), imposed by France on the Austrians, brought to a conclusion the first phase of the revolutionary wars. France gained Venice and the Ionian Islands in the Adriatic, and took control of Austria's former Belgian provinces. Northern Italy fell more firmly into the French sphere of influence, too, as the Cisalpine and Ligurian Republics were set up to replace former monarchical regimes.

NORWAY
(Danish)
Trondhjem
Christiania

SWEDEN

Åbo
Helsingfors
St. Petersburg

Stockholm
Revel

Gothenburg

Archangel

Perm

Aarhus
DENMARK
Copenhagen
Malmö

BALTIC
SEA

Riga

Pskov

Dvinsk

Moscow

Nizhniy
Novgorod
Volga

Samara

SWEDISH
POMERANIA

Königsberg

Vilna

Vitebsk

Smolensk

Tula

Small
Horde

mburg

Danzig

Minsk

Kursk

Saratov

ANOVER
emen
Hanover
Berlin
SAXONY
Dresden

Stettin

PRUSSIA

Posen
Warsaw
Lodz

Breslau

Vistula

Bug

Oder

Elbe

Kiev

Kharkov

RUSSIAN
EMPIRE

Don

Volga

frt
Nuremberg

art

BAVARIA
Munich

BOHEMIA
Prague

MORAVIA
Brünn

Cracow

Lemberg

GALICIA

Vinnitsa

Ekaterinoslav

Dnieper

Astrakhan

Vienna
Pozsony
SBURG POSSESSIONS

AUSTRIA
Salzburg
Innsbruck

Graz

Buda Pest

Debrecen

Kolozsvár

HUNGARY

Jassy

MOLDAVIA

Dniester

Odessa

Szeged

TRANSYLVANIA

HA
Campo Formio
Trieste
Venice

Zágráb

Temesvár

Pécs

Military

WALLACHIA

Sebastopol

Great Kabardia
Circassians
Daghestan

Frontier
Belgrade

Bucharest

Ruschuk

GEORGIA

ALPINE
REP.
Bologna

nce
ny
PAPAL
STATES

SAN MARINO

Zara

Besna Saray

Spalato

Mostar

REPUBLIC
OF RAGUSA

MONTENEGRO

Nish

Danube

Sofia

Varna

Burgas

BLACK SEA

Trebzond

PERSIA

Rome

Naples

Bari

Taranto

KINGDOM OF NAPLES
AND SICILY

Palermo

Messina

Catania

SEA

MALTA
(Knights of
St John)

Corfu

Ionian Islands
(Fr.)

Janina

Úsküb

Philippopolis

Adrianople

Constantinople

Salonica

OTTOMAN

EMPIRE

Ankara

Mosul

Smyrna

Adana

Euphrates

Tigris

Athens

Crete

Nicosia

Beirut
Damascus

Bedouins

145

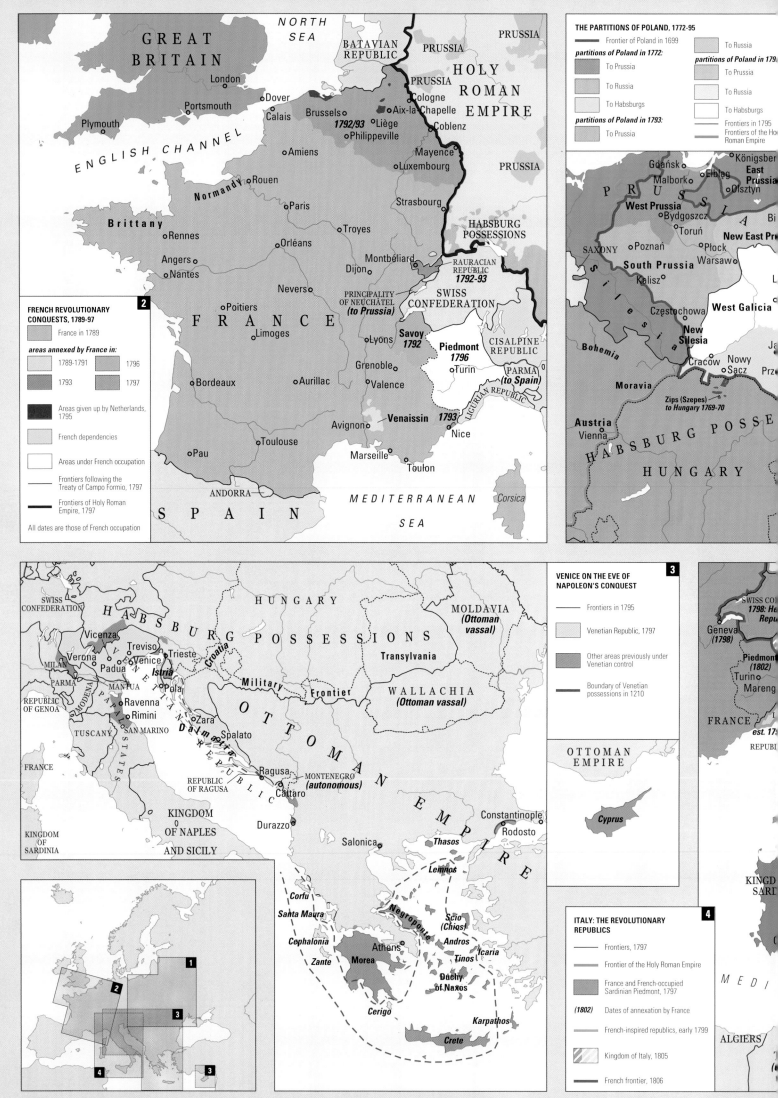

FRENCH REVOLUTIONARY CONQUESTS, 1789-97

- France in 1789

areas annexed by France in:
- 1789-1791
- 1793
- 1796
- 1797
- Areas given up by Netherlands, 1795
- French dependencies
- Areas under French occupation
- Frontiers following the Treaty of Campo Formio, 1797
- Frontiers of Holy Roman Empire, 1797

All dates are those of French occupation

THE PARTITIONS OF POLAND, 1772-95

- Frontier of Poland in 1699

partitions of Poland in 1772:
- To Prussia
- To Russia
- To Habsburgs

partitions of Poland in 1793:
- To Prussia

partitions of Poland in 179[5]:
- To Prussia
- To Russia
- To Habsburgs
- Frontiers in 1795
- Frontiers of the Ho[ly] Roman Empire

VENICE ON THE EVE OF NAPOLEON'S CONQUEST

- Frontiers in 1795
- Venetian Republic, 1797
- Other areas previously under Venetian control
- Boundary of Venetian possessions in 1210

ITALY: THE REVOLUTIONARY REPUBLICS

- Frontiers, 1797
- Frontier of the Holy Roman Empire
- France and French-occupied Sardinian Piedmont, 1797
- (1802) Dates of annexation by France
- French-inspired republics, early 1799
- Kingdom of Italy, 1805
- French frontier, 1806

The Partitions of Poland, 1772-95

1 By the mid-18th century, Augustus the Strong's ambitions to create a great Saxon-Polish power under his dynasty had come to nothing. The elective nature of the Polish monarchy combined with the fractious behaviour of much of the Polish nobility meant that the vast and strategically valuable lands between Poznán and Kiev were an attractive target for other states' ambitions.

In 1772, Russia and Austria, the erstwhile enemies of Prussia, joined Frederick II of Prussia in detaching significant territories from the Polish Commonwealth. Prussia took West Prussia, though without the valuable port of Gdańsk, which she only acquired in 1793. Catherine obtained a large tract of land around Witebsk, while Maria Theresa of Austria received the valuable province of Galicia.

Poland could only survive so long as her independence did not threaten to reverse the three powers' gains. But when serious reforms, including Europe's first written constitution (of May 1791), got underway, Prussia and Russia acted to forestall any chance of a revitalised Poland re-asserting herself.

Austria was distracted by the fate of the Emperor's sister, Marie-Antoinette, in France, but in 1793 Prussia and Russia seized further extensive territories in Poland. Influenced by French revolutionary success, the Poles revolted in 1794. They were swiftly and brutally defeated by the combined powers. Austria and Prussia in particular were anxious to compensate themselves for their losses to France, sharing out what remained of Poland with Russia in 1795. Even Warsaw passed into Prussian hands.

French Revolutionary Conquests, 1789-97

2 Using Louis XVI's military build-up as a basis for their own army, the French revolutionaries showed a genius for organisation after 1792. Conscription (*levée en masse*) was introduced, and the advantage in numbers this gave, combined with revolutionary élan and outstanding generalship, quickly led to the French conquest of neighbouring states.

By 1793, France had annexed the Venaissin (including Avignon), Savoy, Montbéliard, and an area north of Nizza, as well as a patchwork of clerical electorates and other territories in the Rhineland. The occupied territories were, in due course, mostly annexed to the French empire, so that by 1797, when the Austrian Netherlands were annexed, France had acquired her "natural frontiers" from the Channel coast down the Rhine. The Netherlands were allowed nominal independence as the Batavian Republic, while Piedmont was occupied in 1796, although not yet annexed to France.

Venice on the Eve of Napoleon's Conquest

3 Even though Venice had lost much of her former commercial wealth by the late 18th century, she still remained a valuable prize for any conqueror. Ironically, after centuries of defying

would-be conquerors, Venice fell even though she was not formally at war with France. Napoleon decided to eradicate Venice's independence along with that of her ancient rival, Genoa, as part of the Campo Formio settlement which he imposed on Austria in 1797. In order to persuade Austria to accept his creation of French-controlled republics elsewhere in northern Italy, Bonaparte granted Venice herself to the Habsburgs.

Venice's rise to occupy the position of the most powerful republic in Italy and a Mediterranean power in her own right owed everything to her position as an easily defended but highly accessible entrepôt for trade between the European mainland and the Mediterranean. Through her participation in the Fourth Crusade (1204) and the conquest of commercially valuable Constantinople rather than the holy city of Jerusalem, Venice gained a significant empire in the Aegean and the Morea.

Rising Ottoman power and the decline in Venetian wealth due to the shift to trans-Atlantic trade had led, by the start of 1797, to the loss of all but the Ionian Islands (Corfu, Cephalonia and Zante), and several footholds on the Adriatic. Crete had been lost by 1669 and the whole of the Morea by 1715. But Venice clung on to much of Dalmatia (around Zara and Spalato) as well as Istria until 1797. They then fell to Austria before Napoleon incorporated them into his French Empire. Already in 1797, Napoleon had taken the Ionian Islands for France as a stepping stone for his attempted conquest of Egypt.

Italy: the Revolutionary Republics

4 French victories over the Austrians in the 1790s led to a dramatic reordering of the map of Italy. Just as in the Low Countries and Switzerland, Bonaparte redrafted the constitutional as well as the political map of Italy. In fact, he went much further than the Directory in Paris had expected or desired. His Italian settlement of 1797 was the first sign that he intended to pursue his own political goals, albeit still under the guise of serving the French state.

Genoa became the Ligurian Republic, while a Cisalpine Republic was created out of the former duchies of Milan, France's share of the Venetian Republic plus Modena and the Papal territories in the Romagna, including Bologna. At first, the south of the Italian peninsula was left in monarchical hands, but the French soon moved to suppress that compromise. The Kingdom of Naples was turned into the Parthenopean Republic in 1799 while the Papal States around Rome became a republic, too – though both lacked sufficient local republican enthusiasm to make them anything other than French satellites. In 1801, the Kingdom of Etruria was formed out of Tuscany, as compensation for the Bourbon rulers of Parma, which Napoleon planned to annex (and did so in 1805). Only the kingdoms of Sardinia and Sicily remained outside the French republican system of satellites.

Napoleonic Europe

In mid-June 1812, Napoleon's empire dominated Europe, but even as he invaded Russia, cracks were showing in the hastily established edifice of French imperial power. Napoleon found it far easier to conquer than to control the vast territories which his military genius and the superior organisation of the French armies had secured. Yet as his troops advanced on Moscow, Wellington's British forces, with local Portuguese and Spanish allies, were already gnawing away at French control of Spain.

Napoleon's rise to power would have been impossible without the forces unleashed by the French Revolution, but after he had established himself as a dictator (in November 1799), he was confronted by the challenge of making his power permanent. Within five years, he rose from revolutionary consul to self-proclaimed Emperor. Although he staged a referendum to legitimise his accession to the throne and insisted that he was "Emperor of the French" rather than "King of France", his regime increasingly aped old monarchical ways.

Furthermore, whatever his support inside French-speaking Europe, Napoleon insisted on installing his brothers and his sister on the thrones of occupied territories. This old-fashioned dynastic policy backfired most badly in Spain where the brutal deposition of the Spanish Bourbons in 1808 provoked a popular revolt and the first so-called guerrilla war in Europe. Elsewhere, Napoleon placed his brother Louis on the throne of Holland and Jerome on that of the specially created Westphalia. His brother-in-law, Joachim Murat, became King of Naples. These novel monarchies did much to destabilise Napoleon's power-base without legitimising it in the eyes of new subjects.

While Napoleon concentrated on Central Europe and Italy, the Tsar asserted Russian power in the Baltic and against Turkey. Alexander I, who became Tsar after the assassination of his father Paul I in 1801, at first opposed France, but after the drubbing received by the Austro-Russian army at Austerlitz in 1805, and the defeat of a Prussian-Russian force at Friedland in 1806, his mood changed. Following a meeting with Napoleon at Tilsit, the boundary between French conquest and Russia, Europe was divided into spheres of influence. In 1809, Sweden was forced to cede Finland to the Russian Tsar, though Alexander and his successors ruled it as a separate Grand Duchy with its own laws. The Tsar's forces occupied largely Romanian-speaking Bessarabia and forced the Sultan to give it to Russia in 1812.

In 1807, Napoleon was still primarily concerned with his plans for the re-ordering of Germany and Italy (*see* map 2, page 151). He was content to leave Russia alone, particularly as he hoped that Alexander's evident ambitions with regard to Turkey might bring Russia into conflict with France's most persistent enemy, Britain. Russia's war with Turkey was a distraction for Alexander I, but nothing could disguise Napoleon's determination to draw Russia into his Continental System, designed to choke off British trade to Europe. Alexander did not wish to be used as cannon-fodder in France's quarrel with Britain, but nor could Russia afford to be cut off from trade through the Baltic with Britain. Finally, in 1812, Napoleon lost patience and invaded Russia.

Jealousy of Napoleon's unprecedented empire and the humiliation of ancient families serving as his unwilling allies combined to create an unstable situation in 1812, as Prussia and Austria bided their time to see how the invasion of Russia would turn out.

NORWAY

Trondhjem

Christiania

SWEDEN

(Danish)

DENMARK

Gothenburg

Aarhus

Copenhagen • Malmö

Stockholm

BALTIC
SEA

FINLAND

Åbo

Helsingfors

Revel

St. Petersburg

Archangel

Perm

amburg

Bremen

ero

REPUBLIC
OF DANZIG

Danzig

Stettin

Berlin

FEDERATION

Elbe

Dresden

PRUSSIA

Poznań GRAND DUCHY

Oder

OF

WARSAW

Tilsit

Königsberg

Friedland

Vistula

Warsaw

Pskov

Riga

Dvinsk

Vilna

Vitebsk

Minsk

Smolensk

Moscow

Nizhniy
Novgorod

Volga

Samara

Tula

Saratov

Brest-Litovsk

nkfurt

THE RHINE

ttgart

Nuremberg

Munich

Salzburg

Innsbruck

Danube

Prague

Austerlitz

Vienna

Graz

Pozsony

AUSTRIAN EMPIRE

Buda Pest

HUNGARY

Cracow

Debrecen

Kolozsvár

TRANSYLVANIA

Szeged

Temesvár

Brassó

Kiev

Kharkov

Vinnitsa

Dnieper

Ekaterinoslav

RUSSIAN

EMPIRE

Volga

Astrakhan

Small
Horde

Kursk

Rostov

Bessarabia

Kishinev

MOLDAVIA

Jassy

Dniester

Odessa

Sebastopol

Great Kabardia

Circassians

Daghestan

NGDOM

ITALY

Verona

Venice

Trieste

Bologna

San Marino

OMBINO

RENCH

MPIRE

Rome

PONTECORVO

BENEVENTO

Naples

KINGDOM OF

NAPLES

Bari

Taranto

French Empire

Illyrian

Provinces

Zágráb

Military

Frontier

Bosna
Saray

Belgrade

Zara

Spalato

Mostar

MONTENEGRO

Janina

Corfu

Nish

WALLACHIA

Bucharest

Danube

Ruschuk

Sofia

Philippopolis

Üsküb

Adrianople

OTTOMAN

Salonica

Ionian Islands
(Br.)

Varna

Burgas

BLACK SEA

EMPIRE

Constantinople

Angora

Trebizond

Tiflis

Erivan

PERSIA

Tigris

Mosul

KINGDOM OF
SICILY

Palermo

Messina

Catania

Patras

Athens

SEA

MALTA
(Br.)

Crete

Smyrna

Adana

Euphrates

Nicosia

Beirut

Damascus

Bedouins

Map 1 — CENTRAL EUROPE AND ITALY, 1806

Holy Roman Empire, 1797-1806

Small German states outside the Confederation of the Rhine

Jever (to Russia)

DENMARK
Copenhagen
Amsterdam
KINGDOM OF HOLLAND
Hamburg
Lübeck
Bremen
Hanover
SWEDEN
Danzig
Stettin
PRUSSIA
Berlin
Leipzig
Dresden
Belostok
RUSSIA
Warsaw
Brussels
Luxembourg
Mayence
Frankfurt
FRENCH EMPIRE
CONFEDERATION OF THE RHINE
Breslau
Nuremberg
Prague
BOHEMIA
Cracow
Stuttgart
Ratisbon
MORAVIA
Austerlitz
PR. OF NEUCHÂTEL
Berne
Munich
Salzburg
Vienna
HELVETIA
REP. OF VALAIS
Milan
Venice
Trieste
Buda Pest
AUSTRIAN EMPIRE
Hungary
Transylvania
Genoa
KINGDOM OF ITALY
Military Frontier
Wallachia (occupied by Russia)
Belgrade
PR. OF LUCCA
Florence
SAN MARINO
KGDM. OF ETRURIA
Zara
Dalmatia
OTTOMAN EMPIRE
PR. OF PIOMBINO
PAPAL STATES
Rome
KINGDOM OF SARDINIA
PR. OF PONTECORVO
KINGDOM OF NAPLES
PR. OF BENEVENTO
REP. OF RAGUSA
Ragusa
Montenegro
(occupied by Russia)

Map 2 — CENTRAL EUROPE AND ITALY, 1807

Added to the Confederation of the Rhine

Small German states outside the Confederation of the Rhine

Added to French Empire

Under French administration

Annexations by other states

DENMARK
Hamburg
Bremen
Hanover
CONFEDERATION
Erfurt
Frankfurt
Luxembourg
Mayence
FRENCH EMPIRE
OF THE RH...
Stuttgart
Nure...
Ratisb...
Munich
PR. OF NEUCHÂTEL
Berne
HELVETIA
Sa...
REP. OF VALAIS
Milan
Ven...
KING...
Genoa
PR. OF LUCCA
Florence
Rome
PR. OF PONTEC...
PA... STA...

Map 3 — CENTRAL EUROPE AND ITALY, 1809

Added to the Confederation of the Rhine

Added to French Empire

Under French administration

Annexations by other states

DENMARK
Copenhagen
Amsterdam
KINGDOM OF HOLLAND
Hamburg
Lübeck
Bremen
Hanover
SWEDEN
REP. OF DANZIG
Danzig
Stettin
PRUSSIA
Berlin
GRAND DUCHY
Warsaw
OF WARSAW
West Galicia
RUSSIA
Belostok
Brussels
CONFEDERATION
Erfurt
Leipzig
Dresden
Breslau
Cracow
Luxembourg
Mayence
Frankfurt
OF
FRENCH EMPIRE
THE RHINE
Prague
Stuttgart
Nuremberg
Ratisbon
Munich
Austerlitz
Wagram
Vienna
PR. OF NEUCHÂTEL
Berne
Salzburg
HELVETIA
Tyrol
REP. OF VALAIS
Buda Pest
AUSTRIAN EMPIRE
Hungary
Milan
Venice
Trieste
KINGDOM OF ITALY
Transylvania
Genoa
FRENCH EMPIRE
Military Frontier
Wallachia (occupied by Russia)
Belgrade
PR. OF LUCCA
Florence
SAN MARINO
Zara
OTTOMAN EMPIRE
FRENCH EMPIRE
PR. OF PIOMBINO
Rome
KINGDOM OF NAPLES
Ragusa
Montenegro
PR. OF PONTECORVO
PR. OF BENEVENTO

Map 4 — CENTRAL EUROPE AND ITALY, 1810

Added to the Confederation of the Rhine

Added to French Empire

DENMARK
Hamburg
Bremen
Hanover
Amsterdam
Netherlands
CONFEDERATI...
Erfurt
Brussels
Frankf...
Luxembourg
Mayence
OF
FRENCH EMPIRE
THE RHINE
Stuttgart
Nure...
Ratisb...
Munich
PR. OF NEUCHÂTEL
Berne
HELVETIA
Sa...
Tyrol
Valais
Milan
Venic...
KINGDOM OF ITALY
Genoa
PR. OF LUCCA
FRENCH EMPIRE
Florence
PR. OF PIOMBINO
Rome
PR. OF PONTEC...

Central Europe and Italy, 1806

1 Like many shadowy institutions, the Holy Roman Empire served a purpose even during long decades of decline: its institutions provided a pan-German forum for diplomatic discussions without imposing any effective control on the individual states. However, by the beginning of the 19th century, the Empire had become a dangerous political vacuum on the edge of the French state.

Despite their long hold on the Imperial Crown, the Habsburgs recognised that their own collection of personal dominions might prove fragile if they lost the Holy Roman title, with the result that Francis I of Austria tried to reform in a bid to pre-empt Napoleon's threat of abolition. Already in 1803, the Emperor had accepted a radical revision of the old Imperial order. Only three Church states survived out of 81 and the number of free cities sank from 51 to six. In 1804 Francis declared himself "Emperor of Austria", although in doing so he at least clung to a territorial identity for the Habsburg lands, a contrast with Napoleon's title as "Emperor of the French."

On 26 December 1805, just three weeks after Napoleon's crushing victory over an Austrian and Russian army at Austerlitz, Francis agreed to cede all Habsburg territory south of the Alps to France. Napoleon gained Venice and Dalmatia, which he incorporated into the newly formed Kingdom of Italy. The Emperor also had to recognise the rulers of southern Germany as independent sovereigns (though they were in fact puppets of Napoleon). In the meantime, Napoleon had established his own Confederation of the Rhine to co-ordinate his puppets and allies in the German-speaking lands between the Rhine and Prussia. This marked the effective death of any Holy Roman Empire. Francis I formally abrogated its existence on 6 August 1806, at French insistence.

Central Europe and Italy, 1807

2 While he had to confront the Austro-Russian alliance, Napoleon had been willing to bribe Prussia to remain neutral (with, for instance, the offer of George III of England's other kingdom, Hanover), but after his victory over the Austrians and Russians at Austerlitz, he was more willing to dictate terms to the Prussians. Foolishly, Prussia declared war on France in August 1806, even though she was diplomatically isolated.

The shattering defeat of Prussia's much-vaunted army at Jena in October, 1806, left Napoleon free to dispose of Prussian territory and other northern and central German states at will. Napoleon left the Prussian king, Frederick William III, his traditional territories in the east, but took away Prussia's western provinces to provide the core of his brother Jerome's new kingdom of Westphalia. Saxony became a member of the Confederation of the Rhine in 1807, while several of the German states (including Hamburg) were brought under French administration, although not annexed. Prussia also lost the bulk of its gains from the partitions of Poland to the newly created French puppet-state, the Grand Duchy of Warsaw. Danzig, too, was removed from Prussian control and became an independent republic.

At Tilsit, Russia lost some recently gained outposts on the Adriatic to France, though Napoleon gave the Tsar the district around Belostok. In return, the Tsar accepted the existence of the Grand Duchy of Warsaw, a potential threat to Russia's Polish lands. Napoleon also consolidated his position by annexing the Kingdom of Etruria directly to France, and adding East Friesland to the French client kingdom of Holland.

Central Europe and Italy, 1809

3 After his establishment of an informal alliance with the Russian Tsar at Tilsit in 1807, Napoleon turned to mopping up the smaller states which bordered his empire. In May 1809 he annexed the bulk of the Papal States directly to the French empire. His brother, Joseph, already ruled southern Italy from Naples, while his stepson, Eugene de Beauharnais, acted as Viceroy of the Kingdom of Italy.

Napoleon's confiscation of so many Austrian states and properties after Austerlitz encouraged plans for revenge. After 1805, the Austrian military system was much reformed. Austria resumed her war effort against France in 1809, but despite inflicting severe losses on Napoleon's increasingly raw recruits, the Habsburgs' army was defeated at Wagram and Francis I forced to make peace.

Napoleon obliged Austria to cede her remaining Adriatic territories to his puppet Kingdom of Italy and her Polish lands (West Galicia) to the Grand Duchy of Warsaw. He rewarded his ally Bavaria with a swathe of Austrian territory stretching southwards into the Tyrol and including Salzburg. Apart from Britain, Portugal, Sweden and the Ottoman Empire, and a few offshore islands such as Sicily and Sardinia, all of Europe was either ruled by Napoleon or in alliance with him.

Central Europe and Italy, 1810

4 Napoleon's allies were rarely reliable once he faced difficulties. Even his brother Louis sided too often with his Dutch subjects for Napoleon's liking, so in 1810 he was unceremoniously deposed and his Kingdom of Holland incorporated directly into the French Empire, along with a large section of northwest Germany.

Napoleon's attempt to blockade Britain through the enforcement of his "Continental System", designed to destroy British commerce by closing the entire European continent to British trade, led him to occupy even the Duchy of Oldenburg in 1810. This offended the Tsar, since the Duchy was ruled by the family of his grandmother, Catherine the Great. Russia, like France's other unwilling allies, was not prepared to forego the benefits of trade with Britain and war became inevitable.

1815

The Treaty of Vienna

From 1812, with Napoleon's catastrophic defeat in Russia, in which an army of 600,000 vanished into the steppe and the snow, the defeat of Napoleonic France became suddenly probable. Driven out of Spain and then defeated by a coalition army at Leipzig in 1813, in 1815 the revolutionary French forces suffered their final defeat at Waterloo.

Since 1789, Europe had undergone a generation-long convulsion which had left nothing untouched. Old states had been abolished, the world of the *ancien régime* was gone for ever. Yet though the representatives of the victorious powers who assembled in Vienna in 1815 to determine the future of Europe were joined by a common desire to restore the world lost after 1789, they were forced to recognise that no such course was in practice open to them. Thus the the Holy Roman Empire and its constellation of feudal principalities and mini-states summarily abolished by Napoleon in 1806 (*see* map 1, page 150) was not restored. Instead, they drafted the boundaries of a 39-member German Confederation, which paid lip-service both to the defunct Holy Roman past (even as it pronounced the last rites over the vast majority of its members) and to the notion of a common German identity so strongly displayed during the war of liberation against Napoleon after 1812.

At the same time, not least under the persuasive prompting of the central architect of the new order, Prince Metternich of Austria, the new order was profoundly conservative. At Vienna, the victorious allies agreed to meet periodically to settle disputes which might threaten the peace. This "Congress System" proved inadequate for dealing with the crises which arose after 1815. It soon became clear that it was only the overwhelming threat of Napoleonic France which had kept the Allies united. The disappearance of that threat after Waterloo revealed the rivalries and differing interests of the four Great Powers who had defeated the French. Britain's primary concern was to prevent the revival of a French threat to her own independence. So long as the danger of any power exercising hegemony across the continent of Europe was kept in check, Britain was satisfied. Her continental Allies had ideological concerns, too. Francis I's chief minister, Metternich, was determined to prevent any kind of constitutional changes, let alone revolutionary developments, which might threaten the Vienna settlement. By making opposition to internal political change a key principle of the post-Vienna system, Metternich risked committing the Allies to constant police actions and interference in the internal developments of states anywhere in Europe. Particularly after the suicide of the British Foreign Minister Castlereagh in 1822 and his replacement by Canning, the British government was out of sympathy with Metternich's ambition to hinder all change.

At first, Metternich had the support of Russia and Prussia in establishing the Holy Alliance – although Britain refused to join – which was committed to the maintenance of the Vienna settlement in its entirety. The Alliance even wanted to intervene to prevent successful rebellions in Spain's Latin American colonies, but were prevented from doing so by the logistical difficulties involved in such an undertaking, compounded by British and US opposition. The boundaries established between the Great Powers in Europe in 1815, however, proved remarkably stable over the next century by comparison with the 20 years of turbulence which had preceded the Congress of Vienna.

Trondhjem

Christiania

NORWAY

SWEDEN

FINLAND

Archangel

Perm

Åbo

Helsingfors

St. Petersburg

Stockholm

Revel

Nizhniy
Novgorod

Volga

Gothenburg

Pskov

Riga

Moscow

Samara

Aarhus

Copenhagen

Malmö

BALTIC
SEA

Dvinsk

Tula

R U S S I A N

DENMARK

Vilna

Vitebsk

Smolensk

Small
Horde

Hamburg

Königsberg

Danzig

Bremen

Stettin

Minsk

Kursk

Saratov

NOVER

PRUSSIA

Vistula

Warsaw

Brest-Litovsk

E M P I R E

Hanover

Berlin

Posen

Lodz

Don

Leipzig

Dresden

Oder

POLAND

SAXONY

Breslau

REPUBLIC
OF CRACOW

Kiev

Kharkov

Volga

kfurt

Nuremberg

Prague

Elbe

Brünn

Cracow

Vinnitsa

Ekaterinoslav

Rostov

Astrakhan

BAVARIA

Danube

Vienna

Pozsony

A U S T R I A N   E M P I R E

Dnieper

WÜRTTEMBERG

Munich

Salzburg

Graz

Debrecen

Buda   Pest

HUNGARY

Kolozsvár

MOLDAVIA

Jassy

Kishinev

Odessa

Dniester

Kabardia

start

nnsbruck

STEIN

Zágráb

Szeged

Temesvár

TRANSYLVANIA

Brassó

Circassians

Daghestan

DY-VENETIA

Trieste

Venice

ILLYRIAN KINGDOM

Military

Frontier

WALLACHIA

Sebastopol

Tiflis

PARMA

MODENA

Bologna

Zara

Bosna Saray

Belgrade

Bucharest

Danube

Ruschuk

Varna

B L A C K   S E A

ence

ANY

San Marino

PAPAL
STATES

Spalato

Mostar

Nish

Sofia

Philippopolis

Burgas

Trebizond

Erivan

Rome

MONTENEGRO

Üsküb

O
T
T
O
M
A
N

Adrianople

Constantinople

Angora

PERSIA

Naples

Taranto

KINGDOM OF THE
TWO SICILIES

Salonica

Janina

Corfu

Ionian Islands
(Br.)

E
M
P
I
R
E

Smyrna

Adana

Tigris

Mosul

alermo

Messina

Sicily

Catania

Patras

Athens

Euphrates

MALTA
(Br.)

Crete

Nicosia

Beirut

Damascus

Bedouins

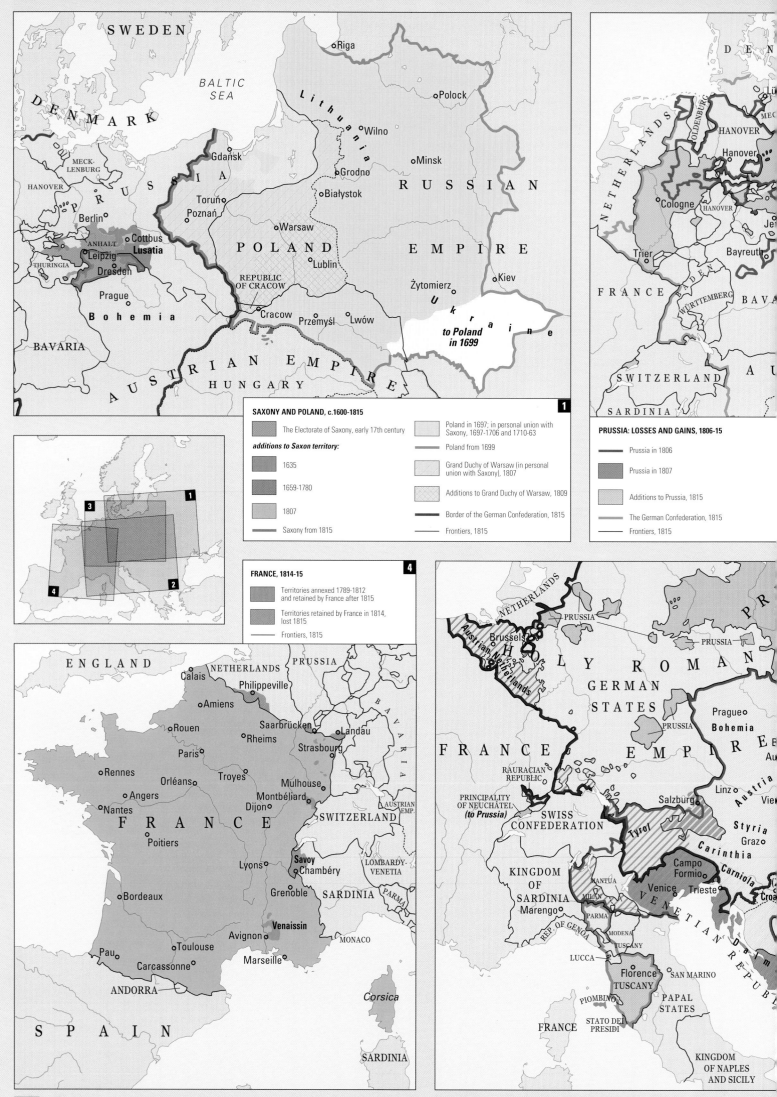

SAXONY AND POLAND, c.1600-1815 [1]

The Electorate of Saxony, early 17th century

additions to Saxon territory:

1635

1659-1780

1807

Saxony from 1815

Poland in 1697; in personal union with Saxony, 1697-1706 and 1710-63

Poland from 1699

Grand Duchy of Warsaw (in personal union with Saxony), 1807

Additions to Grand Duchy of Warsaw, 1809

Border of the German Confederation, 1815

Frontiers, 1815

PRUSSIA: LOSSES AND GAINS, 1806-15

Prussia in 1806

Prussia in 1807

Additions to Prussia, 1815

The German Confederation, 1815

Frontiers, 1815

FRANCE, 1814-15 [4]

Territories annexed 1789-1812 and retained by France after 1815

Territories retained by France in 1814, lost 1815

Frontiers, 1815

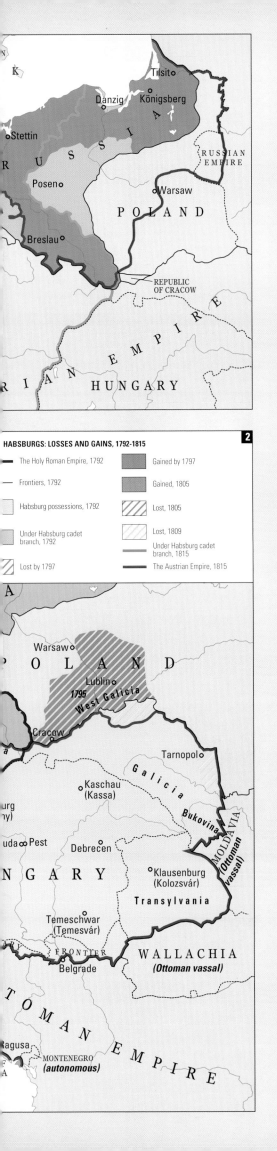

HABSBURGS: LOSSES AND GAINS, 1792-1815 **2**

- ▬ The Holy Roman Empire, 1792
- — Frontiers, 1792
- ☐ Habsburg possessions, 1792
- ☐ Under Habsburg cadet branch, 1792
- ▨ Lost by 1797
- ☐ Gained by 1797
- ▦ Gained, 1805
- ▨ Lost, 1805
- ▨ Lost, 1809
- — Under Habsburg cadet branch, 1815
- ▬ The Austrian Empire, 1815

Saxony and Poland, c. 1600-1815

1 In retrospect, the domination of German history by Prussia seems a quite natural development, but other principalities challenged her and fell by the wayside. The Electorate of Saxony was perhaps the strongest alternative contender for the title of champion of Protestant Germany, but its rulers failed to capitalise on its natural wealth and strategic position. This failure by Augustus the Strong (1694-1733) and his successor Augustus III (1733-63) to achieve the status of a major European power, was all the more striking because the Saxon monarchs ruled the vast territory of Poland, too, from 1697 to 1706 and from 1710 to 1763. They struggled, however, to turn their dual realm into a rival to the Austrian Habsburgs and the Hohenzollerns of Prussia. The Polish constitution limited the powers of the monarchs severely, exposing the folly of the two Augustuses in devoting so many resources to buying the throne of Poland. Saxony and Poland became, instead, the battle-ground in the struggles between Frederick the Great of Prussia and Maria-Theresa of Austria. Poland, in particular, suffered great depopulation and economic damage.

During the French Revolutionary wars, the Saxon rulers sided with Napoleon, and were rewarded with the acquisition of the Grand Duchy of Warsaw in 1807. Saxony, however, failed to change sides as deftly as some of the other German princes after Napoleon's débâcle in Russia in 1812 and was punished by the victorious allies after the final French defeat in 1815. Although Austria and Britain refused to permit the total annexation of Saxony by the Prussians, the Hohenzollerns of Prussia did take the northern half of pre-war Saxony.

The Habsburgs: Losses and Gains, 1792-1815

2 The peace settlement of 1815 saw the restoration to Austria of some of the territories Napoleon had deprived her of. West Galicia, lost in 1809 to the Grand Duchy of Warsaw, was not regained, although the province of Tarnopol, awarded to Russia in 1809 after Napoleon's victory against the Austrians, was recovered by the Habsburgs. The Venetian territories, acquired by the Campo Formio settlement in 1797, but lost again in 1805, returned to Austrian rule. The Austrian Netherlands, lost in 1797, were attached to the Dutch state.

After the abolition of the Holy Roman Empire in 1806, the Habsburgs in effect renounced any ambitions to pursue territorial expansion to the northwest into Germany, relieving long-standing pressure on Bavaria, and opening the way for Prussia to assert its dominance within Germany.

In Italy, Francis I recovered Lombardy and Venetia, while his daughter Marie Louise ruled Parma and his brother Ferdinand restored Tuscany to Habsburg rule. Austrian political and military superiority also ensured the restoration of most of the non-Habsburg monarchs in Italy.

Prussia: Losses and Gains, 1806-15

3 Prussia's role in the Revolutionary and Napoleonic Wars had often been ambivalent, but her decisive participation in the final battle against Napoleon at Waterloo gave her considerable claims both to rewards for her share in the Allied war effort and to a new role as a guarantor of the peace settlement. The Hohenzollern family had long held possessions in western Germany between the Rhine and the Netherlands, but in 1815 Prussia received a large tract of territory, including Trier and Cologne as well as the Saarland. This gave Prussia a wedge of territory intended to back up the United Netherlands as a barrier to any future French attempts at expansion.

These western lands were separated from the rest of Prussia by other newly restored or created states belonging to the German Confederation. This corridor of non-Prussian territory offered a temptation to any ruler in Berlin anxious to consolidate and link his dominions. The key obstacle was the restored Kingdom of Hanover, which was still ruled in personal union by George III of England.

The integration of the western provinces into Prussia posed other problems than their physical separation from the centre. The Rhinelanders had often welcomed the French invaders, for example, and the legacy of prolonged French occupation was not easy to erase. The French-imposed legal system survived, as did metric weights and measures in Prussia to the west of the Rhine.

France, 1814-15

4 At first, the Allies assembled at Vienna in 1814 treated defeated France with remarkable moderation. The Treaty of Paris (30 May 1814) treated France very leniently, largely in the hope of stabilising the restoration of the Bourbons, but a more severe settlement was imposed in November 1815, after the final French defeat at Waterloo, as a retribution for the support given to Napoleon during "The Hundred Days" (his return from Elba).

In 1814, at the insistence of his erstwhile ally, Alexander I of Russia, Napoleon himself had been treated with remarkable clemency by his conquerors. He was exiled to the island of Elba as its nominal emperor, but after Waterloo the defeated Napoleon disappeared into captivity on the British island of St Helena in the South Atlantic.

France was now deprived of strategically important territories on her northeastern frontier, including Philippeville, Landau and part of Savoy. She was in effect pushed back to her borders in 1790, and had to submit to a temporary occupation of Paris, and to pay a large indemnity to the Allies.

1815

The Unification of Italy

The statesmen who gathered at Vienna in 1814-15 after Napoleon's final defeat had been guided by the ambition to stifle the threat of nationalism and revolution to the newly won European order as much as to ensure that France should never again be able to threaten Europe militarily. In practice, the capacity of France to dominate Europe again was already waning. At the start of the century, France's population of some 30 million had overshadowed its neighbours and provided Napoleon with the manpower for his *grande armée*. But thereafter the French population rose only slowly, to around 36 million, while other countries, most notably Prussia, saw their birthrates rise rapidly. France's stagnant birthrate, combined with her relatively slow industrialisation, meant that the threat of French expansion was growing ever weaker.

However, the experience of the French revolution and Napoleonic expansion had given enormous impetus to nationalism: the overthrow of traditional ruling élites in territories overrun by the French armies had a profound effect across Europe. In some states, such as Prussia, resentment of French influence had helped promote a militant patriotism. But whereas nationalism in these countries, in reflecting a reaction against French-imposed change, sought to reinforce existing social orders, in other parts of Europe, especially Italy and Poland, its effect was much more challenging to the status quo. Having tasted the social changes promoted by Napoleon following the French invasions, and in some cases having been granted a degree of autonomy by the invaders, nationalists there naturally reacted against the Vienna settlement, especially as it meant the restoration of traditional rulers (in Italy) and the loss of territory to the victors of the Napoleonic wars (in Poland). Likewise, in 1830, the Belgians revolted and won their independence the following year from the Dutch king, William I, who had been awarded Belgium by the Vienna settlement.

Even in the Balkans, where the slogan of "Liberté, Egalité et Fraternité" and the name of Bonaparte were distant echoes, the stirrings of nationalism appeared, above all in Greece, which achieved its independence from the Turks in 1830. This coincided with a further decline in the cohesion of the Ottoman Empire and with an inability on the part of Austria, faced with nationalist challenges to its own rule, to fill the growing political vacuum to the southeast. A series of revolutions in 1848 rapidly engulfed Austria and Hungary and spread throughout Central Europe. These, and the strains imposed on the Russians in fighting the Crimean War (1854-6) against a coalition of France, Britain and Turkey, showed that neither the Habsburgs nor the Russian Tsar remained strong enough to preserve the Vienna system by force. They had, however, retained sufficient power to hold the line in 1848-9, albeit at great cost and in part because of divisions within nationalist ranks, which in Germany centred on those favouring the inclusion of Austria within a greater German state and those wanting to exclude it.

But relations between Vienna and St Petersburg cooled rapidly, opening the way for the French emperor Napoleon III's campaigns against Russia (1854-56) and then Austria (1859), when neither supported the other against France. The Austrian defeat by the French in 1859 undermined the stability of the central Italian states, which voted for unification with Sardinia-Piedmont. Sicily and Naples were taken in 1860 by an Italian expeditionary force led by Garibaldi, and by 1861 a united Kingdom of Italy had emerged, excluding only the rump Papal States and Venice.

Small German States

The German Confederation

NORWAY

Trondhjem

SWEDEN

FINLAND

Christiania

Åbo

Helsingfors

St. Petersburg

Stockholm

Revel

Perm

Pskov

Riga

Moscow

Samara

BALTIC
SEA

Dvinsk

R U S S I A N

Gothenburg

Aarhus

Copenhagen

Malmö

DENMARK

Königsberg

Danzig

Vilna

Vitebsk

Smolensk

Tula

Nizhniy
Novgorod

Volga

Hamburg

Stettin

Minsk

Saratov

Bremen

NOVER

Berlin

Posen

PRUSSIA

Warsaw

Brest-Litovsk

E M P I R E

Kursk

Hanover

Vistula

Kharkov

Leipzig

Dresden

Oder

Lodz

POLAND

Elbe

Breslau

SAXONY

Don

Frankfurt

Nuremberg

Prague

Cracow

Lemberg

Kiev

Vinnitsa

Volga

Astrakhan

Brünn

Kaschau

Dniester

Ekaterinoslav

Dnieper

Rostov

BAVARIA

AUSTRIAN

Vienna

Pressburg

art

Munich

Danube

Salzburg

Ofen

Pest

Debreczen

Kishinev

Odessa

RG

Innsbruck

Graz

E M P I R E

Szegedin

Klausenburg

Jassy

IN

Laibach

Agram

Fünfkirchen

Temeschwar

Kronstadt

Sebastopol

Circassians

Tiflis

Venice

Trieste

Villafranca

Zara

Szegedin

ROMANIA

B L A C K   S E A

Bologna

SAN MARINO

Bosna Saray

Belgrade

Bucharest

Erivan

Florence

Spalato

SERBIA

Danube

Ruschuk

Varna

Perugia

Mostar

Nish

Sofia

Burgas

PERSIA

ITALY

MONTENEGRO

Üsküb

Philippopolis

Adrianople

Trebizond

Rome

PAPAL
STATES

Gaeta

O

Salonica

Constantinople

Naples

Bari

T

Ankara

Mosul

Taranto

Janina

T

Smyrna

Adana

Palermo

Messina

O

Euphrates

Sicily

Catania

IONIAN ISLANDS

M

Patras

Athens

A

GREECE

(Br.)

N

E M P I R E

Tigris

Nicosia

SEA

MALTA

(Br.)

Crete

Beirut

Damascus

Bedouins

157

POLAND, 1807-47 `1`
- Grand Duchy of Warsaw, established 1807
- From Prussia to Russia, 1807
- Added to Grand Duchy of Warsaw, 1809
- The kingdom of Poland, established 1815
- Prussia from 1815
- Frontiers, 1815

BELGIAN INDEPENDENCE, 1831-39 `4`
- The Netherlands, 1815-39
- Disputed: to Belgium, 1839
- Disputed: to Netherlands, 1839
- Western frontier of German Confederation to 1839
- Adjustments to frontier of German Confederation from 1839
- Frontiers, 1839

ITALY, 1815-61 `2`
- Frontiers in 1822
- Added to Sardinia, 1859
- The Kingdom of Italy, 1861

THE BALKANS, 1815-61 `3`
- Frontiers in 1815
- Autonomous from 17th century
- Ottoman vassals, 1815
- Independent, 1830
- Autonomous (with dates)
- Transferred to autonomous states (with date)
- Lost by Ottomans to Russia 1829, regained 1856
- Lost by Russia to Moldavia, 1856
- United Principalities 1859; from 1861, Romania
- Frontier of Ottoman Empire, 1861

SWEDEN
BALTIC SEA
DENMARK
Kovno
Tilsit
Vilna
PRUSSIA
Gdańsk (Danzig) *(independent from Prussia 1807-14)*
Grodno
Belostok
Bydgoszcz
Toruń
Ostrołęka
RUSSIA
(to Prussia 1815)
Poznań
Płock
Kalisz
Warsaw
Brest-Litovsk
Poland
West Galicia
Częstochowa
Lublin
Chełm
Zamość
Cracow
Lemberg
REPUBLIC OF CRACOW *(independent 1815-47, to Austria 1847)*
Tarnopol *(to Russia 1809, to Austria 1815)*
AUSTRIAN EMPIRE
Hungary

SWITZERLAND
Savoy *(to France 1860)*
Kingdom of Lombardy and Venetia
AUSTRIAN EMPIRE
Milan
Magenta
Solferino
(to Modena, 1847)
Verona
Villafranca
Venice
Hungary
Military Frontier
Turin
SARDINIA
(to Parma, 1847)
PARMA
Parma
MODENA
OTTOMAN EMPIRE
SERBIA
Genoa
(to Modena, 1847)
Modena
Dalmatia
MONACO
MASSA AND CARRARA *(to Modena, 1829)*
Massa
LUCCA
Lucca
SAN MARINO
Nizza (Nice) *(to France 1860)*
Florence
Ancona
MONTENEGRO
FRANCE
TUSCANY
Siena
PAPAL STATES
Castelfidardo
Perugia
FRANCE
Corsica
Rome
KINGDOM OF THE TWO SICILIES
Gaeta
Naples
Bari
Sassari
SARDINIA
Taranto
Cagliari
MEDITERRANEAN SEA
Palermo
Messina
ALGIERS *(to France, 1830)*
TUNIS *(vassal of Ottoman Empire)*
Marsala
Calatafimi
Catania
Malta *(Br.)*

AUSTRIAN Hung
Illyrian Kingdom
Military
(to Serbia 1833) Bosnia
Bosna Saray (Sarejevo)
Dalmatia
Mostar
(to Montenegro 1860)
Cetinje
MONTENEGRO
Scutari
Durazzo
KINGDOM OF THE TWO SICILIES
Ionian Islands (Br.)

Poland, 1807-47

1 After Napoleon's crushing defeat of Prussia in the autumn of 1806 and his rapprochement with Alexander I of Russia at Tilsit in 1807, Poland's chances of regaining her independence barely a decade after her extinction by the Third Partition seemed strong. Napoleon did, indeed, establish a Grand Duchy of Warsaw (*see* map 2, page 151) composed of territories taken from Prussia's share of the last partition, but he showed no inclination to permit a genuinely independent Poland, preferring instead to punish his enemies among the former partitioning powers. Thus, after Austria's defeat by Napoleon in 1809, she lost West Galicia to the Grand Duchy.

Napoleon's defeat in 1815 meant a restoration of tripartite control of Poland by Russia, Austria and Prussia. The new division of spoils gave west Poland and Gdańsk to Prussia while Austria surrendered her claims to West Galicia, which in common with the remainder of the Grand Duchy came under Russian hegemony, in exchange for Tarnopol. Alexander ruled this so-called "Congress Kingdom" of Poland as just another part of his empire, despite its constitution which made it a personal union with Russia. The great Polish rebellion of 1831 was easily defeated by the powerful Russian army and provided Alexander's successor, Nicholas I, with an excuse to tighten his control.

The ancient university city of Cracow had survived 1815 as the Republic of Cracow, the last remnant of self-governed Polish territory. In 1847, Austria annexed it in agreement with Prussia and Russia, despite the protests of France and Britain.

Italy, 1815-61

2 The defeat of Napoleon brought most of the former ruling families of Italy back to their thrones. The role of Austrian troops in restoring the old dynasties, however, illustrated the fragility of the Italian state system. Ultimately the rulers' thrones now rested on the ability of Austria to prop them up.

The Kingdom of Sardinia, which became the driving force behind Italian unification, was ruled by a native Italian dynasty and so faced no nationalist challenges, such as those experienced by the Bourbon and Habsburg rulers in southern Italy. In 1849, Charles Albert of Sardinia unsuccessfully tried to seize Lombardy from the Austrians, but even failure established the Sardinian's credentials as the "natural" leader of Italy. In 1859, with the support of Napoleon III, he gained Milan and Lombardy from the Austrians. Part of Savoy and Nizza were handed over to France to repay her aid. The Austrian defeat destabilised the central Italian states, and under Sardinian pressure they voted for unification. Sicily and Naples were conquered by Garibaldi and his thousand volunteers in 1860 and then handed over to the Sardinian government. The Kingdom of Italy thus came into being in 1861. With the acquisition of Venetia from the Austrians in 1866, and the rump of the Papal States by 1870, unification was almost complete. San Marino, Corsica and some frontier zones of Austria were the only Italian-speaking areas remaining outside Italy's borders.

The Balkans, 1815-61

3 The decay of Ottoman power in Europe during the 19th century was perhaps the key factor in destabilising post-Napoleonic Europe. The emergence of Balkan nationalism occurred in territories far less ethnically homogeneous than those areas in Western Europe which had experienced nationalist movements. Furthermore, the Great Powers of Europe had some sympathy with the nationalist aspirations of the Christian subjects of the Muslim Sultan, above all with the Greeks, modern heirs of the classical civilization of ancient Greece, which outweighed their instinctive desire to maintain the existing order.

Moldavia and Wallachia were the first to rebel (with encouragement from Alexander I of Russia's Greek minister, Capodistria), in 1821. Despite the failure of these uprisings, the Greeks then started a more effective rebellion, backed by idealists such as the English poet Lord Byron. The British, French and Russians sought to temper Turkish reprisals for these revolts, leading to the annihilation of the Ottoman fleet at the decisive, if unintended, battle of Navarino in 1827. The way was cleared for an independent Greece, which emerged in 1830. Many Greek-speaking islands (including Crete), however, remained Ottoman possessions for decades.

Serbia achieved autonomous status after 1817, followed by Wallachia and Moldavia in 1829, the latter two emerging as the United Principalities in 1859 and as Romania in 1861. Serbia, despite further expansion in 1833, remained confined to a small territory north of Nish and south of the Danube.

Belgian Independence, 1831-39

4 The unification of the Low Countries under the House of Orange after 1815 had been intended as an obstacle to revived French expansionism. It was backed up by the garrisoning of the great fortresses at Luxembourg with Prussian troops.

The instability of the new state was revealed when the Belgians, encouraged by the July Revolution in Paris which toppled the Bourbons, rose up against the House of Orange in August 1830. The Belgian revolt combined liberal radicalism, local resentment of Dutch domination and Catholic anti-Orange feeling which united the French-speaking Walloons and the Flemings against the Dutch. The Dutch appealed to Prussia to send troops to crush the rebellion, but Britain persuaded the other Great Powers (France, Prussia, Austria and Russia) to accept an independent Belgium with the proviso that it would be perpetually neutral. The Dutch bitterly opposed the settlement and the new Belgian state achieved full international recognition only in 1839. The Netherlands, meanwhile, were reduced to their borders of 1790, while the Grand Duchy of Luxembourg became a personal union with the Dutch crown.

1861

1871

The Unification of Germany

During the 1860s, Prussia experienced an astonishingly rapid transformation from the least of the five recognised Great Powers to become the motor of a united German state whose military and economic power overshadowed her neighbours. Prussia's rise was based on the rapid growth of her industrial base, which provided the revenues to fund an expanded conscript army equipped with the most modern weaponry. However, without the political genius of Otto von Bismarck, the Prussian Chancellor and architect of German unification, and the military skills of the Prussian General Staff, the unification of Germany to the exclusion of the Habsburg Austrian empire, much of it as "German" as Prussia, could not have come about.

Military reforms begun at the end of the 1850s meant Bismarck was able to elevate Prussia to a dominant position in the German Confederation. Allying himself with Austria against Denmark in 1864, Bismarck tested the new Prussian army successfully. In 1866, it was turned against Austria and those other German states – a majority of them – who opposed the Prussians. In only seven weeks, Prussia routed her enemies and created the North German Confederation.

The settlement which ended the war, the Treaty of Prague, saw Austria excluded from the new Confederation and forbidden to ally herself with the three southern German states (Bavaria, Baden and Wurttemberg). But Bismarck held back from humiliating Austria: Franz Josef did not lose any territory to Prussia (though he had to cede Venetia to Italy).

Bismarck's magnanimity meant that Austria was not inclined to attack Prussia in 1870, when she was at war with France. By contrast, Napoleon III's inept diplomacy left France without allies against the Prussians. Russia refused to help because of Napoleon's support for the Polish rebels against Russia in 1863, while Austria resented the French refusal to help her in 1866. Britain, meanwhile, distrusted the French Emperor's designs on the Low Countries. Italy similarly took advantage of Napoleon III's predicament, seizing French-garrisoned Rome. Bismarck's forces rapidly overran the French and encircled Paris. The following year, Napoleon III was obliged, humiliatingly, to sue for peace. The Treaty of Frankfurt, which followed the war, saw Alsace-Lorraine ceded to Germany, adding to French resentment.

France had for so many generations held the position of chief threat in the minds of other European rulers that the implications of a united Germany went largely unnoticed. The new nation-state had a population of 41 million, larger than any other country west of Russia. Furthermore, Germany's economy was growing as rapidly as her population. But while the new Germany was too large to be a comfortable neighbour, she was too small to exercise hegemony over the rest of Europe. The resulting tension was increasingly to dominate Great Power diplomacy in Europe.

To counter Prussian military success, the great Continental Powers sought to emulate what they perceived as the roots of German success. Instead of relying on a professional army, which the Germans had swept aside, France returned to her revolutionary tradition of conscription, which Prussia had adapted after 1859 to such deadly effect. Even relatively poor Austria and Russia followed the Prussian model. Mass armies became instruments of national power as well as, in states such as France and Italy, schools of nationalism for still largely illiterate peasant soldiers.

NORWAY
Trondhjem
SWEDEN
FINLAND
Christiania
Stockholm
Gothenburg
Åbo
Helsingfors
St. Petersburg
Revel
Pskov
Riga
MARK
Copenhagen
Malmö
Dvinsk
Königsberg
Hamburg
Danzig
Vilna
Vitebsk
Smolensk
Moscow
Tula
RUSSIAN
Nizhniy
Novgorod
Samara
Bremen
Stettin
Berlin
EMPIRE
Minsk
Saratov
Leipzig
Posen
Warsaw
Brest-Litovsk
Kursk
Dresden
Lodz
POLAND
Breslau
Königgrätz
Nuremberg
Prague
Cracow
Lemberg
Vinnitsa
Kiev
Kharkov
EMPIRE
Ekaterinoslav
Astrakhan
gart
Brünn
Kassa
Rostov
Munich
AUSTRO-HUNGARIAN
Innsbruck
Salzburg
Vienna
Pozsony
Buda
Pest
Debrecen
EMPIRE
Kolozsvár
Jassy
Kishinev
Odessa
NSTEIN
Laibach
Pécs
Szeged
Graz
Venice
Trieste
Zágráb
Újvidék
Temesvár
Brassó
Bologna
ROMANIA
Sebastopol
Tiflis
SAN MARINO
Zara
Belgrade
Bucharest
Perugia
Bosna Saray
SERBIA
Erivan
Rome
Spalato
Mostar
Nish
Ruschuk
Varna
PERSIA
MONTENEGRO
Üsküb
Sofia
Burgas
Trebizond
Naples
Bari
Philippopolis
Taranto
Salonica
Adrianople
Constantinople
Angora
Mosul
Janina
Smyrna
Adana
Palermo
Messina
Patras
Athens
Sicily
Catania
GREECE
Cyprus
Beirut
MALTA
(Br.)
Crete
Nicosia
Damascus
Bedouins
161
ITALY
OTTOMAN
EMPIRE

THE HABSBURG EMPIRE, 1849-68 [2]

Map labels:

SWEDEN

NORTH SEA

DENMARK

BALTIC SEA

Copenhagen

Schleswig

GRAND DUCHY OF OLDENBURG

Holstein *(to Austria in 1865)*

Lübeck

Lauenburg

GRAND DUCHY OF MECKLENBURG-SCHWERIN

Hamburg

Bremen

Königsberg

Danzig

NETHERLANDS

Kingdom of Hanover *(to 1866)*

Stettin

GRAND DUCHY OF MECKLENBURG-STRELITZ

PR. OF SCHAUMBURG-LIPPE

PR. OF LIPPE-DETMOLD

DUCHY OF BRUNSWICK

Berlin

DUCHY OF ANHALT

Posen

RUSSIAN EMPIRE

PR. OF WALDECK

LIMBOURG

Cologne

BELGIUM

Elect. of Hesse *(to 1866)*

THURINGIAN STATES

Leipzig

KGDM OF SAXONY

Dresden

Breslau

D. of Nassau *(to 1866)*

Frankfurt

GRAND DUCHY OF HESSE

Prague

Königgrätz

Cracow

Lemberg

LUXEMBOURG

BAVARIA

GRAND DUCHY OF BADEN

Nuremberg

Bohemia

Moravia

Galicia

FRANCE

Stuttgart

KGDM OF WÜRTTEM-BERG

KINGDOM OF BAVARIA

Brünn

Nikolsburg

AUSTRIAN EMPIRE

Munich

Vienna

Pozsony

LIECHTENSTEIN

Gastein

Buda

Pest

SWITZERLAND

Graz

Hungary

Turin

Venetia

Venice

Custozza

Verona

Trieste

Istria

Croatia

Slavonia

Military Frontier

ITALY

MONACO

SAN MARINO

OTTOMAN EMPIRE

GERMANY, 1864-66 [3]

- Lost by Denmark, 1864
- Prussia, 1865
- Additions to Prussia, 1866
- Other German states
- Additions to Italy, 1866
- Austrian possessions from 1866
- The German Confederation to 1866
- Frontiers, 1866
- The North German Confederation from 1867

THE HABSBURG EMPIRE, 1849-68 [2]

- Lost to Sardinia, 1859
- Under Habsburg cadet branch to 1860
- Lost to Italy and Prussia, 1866
- The German Confederation, to 1866
- Serbian Voivodina and Banat of Temesvár (1849-60)

Hungarian territory :

- Detached 1849, reunited 1860
- Detached 1849, reunited 1867
- Autonomous within Hungary, from 1868
- Brought under civil administration, by 1882
- Hungarian crownlands
- Areas represented in the Viennese Imperial Council
- Frontiers, 1868

NORTH GERMAN CONFEDER

BAVARIA

Linz

Salzburg

Innsbruck

Trent

Trieste

Venice

Fiur

San Marino

PAPAL STATES

AUSTRIA-HUNGARY: ETHNIC DIVISIONS

- German
- Hungarian
- Cze
- Poli

DENMARK

Holstein *(to Austria in 1865)*

NETHERLANDS

NORTH GERMAN CONF

Prague

HESSE

BAVARIA

Bohemia

Brünn

Mo

FRANCE

BADEN

WÜRTTEMBERG

NORTH GERMAN CONFEDERATION

Linz

Upper Austria

Lower Austria

Vienna

LIECHTENSTEIN

Vorarlberg

Salzburg

Salzburg

Styria

SWITZERLAND

Innsbruck

Tyrol

Carinthia

Graz

Lombardy

Venetia

Carniola

Milan

Solferino

Trieste

Venice

Croa

Küstenland

Fiume

(detached from Hungary 1849, reunited 1868)

ITALY

San Marino

Dalmati

Florence

Tuscany

Zara

Spalato

Corsica

PAPAL STATES

Slovakian
Ukranian
Serbian
Croatian
Slovenian
Italian
Ladin & Friulian
Romanian
Frontiers, 1868

Austria-Hungary: Ethnic Divisions

1 Franz Josef's empire was a denial of the fashionable 19th-century doctrine of national self-determination. His subjects spoke at least 12 languages and adhered to four major religions (Catholicism, Protestantism, Orthodoxy and Judaism). The Habsburgs had long recognised that nationalism was their deadly enemy, but even an empire based on loyalty to a dynasty rather than a national ideal could not avoid the issue of language rights.

Although some Habsburg dominions possessed clear linguistic majorities, such as the overwhelmingly German-speaking provinces in the Alpine west or the Hungarian-speaking villages of the plains, most parts of the empire contained a mixture of peoples and faiths. As the 19th century progressed, the Habsburgs' Slav subjects began to assert their own identity through new national literatures, music and political organisations.

German-speaking Vienna's difficulties with Budapest over the Hungarians' rights to self-rule made dealing with the other peoples still more complicated. Although Hungarian liberals demanded that the crownlands of St Stephen should enjoy self-rule, they were not happy to extend equal political rights to their large Slovak, Romanian or Serb minorities.

The Habsburg Empire, 1849-68

2 Hungary's relationship with the Habsburg monarchy had always been voluntary – at least in Hungarian eyes. Vienna's efforts to Germanise the Magyars had been resisted both under Joseph II in the 1790s and his successors. 1848 saw a liberal-nationalist revolution in Hungary. For a few months Habsburg rule was overthrown, but in 1849 the Russian army intervened to restore the Habsburg monarchy. Having defeated Hungary, the Habsburgs detached Transylvania from her, augmented Croatia at Hungarian expense, created the new crownlands of Serbian Voivodina and the Banat of Temesvár from former Hungarian territory, and suppressed even nominal Hungarian autonomy. This situation continued until after the Austrian defeat in Italy in 1859, when the Habsburgs, aware of their vulnerable position, agreed a compromise with the Hungarians, by which Serbian Voivodina and the Banat of Temesvár were returned to Hungary and the jurisdiction of the Hungarian parliament was recognised.

Austria's defeat by Prussia in 1866 opened the way for renewed Hungarian demands for self-rule which Franz Josef in Vienna could not resist. The Emperor abandoned any aspiration for centralised rule from Vienna and restored self-government to Hungary by the so-called "Compromise" (*Ausgleich*) of 1867, which granted complete independence to Hungary, leaving only foreign affairs and military policy in common with the lands of the Austrian Crown. Transylvania and other areas were returned to Hungary, including Croatia, which enjoyed a relatively privileged status even in the newly re-founded Magyar national component of the Dual Monarchy (in which the reigning Habsburg was Emperor of Austria, but King of Hungary). The Croatian kingdom had been associated with the Crown of St Stephen for over 700 years and it was only briefly subject to Vienna after 1849. Ironically, Croatian military support for the Habsburgs against the Magyar rebels had been vital to saving the monarchy then, but the Habsburgs proved as ungrateful to the Croats as to the Tsar.

After 1867, the Hungarians conceded more: by the "Agreement" (*Nagoda*) of 1868, Budapest granted Croatia an assembly (*Sabor*) with limited local government powers. By 1882, the "Military Frontier" had been put under civilian administration. Mutual fear of disintegration kept Vienna and Budapest together after 1867, despite petty disputes about the title of the common army (Imperial or Royal according to where it was stationed) and the language of command.

Germany, 1864-66

3 Palmerston once remarked that only three people had ever understood the answer to the Schleswig-Holstein question: the first had gone mad; the second, Queen Victoria's Prince Consort, had since died; while the third, Palmerston himself, had forgotten it. This apparently obscure issue was a classic illustration of the tension between dynastic rights and national identity which became more and more acute during the course of the 19th century.

Danish ambitions to incorporate the two duchies of Schleswig and Holstein went against the grain of German nationalism. The bulk of the duchies' populations was German-speaking, and already by 1848 defending their rights against Danish encroachments had become a popular cause in Germany. Bismarck used the issue to divide his liberal opponents, many of whom felt unable to oppose military intervention on behalf of the Germans there. Austria went along with Bismarck's war against Denmark in 1864 and the re-drawing of boundaries which followed. Austria administered Holstein while Prussia held Schleswig. But friction rapidly developed between Vienna and Berlin leading to the Seven Weeks' War in 1866, after which Prussia annexed the Kingdom of Hanover, Nassau, the Electorate of Hesse and the free city of Frankfurt. In Hanover, political opposition to incorporation into Prussia was particularly persistent. Neither Luxembourg nor Limbourg, which belonged to the King of the Netherlands, joined the North German Confederation after 1866. Limbourg joined the Netherlands, while Luxembourg remained in personal union with the Dutch crown until 1890.

The Prussian dominated 23-state North German Confederation became the German Empire in January 1871 when the principal south German states – Bavaria, Wurttemburg, Baden and Hesse – joined it. Alsace and Lorraine were taken from France and added to the new Reich. The exclusion of the German-speaking Austrians from what was soon to become a united "little Germany" (*Kleindeutschland*) left an anomaly of national self-determination unfulfilled to haunt the 20th century.

1871

Imperial Europe

The years 1871 to 1914 saw Imperial Europe at its zenith. Outside Europe, all the Great Powers bar Austria-Hungary – Britain, Germany, France, Italy, and Russia – established empires that extended across the globe; within Europe, they co-existed uneasily. With none powerful enough to defeat the others unaided and with Britain, the most powerful of all, continuing her traditional concern with her colonies overseas rather than with Europe, each sought advantage in a system of complex and shifting alliances. The principal architect of this armed peace was Germany, concerned above all to safeguard her new territorial gains. But these alliances never included France. The humiliating defeat of 1870-71 and the loss of Alsace-Lorraine were hard enough for France to bear, but far worse was her loss of primacy in Europe. Between 1870 and 1914, Germany's population doubled (from 33 to 65 million; in the same period France's population remained static at around 40 million) and her industrial output quadrupled. She also built up impressive armed forces. Her army, at 95 divisions, was twice the size of France's and 12 times the size of Britain's, while her navy was second only to Britain's. Franco-German estrangement was the one fixed point among the shifting alliances of the Great Powers. For 20 years after 1871 Germany succeeded in convincing most of Europe of her conservative and pacific intentions, and France remained isolated. The balance of power that resulted in Western Europe preserved the peace for 43 years and for most governments territorial questions ceased to be a major issue.

Less intractable than the Franco-German rivalry but equally permanent and sometimes threatening to combine with it was the potential clash of Austro-Hungarian and Russian interests in the Balkans. Here, the combination of Ottoman misgovernment and insurgent nationalism speeded the erosion of Ottoman rule that had already seen Greece achieve independence in 1830, and which culminated in the Treaty of San Stefano in 1878, following a Russo-Ottoman war. The terms of the treaty were considered too favourable to Russia and Bulgaria for Austria-Hungary to accept, and were revised by the Treaty of Berlin the same year (*see* map 3, page 167). Ottoman control of the central Balkans was, though still much weakened, for the time being rescued.

Russia considered it essential that no other power achieved a position from which it could control the straits at Constantinople, through which passed most of the grain on which her economy (and hence her Great Power status) depended. Russia's fundamental motive may thus have been defensive but in practice she varied between attempting to stabilise Ottoman rule and to overthrow it in the hope of replacing the empire with a string of submissive satellites. To Habsburg Austria-Hungary, Russia's efforts seemed a dangerously threatening attempt to encircle the Habsburg monarchy with a crowd of irredentist Slav states under Russian protection. Britain, too, found itself drawn into the conflict. Many saw Russia's interest in the Ottoman Empire as a threat to the overland and Suez routes to India, already endangered in their view by Russian expansion towards Persia and Afghanistan. For the most part, however, as the Great Powers became aware of the complexities of the Balkans, the threats posed by emerging national movements, and of the dangerous incompatibilities of their own ambitions there, they clung stubbornly to the status quo.

NORWAY

SWEDEN

FINLAND

Narvik

Trondhjem

Christiania

Stockholm

Gothenburg

Aarhus
Copenhagen
Malmo

DENMARK

Hamburg
Bremen

Hanover
Berlin

Nuremberg

Stuttgart

Munich

LIECHTENSTEIN

Innsbruck

Venice
Verona

Bologna

Florence

San Marino

Perugia

ITALY

Rome

Naples

Palermo

Messina

Catania

Sicily

MALTA
(Br.)

Åbo

Helsingfors

Revel

Pskov

Riga

BALTIC
SEA

Königsberg

Danzig

Stettin

GERMAN EMPIRE

Posen

Leipzig
Dresden

Breslau

Prague

Brünn

Vienna

Salzburg

Graz

Laibach

Trieste

Zágráb

Zara

BOSNIA-
HERZEGOVINA

Spalato

Mostar

Sarajevo

MONTE-
NEGRO

St. Petersburg

Vilna

Minsk

Oder

Vistula

Elbe

Danube

Pozsony

Budapest

AUSTRO-HUNGARIAN

EMPIRE

Pécs

Szeged

Újvidék

Belgrade

SERBIA

Nish

Üsküb

Dvinsk

Vitebsk

Smolensk

Warsaw

Brest-Litovsk

POLAND

Lodz

Cracow

Lemberg

Kassa

Debrecen

Kolozsvár

Temesvár

Brassó

ROMANIA

Bucharest

BULGARIA

Danube

Ruse

Sofia

Plovdiv

Üsküb

Janina

GREECE

Patras

Athens

Crete

Moscow

Tula

RUSSIAN

Kursk

EMPIRE

Kiev

Kharkov

Vinnitsa

Dnieper

Ekaterinoslav

Dniester

Kishinev

Odessa

Jassy

Varna

Burgas

Adrianople

Constantinople

Salonica

Smyrna

OTTOMAN

Archangel

Nizhniy
Novgorod

Volga

Samara

Saratov

Don

Rostov

Volga

Astrakhan

Sebastopol

BLACK   SEA

EMPIRE

Angora

Trebizond

Adana

Euphrates

Tigris

CYPRUS
(Br.)

Nicosia

Tiflis

Erivan

PERSI

Mosul

Bedouins

SEA

Bari

Taranto

165

SOUTHERN HUNGARY: THE DISSOLUTION OF THE MILITARY FRONTIER. 1873-82

3

Frontier, Hungarian crownlands

Military frontier, to 1873

Tributaries lost by Ottoman Empire, 1878

Territory lost by Ottoman Empire, 1878

Territory brought under civil administration, with date:

To Hungary, 1873

To Croatia-Slavonia, 1873

To Croatia-Slavonia, 1882

Frontiers from 1878

Map 1 (top left)

AUSTRIAN CROWNLANDS

Klagenfurt

Zágráb

Croatia-Slavonia

Fiume

Szíszek

Zengg

Pécs

HUNGARY

Eszék

Temesvár

Újvidék

Pétervárad

Zimony

Pancsova

Banja Luka

Belgrade

SERBIA

Knin

Zara

Bosnia-Herzegovina

Sarajevo

(Austro-Hungarian occupation from 1878)

Spalato

Dalmatia

Mostar

Novibazar

Sanjak of Novibazar

Nish

Ragusa

MONTE-NEGRO

ADRIATIC SEA

Scutari

Üsküb

ITALY

OTTOMAN EMPIRE

Map 2 (top right)

Pécs

AUSTRO-HUNGARIAN EMPIRE

Eszék

Temesvár

Újvidék

Bosnia

Belgrade

Herzegovina

Sarejevo

SERBIA

Spalato

Sanjak of Novibazar

Mostar

Novibazar

Nish

Ragusa

MONTENEGRO

Scutari

Sofi

ADRIATIC SEA

Durazzo

Üsküb

ITALY

Tirana

Macedonia

O T T O

Sa

Janina

Thessaly (to Greece, 1881)

Map 3 (bottom)

NORTH SEA

DENMARK

SWEDEN

BALTIC SEA

Königsberg

Lübeck

Hamburg

GRAND DUCHY OF OLDENBURG

Bremen

GRAND DUCHY OF MECKLENBURG-SCHWERIN

Stettin

GRAND DUCHY OF MECKLENBURG-STRELITZ

Vistula

NETHERLANDS

PRINCIPALITY OF SCHAUMBURG-LIPPE

Elbe

KINGDOM OF PRUSSIA

PRINCIPALITY OF LIPPE-DETMOLD

DUCHY OF BRUNSWICK

Berlin

Posen

DUCHY OF ANHALT

RUSSIAN

BELGIUM

PRINCIPALITY OF WALDECK

Cologne

Rhine

Leipzig

KINGDOM OF SAXONY

EMPIRE

GRAND DUCHY

THURINGIAN STATES

Breslau

Frankfurt

OF HESSE

LUXEMBOURG

KINGDOM OF BAVARIA

ALSACE-LORRAINE Imperial Territory

GRAND DUCHY OF BADEN

KINGDOM OF WÜRTTEMBERG

Stuttgart

KINGDOM OF BAVARIA

FRANCE

Danube

Munich

AUSTRO-HUNGARIAN

LIECHTENSTEIN

SWITZERLAND

EMPIRE

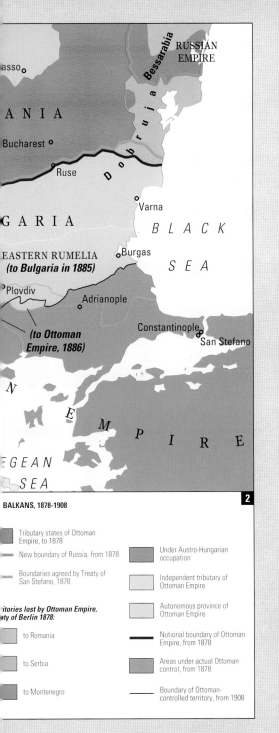

BALKANS, 1878-1908

Tributary states of Ottoman
Empire, to 1878

New boundary of Russia, from 1878

Boundaries agreed by Treaty of
San Stefano, 1878

Territories lost by Ottoman Empire,
Treaty of Berlin 1878:

to Romania

to Serbia

to Montenegro

Under Austro-Hungarian
occupation

Independent tributary of
Ottoman Empire

Autonomous province of
Ottoman Empire

Notional boundary of Ottoman
Empire, from 1878

Areas under actual Ottoman
control, from 1878

Boundary of Ottoman-
controlled territory, from 1908

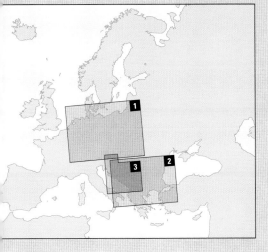

IMPERIAL GERMANY, 1871

Boundary of German Empire from 1871

Free cities

Imperial Germany, 1871

1 The notion that unified Germany was no more than Prussia in another guise gained such rapid acceptance that it was easily and frequently overlooked that Imperial Germany was in fact a federal state in which the 26 individual states had an equal voice. That said, Prussia's remained the dominant influence. Not only was it the largest state, stretching across the whole of the north of the country from the Low Countries in the west to Russia in the east, with the lion's share of the new country's rapidly developing industrial base it had a decisive voice in decision-making.

Yet however inevitable the dominance of Prussia, Bismarck had nonetheless been fearful that the new state would erode Prussia's leading role and that a federal constitution was essential to maintain her identity. (At the same time, he similarly recognised that such an arrangement would allay fears on the part of the smaller states that they would be swallowed whole by Prussia.)

The constitutional arrangements of Prussia itself were significantly different in several important ways from those of the most other German states, not least in regard to the development of democracy. Prussia's parliament (*Landtag*), unlike those of the other German states (save defiantly feudal Mecklenburg-Schwerin), was not elected by universal male suffrage but by a three-tier voting system dating from 1849 and based on taxable income. In consequence, power was largely concentrated in the hands of Bismarck and his successors. Control of the *Landtag* in each state was important because only the local parliaments could raise direct taxes. The fiscal powers of the Imperial Parliament (*Reichstag*) were limited to indirect taxes, such as customs duties. Most important, the army was paid for at a state level and each state had its own army. Nonetheless, all but the Bavarian army were controlled by Prussian superiors, and even this was subordinate to the Prussian General Staff, which co-ordinated all military operations.

Ironically, the only part of the Reich which was not a federal state in its own right with its own constitution and monarch was the Imperial Territory (*Reichsland*) of Alsace-Lorraine, ceded by France under the Treaty of Frankfurt in 1871 (and returned to France at the end of the First World War).

The Balkans, 1878-1908

2 As revolts against Ottoman rule spread through the Balkans in the mid-1870s, Austria was reassured by Russia's apparent lack of direct ambition there. St. Petersburg agreed that no new large-scale Christian state should be created which might thwart Austria's ambitions but that instead Turkey should reform itself.

But by 1877 Russian public opinion had pushed the Tsar into war in support of the Christian Slav rebels. Under the Treaty of San Stefano in 1878 which concluded the war, the Russians chose to create a "Big Bulgaria" stretching across the southern Balkans. This immediately sparked crisis among the Great Powers. Neither Austria-Hungary nor Britain would accept such a Russian puppet-state, particularly as it left Constantinople vulnerable to sudden attack. Playing on Germany's lack of interest in the Balkans, in the same year Bismarck, offering his services as an "honest broker", stepped in to separate his two imperial allies before a further war broke out.

The Treaty of Berlin (1878) overturned much of the San Stefano agreements. Instead, while it ratified the independent status of Serbia and Romania, it preserved the fiction of Ottoman suzerainty over a much-reduced Bulgarian principality. It also created a special status for Bulgarian-inhabited Eastern Rumelia, though this became wholly Bulgarian in 1885.

The decision to reduce Bulgaria and to restore Macedonia to Turkey (as well as to end the Austrian occupation of Bosnia-Herzegovina) proved a costly error in the long term. Bulgaria naturally aspired to recover what had been awarded to her by the Treaty of San Stefano, while Serbia similarly regarded Macedonia and other San Stefano territories as legitimate objects of her ambition. This brought her into direct conflict with Greece, which had, since her own independence in 1830, nursed claims to Macedonia on the ground that it was part of the historic territory of Greece. (Greece made partial amends with her seizure of Thessaly in 1881.)

Meanwhile, no one could agree the fate the Christian populations of the Balkans beyond a pious regret that they should have to remain under Muslim rule. However understandable the failure to grasp the Balkan nettle at Berlin in 1878, the problems of the region's numerous ethnic, nationalist, religious and imperial rivalries were to fester unchecked into the 20th century to everyone's disadvantage.

Southern Hungary: the Dissolution of the Military Frontier, 1873-82

3 The border between Christian Europe and the Muslim Ottoman Empire – the Military Frontier – was one of the great fault lines of Europe. It was established by the Habsburgs in Croatia in the mid-16th century to guard the Habsburg lands against Ottoman incursion and then greatly expanded after 1699 following the expulsion of the Ottomans from the most of Hungary by Prince Eugene. By the mid-19th century, with the Ottoman Empire in terminal decline, Hungarian demands for the return of the Frontier lands to civilian administration increased and from 1873 the Military Frontier was accordingly parcelled among Hungary and Croatia-Slavonia.

1914

The Eve of the First World War

The boundaries between the Great Powers changed little in the century after the Congress of Vienna (1815). Germany, although now unified, Austria-Hungary and Russia still shared largely the same frontiers established at Vienna, and most observers could be forgiven for regarding them as permanent. But in practice the emergence of small states on the periphery of the Powers, allied to tensions created by conflicting aspirations for autonomy and independence on the part of the many ethnic groups within the Austro-Hungarian and Russian empires, marked the beginning of a process that threatened the empires' territorial integrity. In tandem with Great Power rivalry, it created the conditions that were to lead to the cataclysms of the First World War.

Whatever its problems with nationalism, Russia at least had a majority ethnic group. Austria-Hungary lacked even this. The largest group in Hungary were the Magyars, who made up just under half the population. Slovaks, Romanians, Serbs and Croats as well as two-million Germans formed the other half. In the Austrian part of the empire, Germans amounted to only about 35 per cent of the population. Czechs, Poles, Slovenes, Italians and several smaller groups comprised the remainder. The very principle of national self-determination which had justified the unification of Germany was a threat to its Habsburg ally. Nationalist goals were satisfied in Norway, however, which in 1905 was granted full independence by Sweden.

But it was in the Balkans that nationalist aspirations were to prove most volatile. Newly independent Serbia, Bulgaria and Greece all saw the decline of the Turkish Ottoman Empire as an opportunity to extend their territories at the expense of the Turks. At the same, Austria-Hungary and Russia both sought to increase their influence in the region. With Britain's abandonment of its role as protector of the Turkish sultan (a policy intended chiefly to contain Russian ambitions), the way was left open for Serbia, Bulgaria and Greece in 1912 to attack the Ottomans. Dividing the spoils proved harder, however (*see* maps 2 and 3, page 171), and led to further fighting the following year. More threatening still, however, was the involvement of Austria-Hungary and Russia. While the former feared the destabilising effect Serbia might have on its large South Slav population, especially in Bosnia-Herzegovina (provocatively annexed by Austria-Hungary in 1908), the latter was determined to resume her role as protector of Orthodox Christians in the region – if necessary against Catholic Austria-Hungary rather than Muslim Turkey. With Austria and Russia members respectively of the Triple Alliance and the Triple Entente (*see* map 1, page 171), their rivalry in the Balkans increasingly threatened to suck the whole of Europe into conflict. Austria-Hungary's declaration of war against Serbia in July 1914 following the Serbian-sponsored assassination of the Archduke Ferdinand in Sarajevo the previous month was the spark that lit the the conflagration. Russia ordered a general mobilisation. Germany, Austria's ally, mobilised in turn, and on August 1 declared war on Russia. Three days later, Germany also declared war on France. The following day, the Germans invaded Belgium, determined to smash the Triple Entente. Britain promptly declared war on Germany and Austria on Russia. The First World War had begun.

NORWAY

Narvik

Trondhjem

Christiania

SWEDEN

FINLAND

Åbo

Helsingfors

St. Petersburg

Stockholm

Revel

Pskov

Gothenburg

Riga

Aarhus

Copenhagen

Malmo

BALTIC SEA

DENMARK

Hamburg

Bremen

Hanover

Berlin

Stettin

Königsberg

Danzig

EMPIRE

Posen

Warsaw

Brest-Litovsk

Oder

Dresden

Leipzig

RMAN EMPIRE

Elbe

POLAND

Lodz

Vistula

Nuremberg

Prague

Breslau

Cracow

Lemberg

gart

Munich

Danube

AUSTRO-HUNGARIAN

Kassa

Pozsony

TENSTEIN

Salzburg

Vienna

Budapest

Debrecen

EMPIRE

Kolozsvár

Innsbruck

Graz

Pécs

Szeged

Laibach

Zágráb

Temesvár

Venice

Trieste

Újvidék

Verona

Brassó

ROMANIA

Bologna

ence

Zara

BOSNIA-

HERZEGOVINA

Belgrade

Bucharest

SAN MARINO

Spalato

Sarajevo

SERBIA

Danube Ruse

ITALY

Perugia

Mostar

MONTE

NEGRO

Nish

Sofia

BULGARIA

Varna

Burgas

ome

Naples

Bari

Tirana

ALBANIA

Skopje

Plovdiv

Adrianople

Taranto

Janina

Salonica

Constantinople

GREECE

Smyrna

Angora

alermo

Messina

Sicily

Catania

Patras

Athens

SEA

MALTA

(Br.)

DODECANESE

(It.)

Crete

CYPRUS

(Br.)

Archangel

Perm

Nizhniy

Novgorod

Volga

Moscow

Samara

Tula

R U S S I A N

Vilna

Vitebsk

Smolensk

Minsk

Kursk

Saratov

E M P I R E

Don

Kiev

Kharkov

Vinnitsa

Dnieper

Ekaterinoslav

Volga

Dniester

Rostov

Astrakhan

Kishinev

Odessa

Jassy

Sebastopol

BLACK SEA

Tiflis

Erivan

Trebizond

PERSIA

OTTOMAN

EMPIRE

Tigris

Mosul

Adana

Euphrates

Nicosia

Beirut

Damascus

Bedouins

169

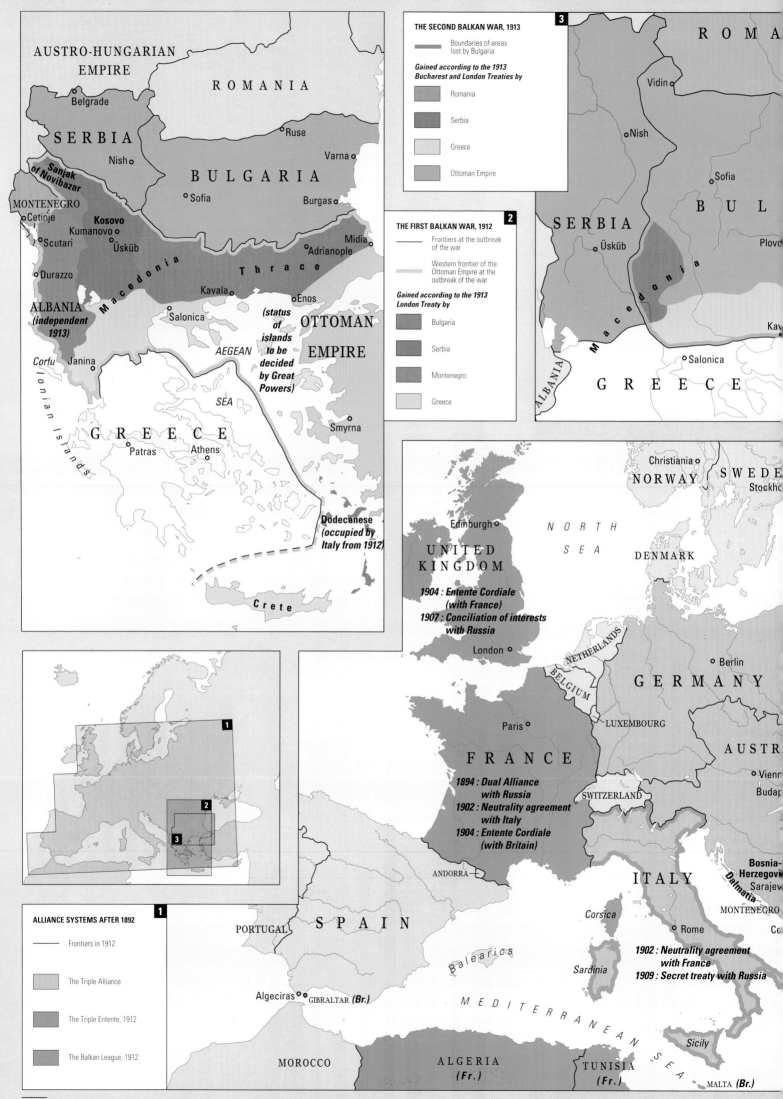

AUSTRO-HUNGARIAN
EMPIRE

Belgrade

SERBIA

Sanjak
of Novibazar

Nish

MONTENEGRO
Cetinje

Kosovo
Kumanovo
Scutari
Üsküb

Durazzo

ALBANIA
(independent
1913)

Janina

Macedonia

Corfu

Ionian Islands

GREECE

Patras

Athens

AEGEAN

SEA

ROMANIA

Ruse

BULGARIA

Sofia

Burgas

Varna

Kavala

Salonica

Thrace

Midia
Adrianople

Enos

(status
of
islands
to be
decided
by Great
Powers)

OTTOMAN

EMPIRE

Smyrna

Dodecanese
(occupied by
Italy from 1912)

Crete

THE SECOND BALKAN WAR, 1913 `3`

Boundaries of areas
lost by Bulgaria

Gained according to the 1913
Bucharest and London Treaties by

Romania

Serbia

Greece

Ottoman Empire

ROMA

Vidin

Nish

Sofia

SERBIA

B U L

Üsküb

Macedonia

Plov

Macedonia

Kav

Salonica

ALBANIA

GREECE

THE FIRST BALKAN WAR, 1912 `2`

Frontiers at the outbreak
of the war

Western frontier of the
Ottoman Empire at the
outbreak of the war

Gained according to the 1913
London Treaty by

Bulgaria

Serbia

Montenegro

Greece

Christiania

NORWAY

SWEDE

Stockho

NORTH

SEA

Edinburgh

UNITED
KINGDOM

DENMARK

1904 : Entente Cordiale
(with France)
1907 : Conciliation of interests
with Russia

London

NETHERLANDS

Berlin

BELGIUM

GERMANY

Paris

LUXEMBOURG

FRANCE

AUSTR

1894 : Dual Alliance
with Russia
1902 : Neutrality agreement
with Italy
1904 : Entente Cordiale
(with Britain)

SWITZERLAND

Vienr

Budap

ANDORRA

Bosnia-
Herzegovi
Sarajev

ITALY

Dalmatia

MONTENEGRO

Corsica

Rome

Ce

SPAIN

PORTUGAL

Sardinia

1902 : Neutrality agreement
with France
1909 : Secret treaty with Russia

Balearics

Algeciras
GIBRALTAR (Br.)

M E D I T E R R A N E A N

S E A

Sicily

MOROCCO

ALGERIA
(Fr.)

TUNISIA
(Fr.)

MALTA (Br.)

ALLIANCE SYSTEMS AFTER 1892 `1`

Frontiers in 1912

The Triple Alliance

The Triple Entente, 1912

The Balkan League, 1912

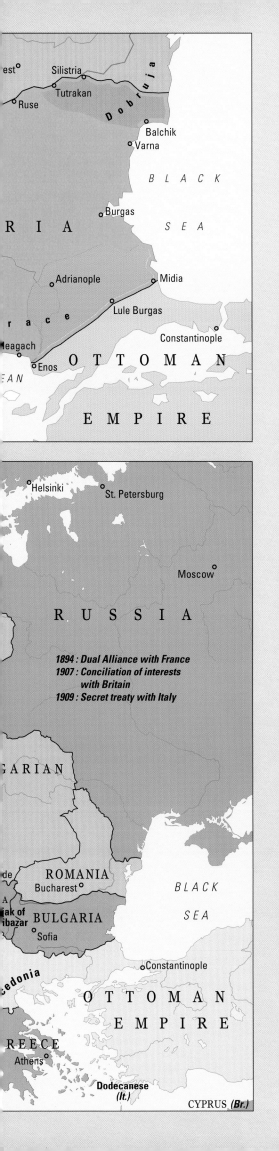

Alliance Systems after 1892

1 By the latter part of the 19th century dynastic ties and fear of unrest had served to draw together the Great Powers to promote an essentially stable order across Europe through a multi-faceted series of diplomatic alliances and alignments. This was the apogee of the European state system. But whatever its apparent stability, the system was permanently threatened by French resentment of Germany's growing primacy among the Continental powers (even if for much of the period France was unable to challenge Germany's fast increasing industrial and military might) and by instability in the Balkans, where an already heady cocktail of dissatisfied and mutually antagonistic states was made more potent still by the rival ambitions of Austria-Hungary and Russia. Both exploited every opportunity to destabilise the new independent states and to occupy disputed frontier areas.

By 1894 Germany's expanding military strength caused France and Russia to become nervous allies. In 1904, alarmed by the equally rapid growth of German naval power, Britain abandoned its "splendid isolation" and also allied itself with France, despite previously strained relations. In 1907 Britain then patched up its differences with Russia to form, with France, the Triple Entente to assure mutual defence against German attack. In Berlin, these measures of alleged self-defence were viewed more as encirclement. Facing declared enemies to the west and the east, Germany drew closer to Austria, whose strained relations with Russia finally cracked in 1908 following the Austrian annexation of Bosnia-Herzegovina. Though Italy had claims on Habsburg territory up to the Alps and in Dalmatia – and was also secretly allied with France and Russia – she, too, was at least nominally allied with Germany and Austria-Hungary in the Triple Alliance, as was Romania. By 1914, Austria-Hungary was Germany's only reliable ally. In the crisis after the murder of the Archduke Ferdinand, Germany could not afford to abandon her even at the risk of a general European war. Furthermore, if war did come, the Kaiser's generals wanted it sooner rather than later: the German army was increasingly certain that it could defeat France and Russia.

The First Balkan War, 1912

2 The new Balkan states – Serbia, Bulgaria and Greece – were united only by their hostility towards the Ottoman Empire, which in 1912 still held Albania and Macedonia. The Italian defeat of the Ottomans in Libya in 1912 encouraged Serbia, Bulgaria and Greece to activate their anti-Ottoman alliance in the hope of dividing the Sultan's European territories between them. The Turkish armies were swiftly defeated. The Treaty of London (1913), mediated by a committee of the Great Powers and chaired by Britain, oversaw the division of the spoils. It left everyone dissatisfied. The great Aegean port of Salonica

was coveted by all three victors. In the event, the Greek army had reached it just hours before the Bulgarians. To bitter Bulgarian resentment, Greek possession was confirmed in London. Bulgaria did, however, take possession of a large tract of land from the Black Sea to Kavala on the Aegean, including Adrianople. The province of Macedonia, which had a mixed population of Slavs, Turks, Jews and Greeks, was claimed by all three states, each with varying degrees of justice and all indifferent to the wishes of its inhabitants. Conquest confirmed its division between Serbia, Bulgaria and Greece. The Treaty of London also confirmed the creation of the independent principality of Albania, a development resented by both Greece and Serbia. Serbia wanted a port on the Adriatic at Albania's expense and feared moreover that an independent Albania would make her substantial Albanian minorities in Kosovo and Macedonia restive. Greece laid claim to northern Epirus (ie, southern Albania), basing her claim on the Greek Orthodox community there. Threatened by hostile neighbours, Albania was pushed into looking first to Austria-Hungary for protection and then to Italy.

The Sanjak of Novibazar, held by Austria-Hungary until 1908, was divided between Serbia and Montenegro. In thus closing the gap between them, their acquisition was crucial in increasing tension between Vienna and Belgrade. Serbia and Montenegro could now co-operate across a common border against their northern neighbour, Austria-Hungary, and seek to stir up the discontents of the South Slavs there. They also blocked further Austro-Hungarian expansion into the Balkans. The clash between Serbian nationalism in full flood and Habsburg expansion culminated in the assassination of the Archduke Ferdinand in Sarajevo in June 1914.

The Second Balkan War, 1913

3 Resentment with the Treaty of London quickly flared into a new war. Determined to right the wrongs done to it in London, in June 1913 Bulgaria attacked its erstwhile allies, Greece and Serbia. Bulgarian military optimism was soon shown to be misplaced. The Greeks and Serbians, aided by Romania and Turkey, who swiftly appreciated the opportunity the Bulgarian attack presented, had little difficulty repulsing the Bulgarians. Bulgaria was as rapidly defeated as Turkey had been the year before. Serbia partitioned much of the former Bulgarian-held areas of Macedonia with Greece. Greece kept Salonica and took western Thrace. Resentful Bulgaria was confined to a barren stretch of the Aegean coast while Turkey recovered Adrianople in Thrace, preserving the foothold in Europe she maintains today. Romania, a non-combatant in the first Balkan War, received southern Dobruja for her efforts in the second.

The Aftermath of the First World War

Despite the defeat of Germany and her allies in the autumn of 1918 and the signing of a string of peace treaties in Paris between the victorious allies and the defeated states in 1919 and 1920, it was several years before the boundaries of the new Europe were clearly established. Revolution and civil war plunged Russia, Germany and much of what had been Austria-Hungary into chaos.

The Europe that emerged was radically different. Russia and Germany had shrunk dramatically; the Austro-Hungarian and Ottoman empires had disappeared; a host of mostly smaller states had appeared. And in Soviet Russia a communist government now ruled in place of the Tsar. The civil war of 1918-20 that followed the 1917 revolution in Russia found counterparts in Hungary (1919), and in Germany (1918-23), where the new democratic government faced threats from both extreme right and left. Until 1923 Germany and parts of central Europe were also afflicted by hyper-inflation, which further destabilised these already fragile regions. Italy, too, was effectively gripped by revolution between 1920 and 1922, when Mussolini's Fascist party seized power. Among the combatants, only in Britain and France was there no serious threat to the political order, though civil war preceded and followed the creation of the Irish Free State in 1922.

The principal treaties agreed at Paris were those of Versailles (1919, with Germany); St-Germain (1919, with Austria); Neuilly (1919, with Bulgaria); Trianon (1920, with Hungary, *see* map 5, page 175); and Sèvres (1920, with Turkey), this last modified after the Greek-Turkish war of 1920-22 by the Treaty of Lausanne (1923).

As members of the victorious alliance, France and Italy gained what nationalists had long regarded as their "natural" frontiers. France regained her Rhine frontier. Italy gained an Alpine frontier (as well as a substantial German-speaking minority). Italy also acquired Istria and the port of Fiume along with Zara (Zadar) on the Dalmatian coast.

The most obviously dramatic effects of the Paris Settlement were the resurrection of Poland as an independent state more than a century after its partition between Austria, Prussia and Russia (*see* map 1, page 147) and the establishment of two new states: Czechoslovakia and Yugoslavia. Yugoslavia was officially a new kingdom of "Serbs, Croats and Slovenes" but was dominated by its old Serbian core. Of equal importance, the Paris Settlement left every post-war state in central Europe with internal problems and potential border disputes. It proved easier to break up multi-national empires than to replace them with ethnically homogeneous states. Poland and Czechoslovakia both had large German minorities after 1919, as well as disgruntled Slav minorities. Czechoslovakia and Yugoslavia also had substantial Hungarian minorities. Furthermore, neither Czechs and Slovaks, nor Serbs, Croats and Slovenes had any experience of living under a common government. Romania, too, inherited large Hungarian and German minorities.

In 1925 the Treaty of Locarno put relations with Germany and the allies on a new basis. But Germany was a reluctant signatory, accepting only her western borders as defined at Locarno. The question of her eastern borders would fester until Hitler resolved them by force.

Narvik

NORWAY

SWEDEN

Trondheim

Oslo

Stockholm

Gothenburg

DENMARK

Aarhus
Copenhagen
Malmo

BALTIC
SEA

FINLAND

Turku

Helsinki

Murmansk

Archangel

Leningrad

Tallinn
ESTONIA

Pskov

Riga LATVIA

LITHUANIA

Daugavpils

FREE CITY
OF DANZIG

Königsberg

Danzig

(Germany)

Wilno

Vitebsk

Minsk

UNION OF

SOVIET

Nizhniy
Novgorod

Volga

Moscow

Smolensk

Tula

Perm

Samara

Hamburg
ERMANY
Bremen
Hanover
Berlin

Elbe
Stettin

Oder

Poznań

Vistula

Warsaw

Brześć

Saratov

Dresden
Leipzig
kfurt
Nuremberg

Breslau
POLAND

Łódź

Kursk

SOCIALIST

Don

Prague
CZECHOSLOVAKIA

ttgart
Munich

Brno

Danube
Vienna

Cracow

Lwów

Kiev

Kharkov

Vinnitsa

Dnieper Dnepropetrovsk

REPUBLICS

Volga

Astrakhan

Innsbruck
ENSTEIN

Salzburg
AUSTRIA
Graz

Ljubljana

Košice

Bratislava

Debrecen

Budapest
HUNGARY

Pécs
Szeged

Cluj

Dniester

Iaşi

Chriştinău

Rostov

Venice
Verona
Trieste

Novi Sad

Timişoara

ROMANIA

Braşov

Odessa

Sebastopol

BLACK

SEA

Tbilisi

Bologna
rence

Zara
SAN MARINO

Zagreb

Belgrade

Bucharest

Yerevan

Perugia

ITALY
Rome

Split
Mostar

KINGDOM OF THE
Sarajevo
SERBS, CROATS,
AND SLOVENES

Danube Ruse

BULGARIA

Varna

Nish

Sofia

Burgas

Trabzon

PERSIA

Palermo

Tirana

ALBANIA

Naples
Bari
Taranto

Messina
Sicily
Catania

SEA

MALTA
(Br.)

Skoplje

Plovdiv

Adrianople

Istanbul

Ankara

TURKEY

Adana

Ioannina

GREECE

Izmir

Thessaloniki

Patrai Athens

DODECANESE

(It.)

Cyprus
(Br.)

Nicosia

Crete

Tigris

Euphrates

Mosul
IRAQ
(Br. Mandate)

SYRIA
(Fr. Mandate)

Beirut
Damascus

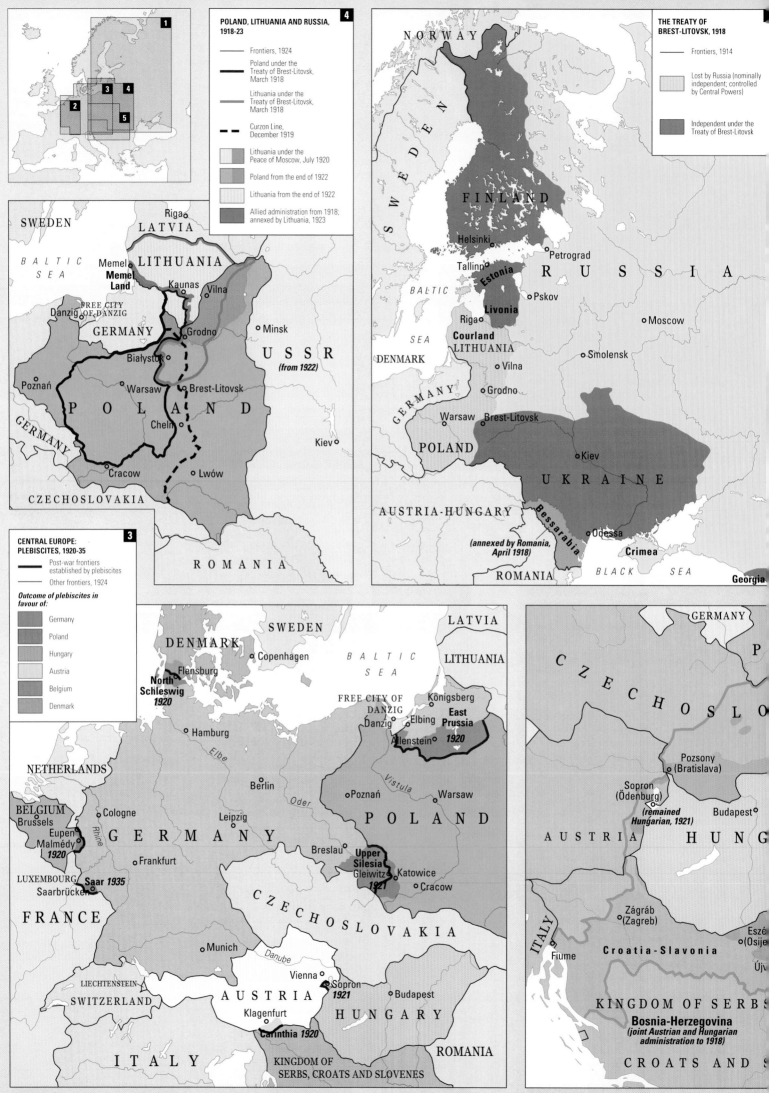

POLAND, LITHUANIA AND RUSSIA, 1918-23

- Frontiers, 1924
- Poland under the Treaty of Brest-Litovsk, March 1918
- Lithuania under the Treaty of Brest-Litovsk, March 1918
- Curzon Line, December 1919
- Lithuania under the Peace of Moscow, July 1920
- Poland from the end of 1922
- Lithuania from the end of 1922
- Allied administration from 1918; annexed by Lithuania, 1923

4

THE TREATY OF BREST-LITOVSK, 1918

- Frontiers, 1914
- Lost by Russia (nominally independent; controlled by Central Powers)
- Independent under the Treaty of Brest-Litovsk

CENTRAL EUROPE: PLEBISCITES, 1920-35

3

- Post-war frontiers established by plebiscites
- Other frontiers, 1924

Outcome of plebiscites in favour of:
- Germany
- Poland
- Hungary
- Austria
- Belgium
- Denmark

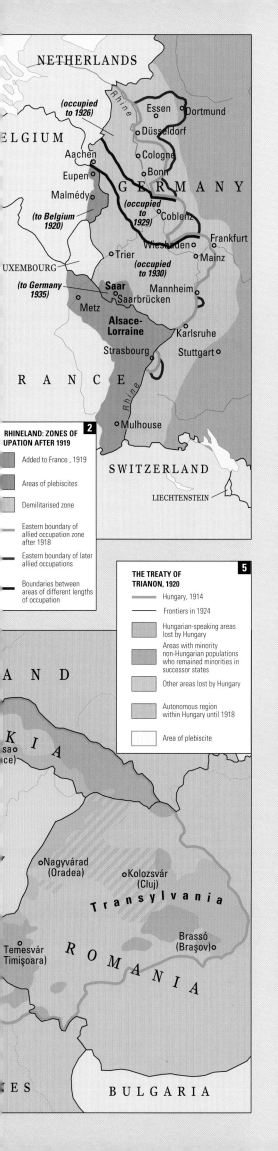

RHINELAND: ZONES OF OCCUPATION AFTER 1919 **2**

- Added to France , 1919
- Areas of plebiscites
- Demilitarised zone
- Eastern boundary of allied occupation zone after 1918
- Eastern boundary of later allied occupations
- Boundaries between areas of different lengths of occupation

THE TREATY OF TRIANON, 1920 **5**

- Hungary, 1914
- Frontiers in 1924
- Hungarian-speaking areas lost by Hungary
- Areas with minority non-Hungarian populations who remained minorities in successor states
- Other areas lost by Hungary
- Autonomous region within Hungary until 1918
- Area of plebiscite

The Treaty of Brest-Litovsk, 1918

1 Russia's withdrawal from the First World War after the Bolshevik takeover was formalised by the settlement between Lenin's Russia and Germany and her allies on 3 March 1918 at Brest-Litovsk. The treaty, deeply unfavourable to Russia, revealed in part the Europe Berlin hoped would be the outcome of the war. Russia lost all its western provinces: Finland, the Baltic states, Poland and the Ukraine (as well as Georgia under the Treaty of Berlin of August 1918). Germany's subsequent defeat was to mean that little could be done to exploit the territories lost by Russia, all of which, other than Georgia and the bulk of the Ukraine, remained independent at least until 1939. Nonetheless, the German desire to lay claim to the resources of this vast region foreshadowed Hitler's obsession with it 20 years later.

The Rhineland: Zones of Occupation after 1919

2 The demilitarisation of Germany was among the key objectives of Versailles, with France in particular anxious that Germany should never again be able to launch an attack across its eastern frontier. In addition to restrictions on the size of the German army, German forces were banned permanently from a wide band of the Rhineland from the Netherlands to Switzerland. To enforce the demilitarisation, allied troops (predominantly French) were stationed in three zones in the demilitarised area, from which they were to withdraw at five-year intervals until 1935. The allied occupation was also intended to ensure that Germany met the huge reparations bill demanded by the allies in compensation for their war losses. It was at least in part the scale of these that accelerated the economic catastrophe that overtook Germany in the early 1920s, leading the country to renege on her payments in 1923. In response, French and Belgian troops occupied further areas, principally in the Ruhr. The following year, Germany accepted a compromise reparations package. A further settlement was reached in 1928. Confident that the question had been settled and anxious to renew good relations with Germany, the withdrawal of the occupying forces was accelerated and the last troops were withdrawn in 1930. In March 1936, Hitler marched his troops back into the Rhineland.

Central Europe: Plebiscites, 1920-35

3 In accordance with the doctrine of self-determination championed by US President Wilson at the Paris Peace Settlement, the victorious allies permitted plebiscites to be held in certain hotly disputed territories to allow their inhabitants to decide which country they wished to live in. This was a novel idea, largely untried before 1919, though even now the allies generally redistributed territory without reference to its inhabitants. In almost every case, the plebiscites were decided along language lines. But there were exceptions. The Protestant Masurians of southern East Prussia, for example, preferred to remain in Germany rather than join Catholic Poland. Furthermore, a simple majority of one group over another could often disguise considerable complications on the ground. In the southeast corner of Upper Silesia, for example, mainly German-speaking towns were surrounded by predominantly Polish-speaking rural areas. As it was clearly impossible to give the rural areas to Poland and the towns to Germany, the Polish majority ensured that the whole area went to Poland. This was a source of enduring German resentment, as was the decision to entrust Danzig to the control of the League of Nations despite its overwhelming German character. Just as economic reasons dictated much of the Polish-German border, so the coal-rich Saarland was also placed under League of Nations control, allowing France to exercise *de facto* economic control. The last of the plebiscites promised at Versailles took place in 1935 when the Saarlanders voted overwhelmingly to return to German rule.

Poland, Lithuania and Russia, 1918-23

4 The defeat of the Red Army outside Warsaw in 1920 ended any prospect of the spread of communism to the West by "armed missionaries". The settlement between Poland and Soviet Russia agreed at Riga in 1921 was surpassed in its harshness to Lenin's Russia only by Brest-Litovsk. Having been obliged to accept the independence of the Baltic States the previous year, Russia now found itself having to accept a greatly expanded Poland, whose eastern border was pushed 200 miles beyond the Curzon Line, the border proposed by Poland's allies at the Paris Peace Settlement. Thus encouraged, the following year Polish forces seized southern Lithuania. (Lithuanian resentment at Poland's gains was such that the two were technically in a state of war until 1939). Lithuania responded by seizing the formerly German port of Memel in 1923, giving rise to further German resentment of the post-war settlement.

The Treaty of Trianon, 1920

5 The truncation of the ancient kingdom of Hungary was one of the most significant results of the First World War. Post-war Hungary lost not only its non-Magyar regions but vast Hungarian-speaking areas as well. The country even lost territory to its former partner, Austria, though Hungary was allowed to retain territory around Sopron after a plebiscite (*see* map 3). Hungarian resentment at the loss of over two-thirds of its pre-war territory and at the fate of more than one-third of the Hungarian-speaking population now under foreign rule simmered throughout the inter-war period.

1940

The Nazi Conquests

Resentment against the terms of the Versailles Settlement was widespread in Weimar Germany. The failure of the new democratic governments there to achieve any significant change in its terms, combined with the effects of the Great Depression after 1929, facilitated the rise to power of Adolf Hitler and the Nazi Party in 1933, which used anti-Versailles rhetoric as an essential ingredient in its election campaigns.

For the first five years of his rule, the Nazi dictator confined himself to chipping away at the restrictions imposed on Germany at Versailles. He refused, for example, to resume the reparations payments imposed at Versailles, while in 1933 he took Germany out of the League of Nations, to which she had been admitted only in 1926. More seriously, in March 1935 Hitler reintroduced conscription and an airforce, both forbidden in 1919, while the following March, more provocatively still, he re-occupied the demilitarised Rhineland.

In March 1938, Hitler's pan-German ambitions became more apparent when, again in direct contravention of the Versailles Treaty, he engineered the unification (*Anschluss*) of his native Austria with Germany. By the following March, with the tacit blessing of Britain and France, who were anxious at all costs to avoid war, Hitler had also occupied the Czech lands (*see* map 2, page 179), using at first the excuse that the country's three-and-a-half-million German speakers had been persecuted by the Czechoslovakian government.

Alerted at last by this occupation of non-German-speaking territory to the real dangers posed by Germany, Britain and France pledged to defend Poland, Greece and Romania from similar Nazi aggression and embarked on crash programmes of military spending. Again, Hitler wrong-footed them. In August, he signed a non-aggression pact with the Soviet Union (*see* map 3, page 178), despite his previous unwavering hostility to communism, neatly sidelining the one country he took to be his most serious enemy. Thus guaranteed, on 1 September Hitler invaded Poland. When their demands that Germany withdraw were ignored, Britain and France declared war. Though taken somewhat by surprise by this new Anglo-French resolve, Hitler's invasion of Poland continued, indeed was augmented by the Soviet invasion of eastern Poland in mid-September. By 29 September, Germany and the Soviet Union had partitioned Poland between them.

Hitler had now to deal with his enemies in the west before they had time to gather strength. In April 1940, his forces rapidly overran Denmark and Norway. On 10 May, they opened a devastating offensive against Holland, Belgium and France. The inadequate defence mounted by British and French forces was brushed aside. Precipitately, the remnants of the British army withdrew to Dunkirk and were evacuated. By mid-June France had effectively been defeated. The Government, now led by Marshal Pétain (a hero of the First World War), requested an armistice and subsequently established itself at Vichy, while the Germans continued to occupy northern and western parts of France.

By July 1940, when Hitler held victory celebrations in Berlin, Germany and her ally, Italy – the "Axis" – were masters, directly or indirectly, of the whole of Western and Central as well as much of Eastern Europe. The Soviet Union, it is true, had made use of Hitler's western offensive in order to occupy Finland and the Baltic states. But the difficulties experienced by the Soviet army in attaining these objectives suggested that it posed no threat to Germany. Hitler's rhetoric about acquiring *Lebensraum* (living space) for German colonisation seemed about to become reality.

NORWAY

Trondheim

Narvik

SWEDEN

Oslo

FINLAND

Murmansk

Archangel

Perm

Turku

Vyborg

Helsinki

Leningrad

Hangö

Stockholm

Tallinn

UNION OF

Gothenburg

Pskov

Nizhniy
Novgorod

Volga

Aarhus

Riga

Moscow

Kuybyshev

Copenhagen

Malmö

BALTIC
SEA

Daugavpils

Tula

SOVIET

DENMARK

Vilnius

Vitebsk

Smolensk

Hamburg

Königsberg

Minsk

Kursk

Saratov

Bremen

Stettin

Danzig

Berlin

Hanover

Vistula

Kharkov

SOCIALIST

Leipzig

Dresden

Posen

Warsaw

Brest

Kiev

Volga

Lodz

GENERAL
GOVERNMENT

Frankfurt

ERMAN EMPIRE

Breslau

Nuremberg

Prague

PROTECTORATE
OF BOHEMIA
AND MORAVIA

Cracow

L'vov

Vinnitsa

Dnieper

Dnepropetrovsk

REPUBLICS

Astrakhan

Stuttgart

Brünn

SLOVAKIA

Kassa

Dniester

Rostov

Munich

Vienna

Bratislava

Debrecen

Iaşi

Odessa

ENSTEIN

Salzburg

Budapest

Kolozsvár

Kishinev

Innsbruck

Graz

HUNGARY

Szeged

Ljubljana

Pécs

Venice

Trieste

Zagreb

Novi Sad

Timişoara

Braşov

Verona

ROMANIA

Sebastopol

Bologna

Zara

Belgrade

Bucharest

BLACK SEA

Tbilisi

rence

SAN MARINO

YUGOSLAVIA

Sarajevo

Danube

Ruse

Perugia

Split

Mostar

Nish

Varna

Yerevan

Rome

Bari

ITALY

ALBANIA

Skoplje

Sofia

BULGARIA

Burgas

Trabzon

IRAN

Tirana

Plovdiv

Edirne

Istanbul

Ankara

Naples

Taranto

Thessaloniki

TURKEY

Messina

Ioannina

Mosul

Palermo

Sicily

Catania

GREECE

Izmir

Adana

IRAQ

Patraí

Athens

SEA

DODECANESE
(It.)

Nicosia

SYRIA
(Fr. Mandate)

MALTA
(Br.)

Crete

CYPRUS
(Br.)

Damascus

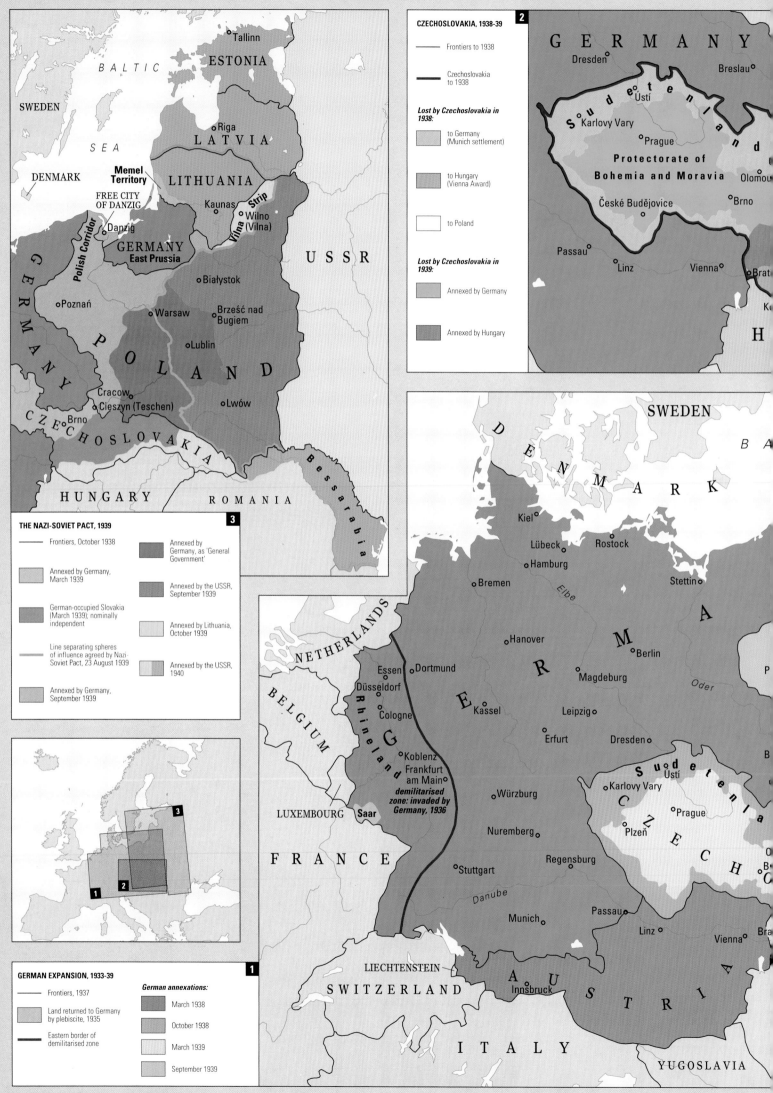

CZECHOSLOVAKIA, 1938-39 `2`

— Frontiers to 1938

— Czechoslovakia to 1938

Lost by Czechoslovakia in 1938:

- to Germany (Munich settlement)
- to Hungary (Vienna Award)
- to Poland

Lost by Czechoslovakia in 1939:

- Annexed by Germany
- Annexed by Hungary

THE NAZI-SOVIET PACT, 1939 `3`

— Frontiers, October 1938

- Annexed by Germany, March 1939
- German-occupied Slovakia (March 1939); nominally independent
- — Line separating spheres of influence agreed by Nazi-Soviet Pact, 23 August 1939
- Annexed by Germany, September 1939
- Annexed by Germany, as 'General Government'
- Annexed by the USSR, September 1939
- Annexed by Lithuania, October 1939
- Annexed by the USSR, 1940

GERMAN EXPANSION, 1933-39 `1`

— Frontiers, 1937

- Land returned to Germany by plebiscite, 1935
- — Eastern border of demilitarised zone

German annexations:

- March 1938
- October 1938
- March 1939
- September 1939

German Expansion, 1933-39

1 If the causes of the First World War were a complex and increasingly unstable series of Great Power rivalries which finally debalanced when Austria-Hungary and Russia clashed in the Balkans, the cause of the Second World War was far more clear-cut: Hitler's determination to ensure German domination of Europe. While Hitler, at any rate to begin with, sought only to overturn the punitive terms of the Paris Peace Settlement, his early successes – the overwhelming vote in favour of rejoining Germany by the Saarlanders in the 1935 referendum; rearmament; and the remilitarisation of the Rhine – rapidly persuaded him to widen his ambitions. Support from his fellow Fascist leader Mussolini in Italy, the distractions caused by the Civil War in Spain (1936-39), the chaos unleashed in the Soviet Union by Stalin's purges, and the reluctance of Britain and France to take seriously the threat of German expansion combined to make his task substantially easier.

Between March 1938 and March 1939, Hitler absorbed into his new *Reich* not only Austria and the Sudentenland, both of which could be claimed to be historically German, but, under its new name of the Protectorate of Bohemia and Moravia, the remainder of the Czech lands as well as the Lithuanian Baltic port of Memel with its surrounding lands. The bridging of the Danzig corridor in Poland, which separated East Prussia from the rest of Germany, was the logical next step, duly taken in September 1939.

Czechoslovakia, 1938-39

2 After 1918, the newly created Czechoslovak state was beset by the problems of incorporating successfully the ethnic groups who found themselves within its borders, above all the three-million-plus Germans in the prosperous industrialised Czech territories of Bohemia and Moravia. By 1938, the combination of economic depression and frustration with the Czech-speaking bureaucracy had produced a vigorous movement among them for unification with neighbouring Germany. At the same time, many Slovaks resented Czech domination of industry and government and the second-class status to which they felt inevitably relegated. Despite a mutually intelligible language, Czechs and Slovaks had little common history.

In September 1938, Hitler engineered the take-over of the Sudetenland as well as much of the south of the frontier lands of the Czech half of the country. As with the *Anschluss* with Austria the previous year, Hitler's was not a military operation. Rather, having co-opted Britain and France to approve his annexation in return for a promise of no further German expansion, it was an entirely peaceful manoeuvre. Its result, however, was to make what remained of the country effectively indefensible, depriving Czechoslovakia not only of her fortifications but, with her abandonment by her allies, of her will to resist. In

addition, the Munich Settlement, as it came to be called, greatly encouraged separatists in Slovakia to break away from the rump Czech lands. By March 1939, they felt secure enough to proclaim an independent Slovakia under German protection. By the middle of the month, Hitler had marched his troops into what remained of the independent Czech lands. Both Poland and Hungary found the prospect of grabbing parts of the dying Czechoslovakia irresistible. Poland seized Cieszyn (Teschen), while Hungary obtained parts of southern Slovakia and Ruthenia, which had substantial Hungarian minorities and had belonged to the Crown Lands of St Stephen before 1918.

The Nazi-Soviet Pact, 1939

3 Although he had loudly condemned appeasement of Germany before Munich, Stalin showed less enthusiasm for confronting Hitler once the Anglo-French capitalists had announced their guarantees of Polish, Romanian and Greek sovereignty following the Nazi occupation of Prague. However, such had been the vocal animosity between Nazi Germany and Soviet Russia that few people were prepared for the sudden reversal of policy announced on 23 August 1939. By then Hitler's demands that Poland agree to the incorporation into his Reich of the overwhelmingly German Free City of Danzig, along with the territory separating it and East Prussia from the rest of Germany, had produced a crisis. The Poles refused to negotiate and were backed up by London and Paris.

Unfortunately, the Western allies were in no position to offer Stalin inducements to co-operate and the Poles, remembering the war of 1919-20, showed no desire to allow Soviet troops into their country. Hitler, however, had no compunction about offering Stalin incentives to adopt a benevolent neutrality in the event of a German-Polish war. In fact, secret protocols to the Nazi-Soviet Non-Aggression Pact of 23 August envisaged the division of the Baltic states and Eastern Europe into German and Soviet spheres. On 1 September, Germany invaded and rapidly overran western Poland. On 17 September, the Red Army moved into the east of the country.

Unlike the German conquerors, the Soviet forces went through the motions of organising plebiscites to confirm the popular will to join the Soviet Union in the areas it occupied. Stalin also demanded that the three Baltic republics permit the entry of Soviet forces to protect them. The following June, as Hitler's troops entered Paris, Lithuania, Latvia and Estonia all "voted" to join the Soviet Union. A rump area of Poland was not annexed directly to the German Reich. Known as the General Government, it was ruled from Cracow.

1940

Hitler's Europe

By the autumn of 1942, Hitler's Germany was at the peak of its power. To the conquests of 1939-40 were added those of Yugoslavia and Greece in the spring of 1941, while in North Africa German troops reached the borders of Egypt, threatening Britain's vital links with India, the Far East and Australia and New Zealand. In June 1941, Hitler had also launched his most ambitious military offensive to date, Operation Barbarossa – the invasion of the Soviet Union.

Hitler's crusade against communism, temporarily shelved by the Nazi-Soviet Pact of 1939, made his invasion of the Soviet Union inevitable. Given his successes by 1941 and the almost complete disorganisation of the Soviet army after Stalin's purges, it must have seemed a realistic prospect, however daunting. Yet in the event the Germans were to be defeated by the immensity of the task they had set themselves: the enormous distances involved, the severity of the Russian winter, the seemingly limitless manpower of the Russians. To begin with, however, it was a remarkable success. The invasion was launched on 22 June with three-million men advancing along a 2,000-mile front. Heavily defended Smolensk, 400 miles behind the Russian frontier, fell within a month. By late November, having taken three-million prisoners and destroyed or captured 18,000 tanks and 20,000 planes, the Germans stood at the gates of Leningrad and Moscow. But as the winter set in, there they remained. In December, the Russians counter-attacked, driving the Germans back more than 100 miles and giving Stalin time to reorganise his shattered defences.

With the Japanese attack on the US Pacific naval base at Pearl Harbor and America's entry into the war against Japan, Hitler then declared war against America. For the first time, the tide was poised to turn against him. The immense resources America was able to deploy combined with the Soviet Union's rapidly increasing military muscle to stretch the Germans to breaking point and beyond. Despite a renewed German offensive against the Soviet Union in the spring of 1942, which saw four-million Axis troops thrust south and west, Hitler was by now fatally over-committed. By October, the German attack had faltered at Stalingrad. As winter closed in once more, half-a-million Axis troops struggled to take the city. By February, the battle had been lost and the starving survivors of 20 German divisions surrendered. It had been the greatest battle in history, claiming one million lives.

But if short-lived, the Nazi re-ordering of Europe was significant. Through a mixture of racial extermination, deportations and boundary adjustments, the Germans tried to establish a new system of states in Europe. The key difference to any previous system was that no freedom was to be permitted to Germany's allies or satellites even if they retained a nominal independence. Vichy France and Denmark, for example, were both permitted self-government, the former until November 1942, the latter until November 1943. Poland, by contrast, was permitted no trace of autonomy after 1939. But even territories with nominal self-government imposed Nazi measures, especially against Jews, which some (such as Vichy France) did with more enthusiasm than the Germans themselves might have expected. These states were also obliged to co-ordinate their economies with Germany's war effort and to provide forced labour in German factories to fill in for German soldiers at the front. These war-time measures foreshadowed the way in which Nazi planners expected to direct a Europe-wide New Order after their final victory.

NORWAY
Trondheim
Oslo
Narvik

SWEDEN
Gothenburg
Stockholm

DENMARK
Aarhus
Copenhagen
Malmö

FINLAND
Turku
Helsinki
Viipuri

Murmansk

Archangel

BALTIC
SEA

Reval
Riga

Leningrad

Pskov

UNION OF

Molotov

SOVIET

Moscow
Gorkiy
Volga

Kuybyshev

Tula

Saratov

REICHSKOMMISSARIAT

Dünaburg
Wilna
OSTLAND
Minsk

Vitebsk

Smolensk

SOCIALIST

Kursk

Königsberg
Danzig

Hamburg
Bremen
Hanover
Berlin
Stettin
Posen
Vistula

Leipzig
Dresden
Breslau
Elbe
Oder
Lodz
Warsaw
Brest
GENERAL
GOVERNMENT

REICHSKOMMISSARIAT

Kiev

Kharkov

Don

Stalingrad
Volga

REPUBLICS

Astrakhan

kfurt
Nuremberg
Prague
PROTECTORATE
OF BOHEMIA
AND MORAVIA
Cracow
Brünn

RMAN EMPIRE

Lemberg

Vinnitsa

UKRAINE

Dnepropetrovsk

Dnieper

Rostov

tgart
Munich
Vienna
Danube
Salzburg
SLOVAKIA
Bratislava
Kassa

Transnistria
Dniester

Innsbruck
NSTEIN
Graz
Lubiana
Venice
Verona
Trieste
Budapest
Szeged
Debrecen
HUNGARY
Pécs
Zagreb
Újvidék
Banat
Timişoara
Belgrade
CROATIA
SERBIA
Kolozsvár
Iaşi
Chişinău
Odessa

Braşov
ROMANIA
Bucharest

Sebastopol

BLACK SEA

Bologna
rence
Zara
SAN MARINO
Spalato
Sarajevo
Mostar
MONTENEGRO
Danube
Ruse
Nish
BULGARIA
Sofia
Varna
Burgas

Perugia
Rome
ITALY

ALBANIA
Skopje
Tirana
Plovdiv
Edirne

Istanbul

Trabzon

Tiblisi

Yerevan

IRAN

Naples
Bari
Taranto

Thessaloniki

Ioannina

Ankara

TURKEY

Mosul
IRAQ

Palermo
Messina
Sicily
Catania

GREECE

Izmir

Adana

Euphrates

Tigris

SEA

MALTA
(Br.)

Patrai
Athens

Crete

DODECANESE
(It.)

CYPRUS
(Br.)

Nicosia

SYRIA
(Fr. Mandate)

LEBANON
Damascus

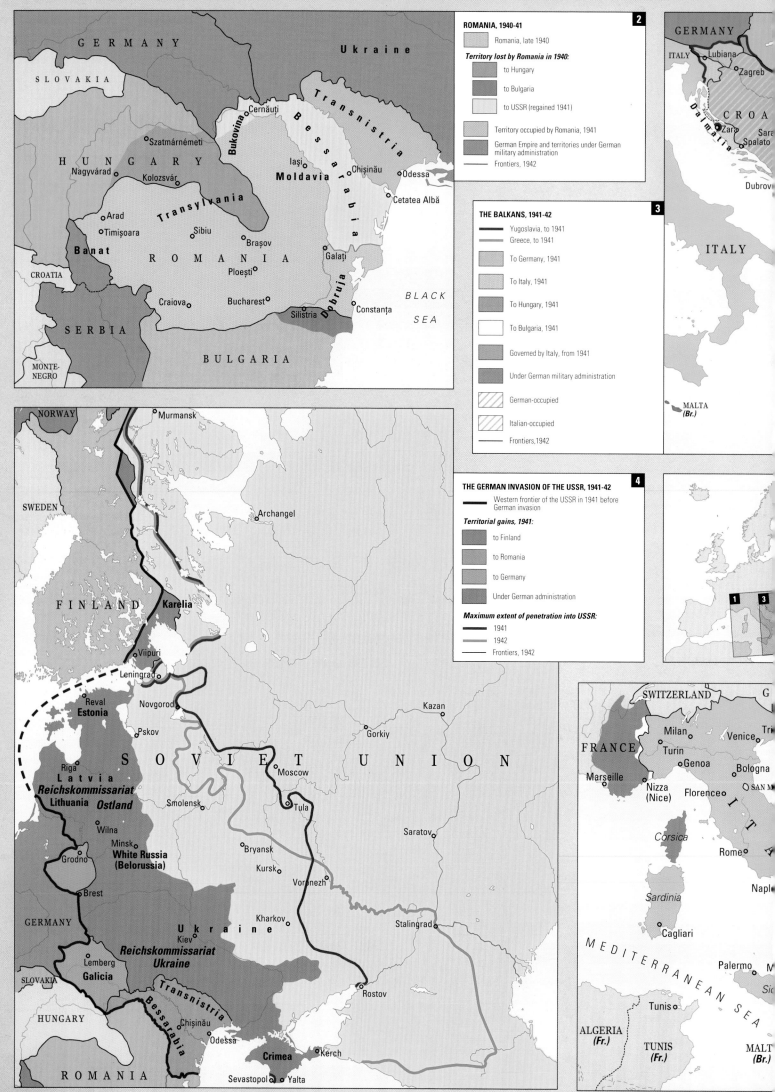

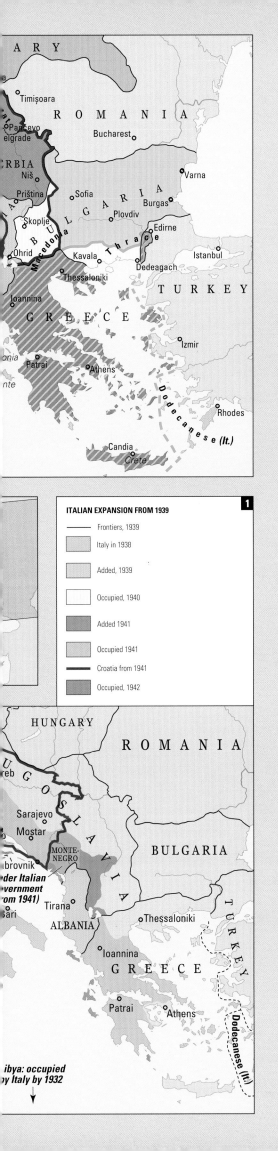

ITALIAN EXPANSION FROM 1939 [1]

- Frontiers, 1939
- Italy in 1938
- Added, 1939
- Occupied, 1940
- Added 1941
- Occupied 1941
- Croatia from 1941
- Occupied, 1942

Italian Expansion from 1939

1 Following the Italian occupation of Albania on Good Friday 1939, Mussolini hoped for further Italian expansion into the Balkans. Playing on Italy's Roman heritage and the medieval empires of Venice and Genoa in the Adriatic and eastern Mediterranean, the fascist regime ringingly asserted the Mediterranean to be Mare Nostrum ("Our Sea"). It also hoped to link the Dodecanese, Italian since 1912, through a corridor of Italian-controlled islands with Italy proper.

However, Mussolini's ambitions could only be realised with German aid, as his bungled invasion of Greece in October 1940 made clear. In April 1941 the German army destroyed both Yugoslav and Greek resistance and placed western Croatia and much of Greece under Italian occupation. The following year, Italy also occupied a swathe of French territory between the Mediterranean and Switzerland as well as the island of Corsica.

Romania, 1940-41

2 Like other weak states in Eastern Europe, Romania came increasingly under German domination in the late 1930s. But German influence did little to diminish long-standing rivalries between these ostensible allies of Hitler. Hungary, for example, aspired to recover territories lost at Trianon (*see* map 5, page 175). The Nazi-Soviet Pact also conspired to weaken Romania: Hitler refused to support Romania when Stalin demanded that she cede Bessarabia to the Soviet Union in June 1940. Taking advantage of Romania's evident weakness, Hungary then demanded that Transylvania be returned. Germany and Italy mediated between their allies and on 30 August 1940 under the Vienna Award gave Hungary a finger of territory from the northwest towards Braşov. At the same time, Bulgaria also recovered southern Dobruja. The effect of these truncations was to leave Romania more dependent on Germany but anxious to recover territory where she could. Hitler's invasion of the Soviet Union gave Romania the chance not only to recover Bessarabia but to seize Transnistria, both of which she held until 1944.

The Balkans, 1941-42

3 The Balkan states had not figured greatly in Hitler's strategy. The role of minor satrapies in the future New Order was the best they could hope for. However, Italy's ambitions in the area, which considerably outstripped her abilities to put them into practice, forced Hitler's hand, though at the same time Hitler was conscious to need to protect his flank for his invasion of the Soviet Union. In March 1941, a coup d'etat saw the overthrow of the Yugoslav government by one more favourable to the Allies. In April, Hitler ordered the invasion of Yugoslavia, which capitulated within 10 days. The German army went on to drive the British out of Greece.

Yugoslavia was divided into zones of occupation shared between Germany, Italy, Hungary and Bulgaria. Germany annexed northern Carinthia and Slovenia but Italy took the capital, Lubiana. Hungary recovered Bácska while Bulgaria occupied the bulk of Macedonia. The Germans established the so-called "Independent State of Croatia" led by the local Fascist leader, Ante Pavelić. Italy took over much of Croatia's coastal territories while Germany occupied the inland areas. Partisan warfare limited the effective control of Pavelić's government, which needed German and Italian forces to prop it up. Its savage atrocities against Serbs, Jews and other minorities made the Croatian regime notorious. A collaborative regime under Nedić was established in a rump Serbia. Greece was largely occupied by Italian forces, with the Germans controlling Athens and Thessaloniki as well as some Aegean islands and Crete. Nonetheless, the increasing success of partisan guerrilla forces coupled with the shortage of German troops to garrison the Balkans meant that large areas were effectively outside Axis control.

The German Invasion of the USSR, 1941-42

4 The occupation and exploitation of the western Soviet Union had long been the goal of Hitler's *Lebensraum* policy. Although German forces never reached the line from Archangel to Astrakhan which Hitler set as the eastern boundary of his future empire, the organisation and exploitation of the occupied territories was started. A fluid area immediately behind the front line was under military administration, but two Reichskommisariats were established: *Reichskommisariat Ostland* administered the territories of the three former Baltic States plus Belorussia; *Reichskommissariat Ukraine* administered the bulk of the Ukraine. (The Crimea remained under military administration.)

In practice, the wartime situation, partisan resistance and Soviet military recovery meant that the German plans to exploit these regions were hardly begun. Only the "negative" policy of mass extermination of Jews and other groups targeted as enemies by the Nazis was carried out on a huge scale. Apart from inflicting enormous loss of life and massive damage to property, the German occupation of Russia left no traces on the ground. After the expulsion of the Germans, the Soviet forces rapidly restored the former Soviet administration, albeit in areas racked by depopulation.

Like the Romanians, the Finns took advantage of the German invasion to recover territory lost to the Soviet Union in 1940, though they advanced only to the border as it had been before the Winter War of 1939-40 in which the Finns, though heavily outnumbered, successfully repulsed a Russian offensive before being obliged by sheer weight of numbers to sue for peace and yield the southeastern corner of the country to Stalin.

Cold War Europe

The Allies had considered the question of the post-war order in Europe as early as 1943. At Tehran in November that year, Churchill and US President Roosevelt had agreed with Stalin that should Hitler be defeated the Soviet Union would be permitted to return to its 1941 borders, thus tacitly allowing Stalin to retain his gains under the Nazi-Soviet Pact of 1939. At subsequent Allied conferences – Yalta in February 1945 and, in the immediate aftermath of the war, Potsdam – Britain and the United States went further still, agreeing that the Soviet Union be allowed to treat the Eastern European territories its army had conquered as belonging to a Soviet sphere of influence. Whatever misgivings the Allies may have felt, and however much they may later have claimed that they were in no position to refuse Stalin's demands, in allowing the Soviet Union to dominate Eastern Europe, the map of the continent was radically transformed following Hitler's defeat.

The most striking result was the shrinking of Germany, with Poland the principal beneficiary, and the division of what remained into two countries. West Germany (the Federal Republic) was formed from the American, French and British areas of occupied Germany, East Germany (the Democratic Republic) from the Soviet occupied zone (*see* map 2, page 186). The former German capital, Berlin, followed this pattern in miniature. As significant, however, was the swallowing whole by the Soviet Union of practically all those states granted independence by the Versailles Settlement after the First World War. Thus Estonia, Latvia and Lithuania and the Ukraine were all incorporated into the Soviet Union, as was Bessarabia, given up by Romania (on Hitler's orders) to the Soviet Union in 1940, seized back by it in 1941 and retaken by Stalin in 1944. Both Poland and Czechoslovakia were revived, though where the latter was reformed largely as it had been in 1919, the former was granted Silesia and Pomerania, areas long inhabited almost exclusively by Germans, and the southern part of East Prussia and Danzig (Gdańsk); but Poland lost vast territories on her eastern border to the Soviet Union. At the same the Soviet Union occupied northern East Prussia, including Königsberg (Kaliningrad). But rather than incorporate the region into neighbouring Lithuania it became part of Russia itself, creating an anomaly of some strategic significance after the collapse of the Soviet Union in 1991 (*see* page 188). Hungary, meanwhile, was restored to the borders established by the Treaty of Trianon (*see* map 5, page 175). Yugoslavia, too, was reformed. Austria was detached from Germany and restored to independence, albeit initially under a Russian-sponsored government recognised only reluctantly by the western powers. In elections held in November 1945 a democratic government was returned and Austria gradually moved away from Soviet influence.

The two zones of Germany followed wholly divergent paths: while denazification in the west followed the Austrian model, with the first free elections permitted in January 1946, in the east the Soviets moved quickly to eradicate all pre-war political parties other than the communists, simultaneously stripping the country of industrial plunder for war reparation. Much the same was true of the rest of Eastern Europe. Indeed by 1949 it was clear that Stalin had created what was in effect a massive extension of the Soviet Empire, as well as a substantial buffer zone between the Soviet Union proper and the West. Western-Soviet relations were plunged into a freeze from which they would not emerge for decades: the Cold War. In escaping Nazi occupation, much of Europe had simply exchanged one tyranny for another.

Trondhjem

Narvik

Murmansk

N O R W A Y

Oslo

S W E D E N

FINLAND

Archangel

Perm

Trondhjem

Gothenburg

Turku

Vyborg

Helsinki

Leningrad

UNION OF

Porkkala

Stockholm

Tallinn

Gorkiy
Volga

Aarhus

Pskov

Moscow

Copenhagen

BALTIC

Riga

S O V I E T

Kuybyshev

Malmo

SEA

Daugavpils

Tula

DENMARK

Vilnius

Vitebsk

Smolensk

S O C I A L I S T

Saratov

Hamburg

Gdańsk

Kaliningrad

Minsk

Bremen

GERMAN

Szczecin

P O L A N D

Kursk

Hanover

DEMOCRATIC

Berlin

Brest

R E P U B L I C S

Volga

Poznań

Warsaw

(under four-

REPUBLIC

power control)

Łódź

Kiev

Kharkov

Leipzig

Dresden

Wrocław

furt

Elbe

Oder

Vistula

Astrakhan

NY

Prague

Cracow

Lvov

Dnieper

Nuremberg

CZECHOSLOVAKIA

Vinnitsa

tgart

Brno

Košice

Dnepropetrovsk

Rostov

Danube

Dniester

unich

Vienna

Bratislava

Salzburg

AUSTRIA

Debrecen

Iași

Odessa

Innsbruck

(under four-

Budapest

Kishinev

power control)

ENSTEIN

Graz

Szeged

Cluj

Sevastopol

FREE STATE

H U N G A R Y

OF TRIESTE

Ljubljana

Pécs

B L A C K   S E A

Venice

Trieste

R O M A N I A

Verona

Zagreb

Tbilisi

Bologna

Novi Sad

Timişoara

Brașov

rence

Zadar

Y U G O S L A V I A

Belgrade

Yerevan

SAN MARINO

Bucharest

Perugia

Sarajevo

Danube

Ruse

IRAN

Split

Niš

Varna

I T A L Y

Mostar

Sofia

Trabzon

Rome

A L B A N I A

Skopje

B U L G A R I A

Burgas

Plovdiv

Edirne

Naples

Bari

Tirana

Istanbul

Ankara

T U R K E Y

Taranto

Thessaloniki

Mosul

IRAQ

Ioannina

Adana

Palermo

Messina

G R E E C E

Izmir

Euphrates

Tigris

Sicily

Catania

SYRIA

Patrai

Athens

SEA

MALTA

Crete

CYPRUS

Nicosia

(Br.)

(Br.)

LEBANON

185

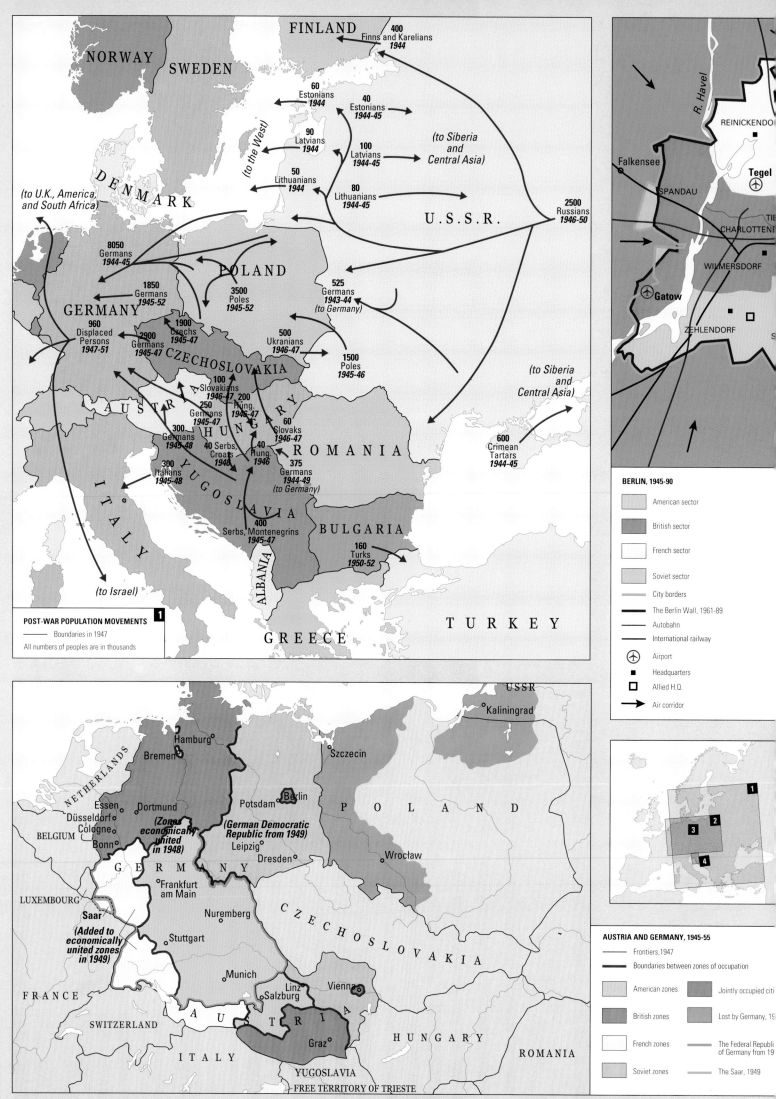

POST-WAR POPULATION MOVEMENTS

NORWAY

SWEDEN

FINLAND

400
Finns and Karelians
1944

60
Estonians
1944

40
Estonians
1944-45

90
Latvians
1944

100
Latvians
1944-45

50
Lithuanians
1944

80
Lithuanians
1944-45

(to the West)

(to Siberia and Central Asia)

U.S.S.R.

2500
Russians
1946-50

DENMARK

(to U.K., America, and South Africa)

8050
Germans
1944-45

POLAND

1850
Germans
1945-52

3500
Poles
1945-52

525
Germans
1943-44
(to Germany)

GERMANY

960
Displaced
Persons
1947-51

2900
Germans
1945-47

1900
Czechs
1945-47

CZECHOSLOVAKIA

500
Ukranians
1946-47

1500
Poles
1945-46

(to Siberia and Central Asia)

AUSTRIA

100
Slovakians
1946-47

200
Hung.
1946-47

250
Germans
1945-47

HUNGARY

300
Germans
1945-48

40 Serbs,
Croats
1946

40
Hung.
1946

60
Slovaks
1946-47

ROMANIA

375
Germans
1944-49
(to Germany)

600
Crimean
Tartars
1944-45

300
Italians
1945-48

YUGOSLAVIA

400
Serbs, Montenegrins
1945-47

BULGARIA

160
Turks
1950-52

ALBANIA

(to Israel)

ITALY

GREECE

TURKEY

POST-WAR POPULATION MOVEMENTS 1

— Boundaries in 1947

All numbers of peoples are in thousands

BERLIN, 1945-90 (inset top right)

NORWAY — *R. Havel*

REINICKENDO

Falkensee

Tegel

SPANDAU

CHARLOTTEN

WILMERSDORF

Gatow

ZEHLENDORF

BERLIN, 1945-90

	American sector
	British sector
	French sector
	Soviet sector
	City borders
	The Berlin Wall, 1961-89
	Autobahn
	International railway
✈	Airport
■	Headquarters
◻	Allied H.Q.
→	Air corridor

AUSTRIA AND GERMANY, 1945-55 (lower map)

USSR

Kaliningrad

Hamburg

Bremen

Szczecin

NETHERLANDS

Essen

Dortmund

Berlin

Potsdam

P O L A N D

Düsseldorf

Cologne

(Zones economically united in 1948)

(German Democratic Republic from 1949)

BELGIUM

Bonn

Leipzig

Dresden

Wrocław

G E R M A N Y

Frankfurt
am Main

LUXEMBOURG

Saar

(Added to economically united zones in 1949)

Nuremberg

C Z E C H O S L O V A K I A

Stuttgart

FRANCE

Munich

Linz

Salzburg

Vienna

A U S T R I A

H U N G A R Y

SWITZERLAND

Graz

ROMANIA

ITALY

YUGOSLAVIA

FREE TERRITORY OF TRIESTE

AUSTRIA AND GERMANY, 1945-55

—	Frontiers,1947
—	Boundaries between zones of occupation
	American zones
	British zones
	French zones
	Soviet zones
	Jointly occupied citi
	Lost by Germany, 19
	The Federal Republi of Germany from 19
	The Saar, 1949

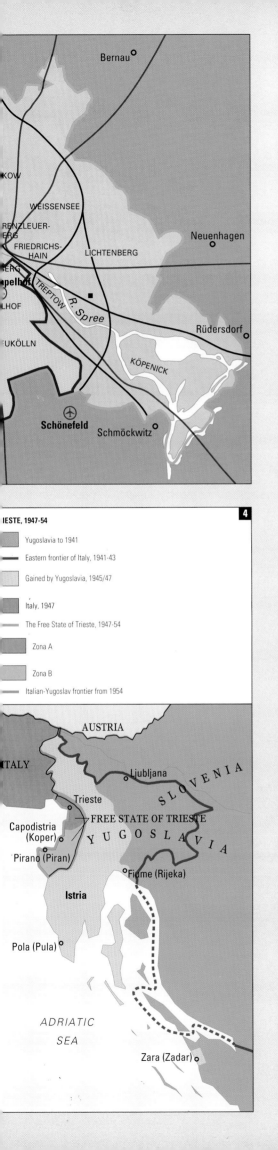

Post-War Population Movements

1 The erasure of the Nazi map of Europe involved vast movements of populations. Germans were expelled from Czechoslovakia and Poland (making the latter an overwhelmingly Polish society for the first time), while many ethnic Germans fled from Yugoslavia, Hungary, Romania, the Baltic States and the Soviet Union. Large-scale German emigration also occurred from France, Belgium and Holland. In all, around 10 million Germans reached the Western zones of occupation, but as many as three million may have died en route. At the same time, several million Russians who had made their way westward during the war were returned to the Soviet Union, as had been agreed at Yalta, many to certain death. Similarly, many thousands of Yugoslavs who had chosen the wrong side in the Partisan war were returned to the new Communist Yugoslav government headed by the successful guerrilla leader, Tito. In Finland, around 400,000 Finns were displaced by the Soviet occupation of Karelia. In the Baltic states, the Soviet government forcibly uprooted 200,000 Balts – an equal number had fled to Germany – and compulsorily resettled or exiled minorities suspected of collaborating with the Germans. About one million "Displaced Persons" of many nationalities were resettled in a variety of western countries. Many Jewish survivors of the Holocaust made their way to Palestine (Israel from May 1948).

Austria and Germany, 1945-55

2 The original hope of the Western Allies was that Germany, once cleansed of Nazism, would be established as a united democratic state. As proposed at the Tehran Conference and agreed at the Yalta Conference in February 1945, the Allies divided Germany and Austria into zones of occupation. The plans, anticipating the advance of the Soviet army from the east and the British and Americans from the west, allotted the eastern part of Germany to the Russians, the north of Germany to the British and southern Germany to the Americans. Berlin was to be under tripartite control. An American proposal for a corridor linking Berlin to the British and American zones was not accepted. At Yalta, it was also agreed that France be allocated an occupation zone, with the British and American sectors reduced to accommodate it, and a sector of Berlin. Similar plans were agreed for the occupation of Austria.

It rapidly became clear, however, that Stalin's intentions toward eastern Germany were wholly at variance with the West's goals for western Germany. Stalin acted almost at once to ensure Communist dominance in his zone, sponsoring the German Communist party – which was relaunched as the Socialist Unity Party in April 1946 – and suppressing all other political organisations by November 1947. As it became clear that the western and eastern halves of the country were destined for separate futures, so relations between the former Allies deteriorated. Germany rapidly became one of the major theatres of conflict in the Cold War, as the growing hostility came to be called, with Berlin the focal point as Stalin strove in the winter of 1948-49 to force the Western Allies out of the city (*see* map 3, below). In September 1949, the Western Allies, abandoning for good hopes of rapprochement with Stalin, announced the creation of the Federal Republic of Germany. Not to be outdone, the next month the Soviet government sponsored the creation of the German Democratic Republic. Both claimed to be the sole legitimate government of Germany.

Austria fared better. Despite Soviet successes elsewhere in Eastern Europe in promoting Communism, they were unable do likewise in Austria. As democracy was re-established, so the occupying forces withdrew. Under the 1955 Treaty of Independence, the last of the occupying troops left, with Austria in turn, at Soviet insistence, accepting irrevocable neutrality and renouncing all rights to renewed *Anshcluss* with Germany.

Berlin, 1945-90

3 Although firmly within the Soviet zone of post-war Germany, Berlin, capital of Germany since 1871, was divided between all four occupying powers. The existence of a Western-controlled island in Soviet territory became an increasing anomaly in Stalin's eyes. Once the economic and monetary division of Germany was sealed in June 1948, Stalin acted to try to push the Western Allies out of their three city zones by blockading Berlin from June 1948 until the spring of 1949. In response, the Western Allies launched an airlift of fuel and food which saved their part of the city from starvation and surrender. West Berlin then entered a twilight period in which, though self-governing, it remained an occupied city. Its isolation increased with the building of the Berlin Wall in 1961. It was the breaching of the Wall in November 1989 that signalled not only the end of the divided city, but the death-knell of the GDR itself.

Trieste, 1947-54

4 In the spring of 1945, both British forces from northern Italy and Tito's partisan forces raced through the disintegrating German armies intent on seizing the port-city of Trieste at the head of the Adriatic. Although the city had an Italian majority, it contained a large Slav minority and its hinterland was largely Slovene-speaking. In the summer of 1945 there was a tense stand-off between the British and Tito's forces. The Partisans could see little reason why their Western ally was supporting the claims of their erstwhile Italian enemies. Trieste threatened to be the first flashpoint of the embryonic Cold War. Only in 1954 was a compromise grudgingly agreed granting the city and a narrow strip of land linking it to the rest of Italy but leaving Trieste still hemmed in by Yugoslav territory. A more amicable agreement was signed in 1979. With the outbreak of the Yugoslav War in 1991, however, some Serb militants announced a revived claim to Trieste.

1949

2001

The Aftermath of the Soviet Union

The post-war borders of Europe proved remarkably resilient. For 40 years after 1949 there were no major changes to the European map. Yet it was mutual hostility that provided the essential stability of the period: the Cold War. Eastern Europe was dominated by the communist Soviet Union, which imposed on it a repressive and economically backward rule. Western Europe, by contrast, was broadly democratic and economically vigorous. These divisions were underlined by rival military and economic blocs: NATO, the EEC and EFTA in the West; and the Warsaw Pact and COMECON in the East.

The most potent symbol of this division was Germany – democratic in the west, communist in the east – and above all its former capital, Berlin, since 1961 literally divided in two by the Berlin Wall. It was only appropriate that the fall of the Wall in November 1989 was to herald the sudden disintegration of the Soviet Union and the post-war division of Europe. Soviet leader Mikhail Gorbachev's attempt to reform the system from within by his policy of *perestroika* (restructuring) failed to stem the tide of nationalism. As remarkable was the sudden appearance, in the wake of the collapse of communist rule in both the USSR and Eastern Europe, of no fewer than 22 new countries (amongst them the 15 republics of the former Soviet Union). Thus the three Baltic states, Belarus, the Ukraine, Moldova, Georgia, Azerbaijan and Armenia gained an independence which they had not known since before the Second World War. These new states were not destined to live in peace. Break-away movements emerged, threatening to inflict on the region a fatal combination of old hatreds and new destructive power: Transnistria declared independence from Moldova; Chechnya declared its independence from Russia; Crimea sought to break away from Ukraine; and Armenia went to war with Azerbaijan over Nagorno-Karabakh.

The fall-out from these sudden events was most extreme in Yugoslavia, which in 1991 simply disintegrated under pressure from the long-suppressed rivalries of its ethnic groups. In June that year the republics of Slovenia and Croatia declared their independence, following which Serbian forces attacked them both. The war in Croatia lasted for seven months. In April 1992 full-scale civil war broke out between Serbs, Croats and Muslims in newly independent Bosnia-Herzegovina. Peace was restored only in November 1995, leaving a fragile Bosnian state divided between the three races. In 1999 bloodshed broke out in Serbia's province of Kosovo, provoking NATO intervention to halt the Serb slaughter of the majority ethnic-Albanian population. Kosovo was left in a state of limbo, in theory still part of Yugoslavia, in practice administered by the international community. Macedonia, too, which remained uneasily free of fighting after its declaration of independence in 1992, suffered an ethnic-Albanian insurgency in 2001. In Czechoslovakia, meanwhile, the general election of June 1992 revealed the tensions between Czechs and Slovaks and the country broke into two, the Czech Republic and Slovakia.

The euphoria following the fall of the Berlin Wall had evaporated by 1993. Parts of eastern Europe were beset by instability, poverty, ethnic tensions and even open warfare; whilst a prosperous western area looked to the European Union. It was no surprise that by 2001 most of the new democracies in Eastern Europe had applied to join the EU. In any case, the ebb and flow of borders, a process which Europe thought it had left behind in 1945, had returned with a vengeance.

Areas not controlled by the states to which they theoretically belong

NORWAY

Trondhjem

Narvik

SWEDEN

FINLAND

Murmansk

Archangel

Perm

Oslo

Stockholm

Turku

Helsinki

Vyborg

St Petersburg

Tallinn

ESTONIA

RUSSIAN

Nizhniy
Novgorod

Volga

Gothenburg

Århus

Copenhagen

Malmö

BALTIC
SEA

Riga

LATVIA

Pskov

Moscow

FEDERATION

Samara

DENMARK

Hamburg

LITHUANIA

Daugavpils

Smolensk

Tula

Saratov

Bremen

Szczecin

Vilnius

RUS.FED.
Kaliningrad

Vitsyebsk

Hanover

Berlin

POLAND

Gdańsk

Minsk

Kursk

Don

50°

KAZAKHSTAN

RMANY

Poznań

Oder

Warsaw

Brest

BELARUS

Leipzig

Dresden

Łódź

Wrocław

Vistula

nkfurt

Prague

CZECH REPUBLIC

Cracow

L'viv

UKRAINE

Kiev

Kharkiv

Volga

Nuremberg

Brno

SLOVAKIA

Košice

Vinnytsya

Dnipropetrovs'k

Astrakhan

ttgart

Danube

Vienna

Bratislava

Dniester

Rostov

Munich

Salzburg

AUSTRIA

Budapest

Debrecen

MOLDOVA

Dnieper

Innsbruck

Graz

HUNGARY

Iași

Chișinău

Odesa

ENSTEIN

SLOVENIA

Zagreb

Pécs

Szeged

Cluj-Napoca

CHECHNYA

Venice

Trieste

Ljubljana

ATIA

Novi Sad

ROMANIA

Brașov

Timișoara

Crimea

GEORGIA

Verona

C

R

O

BOSNIA
HERZEGOVINA

Belgrade

Bucharest

Sevastopol

Tbilisi

AZERBAIJAN

Bologna

Zadar

San Marino

Sarajevo

Danube

Ruse

BLACK SEA

ARMENIA

orence

Split

Mostar

YUGOSLAVIA

Niš

Sofia

Varna

Yerevan

NAGORNO-
KARABAKH

ITALY

Perugia

KOSOVO

Skopje

BULGARIA

Burgas

Trabzon

IRAN

Rome

ALBANIA

Tirana

MACEDONIA

Plovdiv

Edirne

Istanbul

Ankara

TURKEY

Naples

Bari

Taranto

Thessaloniki

Mosul

IRAQ

Joannina

GREECE

Izmir

Adana

SYRIA

Palermo

Messina

Sicily

Catania

Patra

Athens

Euphrates

Tigris

SEA

MALTA

Crete

Nicosia

CYPRUS

LEBANON

189

EUROPEAN ECONOMIC BLOCS, 1947-2000

Benelux customs union, 1947

Council for Mutual Economic Assistance (COMECON)

COMECON members, 1949

subsequent members

YUGO. countries which broke up, 1990–93

The European Free Trade Assocation (EFTA)

EFTA members late 1972

The European Economic Area (EEA)

EEA members April 1997

The European Union

EEC members, 1957

joined, Jan. 1973

joined, Jan. 1981

joined Jan. 1986

admitted Oct. 1990 (East Germany)

joined Jan. 1995

applied by June 1996 for EU membership, with date of application

★ countries beginning accession negotiations, 1998

★ countries beginning accession negotiations, 2000

ICELAND

NORWAY

SWEDEN

FINLAND

RUSSIAN FEDERATION

ESTONIA *1995*

LATVIA

LITHUANIA

RUS. FED.

SOVIET UNION

DENMARK

UNITED KINGDOM

IRELAND

NETHER- LANDS

BELGIUM

LUX.

EAST GERMANY

GERMANY

POLAND *1994*

BELARUS

UKRAINE

CZECH REP. *1996*

CZECHOSLOVAKIA

SLOVAKIA *1995*

MOLDOVA

LIECT.

AUSTRIA

SWITZ.

HUNGARY *1994*

ROMANIA *1995*

FRANCE

SLOVENIA *1996*

CROATIA

YUGOSLAVIA

BOS.- HERZ.

YUGO.

BULGARIA *1995*

TURKEY *1987 customs union with EU effective from 1 Jan. 1996*

MONACO

SAN MARINO

ITALY

ANDORRA

MAC.

ALBANIA

PORTUGAL

SPAIN

GREECE

GIBRALTAR

MALTA *1990*

CYPRUS *1990*

ALBANIANS IN THE BALKANS, 1998-2001

Overwhelmingly Albanian-inhabited areas outside Albania

NATO-occupied Kosovo since June 1999, ethnic Albanians seeking independence

Demilitarized zone since June 1999

Notional frontier of Yugoslavia, 2001

Approximate extent of Albanian guerilla activity, 2001

Frontiers, 2001

SERBIA

Niš

Pirot

Novi Pazar

Leskovac

MONTENEGRO

Mitrovica

Podgorica

KOSOVO

Priština

Vranje

Shkodër

Kukës

Tetovo

Kumanovo

BULGARIA

Skopje

Kočani

MACEDONIA

Durrës

Kičevo

Strumica

Tirana

Prilep

Vardar

ALBANIA

Elbasan

Ohrid

Bitola

Lake Ohrid

Lake Prespa

Korçë

Vlorë

Gjirokastër

GREECE

CENTRAL AND EASTERN EUROPE, 1990-2001

Western border of the USSR to 1991

Former satellite states of the USSR

Former GDR: to the Federal Republic of Germany, 1990

Independent, 1991

Independent, 1992

Independent, 1993

Yugoslavia to 1991

Czechoslovakia to 1993

Chechenia-Ingushetia, November 1991

Independence declared after 1990 but not recognised internationally

Independence asserted after 1990

Under foreign occupation (May 2001)

Frontiers, 2001

Oslo

NORWAY

SWEDEN

FINLAND

Tallinn

ESTONIA

DENMARK

Riga

LATVIA

(independence declared 1990, recognised 1991)

LITHUANIA

Vilnius

RUSSIAN FED.

RUSSIAN

FEDERATION

Moscow

TATARSTAN

BASHKORTOSTAN

GERMANY

Berlin

West Berlin (to 1990)

POLAND

Warsaw

Minsk

BELARUS

CZECH REPUBLIC

Prague

Kiev

KAZAKHSTAN

SLOVAKIA

Bratislava

UKRAINE

AUSTRIA

SLOVENIA

Budapest

Zagreb

HUNGARY

MOLDOVA

TRANSNISTRIA

(at war with invading Russian forces 1994-96; partially successful Russian onslaught 1999, still at war in 2001)

CROATIA

KRAJINA

SERBIAN REP. OF BOSNIA

BOSNIA-

HERZE- GOVINA

Sarajevo

Belgrade

ROMANIA

Bucharest

GAGAUZIA

(Ingushetia: joined Russian Federation, December 1992)

CHECHNYA

HERCEG BOSNA

YUGOSLAVIA

MONTENEGRO

(referendum on separation from Yugoslavia to be held in 2001)

KOSOVO

(occupied by NATO forces 1999)

Sofia

BULGARIA

ABKHAZIA

GEORGIA

ALBANIA

Skopje

MACEDONIA

AZERBAIJAN

NAGORNO- KARABAKH

ARMENIA

GREECE

TURKEY

(occupied by Armenian/Karabakh forces)

AUSTRIA

Maribor

SLOVENIA

Ljubljana

Va[r]

Karlovac

Rijeka

Sisak

Zadar

Kni[n]

Sp[lit]

ITALY

The Aftermath of the Soviet Union

Central and Eastern Europe, 1990-2001

1 The opening of the Berlin Wall on 9 November 1989 marked the dramatic collapse of the East German regime. Faced with a massive wave of emigration to the west and the collapse of its economy, there was little alternative for the GDR but to unite with the West. The restoration of a united Germany on 3 October 1990 marked the end of the limitations on German sovereignty which the four Occupying Powers had exercised since 1945.

Thereafter events in Eastern Europe took increasingly dramatic turns. On 25 December 1991 the USSR came to an end after many of its constituent republics declared independence in the aftermath of a failed hard-line putsch in August. The former republics became 15 independent states. The break-up of the USSR did not bring peace, however: civil war raged in Georgia; Armenian forces occupied most of Nagorno-Karabakh, claiming it from neighbouring Azerbaijan; Chechnya declared its independence and suffered two invasions, in 1994 and 1999, aimed at reincorporating it into Russia; and the Russian majority in Transnistria (eastern Moldova) also declared its independence.

Meanwhile, Czechoslovakia broke up into the Czech republic and Slovakia in January 1993 following a Slovak nationalist victory in elections the previous year. The break-up was largely peaceful, unlike that experienced in Yugoslavia after 1991 (*see* below).

The Break-up of Yugoslavia from 1991

2 Under Tito's rule (1944-80), Yugoslavia was widely held to be a model multi-national state, but after his death the forces holding the country together weakened. A resurgence of Serb nationalism, promoted after 1987 by the leader of the Serbian Communist Party, Slobodan Milošević, alarmed the other republics. In Serbia (and Montenegro), the Communist Party repositioned itself as the guardian of national rather than class interests. In Slovenia, with its homogeneous population (90% Slovene), a non-communist nationalist opposition won power and declared independence in 1991.

After a half-hearted attempt to coerce Slovenia back into Yugoslavia at the end of June 1991, a much more serious war broke out in Croatia during that summer. The Serb minority (12%) which formed the majority in areas such as the Krajina refused to accept the idea of Croatian independence. Serbian forces took military action and conquered about one-third of Croatia's territory at the time of independence (June 1991).

Unlike Serbia and Croatia, Bosnia lacked a numerically dominant group: Serbs constituted about 31% of the population, Croats 17% and Bosnian Muslims 44%. War broke out in 1992 and the inter-mingling of the different groups encouraged the policy of "ethnic cleansing"– the removal or slaughter of populations to create areas with a majority of one ethnic group.

The efforts of international bodies like the UN and EU to resolve the war could not halt the advance of Bosnian Serb forces. By early 1994, the Bosnian Serb army had occupied more than two-thirds of pre-war Bosnia-Herzegovina. More than two million people had been displaced and over 100,000 killed. Against the odds, Bosnia survived. In March 1994 the Bosnian Muslims and Croats formed a fragile federation, and in 1995 Bosnian Serb successes against the Muslim enclaves of Žepa, Srebrenica and Goražde provoked NATO to intervene. In November 1995, facing military defeat, Milošević bowed to American-backed pressure to accept a settlement. Serbs, Croats and Muslims were joined in an uneasy federal system. Meanwhile, Bosnian Serbs and Croats sought closer ties for their respective areas with Serbia and Croatia proper.

European Economic Blocs, 1947-2000

3 The Second World War gave renewed impetus to the idea of preventing future wars by uniting the European states in some form of federal arrangement. In 1957 the European Economic Community was established by the Treaty of Rome to pursue this goal. The Community grew from its original six members (France, Germany, Italy, Belgium, the Netherlands, and Luxembourg) with the accession of Denmark, Ireland and the United Kingdom (1973), Greece (1981), and Spain and Portugal (1986). The EC extended the scope of its operations, too. In 1985 it agreed the creation of a single market under which Europe would become a single free-trade zone. Proposals for further integration bore fruit in the Maastricht Treaty, which, after intense opposition from several members, was ratified in 1993 and committed the EC–which became the EU on 1 January 1994 as one of its terms– to work towards economic and monetary union. Britain and Denmark stood aside from several of the Treaty's provisions.

The European Free Trade Association (EFTA), set up in 1959 by Britain as an alternative to the EC, gradually lost members to it: most of the remaining EFTA countries –Finland, Sweden and Austria– joined the EU in 1995, although Norway rejected membership in a referendum. By 2001 many of the former eastern bloc countries had submitted applications for membership, although none were expected to join before 2004.

Albanians in the Balkans, 1998-2001

4 When Albania won independence from the Ottoman empire in 1912, over half the Albanian community was left outside its borders, largely in the Yugoslav-controlled regions of Kosovo and Macedonia. In 1998 an ethnic Albanian guerrilla group, the Kosovo Liberation Army (KLA), stepped up its campaign to win independence for Kosovo. Serb forces responded by launching a campaign of ethnic cleansing against the Albanians in 1998-99. A NATO-led bombing campaign in early 1999 forced the Yugoslav government to back down and from June 1999 Kosovo found itself administered by the international community. Many Kosovo Serbs fled into Serbia proper. In 2001, another ethnic Albanian insurgent group, the NLA occupied villages in northern Macedonia, threatening to destabilize that country, where over a third of the population is of Albanian origin.

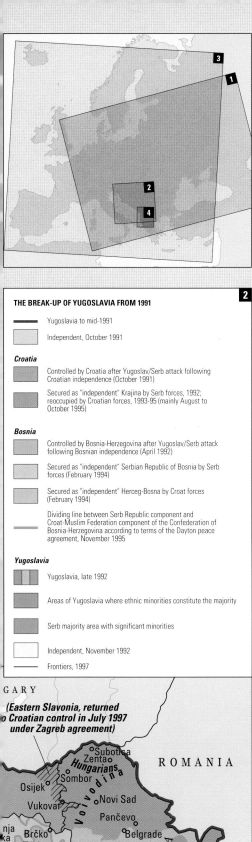

THE BREAK-UP OF YUGOSLAVIA FROM 1991

— Yugoslavia to mid-1991

Independent, October 1991

Croatia

Controlled by Croatia after Yugoslav/Serb attack following Croatian independence (October 1991)

Secured as "independent" Krajina by Serb forces, 1992; reoccupied by Croatian forces, 1993-95 (mainly August to October 1995)

Bosnia

Controlled by Bosnia-Herzegovina after Yugoslav/Serb attack following Bosnian independence (April 1992)

Secured as "independent" Serbian Republic of Bosnia by Serb forces (February 1994)

Secured as "independent" Herceg-Bosna by Croat forces (February 1994)

Dividing line between Serb Republic component and Croat-Muslim Federation component of the Confederation of Bosnia-Herzegovina according to terms of the Dayton peace agreement, November 1995

Yugoslavia

Yugoslavia, late 1992

Areas of Yugoslavia where ethnic minorities constitute the majority

Serb majority area with significant minorities

Independent, November 1992

— Frontiers, 1997

(Eastern Slavonia, returned to Croatian control in July 1997 under Zagreb agreement)

HUNGARY

Subotica, Zenta, Hungarians, Sombor, Osijek, Vojvodina, Vukovar, Novi Sad, Pančevo, Brčko, Tuzla, Belgrade, BOSNIA, Vitez, Sarajevo, Pale, Srebrenica, Romanians, Kragujevac, Žepa, Kruševac, HERZEGOVINA, Goražde, SERBIA, Niš, Mostar, Muslims, Novi Pazar, Bulgarians, MONTENEGRO, Albanians, Priština, Dubrovnik, Podgorica, Kosovo, BULGARIA, Kumanovo, Skopje, MACEDONIA, ALBANIA, Bitola, GREECE, ROMANIA

2001

BIBLIOGRAPHY

Listed below are a range of historical and thematic atlases which contain particularly useful maps, and a basic selection of works for further reading:

I. Historical and Thematic Atlases

Alexis, M.G. *Atlas de Géographie et Historique*, Brussels 1900

Atlante Enciclopedico, Storia Antica e Medievale, Milan 1989

Atlante Enciclopedico, Storia Moderna e Contemporanea, Milan 1990

Atlante Storico Illustrato, Novara 1977

Atlas Historiczny Polski, Warsaw 1973

Atlas Istoriya na Bulgariya, Sofia 1975

Atlas of Modern World History, Oxford 1989

Atlas of the Classical World, London 1959

Atlas zur Geschichte, 2 vols. Leipzig 1976

Atlas zur Universalgeschichte, Munich 1980

Bazilevsky, K.V., Golubtsov, A., Zinoviev, M.A. *Atlas Istorii SSR*, Moscow 1952

Beckingham, C.F. *Atlas of the Arab World and the Middle East*, London 1960

Bjørklund, O., Holmboe, H., Røhr, A. *Historical Atlas of the World*, Edinburgh 1970

Brice, C. (ed.) *An Historical Atlas of Islam*, Leiden 1981

Calmette, J. *Atlas Historique II*, Paris 1959

The Collins Atlas of World History, London 1987

Darby, H.C., Fullard, H. (eds.) *The New Cambridge Modern History* vol. XIV: Atlas, Cambridge 1970

Dockrill, M. *Atlas of Twentieth Century World History*, Glasgow 1991

Duby, G. *Atlas Historique Larousse*, Paris 1978

Edwards, R.D. *An Atlas of Irish History*, London 1973

Fox, E. (ed.) *Atlas of European History*, Oxford 1964

Freeman-Grenville, G.S.P. *Atlas of British History*, London 1979

Gilbert, M. *Russian History Atlas*, London 1993

Gilbert, M. *Recent History Atlas 1860-1960*, London 1966

Gilbert, M. *First World War Atlas*, London 1970

Gilbert, M. *Jewish History Atlas*, London 1973

Griess, T.E. (ed.) *Atlas for the Great War*, Wayne, New Jersey, 1986

Grosser Atlas zur Weltgeschichte, Braunschweig 1972

Grosser Historischer Weltatlas, 3 vols., Munich 1972-81

Hazard, H.W. *Atlas of Islamic History*, Princeton 1952

Hilgemann, *Atlas zur Deutschen Zeitgeschichte*, Munich 1986

Hill, D. *An Atlas of Anglo-Saxon England*, Oxford 1981

Keegan, J. *The Times Atlas of the Second World War*, London 1989

Képes Történelmi Atlasz, Budapest 1976

Kinder, H., Hilgermann, W. *DTV Atlas zur Weltgeschichte* 2 vols. Stuttgart 1964 (published in English as *The Penguin Atlas of World History*, London 1974 & 1978)

Kubijovyč, V. (ed.) *Atlas of Ukraine and Adjoining Countries*, Lviv 1937

Mackay, A., Ditchburn, D. (eds.) *Atlas of Medieval Europe*, London 1977

McEvedy, C. *The Penguin Atlas of Modern History*, Harmondsworth, 1979

McEvedy, C. *The Penguin Atlas of Recent History*, Harmondsworth, 1982

McEvedy, C. *The Penguin Atlas of Medieval History*, Harmondsworth, 1977

McEvedy, C. *The Penguin Atlas of Ancient History*, Harmondsworth 1967

Millî Tarih Atlası, Istanbul 1985

Milner-Gulland, R., Dejevsky N. *Cultural Atlas of Russia*, New York 1989

Nelson's Atlas of the Classical World, London 1959

Nelson's Atlas of the Early Christian World, London 1959

Nelson's Atlas of World History, London 1965

Palmer, R.R. (ed.) *Atlas of World History*, Chicago 1965

Parker, G. (ed.), *The Times Atlas of World History*, 4th edtn., London 1993

Pascu, S. *Atlas Istoric*, Bucharest, 1971

Riley-Smith, J.H. (ed.) *The Atlas of the Crusades*, London 1991

Roaf, M. *Cultural Atlas of Mesopotamia and the Ancient Near East*, Oxford 1990

Robinson, F. *Atlas of the Islamic World since 1500*, Oxford 1982

Scarre, C. (ed.) *The Times Atlas of Past Worlds*, London 1988

Scarre, C. *The Penguin Historical Atlas of Ancient Rome*, London 1995

Sellman, R.R. *A Historical Atlas 1789-1971*, London 1971

Shepherd, W.R. *Historical Atlas*, New York 1964

Sinclair, S. *Atlas de Geographie Historique de la Fance et de la Gaule*, Paris 1985

Školský Atlas Československých Dejín, Bratislava 1970

Stembridge, J.H., *The Oxford War Atlas*, London 1941

Talbert, R.J.A. (ed.) *Atlas of Classical History*, London 1985

The Times Atlas of the World, 9th Comprehensive Edition, London 1992

Tarih Atlası, Istanbul 1989

Toynbee, A.J., Myers, E.D. *A Study of History, Historical Atlas and Gazetteer*, Oxford 1959

Treharne, R.F., Fullard, H. (eds.) *Muir's Historical Atlas*, London 1966

Van der Heyden, A.M., Scullard, H.H. *Atlas of the Classical World*, London 1959

Van Der Meer, F., Mohrmann, C. *Atlas of the Early Christian World*, London 1958

Vermaseren, B.A. *Atlas Algemene en Vaderlandse Geschiedenis*, Groningen 1969

Verzameling, R. *Atlas der Algemene en der Belgische Geschiedenis*, Namen 1985

Vicens Vives, J. *Atlas de Historia de España*, Barcelona 1973

Westermann Grosser Atlas zur Weltgeschichte, Brunswick 1976

Whitehouse, D. & R. *Archaeological Atlas of the World*, London 1975

II. General Works

Clogg, R. *A Concise History of Greece*, Cambridge 1992

Cook, M.A. (ed.) *A History of the Ottoman Empire to 1730*, Cambridge 1976

Darby, H.C. (ed.) *An Historical Geography of England before AD1800*, Cambridge 1936 & 1960

East, W.G. *An Historical Geography of Europe*, London 1967

Freeman, E.A. *The Historical Geography of Europe*, London 1882

Grousset, R. *The Empire of the Steppes: A History of Central Asia*, New Brunswick N.J. 1970

Hearder, H. *Italy, A Short History*, Cambridge 1990

Jelavich, B. *History of the Balkans*, Cambridge 1983

Langer, W.L. *An Encyclopedia of World History*, London 1972

Malcolm, N. *Bosnia, A Short History*, London 1994

Mantram, R. *Histoire de l'Empire Ottoman*, Paris 1989

McNeill, W.H. *A World History*, New York 1971

Miquel, A. *L'Islam et sa Civilisation*, Paris 1968

Ostrogorsky, G. *History of the Byzantine State*, Oxford 1969

Parker, W.H. *An Historical Geography of Russia*, London 1968

Pitcher, D.E. *An Historical Geography of the Ottoman Empire*, Leiden 1973

Roberts, J.M. *The Hutchinson History of the World*, revised ed., London 1987

Seltzer, L.E. (ed.) *The Columbia Lippincott Gazetteer of the World*, New York 1952

Smith, C.T. *An Historical Geography of Western Europe before 1800*, revised ed., London & New York 1978

Wanklyn, W. *The Eastern Marchlands of Europe*, London 1941

III. Classical Europe

Boardman, J. (ed.) *The Oxford History of the Classical World*, Oxford 1989

Bury, J.B., Cook, S.A., Adcock, F.E. (eds.) *The Cambridge Ancient History*, Cambridge 1923, 2nd ed. 1982

Cary M., Scullard H.H. *A History of Rome down to the Reign of Constantine*, London 1975

Ferguson, J. *The Heritage of Hellenism*, London 1973

Jones, A.H.M. *The Late Roman Empire* (3 vols), Oxford 1964

Scullard, H.H. *From the Gracchi to Nero*, London & New York 1959

Snodgrass, A. *Archaic Greece*, London 1989

Tarn, W.W. *Alexander the Great*, Cambridge 1948

IV. Dark Ages Europe

Ahzweiler, H. *L'Asie Mineure et les Invasions Arabes, Revue Historique* 1962

Collins R., *Early Medieval Spain: Unity in Diversity 400-1000*, London 1983

James, E. *The Origins of France*, Oxford 1982

McKitterick, R. *The Frankish Kingdoms under the Carolingians 751-987*, London 1983

Musset, L. *Les Invasions: Les Vagues Germaniques*, Paris 1965

Musset, L. *Les Invasions: Le Second Assaut contre l'Europe Chrétienne*, Paris 1971

Thompson, E.A. *A History of Attila and the Huns*, 1948

Vernadsky, G. *Kievan Russia*, New Haven, Conn. 1972

Wallace-Hadrill, J.M. *The Barbarian West 400-1000*

Wood, I. *The Merovingian Kingdoms 450-751*, London 1994

V. Medieval Europe

Barraclough, G. *Medieval Germany*, Oxford 1938 & 1967

Bauml, F.H. *Medieval Civilization in Germany 800-1273*, London 1969

Brooke, C.N.L. *The Twelfth-century Renaissance*

Bury, J.B., Gwatkin, H.M., Whitney, J.P. (eds.) *The Cambridge Medieval History*, Cambridge 1911-

Christiansen, E. *The Northern Crusades*, 1980

Fowler, K. *The Age of Plantagenet and Valois*, New York 1967

Hay, D. *Europe in the Fourteenth and Fifteenth Centuries*, London 1966

Holmes. G. *Europe, Hierarchy and Revolt 1320-1450*, London 1975

Lomax, D.W. *The Reconquest of Spain*, London 1978

McKitterick, R. (ed.) *The New Cambridge Medieval History II: 700-900*, Cambridge 1995

Moss, H. St. L.B. *The Birth of the Middle Ages*, Oxford 1935

Phillips, J.R.S. *The Medieval Expansion of Europe*, Oxford 1988

Southern, R.W. *The Making of the Middle Ages*, 1953

VI. Early Modern Europe

Boxer, C.R. *The Portuguese Seaborne Empire 1415-1825*, London 1991

Boxer, C.R. *The Dutch Seaborne Empire 1600-1800*, London 1965

Braudel, F. *The Mediterranean and the Mediterranean World in the age of Philip II*, London 1972

Elliott, J.H. *Europe Divided 1559-98*, London 1968

Elton, G.R. *Reformation Europe 1517-59*, London

Evans, R.J.W. *The making of the Habsburg Monarchy 1550-1700*, Oxford 1979

Fletcher, A. *Tudor Rebellions*, 3rd ed., London 1983

Hale. J.R. *Renaissance Europe*, London 1971

Hatton, R.M. *Europe in the age of Louis XIV*, London 1969

Inalcik, H. *The Ottoman Empire: The Classical Age 1300-1600*, London 1973

Koeningsberger, H.G., Mosse, G.L., Bowler G.Q. *Europe in the sixteenth century*, 2nd ed., London 1989

Lockyer, R. *Habsburg & Bourbon Europe*, Harlow 1974

Parker, G. *The Dutch Revolt*, Harmondsworth, 1977

Parker, G. *Europe in Crisis 1598-1648*, London 1979

Parker, G. *Spain and the Netherlands 1559-1659*, London 1979

Stoye, J. *The Siege of Vienna*, London 1964

Stoye, J. *Europe Unfolding, 1648-88*, London

VII. Modern Europe

Calvocoressi, P. *World Politics since 1945*, 6th edtn., London 1993

Churchill, Winston S. *The Second World War*, London 1948-53

Clark, M. *Modern Italy 1871-1982*, London 1984

Grenville, J. *Europe Reshaped 1848-78*, London

Hobsbawm, E.J. *The Age of Revolution*, London 1962

Hufton, O. *Europe: Privilege and Protest 1730-89*, London 1980

Liddell Hart, B. *History of the Second World War*, London 1970

Rudé, G. *Revolutionary Europe 1783-1815*, London, 1972

Stone, N. *Europe Transformed*, London 1983

Taylor, A.J.P. *The First World War*, London 1963

Thomson, D. *Europe Since Napoleon*, (revised edtn.) London 1966

Aachen – Angora

INDEX

1 HISTORICAL PLACE NAMES

Geographical names vary with time and with language, and there is some difficulty in treating them consistently in an historical atlas which covers Europe from 900 BC to the present day. Over these nearly three-thousand years the same place will often have been known by many different names. We have aimed at the simplest possible approach to the names on the maps, using the index to weld together the variations.

On the maps, forms of names will be found in the following hierarchy of preference:

a English conventional names or spellings, in the widest sense, for all principal places and features, e.g. Moscow, Vienna, Munich, Danube (including those that today might be considered obsolete when these are appropriate to the context, e.g. Saragossa).

b Names that are contemporary in terms of the maps concerned. There are here three broad categories:

i names in the ancient world, where the forms used are classical, e.g. Latin or latinised Greek.

ii Names in the post-medieval modern world, which are given in the form (though not necessarily the spelling) current at the time of the map (e.g. Reval or Revel before 1920, not Tallinn) whose language reflects the sovereignty then existing, e.g. Üsküb (Turkish) rather than Skoplje (Serbian) or Skopje (Macedonian) in maps showing Ottoman rule.

iii Names in the present-day world, where the spelling generally follows that of *The Times Atlas of the World.*

Alternative names and spellings have occasionally been shown in brackets on the maps to aid identification.

2 THE INDEX

The index includes all names appearing on the main maps and all those on the subsidiary maps that are pertinent to the events and developments they illustrate. Names of important places which appear successively on main maps are indexed to their first occurrence only, e.g. "**Bremen** N Germany 48-" indicates that this name will be found on all main maps from page 48 onwards.

Where a place is referred to by two or more different names in the course of the atlas, there will be a corresponding number of main entries in the index. The variant names in each case are given in brackets at the beginning of the entry, their different forms and origins being distinguished by such words as *now*, *later*, *formerly* and others included in the list of abbreviations.

"**Vilna** (*Ger.* Wilna, *Pol.* Wilno, *mod.* Vilnius)" means that the page references to that city on maps dealing with periods when it was known as Vilna follow that entry, but the page references pertaining to it when it had other names will be found under those other names.

Places are located generally by reference to the country in which they lie (exceptionally by reference to island groups or sea areas), this being narrowed down where necessary by location as E(ast), N(orth), C(entral), etc. The reference will normally be to the modern state in which the place now falls unless there is a conventional or historical name which conveniently avoids the inevitably anachronistic ring of some modern names, e.g. Anatolia rather than Turkey.

Though page references are generally kept in numerical order, since this corresponds for the most part with chronological order, they have been rearranged occasionally where the chronological sequence would be obviously wrong, or in the interests of grouping appropriate references under a single sub-heading.

All variant names and spellings are cross-referenced in the form "**Bourgogne** (Burgundy)", except those which would immediately precede or follow the main entries to which they refer. The bracketed form has been chosen so that such entries may also serve as quick visual indications of equivalence. Thus Bourgogne (Burgundy) means not only "see under Burgundy" but also that Burgundy is another name for Bourgogne.

Reference to the main maps is by page number(s), e.g. 85 or 97-109; to the subsidiary maps it is by page number/map number, e.g. 135/2. All main entries have been given sub-entries in the form of a relevant date or, where possible, of date + event, e.g. "conquered by Clovis, 507".

3 ABBREVIATIONS

a/c	also called
Alb.	Albanian
anc.	ancient
Ar.	Arabic
a/s	also spelled
Bas.	Basque
Bel.	Belorussian
Bibl.	Biblical
Bret.	Breton
Bulg.	Bulgarian
C	Century (when preceded by 17, 18, etc.)
C	Central
Cat.	Catalan
Cr.	Croat
Cz.	Czech
Dan.	Danish
Dut.	Dutch
E	East(ern)
Eng.	English
Est.	Estonian
f/c	formerly called
Finn.	Finnish
form.	former(ly)
Fr.	French
f/s	formerly spelled
Gal.	Galician
Geor.	Georgian
Ger.	German
Gr.	Greek
Hung.	Hungarian
Ir.	Irish
It.	Italian
Lat.	Latin
Latv.	Latvian
Lith.	Lithuanian
Lus.	Lusatian
Maced.	Macedonian
med.	medieval
mod.	modern
N	North(ern)
n/c	now called
Nor.	Norwegian
n/s	now spelled
obs.	obsolete
Pol.	Polish
Port.	Portuguese
Rom.	Romanian
Russ.	Russian
S	South(ern)
s/c	sometimes called
S.Cr.	Serbo-Croat
Serb.	Serbian
Slvk.	Slovak
Slvn.	Slovene
Sp.	Spanish
Sw.	Swedish
Turk.	Turkish
Ukr.	Ukrainian
var.	variant
W	West(ern)
Wel.	Welsh
WW1	First World War
WW2	Second World War

Aachen (*Fr.* Aix-la-Chapelle, *anc.* Aquis Granum) Frankish Kingdom 511, 54/1, 4

Aargau (*Fr.* Argovie) canton of N Switzerland added to Swiss Confederation 1417, 110/1

Aarhus (*n/s* Århus) C Denmark 60-

Abdera NE Greece Greek colony 9C-6C BC, 14/1; in Persian Empire 480 BC, 18/1; Athenian Empire 431 BC, 22/1

Abkhazia breakaway region of NW Georgia 1993, 190/1

Åbo (*Finn.* Turku) SW Finland 77-

Abydos (*a/s* Abydus) NW Anatolia Ionian revolt against Persians 5C BC, 19/2; Athenian Empire 431 BC, 22/1; Second Macedonian War 202 BC, 30/2

Acanthus NE Greece Greek colony 9C- 6C BC, 14/1

Acarnania region of NW Greece 900-800 BC, 10/4; Persian Wars 490-480 BC, 18/3; Corinthian League 337 BC, 22/3; Second Macedonian War 202 BC, 30/2

Achaea (*a/s* Achaia) region of S Greece 900-800 BC, 10/4; Persian Wars 490-480 BC, 18/3; Athenian Empire 431 BC, 22/1; conquered by Rome 146 BC, 30/3; Roman province AD 180, 38/3

Achaean League W Greece Pyrrhus's Empire 295-275 BC, 26/3; Second Macedonian War 202 BC, 30/2

Achaia, Principality of S Greece state of Latin Empire 1190-1270, 86/4, 90/1

A Coruña (Corunna)

Acragas (Akragas)

Adana S Turkey 85-

Adria (Hadria)

Adrianople (*mod.* Edirne, *anc.* Uskudama, *later* Hadrianopolis) NW Turkey Roman Empire 450, 45; 526, 49; Byzantine Empire 527, 54/2; Ottoman Empire 1389, 107/2

Aegae N Greece Athenian Empire 431 BC, 22/1

Aegean Sea Genoese possessions 500, 107/2; First Balkan War 1912, 170/2

Aegyptus Roman diocese of Egypt and Libya 324-337, 42/3

Aenus (*a/s* Aenos, *MGr.* Ainos, *a/s* Enos, *Turk.* Enez, *f/s* Inoz) NW Turkey Greek colony 9C-6C BC, 14/1; Ionian revolt against Persians 5C BC, 19/2; Athenian Empire 431 BC, 22/1; in Ptolemaic Empire 202 BC, 30/2

Aeolians people of Greece and W Anatolia 800 BC, 10/4

Aeolis region of NW Anatolia 900-800 BC, 10/4

Aetolia region of W Greece Persian Wars 490-480 BC, 18/3

Aetolian League W Greece Pyrrhus's Empire 295-275 BC, 26/3; Second Macedonian War 202 BC, 30/2

Africa Roman diocese of NW Africa 285-337, 42/2,3

Africa Proconsularis Roman province of N Africa AD 180, 38/3

Agathe (*mod.* Agde) S France Greek colony 9C-6C BC, 14/1

Agedincum (*mod.* Sens) NE France conquered by Rome 57 BC, 34/2

Agincourt (*Fr.* Azincourt) N France Hundred Years' War, 102/2

Agram (Zágráb)

Agri Decumates district of SE Germany abandoned by Rome 260, 46/1

Agrigento, Agrigentum (Akragas)

Ainos (Aenus)

Aix-la-Chapelle (*Ger.* Aachen, *anc.* Aquis Granum) in Kingdom of Soissons 481, 51/4; East Frankish kingdoms 870, 66/4; annexed by France 1792-3, 146/1

Akkerman (Cetatea Albă)

Ak-Koyunlu Turcoman principality of E Anatolia 1430, 101

Akragas (*a/s* Acragas, *Lat.* Agrigentum, *mod.* Agrigento, *f/c* Girgenti) Greek colony 9C-6C BC, 14/1; Syracusan rule 375 BC, 22/2; Pyrrhus's Empire 295-275 BC, 26/3

Alalia (*a/c* Aleria) E Corsica Etruscan city 6C BC, 14/3

Alans people of the N Caucasus 395-1003, 41-69

Alba region of N Scotland 908, 64

Alba Fucens (*a/c* Alba Fucentia, *mod.* Alba) Roman colony 300 BC, 26/2

Albania subdued by Macedonia 336 BC, 22/3; temporary Aragonese fief mid-15C, 94/2; Ottoman conquest by 1500, 107/2; independent 1913, 170/2; 1925, 173; annexed by Italy 1939, 182/3, 183/1

Albanians minority within Serbia 1993, 191/2

Albarrazin district of NE Spain 1086, 79/3

Aldborough (Isurium)

Aldeigjuborg (*mod.* Staraya Ladoga) NW Russia Viking town 9-10C, 66/C

Alemannia S Germany 561 55/4; Frankish territory 565, 62/1

Alemans people of S Germany 565, 52; 54/1

Aleria (*a/c* Alalia) E Corsica Roman Empire 238 BC, 30/1

Alexander's Empire 323 BC, 21, 22/4; successor states 301 BC, 26/1

Alexandria (*Ar.* Al Iskandariyah) N Egypt Ptolemy's Empire 301 BC, 26/1; Byzantine Empire 527, 54/2

Alexandria (*a/c* Alexandria Areion, *mod.* Herat) Afghanistan Seleucid Empire 301 BC, 26/1

Alexandria (*a/c* Alexandria ad Issum, *later* Alexandretta, *mod.* Iskenderun) SE Turkey Seleucid Empire 301 BC, 26/1

Alexandria Troas NW Anatolia Roman Empire 29 BC, 30/3; 55 BC, 34/3

Algecrias SW Spain 80-

Alger (Algiers)

Algeria (*Fr.* Algérie) French from1861-1961, 156-185; independence 1962, 189

Alghero NW Sardinia conquered by Aragonese 1322, 94/2

Algiers (*Fr.* Alger) N Algeria to France 1830, 158/2

Al Iskandariyah (Alexandria)

Allenstein (*Pol.* Olsztyn) NW Poland plebiscite 1920, 174/3

Almería, Kingdom of Spain Seleucid Empire 301 BC, 26/1; Spain 1086, 79/3

Almohads, Empire of the S Spain 1180, 82/1

Almoravid Empire northern limits in Spain 1115, 82/1

Alpes Cottiae Roman province of France/Italy AD 180, 38/3

Alpes Graiae et Poeninae Roman province of France/Italy AD 180, 38/3

Alpes Maritimae Roman province of France/Italy AD 180, 38/3

Alpuente district of NE Spain 1086, 79/3

Alsace (*Ger.* Elsass) region of E France added to Burgundy by 1477, 106/1; controlled by France 1648, 131/1

Alsace-Lorraine (*Ger.* Elsass-Lothringen) region of E France in German Empire 1871, 166/1; added to France 1919, 175/2

Al Ushbunah (*mod.* Lisbon) C Portugal Muslim conquest by 732, 56; Muslim rule 60-76

Amalfi S Italy conquered by Normans 1127, 79/1

Amaseia (*a/s* Amasia, *mod.* Amasya) NE Anatolia Empire of Pontus 121 BC, 34/4

Ambracia (*mod.* Arta) NW Greece Greek colony 9C-6C BC, 14/1; Persian Wars 490-480 BC, 18/3; Athenian Empire 431 BC, 22/1; in Molossian Kingdom 334 BC, 22/3; Pyrrhus's Empire 295-275 BC, 26/3; Second Macedonian War 202 BC, 30/2

Amiens (Samarobriva)

Amisus (*mod.* Samsun) N Anatolia Greek colony 9C-6C BC, 14/2; Roman Empire 31 BC, 33; in Persian Empire 480, 17; in Alexander's Empire 323, 21

Amorgos island of S Aegean conquered by Persians 480 BC, 18/3

Ampurias (Emporiae)

Amsterdam C Netherlands 80-; 1648, 123/1

Anatolia Greek colonisation 9C-6C BC, 14/2; Kingdom of Antigonus 323 BC, 22/4; Turcoman principalities 14C, 93-97; Ottoman Empire 1390-1913, 98-170

Ancona C Italy ally of Rome by 270 BC, 26/2; acquired by Papal States 774, 62/3; 1219, 90/3; Hungarian protectorate 1488, 110/1

Ancyra (*mod.* Ankara, *f/c* Angora) C Anatolia Seleucid Empire 301 BC, 26/1; in Roman Empire 395, 41

Andorra condominium 1180, 94/1

Andros island of C Aegean conquered by Persians 480 BC, 18/3; Macedonian dependency 202 BC, 30/2; Venetian possession 1210, 146/3

Angevin Empire England and France growth 1154-80, 83/3

Angles settlement in Britain 350-450, 46/2

Angora (*anc.* Ancyra, *mod.* Ankara) C Turkey 81-

Angoulême – Bergamo

Angoulême region of W France added to Royal Domain by 1226, 114/3
Angoulême, County of W France fief of Duchy of Aquitaine 1030, 74/3
Anhalt, Duchy of N Germany North German Confederation 1867, 162/3; in German Empire 1871, 166/1
Anhalt, Principality of N Germany Holy Roman Empire 1648, 126/2
Anjou region of N France added to Royal Domain by 1223, 86/2; 114/3
Anjou, County of NW France fief of French Crown 74/3; inherited by Henry II by 1154, 83/3
Ankara (Ancyra, Angora)
Annaba (Hippo Regius)
Ansbach, Principality of C Germany Holy Roman Empire 1648, 126/2
Antakya (Antioch)
Antandros NW Anatolia Athenian Empire 431 BC, 22/1
Antigonus, Kingdom of Anatolia 323 BC, 22/4
Antioch (*Lat.* Antiochia, *mod.* Antakya) SE Turkey in Persian Empire 480, 17; in Alexander's Empire 323, 21; Seleucid Empire 301 BC, 26/1; Roman Empire 55 BC, 34/3; Byzantine Empire 527, 54/2
Antioch, Principality of SE Anatolia 1180-1223, 81, 85
Antiochia (*a/c* Antiochia Pisidiae) C Anatolia Roman Empire 55 BC, 34/3
Antium (*mod.* Anzio) Roman control 380 BC, 14/3, 22/2
Antwerp (*Dut.* Antwerpen, *Fr.* Anvers) N Belgium 159/4
Anzio (Antium)
Apamea W Syria Roman Empire 55 BC, 34/3
Aphrodisias SW Anatolia Roman Empire 129 BC, 30/1
Apollonia (*mod.* Sozopol) E Bulgaria Greek colony 9C-6C BC, 14/2; in Persian Empire 480 BC, 18/1; subdued by Macedonia 336 BC, 22/3; Macedonian dependency 202 BC, 30/2; taken by Burebista c. 45 BC, 34/1
Apollonia S Albania Greek colony 9C-6C BC, 14/1; Greek city 275 BC, 26/3
Appenzell canton of E Switzerland joins Swiss Confederation 1411, 110/1
Apulia, County of S Italy secured by Normans 1042, 79/1
Aquae Sulis (*mod.* Bath) SW England Roman Empire AD 80, 39/2
Aquileia NE Italy Roman Empire 55 BC, 34/3; Ostrogothic rule 508, 50/2
Aquileia, Partiarchate of NE Italy church state 1390, 98/3
Aquincum (*mod.* Budapest) Roman Empire 395, 41
Aquis Granum (Aix-la-Chapelle)
Aquitaine region of SW France lost by Franks 670, regained 736, 62/1
Aquitaine, Duchy of SW France added to Angevin Empire 1180, 83/3
Aquitania Roman province of SW France AD 180, 38/3
Arabia Roman province of Egypt/Jordan AD 180 38/3
Aradus (*Bibl.* Arvad, *later* Arwad, *Fr.* Rouad, *a/s* Ruad) W Syria Phoenician city 900 BC, 9
Aragon, Kingdom of N Spain 1030, 74/1; united with Catalonia 1137, 82/1; 1328, 94/1; expansion from 1210-mid-15C, 94/2; Spanish inheritance of Charles V 1516, 114/1
Aramaeans early people of Middle East 9
Arbela (*a/c* Arbailu, *mod.* Arbil) N Iraq Seleucid Empire 301 BC, 26/1
Arcadia region of S Greece peopled by Aeolians 800 BC, 10/4; Persian Wars 490-480 BC, 18/3
Archangel (*Russ.* Arkhangel'sk) N Russia 125-
Arelate (*mod.* Arles) S France Roman Empire 31 BC, 32
Arezzo (Arretium)
Argentorate (*a/c* Argentoratum, *mod.* Strasbourg) E France Roman Empire 31 BC, 32
Argolis region of SE Greece peopled by Dorians 800 BC, 10/4; Persian Wars 490-480 BC, 18/3
Argos S Greece Mycenaean city c.1300 BC, 10/2; city-state 600 BC, 13; ally of Athens 22/1; to Duchy of Athens 1190-1270, 86/4, 90/1; Second Macedonian War 202 BC, 30/2
Argovie (Aargau)
Ariminum (*mod.* Rimini) N Italy Roman colony 300 BC, 26/2; Roman Empire 55 BC, 34/3
Arkhangel'sk (Archangel)
Arles (*anc.* Arelate) S France under the Visigoths 526, 48; in the Frankish kingdoms 565-814, 52, 56, 60; in Burgundy 910, 64
Armagnac region of S France Hundred Years' War 102/2
Armenia country of the Caucasus Alexander's Empire 323 BC, 22/4; Seleucid Empire 301 BC, 26/1; 100 BC, 29; Roman dependency 31 BC, 33; Roman vassal state 114-117, 38/1; independence 189, 37; 1991, 190/1
Arpi S Italy ally of Rome 300 BC, 26/2
Arras (*anc.* Nemetacum, *a/c* Nemetocenna) NE France Hundred Years' War, 102/2; Union of Arras 1579, 123/1
Arretium (*mod.* Arezzo) C Italy Etruscan city 600 BC, 14/3; controlled by Rome 380 Bc, 22/2; ally of Rome by 270 BC, 26/2; Roman Empire 31 BC, 33
Arta (Ambracia)
Artaxata Armenia 189, 37
Artemisium (*mod.* Artemision) E Greece Persian Wars 490-480 BC, 18/3
Artois region of NE France added to France 1659, 13/1; added to Royal Domain by 1223, 86/2; Burgundian control 1404, 106/1; Union of Arras 1579, 123/1
Arvad, Arwad (Aradus)
Asculum (*mod.* Ascoli Satriano) C Italy Pyrrhus's Empire 295-275 BC, 26/3; ally of Rome by 270 BC, 26/2
Ashur (*mod.* Sharqat) N Mesopotamia to Assyrian Empire 934-912 BC, 10/3
Asia region of W Anatolia added to Roman Empire 133-29 BC, 30/2; Roman province of W Anatolia AD180, 38/3
Asiana Roman diocese of W Anatolia 285-337, 42/2,3
Asine (*mod.* Koroni, *It.* Corone) SW Greece Persian Wars 490-480 BC, 18/3
Assisi C Italy added to Papal States by 1219, 90/3
Assos (*a/s* Assus) NW Anatolia Athenian Empire 431 BC, 22/1
Assyrian Empire 10-7C BC, 10/3
Asti (*anc.* Hata) NW Italy under the Visconti 1390, 98/3
Astrakhan S Russia 93-
Astrakhan, Khanate of E Russia 1466-1530, 105-113
Asturias region of N Spain 718-1030, 74/1
Athenopolis S France Greek colony 9C-6C BC, 14/1
Athens (*Lat.* Athenae, *Gr.* Athina, *f/s* Athinai) E Greece Mycenaean city 14C BC, 10/2; city-state 550 BC, 13; Athenian Empire 431 BC, 22/1; Corinthian League 337 BC, 22/3; Cassander's Kingdom 301 BC, 26/1; Second Macedonian War 202 BC, 30/2; Roman Empire 100 BC, 30/3; E Roman Empire 450, 46/1; Byzantine Empire 527, 54/2
Athens, Duchy of State of Latin Empire 1190-1270, 86/4, 90/1; Aragonese possession 1379-90, 94/2; 1360, 98/2
Attica region of E Greece peopled by Ionians 800 BC, 10/4; Persian Wars 490-480 BC, 18/3
Augsburg (*anc.* Augusta Vindelicorum) S Germany conquered by Clovis 507, 51/4; East Frankish Kingdom 870, 66/4; Bishopric 1648, 122/3, 126/2
Augusta Nemetum (Spires)
Augusta Suessionum (Noviodunum)
Augusta Taurinorum (*mod.* Torino, *Eng.* Turin) NW Italy Roman Empire AD 180, 36; Ostrogothic rule 508, 50/2
Augusta Treverorum (*a/c* Treveri, *mod.* Trier, *Eng.* Treves) W Germany Roman Empire AD 180, 36; Empire of Postumus 259-274, 43/1; abandoned by Rome by 3C, 46/1; Byzantine Empire 554, 54/2; taken by Lombards 590, 58/3
Augusta Vindelicum (*a/s* Augusta Vindelicorum, *mod.* Augsburg) S Germany Roman Empire AD 180, 36
Augustobona (*mod.* Troyes) C France Roman Empire AD 180, 36
Augustodunum (*mod.* Autun) C France Roman Empire 180, 36; 395, 40
Augustodurum (*mod.* Bayeux) N France Roman Empire AD 180, 36
Augustoritum (Limoges)
Aurelianum (Cenabum, Orléans)
Aussig (Ústí nad Labem)
Austrasia NE France partition of the Frankish kingdom 561, 55/4
Austria acquired by Bohemia 1251, 91/2; Habsburg possession 1282, 102/1; 1477, 114/1; 1660, 122/2; Archduchy 1648, 126/2; Habsburg territory 1699-1789, 142/2; annexed by Germany 1938, 178/1; Allied zones of occupation 1945, 186/2; EFTA 1993, 190/3
Austria-Hungary administrative divisions 1849-68, 162/2; ethnic divisions 163/1; Austrian Crownlands 166/3; Triple Alliance 170/1
Austrian Empire loss of West Galicia to Warsaw 1809, 151/3; boundaries 1815, 154/2
Austrian Netherlands *see* Netherlands
Autissiodurum (Auxerre)
Autun (Augustodunum)
Auvergne region of C France added to Royal Domain by 1226, 114/3
Auvergne, County of C France fief of Duchy of Aquitaine 1030, 74/3
Auxerre (*anc.* Autissiodurum) E France Hundred Years' War, 102/2
Auxerre, County of C France fief of French Crown 74/3
Avar Kingdom SE Europe 596-732, 58/2
Avaricum (Bourges)
Avars Slav people of C Europe 9C, 66/2
Avenio (Avignon)
Aventicum (*mod.* Avenches, *Ger.* Wifflisburg) W Switzerland settled by Burgundians 450, 46/3
Aversa, County of C Italy conquered by Normans by 1090, 79/1
Avignon (*anc.* Avenio) S France under the Visigoths 526, 48; in the Frankish kingdoms 565-814, 52, 56, 60; in Burgundy 910, 64; added to Royal Domain 1226, 114/3
Avlona (*It.* Valona, *mod.* Vlorë) S Albania in Bulgaria 986, 70/4
Aydin Turcoman principality of W Anatolia 1328-1382, 93, 97
Azerbaijan independence 1991, 190/1
Azincourt (Agincourt)
Azov S Russia Ottoman town 1530-1721, 121-137
Babylon C Mesopotamia to Assyrian Empire 721-705 BC, 10/3
Bácska (*S.Cr.* Vojvodina, *Ger.* Wojwodina) region of N Serbia annexed by Hungary 1941, 182/3
Badajoz, Kingdom of W Iberia 1086, 79/3
Baden, Grand Duchy of SW Germany within German Confederation 1815, 154/3; 1861, 156; 1866, 162/3; in German Empire 1871, 166/1
Baden, Margravate of SW Germany Holy Roman Empire 1648, 126/2
Baecula S Spain Roman Empire 181 BC, 30/1
Baetica Roman province of S Spain AD 180, 38/3
Bagacum (*mod.* Bavay) N France Roman Empire 31 BC, 32
Baiocasses (Bayeux)
Baiona (Bayonne)
Bakhchisaray Crimea Ottoman town 1618-1721, 121-137
Balansiyah (*mod.* Valencia) E Spain Muslim conquest 732, 56; Emirate of Cordova 814, 60; 908, 64
Baleares, Kingdom of the W Mediterranean 1086, 79/3
Balearic Islands (*Sp.* Baleares) W Mediterranean taken by Visigoths c.460, 50/1; Byzantine Empire 554, 54/2
Balkans region of Seleucid Empire Persian expansion 513-480 BC, 18/1; 301 BC, 26/1; Roman expansion 270-31 BC, 30/3; Europe 1140-1240, 86/3,4; on eve of Ottoman conquest 1360, 98/2; Ottoman conquests 1359-1500, 107/2; 1815-61, 159/3; Treaty of San Stefano 1878, 166/2; Balkan League 1912, 170/1; First Balkan War 1912, 170/2; Second Balkan War 1913, 170/3; 1941-42, 182/3, 183/1
Bamberg C Germany Bishopric 1648, 126/2; Archbishopric 1660, 122/3
Banat region of N Serbia/Romania acquired by Habsburgs 1718, 142/2; move from military to civil administration 1751, 142/3; German occupation 1941, 182/2,3
Banja Luka N Bosnia Serbian occupation 1993, 191/2
Bar, Duchy of E France added to Burgundy by 1477, 106/1; occupied by France 1635-61 and 1670, 131/1; lost by France 134/3
Barcelona (*anc.* Barcino) NE Spain 60-; West Frankish Kingdom 880, 66/4; 1030, 74/1
Barcino (*mod.* Barcelona) NE Spain Visigothic rule 475, 50/1
Bari (*anc.* Barium) S Italy 69-; Viking rule 11-12C, 66/D; Byzantine possession 1155-6, 79/1
Barium (*mod.* Bari) S Italy Byzantine Empire 554, 54/2
Bashkortostan (*a/c* Bashkiria) autonomous republic of Russian Federation 1993, 190/1
Basle (*anc.* Basilia, *Ger.* Basel, *Fr.* Bâle) W Switzerland Bishopric 1579, 126/1; 1648, 126/2
Basques 5-6C, 50/1,3; Visigothic rule 624, 58/1
Bastarnae early people of Dacia 34/1
Batavian Republic (*mod.* Netherlands) annexed by France 1789-91, 146/1
Bath (Aquae Sulis)
Baturin (*mod.* Baturyn) N Ukraine in Hetmanate 1667, 135/2
Bavaria (*Ger.* Bayern, *Cz.* Bavorsko) region of S Germany lost by Franks 7C, regained 728, 62/1; 1382, 97; 1660, 122/2; 955-1779, 138/3; in German Confederation 1815, 154/1,3; 1861, 157
Bavaria, Duchy of S Germany Guelph lands 1179, 82/4
Bavaria, Electorate of S Germany Holy Roman Empire 1648, 126/2
Bavaria, Kingdom of 1866, 162/3; in German Empire 1871, 166/1
Bavarians people of S Germany 565, 52
Bavay (Bagacum)
Bayern (Bavaria)
Bayeux (*anc.* Augustodurum, *med.* Baiocasses) N France Viking rule 924-33, 66/A; 64-
Bayonne (*anc.* Lapurdum, *Bas.* Baiona) English in 1223, 86/2; English in 1380, 102/2
Bayreuth S Germany Bishopric 1648, 126/2; in Prussia 1806, 154/3
Bayrūt (Berytus)
Béarn district of SW France Catalan-Aragonese fief 1180, 82/1; Catalan-Aragonese dependency to mid-13C, 94/2; English and Burgundian control 1429, 102/2; outside Royal Domain in 1530, 114/3
Beç, Bécs (Vienna)
Bécsújhely (*Ger.* Wiener Neustadt) E Austria to Hungary from 1485, 110/1
Beirut (Berytus)
Beja S Portugal held by Christians before 1180, 82/1
Belarus (Belorussia)
Belfast N Ireland 136-
Belgica Roman province of France/Belgium/Germany AD 180, 38/3
Belgium part of Austrian Netherlands 1714, 142/2; annexed by France 1792-3, 146/1; independence 1839, 158/4; European Union 1993, 190/3
Belgorod-Dnestrovskiy (Cetatea Albă)
Belgrade (*Serb.* Beograd) N Serbia 77-; in Bulgaria 986, 70/4; annexed by Hungary 1229, 86/3; in Hungary 1490, 110/1; acquired by Habsburgs 1718-39, 138/1; to Serbia 1817, 158/2; 1993, 190/1
Beloozero early principality of W Russia 1270-1328, 89, 93
Belorussia (*a/c* Belarus) independence 1991, 190/1
Belostok (*Pol.* Białystok) E Poland transfer from Prussia to Russia 1807, 158/1
Benevento (*anc.* Beneventum) S Italy taken by Lombards 590, 59/3
Benevento, Duchy of S Italy dependency of Frankish Empire 787, 62/1
Benevento, Principality of S Italy 908, 64; conquered by Normans by 1090, 79/1; 1806-10, 150/1-4
Beneventum (*mod.* Benevento) S Italy Pyrrhus's Empire 295-275 BC, 26/3 Roman colony 300 BC, 26/2; Roman Empire 270 BC, 30/3; 55 BC, 34/3
Beograd (Belgrade)
Berestie early principality of W Russia 1270, 89
Berg, County of NW Germany Bavarian territory 18C, 138/3
Berg, Duchy of NW Germany Holy Roman Empire 1648, 126/2
Bergamo (anc. Bergomum) N Italy under the Visconti 1390, 98/3

Damascus – Frankish Kingdom(s)

of Austria-Hungary 1849-68, 162/2; Austrian Crownlands 166/3; annexed by Italy 1941, 182/3, 183/1
Damascus (*mod.* Dimashq, *a/c* Ash Sham, *Fr.* Damas) SW Syria Seleucid Empire 301 BC, 26/1
Danelaw extent in 886, 70/2
Danzig (*Pol.* Gdańsk) NW Poland 89-101; 145-181
Danzig, Republic of 1807-10, 150/2-4; in Prussia 1807, 155/3; independent from Prussia 1807-14, 158/1; free city 1921, 174/4
Daugavpils (Dünaburg)
Dauphiné region of SE France Hundred Years' War, 102/2; added to Royal Domain by 1530, 114/3
Debrecen (*f/s* Debreczen) E Hungary 69-
Dedeagach (*mod.* Alexandroupoli) NE Greece occupied by Bulgaria 1913, 170/3; occupied by Bulgaria 1941, 182/3
Deira region of NE England Anglo-Saxon by end 6C, 54/3
Delos (*mod.* Dilos, *a/s* Dhilos) S Aegean Athenian Empire 431 BC, 22/1
Delphi (*mod.* Delfoi, *a/s* Dhelfoi) C Greece Persian Wars 490-480 BC, 18/3; Athenian Empire 431 BC, 22/1; Corinthian League 337 BC, 22/3
Demetrias (*mod.* Volos) E Greece Second Macedonian War 202 BC, 30/2; Roman Empire 100 BC, 30/3; 55 BC, 34/3
Denmark Anglo-Saxon settlement 350-450, 46/2; Viking state c.1000, 66/B; expansion 950-1223 87/1; loss of Schleswig-Holstein 1865, 162/3; European Union 1993, 190/3
Deols, County of C France fief of Duchy of Aquitaine 1030, 74/3
Dertosa (*mod.* Tortosa) NE Spain Roman Empire 55 BC, 34/3
Deutsch-Altenburg (Carnuntum)
Deva (*mod.* Chester) C England Roman Empire AD 80, 39/2
Dhilos (Delos)
Dhodhekanisos (Dodecanese)
Dhu'l-Qadr (Dulkadir)
Diadora (Iadena)
Dijon (*anc.* Dibio) E France 48-; in Frankish Kingdom 534, 54/1; Frankish Empire 843, 66/3; Hundred Years' War, 102/2
Dilos (Delos)
Dioscurias (*mod.* Sokhumi, *Russ.* Sukhumi) W Georgia Greek colony 9C-6C BC, 14/2; in Persian Empire 480, 17; in Alexander's Empire 323, 21
Diospolis Magna (Thebes)
Divodurum (Metz)
Djerba S Tunisia Viking rule 1135-60, 66/D
Dnepropetrovsk, Dnipropetrovs'k (Ekaterinoslav)
Dobruja (*a/s* Dobrudja) region of Romania/Bulgaria south gained by Bulgaria 1940, 182/2
Doclea S Montenegro Roman Empire 100 BC, 30/3; 55 BC, 34/3
Dodecanese (*Gr.* Dodekanisos, *f/s* Dhodhekanisos) islands of SE Aegean occupied by Italy 1912, 170/2; 1942, 182/3, 183/1
Doornijk (Tournai)
Dorians people of S Greece 800 BC, 10/4
Doris region of C Greece peopled by Dorians 800 BC, 10/4
Dortmund NW Germany Allied occupation 1920-5, 175/2; British occupation 1945, 186/2
Dorylaeum (*mod.* Eskişehir) W Turkey Roman Empire 55 BC, 34/3
Dovena town of Great Moravia 830, 66/2
Drač (Durazzo)
Drenthe district of N Netherlands independent 1581, 123/1
Dresden E Germany 80-; enters Confederation of the Rhine 1807, 151/2; in German Confederation 1815, 154/1,3; Russian occupation 1945, 186/2
Dublin (*Ir.* Baile Átha Cliath) E Ireland 50-; secured by England by 1172, 83/3
Dublin, Kingdom of E Ireland Viking state 916-980, 66/A
Dubrovnik (*anc.* Ragusium, *mod.* Ragusa) S Croatia occupied by Italy 1941, 182/3, 183/1; 1993, 191/2
Duisburg NW Germany Allied occupation 1923-5, 175/2
Duklja district of W Bulgaria 986, 70/4
Dulkadir (*a/s* Dhu'l-Qadr) Turkoman principality of E Anatolia 1382-1493, 97-109
Dünaburg (*Russ.* Dvinsk, *Latv.* Daugavpils, *Pol.* Dyneburg) SE Latvia 89-113; 1772, 146/2; 1942, 181
Dunkirk (*Fr.* Dunkerque) NE France added to France 1662, 131/1
Durazzo (*anc.* Epidamnus, *later* Dyrrachium, *mod.* Durrës) C Albania 1360, 98/1
Durham N England added to Wessex by 939, 71/2; 124-
Durocortorum (Rheims)
Durostorum (*mod.* Silistra, *f/s* Silistria) NE Bulgaria Roman Empire AD 80, 37
Durovernum (*med. Lat.* Cantuaria, *mod.* Canterbury, *Fr.* Cantorbéry) SE England Roman Empire AD 43, 39/2
Durrës (Durazzo)
Düsseldorf NW Germany Allied occupation 1923-5, 175/2; British occupation 1945, 186/2
Dvinsk (Dünaburg)
Dyfed principality of S Wales 600, 58/4; 796, 62/2; vassal of Wessex 70/2; Welsh unification 800-1057, 74/2
Dyneburg (*Ger.* Dünaburg, *Latv.* Daugavpils, *Russ.* Divinsk) SE Latvia in Poland 1572-1721, 117-137
Dyrrachium (*It.* Durazzo, *mod.* Durrës) C Albania Roman Empire 219 BC, 30/3; 55 BC, 34/3; in Bulgaria 986, 70/4
East Angles people of E England Kentish domination 600, 58/4
East Anglia region of E England Anglo-Saxon state by end 6C, 54/3; added to Mercia by 796, 62/2; added to Wessex by 924, 71/2
Eastern Rumelia region of S Bulgaria to Bulgaria 1885, 166/2
East Frankish Kingdom (mod. West Germany) 870-880, 66/4
East Franks people of W Germany 565, 52
East Friesland (*Ger.* Ostfriesland) region of NW Germany county 1648, 126/2; added to Prussia 1744, 142/1
East Germany (*a/c* German Democratic Republic) joined Federal Republic 1990, 190/1
East Prussia (*Ger.* Ostpreussen) Baltic region of Russia/Poland Polish fief from 1466, 118/3; secular duchy of Prussia from 1525, 119/2; in Prussia 1640, 135/1; 1720, 143/1; plebiscite 1920, 174/3
Eburacum (*a/s* Eboracum, *mod.* York) N England Roman Empire AD 78, 39/2; abandoned by Rome c 400, 46/1; Anglo-Saxon settlement 350-450, 46/2
Ecbatana (*mod.* Hamadan) W Iran Seleucid Empire 301 BC, 26/1
Edinburgh S Scotland 68-; added to Wessex by 939, 71/2
Edirne (Adrianople)
Eflâk (Wallachia)
Eger (*mod.* Cheb) W Bohemia acquired by Luxemburgs 1315, 102/4
Egripo (Euboea)
Egypt (*Lat.* Aegyptus, *Ar.* Misr) ancient Empire, 10/1; Assyrian conquest, 668-627 BC, 10/3; Roman province AD 180, 38/3
Eichstätt C Germany Bishopric 1648, 126/2; 1660, 122/3
Eion NE Greece Athenian Empire 431 BC, 22/1
Eire (*f/c* Irish Free State, *n/c* Republic of Ireland) 1940, 176; 1942, 180
Ekaterinoslav (*Russ.* Dnepropetrovsk, *Ukr.* Dnipropetrovs'k) S Ukraine 141-
Elaea W Anatolia in Pergamum 202 BC, 30/2
Elam country of S Mesopotamia to Assyrian Empire 668-627, 10/3
Elba island of W Italy annexed by France 1803, 146/4
Elbląg (*Ger.* Elbing) N Poland to Prussia 1772, 146/2
Elea (*a/c* Velia) S Italy Greek city-state 6C BC, 14/3; 375 BC, 22/2
Elis region of W Greece 900-800 BC, 10/4; Persian Wars 490-480 BC, 18/3; Second Macedonian War 202 BC, 30/2
Ellipi country of C Mesopotamia to Assyrian Empire 668-627, 10/3
Elmet Celtic state of N England 600, 58/4
Elsass (Alsace)
Elsass-Lothringen (Alsace-Lorraine)
Emerita Augusta (*Ar.* Maridah, *mod.* Mérida) SW Spain Roman Empire 180, 36; Visigothic rule 476, 50/3
Emona (*mod.* Ljubljana) C Slovenia Ostrogothic rule 508, 50/2
Emporiae (*a/s* Emporium, *Gr.* Emporion, *mod.* Ampurias) NE Spain Greek colony 9C-6C BC, 14/1; in Massilia 121 BC, 30/1
Enez (Aenus)
England Anglo-Saxon states 6C, 54/3; the Heptarchy 600, 58/4; supremacy of Mercia 625-796,62/2; Danelaw 917-54, 66/A; 899-1018, 70/2; Norman Conquest 78/2; Angevin Empire 1154-80, 83/3; Hundred Years' War 14-15C, 102/2
Enos (Aenus)
Ephesus (*a/s* Ephesos) W Anatolia Ionian city 800 BC, 10/4; Persian Wars 490-480 BC, 18/3; Athenian Empire 431 BC, 22/1; Kingdom of Lysimachus 301 BC, 26/1; Ptolemaic Empire 202 BC, 30/3; Roman Empire 100 BC, 30/2
Epidamnus (*later* Dyrrachium, *mod.* Durrës, *It.* Durazzo, *SCr.* Drač) C Albania Greek colony 9C-6C BC, 14/1; Greek city 275 BC, 26/3
Epirus (*Gr.* Epiros) region of Greece/Albania Persian Wars 490-480 BC, 18/3; Molossian Kingdom 334 BC, 22/3; Pyrrhus's Empire 295-275 BC, 26/3; Second Macedonian War 202 BC, 30/2; Roman province AD 180, 38/3; Ottoman conquest by 1500, 107/2
Epirus, Despotate of Albania/Greece successor state to Byzantine Empire 1190-1212, 86/4; Byzantine vassal from 1262, 90/1
Erdely (Transylvania)
Ereğli (Heraclea Pontica, Perinthus)
Eretna Turcoman principality of E Anatolia 1382, 97
Eretria E Greece Greek mother-city 9C-6C BC, 14/1,2; Persian Wars 490-480 BC, 18/3
Erfurt C Germany joins Confederation of the Rhine 1807, 150/2
Erivan (*mod.* Yerevan) C Armenia 93-169
Ermeland (*n/s* Ermland) district of N Poland acquired by Prussia 1656-7, 135/1; 1772, 143, 3
Érsekújvár (*Ger.* Neuhäusel, *mod.* Nové Zámky) Slovakia added to Ottoman Empire 1664, 130/3
Erythrae W Anatolia Ionian revolt against Persians 5C BC, 19/2
Eschental S Switzerland added to Swiss Confederation 1403-22, 110/2
Eschental district of N Italy in Swiss Confederation 1512-15, 126/1
Eski Cuma (Târgovişte)
Eskişehir (Dorylaeum)
Esseg (Eszék)
Essen NW Germany Allied occupation 1923-5, 175/2; British occupation 1945, 186/2
Essex region of E England Anglo-Saxon state 530, 54/3; dependency of Kent 600, 58/4; added to Mercia by 796, 62/2
Estonia to Denmark 1219, 87/1; to Sweden 1561, 119/2; added to Sweden 1582-1600, 130/2; independence 1918, 174/1; annexed by USSR 1940, 178/3; occupied by Germany 1942, 182/4; independence 1991, 190/1
Estonians WW2 migration 1944-45, 186/1
Eszék (*mod.* Osijek, *Ger.* Esseg) N Croatia to Croatia-Slavonia 1873, 166/3; Treaty of Trianon 1920, 175/5
Etruria, Kingdom of C Italy new name for Tuscany 1801, 146/4
Etruscan City States N Italy 550 BC, 12; 480 BC, 16; 323 BC, 20
Etruscans early people of N Italy 900 BC, 8; 6C-4C BC, 14/3
Euboea (*Gr.* Evvoia, *It.* Negroponte, *med.* Egripo, Euripos) island of E Greece peopled by Ionians 800 BC, 10/4; Persian Wars 490-480 BC, 18/3; Athenian Empire 431 BC, 22/1; Corinthian League 337 BC, 22/3; Macedonian dependency 202 BC, 30/2; Venetian possession 1190-1270, 86/4, 90/1
Eupen E Belgium to Belgium by plebiscite 1920, 174/3, 175/2
Euripos (Euboea)
Evvoia (Euboea)
Exeter (*anc.* Isca Domnoniorum) SW England 128-
Faeroe Islands (*Dan.* Faerøerne, *Faer.* Fóroyar) Norwegian rule 13-14C, 88; Danish from 15C, 112-
Faesulae (*mod.* Fiesole) N Italy Etruscan city 600 BC, 14/3
Falerio C Italy Roman Empire 270 BC, 30/3; Roman Empire 55 BC, 34/3
Fehérvár (*mod.* Székesfehérvár, *Ger.* Stuhlweissenburg) W Hungary national king crowned 1526, 118/1
Felicitas Julia (*earlier* Olisipo, *Ar.* Al Ushbunah, *mod.* Lisboa, *Eng.* Lisbon) W Portugal Roman Empire 55 BC, 34/3; Kingdom of Sueves 431, 46/3
Felsina (*later* Bononia, *mod.* Bologna) N Italy Etruscan city 600 BC, 14/3
Feodosiya (Theodosia)
Fermo (Firmum)
Ferrara (*anc.* Forum Alieni) N Italy acquired by Papal States 757, 62/3; 278, 90/3; under the Este 1336, 95/3
Ferrara, Duchy of N Italy Treaty of Lodi 1454, 106/4; Venetian possession 1490, 110/1; independence from Papal States by 1559, 114/2
Fiesole (Faesulae)
Filibe (Philippopolis)
Finland part of Sweden 1523-1683, 130/2; independence 1918, 174/1; Karelian territory regained from USSR 1941, 182/4; proposed entry into European Union 1993, 190/3; 1993, 190/3
Finnic peoples NE Europe 565, 53
Finno-Ugrians early people of W Russia 9-
Finns migration 1944, 186/1
Firenze (Florence)
Firmum (*a/c* Firmum Picenum, *mod.* Fermo) C Italy Roman colony 300 BC, 26/2
Fiume (*Cr.* Rijeka) W Croatia acquired by Yugoslavia 1947, 187/4
Flanders (*Fr.* Flandres, *Dut.* Vlaanderen) region of Belgium/France Hundred Years' War, 102/2; Burgundian control 1404, 106/1; 1648, 123/1; added to France 1684, 131/1; lost by France 1697, 134/3; southwest occupied by Italy 1940 and 1942, 183/1
Flanders, County of NE France fief of French Crown 1030, 74/3
Flensburg (*Dan.* Flensborg) NW Germany plebiscite 1920, 174/3
Florence (*anc.* Florentia, *mod.* Firenze) C Italy taken by Lombards 590, 58/3; Frankish rule 774-814, 62/1; Frankish empire 843, 66/3; 1336, 95/3; added to French Empire 1809, 150/3
Florence, Republic of C Italy Treaty of Lodi 1454, 106/4; 1499-1559, 114/2
Florentia (*mod.* Firenze, *Eng.* Florence) Ostrogothic rule 508, 50/2; Byzantine Empire 554, 54/2
Foix region of S France outside Royal Domain in 1530, 114/3
Fokis (Phocis)
Forum Alieni (Ferrara)
Forum Julii (*mod.* Cividale del Friuli) NE Italy taken by Lombards 590, 58/3
Fosdinovo N Italy 1714-21, 138/2
France Greek colonisation in south 9C-6C BC, 14/1; Empire of Postumus 259-274, 43/1; abandoned by Rome by 3C, 46/1; occupied by Teutonic peoples by 475, 46/3; feudal fragmentation 987-1030, 74/3; William the Conqueror 1035-92, 78/2; Angevin Empire 1154-80, 83/3; growth of the Royal Domain to 1223, 86/2; Hundred Years' War 14-15C, 102/2; growth of Royal Domain to 1530, 114/3; expansion under Louis XIV 131/1; territorial losses after 1685, 134/3; revolutionary conquests 1789-97, 146/1; 1814-15, 154/4; alliances 1894-1904, 170/1; southwest occupied by Italy 1940 and 1942, 183/1; European Union 1993, 190/3
Franche-Comté (*Ger.* Freigrafschaft Burgund) region of SE France Habsburg possession 1520, 114/2; Holy Roman Empire 1648, 126/2; added to France 1678/9, 131/1
Franconia region of C Germany 565, 55/4
Franconia, Duchy of C Germany Hohenstaufen land 1179, 82/4
Frankfurt (*a/c* Frankfurt am Main, *Eng.* Frankfort, *Fr.* Francfort) W Germany 58-; American occupation 1945, 186/2
Frankish Empire (*later* called Carolingian Empire) France/Germany to 511, 51/4; partition 561, 55/4; growth to 814, 62/1; partition 843, 66/3; partition 870 and 880, 66/4; southern frontier in Spain 814, 74/1
Frankish Kingdom(s) NE France 476, 50/3; SW France taken from Visigoths 507, 50/1; France and Germany 511, 51/4; expansion to 561, 54/1

Liège, Bishopric of – Messana

Liège, Bishopric of E Belgium added to Burgundy by 1477, 106/1; 1648, 123/1; Holy Roman Empire 1648, 126/2

Liegnitz, Principality of E Germany Holy Roman Empire 1648, 126/2

Ligurian Republic NW Italy established 1797, 146/1; annexed by France 1805, 146/4

Ligurians early people of N Italy 8-; 270 BC, 24

Lilybaeum (*mod.* Marsala) W Sicily Syracusan rule 375 BC, 22/2; Pyrrhus's Empire 295-275 BC, 26/3; Roman Empire 241 BC, 30/1; taken by Vandals c. 460, 50/1

Limburg (*Fr.* Limbourg) region of E Belgium/Netherlands acquired by Luxemburgs 1355, 102/4; to Burgundy 1430, 106/4; 1648, 123/1; divided 1839, 159/4; in German Confederation 1866, 162/3

Limoges (*anc.* Lemovices, Augustoritum) C France Visigothic rule 476, 50/3; conquered by Clovis 507, 50/1, 51/4

Limonum (*mod.* Poitiers) W France Roman Empire AD 180, 36

Limousin region of C France outside Royal Domain in 1530, 114/3

Limousin, County of C France fief of Duchy of Aquitaine 1030, 74/3

Limpurg, County of C Germany added to Prussia 1713, 135/1; lost by Prussia 1742, 142/1

Lincoln (Lindum)

Lindos (*a/s* Lindus) Rhodes Ionian revolt against Persians 5C BC, 19/2

Lindsey district of E England dependency of Kent 600, 58/4

Lindum (*mod.* Lincoln) E England Roman Empire AD 43, 39/2; Roman territory c. 350, 46/2

Lingen NW Germany added to Prussia 1702, 135/1, 142/1

Linz N Austria American occupation 1945, 186/2

Lipova (Lippa)

Lippa (*mod.* Lipova) W Romania added to Ottoman Empire 1618, 130/3

Lippe, County of N Germany Holy Roman Empire 1648, 126/2

Lippe-Detmold, Principality of NW Germany North German Confederation 1867, 162/3

Lisbon (*Ar.* Al Ushbunah, *Port.* Lisboa, *anc.* Olisipo, *later* Felicitas Julia) C Portugal Christian conquest by end 11C, 82/1

Lissa (*mod.* Vis) island of E Adriatic in Austria-Hungary 1868, 162/2

Lithuania (*Lith.* Lietuva, *Ger.* Litauen, *Pol.* Litwa, *Russ.* Litva) growth to 1430, 103/3; growth of Jagiello power 1440-1526, 111/3; Union of Lublin 1569, 118/3; to Russia 1793, 146/2; in Poland 1699, 154/1; 1918-22, 174/1,4; annexed to USSR 1940, 178/3; occupied by Germany 1942, 182/4; independence 1991, 190/1

Lithuanians WW2 migration 1944-45, 186/1

Little Poland (*Pol.* Małopolska) region of S Poland to Poland 999, 74/4

Little Wallachia region of S Romania under Habsburgs 1718-39, 142/2; returned to Ottomans 1739, 142/3

Liverpool NW England 128-

Livonia (*Ger.* Livland) region of Estonia/ Latvia added to Polish-Lithuanian state 1561-85, 118/3; Russian occupation 1558-82, 119/2; added to Sweden 1629, 130/2; independence 1918, 174/1

Livs people of Estonia/Latvia 1180, 81

Ljubljana (*anc.* Emona, *Ger.* Laibach, *It.* Lubiana) W Slovenia 1993, 191/2

Lleida (Lérida)

Locris region of C Greece Athenian Empire 431 BC, 22/1

Łódź (Russ. Lodz) C Poland 133-

Lombards, Kingdom of the E Germany 561, 54/1

Lombardy region of N Italy added to Frankish Mepire 774, 62/1; lost by Austria to Sardinia 1859, 162/2

Lombardy and Venetia, Kingdom of western part added to Sardinia 1859, 158/2

Londinium (*mod.* London, *Fr.* Londres) S England Roman Empire AD 43, 38/1, 39/2; abandoned by Rome c. 400, 46/1; Anglo-Saxon settlement 350-450, 46/2

London (*anc.* Londinium) SE England 52-; Mercian rule 796, 62/2

Lorch S Germany in Frankish Kingdom 561, 54/1

Lorraine (*Ger.* Lothringen) region of NE France Holy Roman Empire 1648, 126/2; duchy under French control 1635-59 and 1670, 131/1; lost by France 1697, 134/3

Lotharingia NE France partition of Frankish Empire 843, 66/3

Lothringen (Lorraine)

Lower Austria province of Austria-Hungary 1849-68, 162/2

Lower Burgundy East Frankish Kingdom 870, 66/2

Lower Lorraine, Duchy of E France Holy Roman Empire 1179, 82/4

Lower Palatinate region of W Germany Holy Roman Empire 1648, 126/2

Lübeck N Germany Bishopric 1660, 122/3; joins Confederation of the Rhine 1809, 150/3; in French Empire 1810, 150/4; in German Confederation 1815, 154/3; free city 1871, 166/1

Lubiana (*Slvn.* Ljubljana, *Ger.* Laibach) W Slovenia annexed to Italy 1941, 182/3, 183/1; 1993, 191/2

Lublin C Poland to Habsburgs 1795, 146/2; occupied by Germany 1939, 178/1

Lucca C Italy under the Scaligers 1336, 95/3; Treaty of Lodi 1454, 106/4

Lucca, Principality of 1806-10, 150/1-4

Lucca, Republic of N Italy 1714-21, 138/2; established 1799, 146/4

Luceria (*mod.* Lucera) S Italy Roman colony 300 BC, 26/2

Lucerne (*Ger.* Luzern) C Switzerland added to Swiss Confederation 1332, 110/2; 1486, 126/1

Lucus Augusti (*mod.* Lugo) NW Spain in Kingdom of Sueves 431, 46/3

Lugano S Switzerland joined Swiss Confederation 1512, 126/1

Lugdunum (*mod.* Lyon, *Eng.* Lyons) E France Roman Empire 31 BC, 32

Lugo (Lucus Augusti)

Luik (Liège)

Lund S Sweden Viking town c.1000, 66/B; in Denmark c. 950, 87/1

Lusatia (*Ger.* Lausitz) region of SE Germany to Poland 1018, 74/4; acquired by Luxemburgs 1366, 102/4; to Hungary 1477-9, 110/1; added to Saxony 1635, 154/1

Lusatia, Margravate of SW Poland Wettin land 1179, 82/4

Lusitania Roman province of Portugal AD 180, 38/3

Lutetia (*mod.* Paris) N France Roman Empire 31 BC, 32, 35/2; Empire of Postumus 259-274, 43/1; abandoned by Rome by 3C, 46/1

Lüttich (Liège)

Luxembourg (*Ger.* Luxemburg) annexed by France 1792-3, 146/1; in French Empire 1806-10, 150/1-4; European Union 1993, 190/3

Luxemburg (*Fr.* Luxembourg) added to Burgundy by 1467, 106/4; 1648, 123/1; occupied by France 1679, 131/1; lost by France 1697, 134/3; part of Austrian Netherlands 1714, 142/2; divided 1839, 159/4

Luxemburg, County of 1307-95, 102/4

Luzern (Lucerne)

L'vov (*Ukr.* L'viv, *Pol.* Lwów, *Ger.* Lemberg) intermittent Hungarian control 1208-34, 86/3

Lwów (*Ukr.* L'viv, *Russ.* L'vov, *Ger.* Lemberg) W Ukraine to Habsburgs 1772, 146/2; annexed by USSR 1939, 178/3

Lycia region of S Anatolia 121 BC, 29; Roman dependency 31 BC, 33

Lycia et Pamphylia Roman province of S Anatolia AD 180, 37

Lydia region of W Anatolia 1350 BC, 13

Lyons (*Fr.* Lyon, *anc.* Lugdunum) E France 48-; in Frankish Kingdom 534, 54/1; Frankish Empire 843, 66/3; Hundred Years' War, 102/2

Lysimachia NW Turkey Kingdom of Lysimachus 323 BC, 22/4; in Ptolemaic Empire 202 BC, 30/2

Lysimachus, Empire of Bulgaria/NW Anatolia 301 BC 26/1

Lysimachus, Kingdom of Alexander's Empire 323 BC, 22/4

Lyubech N Ukraine Lithuanian by 1377, 103/3

Maastricht SE Netherlands added to Netherlands 1648, 123/1; 159/4

Macedon (*Lat.* Macedonia) ancient state of N Greece 270 BC, 25; Second Macedonian War 202 BC, 30/2; added to Rome 148 BC, 30/1,3

Macedonia (*Gr.* Makedonia, *f/s* Makedhonia, *Maced.* Makedonija) region of Greece/Serbia/Macedonia Persian vassal 490 BC, 18/1; rise to 334 BC, 22/3; Alexander's Empire 323 BC, 22/4; Roman province AD 180, 38/3; Roman diocese 324-337, 42/3; First and Second Balkan Wars 1912-13, 170/2,3

Macedonia former republic of Yugoslavia annexed by Bulgaria 1941, 182/3; independence 1992, 191/2

Mâcon (*anc.* Matisco) E France added to Burgundy by 1467, 106/1

Macsó district of S Hungary to Serbia 1339-42, 98/1; 1360, 98/2

Madrid (*Ar.* Majrit) C Spain 68-

Magdeburg E Germany Archbishopric 1648, 126/2; added to Prussia 1680, 135/1

Magenta N Italy to Sardinia 1859, 158/2

Magonsaete early people of W England Mercian rule 796, 62/2

Mahilyow (Mogilev)

Mähren (Morovia)

Mainake S Spain Greek colony 9C-6C BC, 14/1

Maine region of N France Norman control 10-11C, 66/A; Angevin Empire 1154-80, 83/3

Maine, County of NW France fief of French Crown 1030, 74/3

Mainz (*Fr.* Mayence) W Germany in Frankish Kingdom of Soissons 481, 51/4; East Frankish Kingdom 870, 66/4; Archbishopric 1660, 122/3, 126/2; Allied occupation 1918-30, 175/2

Majorca, Kingdom of W Mediterranean 1180, 94/1; Aragonese from 1229, 94/2; 1276-1344, 94/2

Majrit (Madrid)

Malaca (*mod.* Málaga) S Spain Phoenician colony 9C-6C BC, 14/1; Byzantine Empire 554, 54/2

Málaga (*anc.* Malaca, *Ar.* Malaqah) S Spain 88-

Malaqah (*mod.* Málaga) S Spain Muslim rule 68-84

Malatya (Melitene)

Malbork (*Ger.* Marienburg) NW Poland to Prussia 1772, 146/2

Malestroit NW France Hundred Years' War, 102/2

Mallia C Crete Minoan site c.1500 BC, 10/2

Mallorca, Muslim Kingdom of 1180, 82/1

Malmédy E Belgium to Belgium by plebiscite 1920, 174/3, 175/2

Malmö S Sweden 81-

Małopolska (Little Poland)

Malta (*anc.* Melita) island of C Mediterranean Phoenician control 9C BC, 14/1; Carthaginian possession 550 BC, 12-24; Roman occupation 121 BC, 28, 32; Knights of St John 1551, 114/2; 1721, 138/2; British by 1812, 149-; independence 1964, 189

Man, Kingdom of W Scotland Viking state 1113, 66/A; Norwegian from 1075, 78/2

Manchester (*anc.* Mancunium) C England 137-

Mansfeld C Germany acquired by Prussia 1780, 142/1; divided 1839, 159/4

Mantua (*It.* Mantova) N Italy Etruscan control c. 550-400 BC, 14/3; under the Gonzagas 1336, 95/3; Treaty of Lodi 1454, 106/4

Mantua, Duchy of N Italy under the Visconti 1336, 95/3; 1714-21, 138/2; acquired by Habsburgs 1708, 142/2; lost by Habsburgs 1797, 154/2

Marathon E Greece Persian Wars 490-480 BC, 18/3

Marburg (Maribor)

Marengo NW Italy annexed to France 1802, 146/4

Maribor (*Ger.* Marburg) E Slovenia 1993, 191/2

Maridah (*mod.* Mérida) S Spain Muslim rule 1180, 82/1

Marienburg (Malbork)

Marinids Muslim dynasty of NW Africa 1270-1466, 88-106

Mark, County of NW Germany Holy Roman Empire 1648, 126/2; in Prussia 1640, 135/1

Maronea NE Greece Greek colony 9C-6C BC, 14/1; in Persian Empire 480 BC, 18/1; Athenian Empire 431 BC, 22/1; in Ptolemaic Empire 202 BC, 30/2

Marsala (Lilybaeum)

Marseille (*anc.* Massilia) S France under the Ostrogoths 526, 48, 50/3; Visigothic rule 477, 50/1; in Frankish Kingdom 534, 54/1, 56; Frankish Empire 843, 66/3; in Burgundy 910, 64-84; Aragonese dependency to 1258, 94/2

Masovia (*a/s* Mazovia, *Pol.* Mazowsze, *Ger.* Masovien) region of E Poland inherited by Bolesław 1138, 83/2

Massa N Italy 1714-21, 138/2

Massa and Carrara NW Italy to Kingdom of Italy 1861, 158/2

Massilia (*mod.* Marseille, *Eng.* Marseilles) S France Greek colony 9C-6C BC, 14/1; 121 BC, 30/1; Roman Empire 58-55 BC, 34/2,3; Empire of Postumus 259-274, 43/1

Matisco (Mâcon)

Mauretania region of NW Africa Carthaginian control 149 BC, 30/1; Roman province 55 BC, 34/3

Mauretania Caesariensis Roman province of N Algeria AD 180, 38/3

Mauretania Tingitana Roman province of N Morocco AD 180, 38/3

Mauryan Empire NW India Alexander's Empire 323 BC, 22/4

Mayence (*Ger.* Mainz) W Germany annexed to France 1792-3, 146/1; in French Empire 1806-10, 150/1-4

Mazovia, Mazowsze (Masovia)

Meath province of E Ireland 1092, 78/2

Mecklenburg district of N Germany in German Confederation 1815, 154/1,3

Mecklenburg-Schwerin, Grand Duchy of N Germany North German Confederation 1867, 162/3; in German Empire 1871, 166/1

Mecklenburg-Schwerin-Güstrow, Duchy of Holy Roman Empire 1648, 126/2

Mecklenburg-Strelitz, Grand Duchy of N Germany North German Confederation 1867, 162/3; in German Empire 1871, 166/1

Medes, Empire of the E Anatolia 550 BC, 18

Media Atropatene region of N Persia Alexander's Empire 323 BC, 22/4; Seleucid Empire 301 BC, 26/1

Mediolanum (*mod.* Milano, *Eng.* Milan) NW Italy Roman Empire 55 BC, 34/3; 284-337, 42/2,3; Ostrogothic rule 508, 50/2; Byzantine Empire 554, 54/2

Meersen W Germany East Frankish Kingdom 870, 66/4

Megara E Greece Greek mother-city 9C-6C BC, 14/1,2; Persian Wars 490-480 BC, 18/3

Meissen, Margravate of N Germany Wettin land 1179, 82/4

Melita (Malta)

Melitene (*mod.* Malatya) C Turkey Roman Empire AD 180, 37; 395, 41

Melos (*n/s* Milos) island of S Aegean Persian Wars 490-480 BC, 18/3; Athenian Empire 431 BC, 22/1

Memel (*mod.* Klaipėda) W Lithuania added to Sweden 1645, 130/2; Allied administration 1918, annexed by Lithuania 1923, 174/4

Memel Territory (*Ger.* Memelland) in Allied administration 1918, annexed by Lithuania 1923, 174/4; annexed by Germany 1939, 178/3

Memphis N Egypt ancient Eygyptian Empire 10/1; to Assyrian Empire 667-660 BC, 10/3; Ptolemaic Empire 301 BC, 26/1

Menorca (Minorca)

Menteşe (*a/s* Menteshe) Turcoman principality of W Anatolia 1328-82, 93, 97; 1360, 98/2

Mercia kingdom of C England dependency of Kent 600, 58/4; expansion 625-796, 62/2; West Mercia and Danish Mercia added to Wessex 924-939, 71/2

Mercia region of C England Anglo-Saxon state by end 6C, 54/3

Mérida (Emerita Augusta, Maridah)

Mesembria E Bulgaria Greek colony 9C-6C BC, 14/2; in Persian Empire 480 BC, 18/1; Greek city taken by Burebista c. 45 BC, 34/1

Messana (*Gr.* Messene, *f/c* Zankle, *a/s* Zancle, *mod.* Messina) NE Sicily Syracusan rule 375 BC, 22/2; Greek city 275 BC, 26/3; Roman Empire 241 BC, 30/1; Byzantine Empire 535, 54/2

Ofen – Potidaea

Ofen (Buda)
Olbia (*mod.* Mykolayiv, *Russ.* Nikolayev) S Ukraine Greek colony 9C-6C BC, 14/2; 270 CBC, 26/1; Greek city taken by Burebista c45 BC, 34/1
Oldenburg N Germany County 1648, 126/2; in German Confederation 1815, 154/3
Oldenburg, Grand Duchy of NW Germany North German Confederation 1867, 162/3; in German Empire 1871, 166/1
Old Sech S Ukraine 1775, 135/2
Olisipo (Felicitas Julia)
Olmütz (*mod.* Olomouc) N Moravia to Hungary 1477-9, 110/1
Olomouc (*Ger.* Olmütz) annexed by Germany 1939, 178/2
Olsztyn (*Ger.* Allenstein) N Poland to Prussia 1772, 146/2
Olynthus NE Greece Athenian Empire 431 BC, 22/1; subdued by Macedonia 336 BC, 22/3
Opava (Troppau)
Opole (*Ger.* Oppeln) S Poland inherited by Władisław 1138, 83/2
Oporto (*anc.* Portus Cale, *Port.* Porto, *Ar.* Burtuqal) N Portugal 68-
Oppeln (Opole)
Oradea (Nagyvárad)
Orchomenus E Greece Mycenaean city c.1300 BC, 10/2
Oreus E Greece Persian Wars 490-480 BC, 18/3
Oriens Roman diocese and praefectura of E Mediterranean 284-337, 42/2,3
Orkney, Earldom of N Scotland Viking state 10-11C, 60/A; Norwegian possession 1092, 78/2
Orléans (*anc.* Cenabum, *later* Civitas Aurelianum) N France Frankish kingdoms 526, 48-64; French Royal Domain 987, 74/3; 1032, 86/2; Hundred Years' War, 102/2
Orospeda district of SE Spain Visigothic rule 565, 54/2; added to Visigothic Kingdom 571, 58/1
Orvieto (*anc.* Urbs Vetus) C Italy acquired by Papal States 787, 62/3; 1219, 90/3
Ösel (*mod.* Saaremaa) island of W Estonia to Denmark 1573, 119/2
Osijek (*Hung.* Eszék, *Ger.* Esseg) E Croatia held by Serbs 1993, 191/2
Oslo (*f/c* Christiania 1624-1924, *a/s* Kristiania) S Norway 77-; Danish rule 1028-35, 87/1
Osman Ottoman principality of W Anatolia 1328, 93
Osnabrück N Germany 105-; Bishopric 1660, 122/3; 126/2
Osrhoene region of NE Syria Roman dependency 31 BC, 33
Ostfriesland (East Friesland)
Ostia C Italy Roman colony 300 BC, 26/2
Ostland, Reichskommissariat German territory of the Baltic States 1942, 182/1
Ostpreussen (East Prussia)
Ostrogothic Empire N Black Sea 4C, 43/4
Ostrogoths people of E Europe in Hungary/Serbia from 454 , 46/3
Ostrogoths, Kingdom of Italy/Croatia 453-526, 50/2
Otranto (*anc.* Hydruntum) Viking rule 11-12C, 66/D
Ottoman Empire 1390, 98/2; conquests in Balkans 1359-1500, 107/2; northern frontier in Hungary 1568, 118/1; 1683, 129; boundaries at 1861, 159/3; Treaty of San Stefano 1878, 166/2; First and Second Balkan Wars 1912-13, 170/2,3
Overijssel district of E Netherlands Union of Utrecht 1579, 123/1
Ovetum (*mod.* Oviedo) N Spain Kingdom of the Sueves 565, 52
Oviedo (*anc.* Ovetum) N Spain 56-
Oxford S England 104-
Ozora district of S Hungary 14C 98/1,2
Paderborn N Germany Bishopric 1660, 122/3; 126/2
Padova, Padua (Patavium)
Paeonia district of N Greece subdued by Macedonia 336 BC, 22/3
Paestum (Posidonia)
Pagasae N Greece Athenian Empire 431 BC, 22/1; subdued by Macedonia 336 BC, 22/3
Palaiokastro Crete Minoan site c.1500, 10/2
Palatinate (*Ger.* Pfalz) region of NW Germany Protestant in 1600, 122/2; occupied by France 1688, 131/1; lost by France 1697, 134/3; Bavarian territory 18C, 138/2
Pale SE Croatia held by Serbs 1993, 191/2
Palermo (*anc.* Panormus) NW Sicily 69-; Viking rule 11-12C, 66/D
Palestrina (Praeneste)
Palma Balearic Islands Roman Empire 55 BC, 34/3
Pampeluna, Pamplona (Pompaelo)
Pankow district of East Berlin 1945-90, 186/3
Pannonia Slovenia/Croatia lost to Huns by 446, 46/1; added to Frankish Empire 796, 62/1; 9C, 66/2
Pannoniae Roman diocese of Slovenia/Croatia 284-337, 42/2,3
Pannonia Inferior Roman province of Hungary AD 180, 38/3
Pannonia Superior Roman province of Austria/Hungary AD 180, 38
Panormus (*mod.* Palermo) N Sicily Phoenician colony 9C-6C BC, 14/1; Syracusan rule 375 BC, 22/2; Pyrrhus's Empire 295-275 BC, 26/3; 55 BC, 34/3; Byzantine Empire 535, 54/2
Panticapaeum (*mod.* Kerch) S Ukraine Greek colony 9C-6C BC, 14/2; added to Pontus 110 BC, 34/4; Ostrogothic Empire 370, 43/4
Papal States C Italy development 756-814, 62/3; 1156, 79/1; expansion 1178-1278, 90/3; 1336, 95/3; 1390, 98/3; Treaty of Lodi 1454, 106/4; 1513, 114/2; 1683, 128; 1714-21, 138/2; called Roman Republic 1798-1800, 146/4; divided between Italy and French Empire 1809, 150/3; largely integrated into Italy 1861, 158/2
Paphlagonia region of N Anatolia Alexander's Empire 323 BC, 22/4; 270 BC, 25
Parauaea (*a/s* Parauea) region of NW Greece subdued by Macedonia 336 BC, 22/3; Pyrrhus's Empire 295-275 BC, 26/3
Paris (*anc.* Lutetia) N France Frankish kingdoms 526, 48-64; 1030, 74/3; Royal Domain 1032, 86/2; Hundred Years' War, 102/2
Parma N Italy taken by Lombards 605, 58/3; Holy Roman Empire 1336, 95/3
Parma, Duchy of N Italy independence from Papal States 1545, 114/2; 1714-21, 138/2; under Habsburgs 1714-38 and 1748, 142/2; annexed by France 1805, 146/4; to Kingdom of Italy 1861, 158/2
Parolissus (Porolissum)
Paros island of S Aegean conquered by Persians 480 BC, 18/3; Second Macedonian War 202 BC, 30/2
Parthian Empire NW Persia 100 BC-180 AD, 29-37; Roman vassal 115-117, 38/1
Passarowitz (*Serb.* Požarevac) E Serbia acquired by Habsburgs 1718-39, 138/1
Passau (*anc.* Castra Batava) S Germany in Frankish Kingdom 561, 54/1; East Frankish Kingdom 870, 66/4; Bishopric 1660, 122/3
Patavium (*mod.* Padova, *Eng.* Padua, *Fr.* Padoue) N Italy Roman Empire AD 180, 36
Patrae (*mod.* Patra, *f/s* Patrai, *a/c* Patras) SW Greece Roman Empire 55 BC, 34/3; Byzantine Empire 527, 54/2
Patrai (*anc.* Patrae, *n/s* Patra, *a/s* Patras) W Greece occupied by Italy 1941, 182/3, 183/1
Pavia (*anc.* Ticinum) N Italy taken by Lombards 590, 58/3
Pechenegs people of SE Europe 908, 65; 71/4
Pécs (*Ger.* Fünfkirchen) S Hungary 69-
Pella N Greece Cassander's Kingdom 301 BC, 26/1
Peloponnese (*a/c* Morea, *Lat.* Peloponnisus, *mod.* Peloponnisos) region of S Greece Corinthian League 337 BC, 22/3
Pereyaslavl W Russia in Muscovy 1521, 106/3
Pereyaslavl early principality of W Russia 1095-1328, 77-93
Pergamum Greek state of W Anatolia 202 BC, 30/2; Roman Empire 55 BC, 34/3
Periaslav (*mod.* Pereyaslav-Khmel'nyts'kyy) C Ukraine in Hetmanate 1667, 135/2
Périgord, County of SW France fief of Duchy of Aquitaine 1030, 74/3
Perinthus (*mod.* Ereğli) NW Turkey Greek colony 9C-6C BC, 14/2; Ionian revolt against Persians 5C BC, 19/2; Athenian Empire 431 BC, 22/1; subdued by Macedonia 336 BC, 22/3; Roman Empire 31 BC, 30/3; Roman Empire 55 BC, 34/3
Peristeria W Greece Mycenaean city 14C BC, 10/3
Perm (*f/c* Molotov) E Russia 77-
Perrhaebia region of N Greece subdued by Macedonia 336 BC, 22/3
Persepolis (*Pers.* Takht-e Jamshid) S Persia Seleucid Empire 301 BC, 26/1
Persian Empire (*a/c* Sasanian Empire) Anatolia and Balkans 513-480 BC, 18/1,3; 19/2; 450-565, 45-53
Perugia (*anc.* Perusia) C Italy 69-; acquired by Papal States 756, 62/1; 1219, 90/3
Perusia (*mod.* Perugia) N Italy Etruscan city 600 BC, 14/3; Byzantine Empire 554, 54/2
Pesaro (Pisaurum)
Pesto (Posidonia)
Petrograd (St Petersburg)
Pfalz (Palatinate)
Pförten (Brody)
Phaistos (*Lat.* Phaestus) S Crete Minoan site c.1500 BC, 10/2
Phanagoria S Russia Greek colony 9C-6C BC, 14/2
Pharus (*mod.* Hvar, *Ital.* Lesina) island of W Croatia added to Rome 229-191 BC, 30/3
Phasis W Georgia in Persian Empire 480, 17; in Alexander's Empire 323, 21
Pherae (*mod.* Velestinon) N Greece Athenian Empire 431 BC, 22/1; subdued by Macedonia 336 BC, 22/3
Philadelphia W Anatolia Byzantine Empire 1390, 98/2
Philippeville SW Belgium annexed by France 1792-3, 146/1; lost by France 1815, 154/4
Philippi NE Greece subdued by Macedonia 336 BC, 22/3
Philippopolis (*mod.* Plovdiv, *Turk.* Filibe) S Bulgaria 49-; subdued by Macedonia 336 BC, 22/3; Byzantine Empire 527, 54/2; Ottoman Empire 1389, 107/2
Phocaea (*Gr.* Phokaia) W Anatolia Aetolian city 800 BC, 10/4; Athenian Empire 431 BC, 22/1
Phocis (*mod.* Phokis, *a/s* Fokis) region of C Greece Corinthian League 337 BC, 22/3
Phoenicia country of E Mediterranean 900 BC, 9; colonisation in W Mediterranean 9C-6C BC, 14/1
Phokaia (Phocaea)
Phokis (Phocis)
Phrygia region of W Anatolia 900 BC, 9; in Empire of Pontus 129-120 BC, 34/4
Picardy (*Fr.* Picardie) region of NE France Hundred Years' War, 102/2; added to Burgundy by 1467, 106/1; added to Royal Domain by 1226, 114/3
Picts people of N Scotland 732, 56; 796, 62/2
Piedmont (*It.* Piemonte) region of NW Italy within Kingdom of Sardinia 1714-21, 138/2; occupied by France 1796, 146/1; annexed to France 1802, 146/4
Pilos (Pylos)
Pilsen (Plzeň)
Piombino C Italy protectorate of Florence 1454, 106/4; 1714-21, 138/2
Piombino, Principality of C Italy 928-1000, 70/1; added to French Empire 1807, 150/2
Pirano (*Slvn.* Piran) W Slovenia Free Territory of Trieste 1947-54, 187/4
Pisa (*anc.* Pisae) C Italy taken by Lombards 590, 58/3; 1336, 95/3; Holy Roman Empire 1390, 98/3
Pisa, Republic of C Italy added to Florence 1509; 114/2
Pisae (*mod.* Pisa) C Italy ally of Rome by 270 BC, 26/2; Roman Empire 264 BC, 30/1; 55 BC, 34/3
Pisaurum (*mod.* Pesaro) NE Italy Etruscan control c. 550-400 BC, 14/3
Pisidia region of SW Anatolia 100 BC, 29
Plataea (*mod.* Plataiai) E Greece Persian Wars 490-480 BC, 18/3
Płock (*Ger.* Schröttersburg) C Poland to Prussia 1793, 146/2
Plovdiv (Philippopolis)
Plzeň (*Ger.* Pilsen) W Bohemia annexed by Germany 1939, 178/1
Podgorica (*f/c* Titograd) S Montenegro 1993, 191/2
Podolia (*Pol.* Podole, *Russ.* Podolya) region of W Ukraine to Russia 1793
Poitiers (anc. Limonum) C France Hundred Years' War, 102/2
Poitou region of C France added to Royal Domain by 1223, 86/2; 114/3
Poitou, County of W France fief of Duchy of Aquitaine 1030, 74/3
Pola (*Cr.* Pula) W Croatia acquired by Yugoslavia 1947, 187/4
Poland 928-100, 70/1; expansion under Bolesław the Brave 992-1025, 74/4; fragmentation from 1138, 83/2; in personal union with Hungary from 1370, 98/1; in union with Lithuania from 1386, 103/3; growth of Jagiello power 1440-1526, 111/3; Union of Lublin 1569, 118/3; partitions 1772-92, 146/2; borders of 1699, 154/1; personal union with Saxony 1807, 154/1; Grand Duchy of Warsaw 151/3, 155/4; 1807-47, 158/1; Kingdom established 1815, 158/1; Treaty of Brest-Litovsk 1918, Curzon Line 1919, 174/4; east annexed by Germany 1939, 178/1; Nazi-Soviet Pact 1939, 178/3; post-WW2 population movements 186/1; territories acquired from Germany 1945, 186/2
Polatsk (Polotsk)
Poles migration 1945-52, 186/1
Polish Corridor NW Poland annexed by Germany 1939, 178/3
Polock (*mod.* Polatsk, *Russ.* Polotsk) N Belarus in Lithuania under Russian control 1570, 118/3; to Russia 1772, 146/2
Polotsk (*Pol.* Polock, *mod.* Polatsk) N Belarus Lithuanian by 1341 in Kievan Rus 800, 70/1
Polotsk, Principality of W Russia 1095-1270, 77-89
Poltava E Ukraine in Hetmanate 1667, 135/2
Pomerania (*Ger.* Pommern, *Pol.* Pomorze) region of N Germany/Poland added to Prussia 1663-1720, 135/1
Pomerelia (*Ger.* Pomerellen) region of NE Germany 1180, 81
Pommern, Pomorze (Pomerania)
Pompaelo (*mod.* Pamplona, *f/c* Pampeluna, *Fr.* Pampelune) NE Spain Roman Empire AD 180, 36
Pompeii S Italy Etruscan control c. 530 BC, 14/3
Pontecagnano S Italy Etruscans 530 BC, 14/3
Pontecorvo, Principality of W Italy added to French Empire 1807, 150/2
Ponthieu region of N France Hundred Years' War, 102/2; to Burgundy 1435, 106/4
Pontus region of N Anatolia 121 BC, 29; Empire under Mithradates 120 BC, 34/4; Roman dependency 31 BC, 33; Roman diocese 284-337, 42/2,3
Pontus, Empire of under Mithradates Eupator 121-110 BC, 34/4
Populonia E Italy N Italy Etruscan city 600 BC, 14/3; acquired by Papal States 789, 62/1
Porolissum (*a/s* Parolissus) N Romania Roman Empire AD 180, 37
Porto (Oporto)
Portugal partly held by Normans 1086, 78/2; successor state of the Caliphate of Cordova 1086, 79/3; independent from 1143, 82/1; European Union 1993, 190/3
Portus Cale (*mod.* Porto, *Eng.* Oporto) N Portugal in Kingdom of the Sueves 565, 52
Portus Namnetum NW France Roman Empire 31 BC, 32
Posen (Poznań)
Posidonia (*a/s* Poseidonia, *later* Paestum, *mod.* Pesto) Greek city-state 6C Bc, 14/3
Potaissa N Romania Roman Empire AD 180, 37
Potidaea (*later* Cassandreia, *mod.* Nea Potidaia) NE Greece Greek colony 9C-6C BC, 14/1; in Persian Empire 480 BC, 18/1; subdued by Macedonia 336 BC, 22/3

Szörény – Urbs Vetus

Szörény region of SW Romania to Hungary early 13C, 86/3; under Bosnian and Wallachian vassal rulers 1370, 98/1
Taginae Byzantine Empire 554, 54/2
Tallinn (*Ger.* Reval, *Russ.* Revel) N Estonia annexed by USSR 1940, 178/3; occupied by Germany 1942, 182/4
Tanais S Russia Greek colony 9C-6C BC, 14/2
Tangier (*anc.* Tingis, *Fr.* Tanger) N Africa Portuguese possession from 1471, 94/1
Tannenberg (*Pol.* Stębark) E Prussia 1410, 102/1; 1525, 118/2
Taormina E Sicily Byzantine possession 1036-43, 79/1
Tarabulus (Tripolis)
Taranto (*anc.* Taras, *later* Tarentum) S Italy 69-; Viking rule 11-12C, 66/D; Byzantine possession 1155-6, 79/1
Taras (*later* Tarentum, *mod.* Taranto) S Italy Greek colony 9C-6C BC, 14/1; Greek city 375 BC, 22/2
Tarentum (*f/c* Taras, *mod.* Taranto) S Italy ally of Rome by 270 BC, 26/2; Pyrrhus's Empire 295-275 BC, 26/3; Roman Empire 270 BC, 30/1,3; 55 BC, 34/3; Ostrogothic rule 508, 50/2; Byzantine Empire 554, 54/2; taken by Lombards 7C, 58/3
Târgovişte (*f/s* Tîrgovişte, *Turk.* Eski Cuma) S Romania Ottoman Empire end-14C, 107/2
Tarnopol (*Ukr.* Ternopil', *Russ.* Ternopol') W Ukraine lost by Habsburgs 1809, 155/2; to Russia 1809, to Austria 1815, 158/1
Tarquinii (*mod.* Tarquinia, *f/c* Corneto) N Italy Etruscan City 600 BC, 14/3
Tarraco (*mod.* Tarragona, *Ar.* Tarrakunah) NE Spain Roman Empire 197 BC, 30/1; Roman Empire 55 BC, 34/3; Visigothic rule 476, 50/1,3
Tarraconensis Roman province of N and W Spain AD 180, 38/3
Tarragona (*anc.* Tarraco, *Ar.* Tarrakunah) NE Spain Christian conquest by end 11C, 82/1
Tarrakunah (*mod.* Tarragona) NE Spain Muslim conquest 732, 56; Emirate of Cordova 814, 60
Tarsus SE Anatolia Roman Empire 55 BC, 34/3
Tatarstan autonomous republic of Russian Federation 1993, 190/1
Taurasia (Turin)
Tbilisi (*f/c* Tiflis, *Geor.* T'bilisi) E Georgia 173-
Tecklenburg NW Germany added to Prussia 1707, 135/1
Tegea S Greece Persian Wars 490-480 BC, 18/3
Tegel airport in French sector of Berlin 1945 186/3
Teke Turcoman principality of W Anatolia 1328-82, 93, 97
Tekirdağ (Rodosto)
Temeschwar, Banat of region of W Romania 18C, 138/1; 1868, 162/2
Temesvár (*Ger.* Temeschwar, *mod.* Timişoara) SW Romania 69-; to Romania 1920, 175/5
Tempelhof airport in American sector of Berlin 1945 186/3
Tenda (*Fr.* Tende) SE France Treaty of Lodi 1454, 106/4
Tenos (*n/s* Tinos) island of S Aegean conquered by Persians 480 BC, 18/3
Teos W Anatolia Athenian Empire 431 BC, 22/1
Tergeste (Trieste)
Ternopil', Ternopol' (Tarnopol)
Teruel E Spain Christian conquest by end 11C, 82/1
Teschen (Cieszyn)
Těšín (Cieszyn)
Tessin (Ticino)
Teurnia N Austria Roman Empire AD 180, 36
Teutonic Order E and S Baltic 1270-1493, 91-109; collapse 1513-85, 119/2
Teutonic Peoples N Europe 8-
Thasos (*a/s* Thasus) island of N Aegean conquered by Persians 480 BC, 18/3; Second Macedonian War 202 BC, 30/2
Thebes (*mod.* Thivai) E Greece Mycenaean city 14C BC, 10/3; mother-city 550 BC, 13; allied with Persia 480 BC, 18/1,3; Athenian Empire 431 BC, 22/1; Corinthian League 337 BC, 22/3
Thebes (*Lat.* Thebae, *earlier* Diospolis Magna) Upper Egypt ancient Empire 10/1; to Assyrian Empire 667-660 BC, 10/3
Theodosia (*med.* Kaffa, *It.* Caffa, *Turk.* Kefe, *mod.* Feodosiya) S Ukraine Greek colony 9C-6C BC, 14/2; in Byzantine Empire 1031, 70/1
Thera (*mod.* Thira, *It.*. Santorini) Athenian Empire 431 BC, 22/1
Thermopylae C Greece Persian Wars 490-480 BC, 18/3
Thessalonica (*a/c* Salonica, *mod.* Thessaloniki) NE Greece Roman Empire 148 BC, 30/3; 305 AD, 42/2; 55 BC, 34/3
Thessaly (*Gr.* Thessalia) region of C Greece peopled by Aeolians 800 BC, 10/4; Persian Wars 490-480 BC, 18/3; Athenian Empire 431 BC, 22/1; Macedonian dependency 202 BC, 30/3; Ottoman conquest by 1402, 107/2; to Greece 1881, 166/2
Theveste N Africa in Carthage 149 BC, 30/1
Thira (Thera)
Thivai (Thebes)
Thorn (Toruń)
Thrace (*Gr.* Thraki, *Bulg.* Trakiya) region of NE Greece/NW Turkey First and Second Balkan Wars 1912-13, 170/2,3; annexed by Bulgaria 1941, 182/3
Thracia Roman province of Bulgaria/Greece AD 180, 38/3
Thraciae Roman diocese of Bulgaria/Greece 284-337, 42/2,3
Thracians early people of SE Europe 9-
Thurgau canton of E Switzerland added to Swiss Confederation 1460, 110/2
Thurii S Italy Greek city 375 BC, 22/2; Pyrrhus's Empire 295-275 BC, 26/3; ally of Rome by 270 BC, 26/2
Thuringia (*Ger.* Thüringen) state of C Germany added to Frankish Kingdom 531-2, 54/1; in German Confederation 1815, 154/1
Thuringia, Landgraviate of E Germany Holy Roman Empire 1179, 82/4
Thuringians people of C Germany 6C, 49-53
Thuringian States N Germany North German Confederation 1867, 162/3; in German Empire 1871, 166/1
Tibur (*mod.* Tivoli) S Italy Roman control 380 BC, 14/3; ally of Rome 300 BC, 26/2
Ticino (*Fr.* Tessin) canton of S Switzerland joins Swiss Confederation 1513, 126/1
Ticinum (Pavia)
Tiergarten district of West Berlin 1945-90, 186/3
Tiflis (*Russ.* Tbilisi, *Geor.* T'bilisi) E Georgia 60-169
Tilsit (*Russ.* Sovetsk) W Russia in Prussia 1807, 155/3
Timişoara (Temesvár)
Tingis (*mod.* Tanger, *Eng.* Tangier) N Morocco Roman Empire 31 BC, 32
Tinos (*anc.* Tenos) island of C Aegean Venetian possession 1210, 146/3
Tirana (*a/s* Tiranë) C Albania 173-
Tîrgovişte (Târgovişte)
Tiryns S Greece Mycenaean city 14C BC, 10/3
Titograd (Podgorica)
Tivoli (Tibur)
Tmutarakan S Russia in Kievan Rus by 900, 70/1; 1030, 73
Toledo (*anc.* Toletum, *Ar.* Tulaytulah) C Spain 68-; Republic 908, 64
Toledo, Kingdom of C Spain 1031-85, 79/3
Toletum (*Ar.* Tulaytulah, *mod.* Toledo, *Fr.* Tolede) C Spain Roman Empire 55 BC, 34/3; abandoned by Rome by 3C, 46/1; Visigothic rule 476, 50/1,3
Tolosa (*mod.* Toulouse) S France Roman Empire 58 BC, 34/2; abandoned by Rome by 3C, 46/1; in Visigothic kingdom 431, 46/3
Tomi (*mod.* Constanţa) E Romania Greek colony 9C-6C BC, 14/2; in Persian Empire 480 BC, 18/1; Greek city taken by Burebista c45 BC, 34/1
Torino (Turin)
Tortosa (*anc.* Dertosa) NE Spain Christian conquest by end 11C, 82/1
Tortosa, Kingdom of NE Spain 1086, 79/3
Toruń (*Ger.* Thorn) W Poland to Prussia 1772, 146/2; to Prussia 159/1; occupied by Germany 1939, 178/1
Toulouse (*anc.* Tolosa) S France Visigothic rule 476, 50/3; conquered by Franks 507, 50/1, 51/4; West Frankish Kingdom 880, 66/4; Hundred Years' War, 102/2
Toulouse, County of S France fief of Duchy of Aquitaine 1030, 74/3
Touraine region of C France added to Royal Domain by 1223, 86/2
Touraine, County of N France fief of French Crown 1030, 74/3
Tournai (*Dut.* Doornijk) SW Belgium conquered by Franks 476, 50/3, 51/4
Tours (*anc.* Caesarodunum, *later* Urbs Turonum) N France Frankish kingdoms 526, 48-64; Hundred Years' War, 102/2
Trabzon (Trapezus)
Trakiya (Thrace)
Transcarpathia (Ruthenia)
Transnistria region of SW Ukraine occupied by Romania 1941, 182/2
Transnistrian Republic breakaway region of E Moldova 1993, 190/1
Transylvania (*Rom.* Transilvania, *Hung.* Erdély, *Ger.* Siebenbürgen) region of NW Romania principality 1570, 118/1; in personal union with Poland-Lithuania 1576-86, 118/3; returned to Hungary 1750, 138/1; Habsburg territory 1699-1789, 142/2; reunited with Hungary 1860, 163/2; to Hungary 1940, 182/2
Trapezus (*mod.* Trabzon, *Eng.* Trebizond) NE Anatolia Greek colony 9C-6C BC, 14/2; in Persian Empire 480, 17; in Alexander's Empire 323, 21; Greek city 301 BC, 26/1; Byzantine Empire 527, 54/2
Trebizond (Trapezus)
Trebizond, Empire of NE Anatolia Greek successor state to Byzantine Empire 1212, 86/4
Trebizond, Empire of NE Anatolia 1223-1430, 85-101
Trebunia district of W Bulgaria 986, 70/4
Trencsén (*Ger.* Trentschin, *mod.* Trenčin) C Slovakia to Poland 1017-18, 74/4
Trent, Bishopric of N Italy church state 1390, 98/3; Habsburg possession 1400 102/1; 1660, 122/3; Holy Roman Empire 1648, 126/2; Habsburg possession 1721, 138/2
Treveri (*a/c* Augusta Treverorum) Roman Empire 284-337, 42/2,3
Treves (Trier)
Triaditsa (Serdica)
Trier (*Fr.* Trèves, *Eng.* Treves, *anc.* Augusta Treverorum) W Germany Ripuarian Frankish Kingdom 476, 50/3; Luxemburg control 1307-54, 102/4; Bishopric 1660, 122/3; lost by France 1697, 134/3; Allied occupation 1918-30, 175/2
Trieste (*anc.* Tergeste, *Ger.* Triest, *Slvn.* Trst) NE Italy 77-; Habsburg possession 1382, 102/1; lost by Habsburgs 1805, 154/4; Free Territory 1947-54, 187/4
Trimontium S Scotland Roman Empire AD 180, 39/2
Tripolis (*a/c* Oea, *mod.* Tarabulus, *Eng.* Tripoli) Byzantine Empire 527, 54/2
Trondheim (*f/s* Trondhjem, *f/c* Nidaros 11-16C) C Norway 1030-
Trondhjem (n/s Trondheim) C Norway Danish rule 1028-35, 87/1
Troppau (*Cz.* Opava) N Moravia to Hungary 1477-9, 110/1
Troy NW Anatolia 1300 BC, 10/3; Aeolian city 800 BC, 10/4
Troyes (*anc.* Augustobona) E France Hundred Years' War, 102/2
Trst (Trieste)
Tsaritsyn (Stalingrad)
Tschenstochau (Częstochowa)
Tula W Russia 77-
Tulaytulah (*mod.* Toledo) Spain Muslim conquest 732, 56; Emirate of Cordova 814, 60
Tunis region of N Africa Roman Empire 146 BC, 30/1; Viking rule 1146-60, 66/D; disputed by Spain and Ottomans 1551, 114/2; to France by 1885, 164
Tunis (*n/c* Tunisia) region of N Africa Ottoman vassal 1618-1871, 123-163; Frnch by 1885, 164
Turin (*anc.* Taurasia, *later* Augusta Taurinorum, *It.* Torino) NW Italy Kingdom of the Lombards from 590, 56, 58/3; Frankish rule 774-814, 62/1; occupied by France 1796, 146/1; annexed to France 1802, 146/4
Turkey association with European Union 1993, 190/3
Turkic peoples S Russia 565, 53
Turks migration 1950-52, 186/1
Turku (Åbo)
Turov-Pinsk early principality of W Russia 1180-1270, 81-89
Tuscany, Grand Duchy of C Italy 1714-21, 138/2; acquired by Habsburgs 1737, 142/2; called Kingdom of Etruria 1801, 146/4; Habsburg secundogeniture 1792, 154/2; to Kingdom of Italy 1861, 158/2
Tuscany, Kingdom of N Italy Habsburg secundogeniture to 1860, 162/2
Tuzla N Bosnia Muslim enclave 1993, 191/2
Tver early principality of W Russia 1382-1466, 97-105
Tver, Great Principality of W Russia annexed by Muscovy 1485, 106/3
Tver-Dmitrov early principality of W Russia 1270-1328, 89, 93
Two Sicilies, Kingdom of the S Italy to Kingdom of Italy 1861, 158/2
Tylisian Kingdom Bulgaria 270 BC, 25
Tymphaea region of NW Greece Pyrrhus's Empire 295-275 BC, 26/3
Tyras (*mod.* Bilhorod-Dnistrovs'kyy, *Russ.* Belgorod-Dnestrovskiy, *f/c* Akkerman, *Rom.* Cetatea-Albă) SW Ukraine Greek colony 9C-6C BC, 14/2; 270 BC, 26/1; Greek city taken by Burebista c45 BC, 34/1
Tyre (*anc.* Tyrus, *Ar.* Sur) Lebanon to Assyrian Empire 721-705 BC, 10/3
Tyrol (*Ger.* Tirol, *It.* Tirolo) region of Austria/Italy Habsburg possession from 1363, 102/1; 1477, 114/1; 1660, 122/3; Luxemburg control 1335-42, 102/4; County 1648, 126/2; in Bavaria 955, 138/3; Habsburg territory 1699-1789, 142/2; in Confederation of the Rhine 1809-10, 150/3-4; lost by Habsburgs 1805, 154/2; province of Austria-Hungary 1849-68, 162/2
Tyrus (Tyre)
Uglich early principality of W Russia 1270-1328, 89, 93
Ugrians early people of N Russia 565, 53
Újvidék (*now* Novi Sad, *Ger.* Neusatz) N Serbia occupied by Hungary 1941, 182/3
Ukraine in Lithuania 1562, added to Poland 1569, 118/3; Zaporogian Cossacks 1667-1775, 135/2; west part from Poland to Russia 1793-5, 146/2; southeast to Poland 1699, 154/1; independence 1918, 174/1; occupied by Germany 1941-42, 182/4; independence 1991, 190/1
Ukrainians migration 1946-47, 186/1
UlpiaTraiana (Sarmizegethusa)
Ulster province of Ireland 1092, 78/2
United Kingdom Entente Cordiale 1904, 170/1; 1812, 148; European Union 1993, 190/3
Unterwald canton of C Switzerland added to Swiss Confederation 1291, 110/2
Upper Austria province of Austria-Hungary 1849-68, 162/2
Upper Burgundy East Franking Kingdom 66/4
Upper Guelders (*a/c* Upper Gelderland) 1648, 123/1; added to Prussia 1715, 135/1, 142/3
Upper Lorraine, Duchy of E France Holy roman Empire 1179, 82/4
Upper Palatinate (Ger. Oberpfalz) region of C Germany Luxemburg control 1353-73, 102/4; Protestant in 1600, 122/2
Upper Silesia (*Ger.* Oberschlesien, *Pol.* Górny Śląsk) region of SW Poland plebiscite 1921, 174/3
Uppsala E Sweden Viking town c.1000, 66/1B; 69-89
Urartu country of ancient Near East 9
Urbino C Italy acquired by Papal States 756, 62/3; 1219, 90/3
Urbino, Duchy of N Italy independence from Papal States by 1551, 114/2
Urbs Turonum (Tours)
Urbs Vetus (Orvieto)